THINKING THE POETIC MEASURE OF JUSTICE

SUNY series in Contemporary Continental Philosophy

Dennis J. Schmidt, editor

THINKING THE POETIC MEASURE OF JUSTICE

Hölderlin–Heidegger–Celan

CHARLES BAMBACH

STATE UNIVERSITY OF NEW YORK PRESS

Published by
State University of New York Press, Albany

Printed in the United States of America

For information, contact
State University of New York Press, Albany, NY
www.sunypress.edu

Production, Laurie Searl
Marketing, Anne M. Valentine

Library of Congress Cataloging-in-Publication Data

Bambach, Charles R.
Thinking the poetic measure of justice : Hölderlin–Heidegger–Celan / Charles Bambach.
p. cm. — (SUNY series in contemporary continental philosophy)
Includes bibliographical references and index.
ISBN 978-1-4384-4581-6 (hc : alk. paper)—978-1-4384-4580-9 (pb : alk. paper)
1. Heidegger, Martin, 1889–1976. 2. Hölderlin, Friedrich, 1770–1843. 3. Celan, Paul. 4. Justice. I. Title.

B3279.H49B2655 2013
193—dc23 2012015326

10 9 8 7 6 5 4 3 2 1

For Lucy—and for Rolf and my brother John

Justice, justice shall you pursue

—Deuteronomy 16:20

CONTENTS

ABBREVIATIONS

Unless otherwise indicated, all translations are my own. At times I modify existing translations to provide a terminology consistent throughout this book. Sometimes I will also provide alternate translations of the same terms depending on context.

SS	Summer Semester
WS	Winter Semester

HÖLDERLIN

BA	*Bremer* Hölderlin *Ausgabe. Sämtliche Werke, Briefe und Dokumente in zeitlicher Folge*. Ed. D. E. Sattler. 12 Vols. München: Luchterhand, 2004.
BL	Böhlendorff Letter. Trans. Dennis Schmidt. In *On Germans and Other Greeks: Tragedy and Ethical Life*. Bloomington: Indiana University Press, 2001.
DKV	Deutscher Klassiker Verlag Ausgabe. Ed. Jochen Schmidt. In *Sämtliche Werke und Briefe in drei Bänden*. Frankfurt: Deutscher Klassiker Verlag, 2004.
ELT	*Hölderlin: Essays and Letters on Theory*. Ed. Thomas Pfau. Albany: State University of New York Press, 1988.
E&L	*Essays and Letters*. Ed. Jeremy Adler and Charlie Louth. Harmondsworth: Penguin, 2009.
FHA	Frankfurter Hölderlin Ausgabe. *Sämtliche Werke*. Ed. D. E. Sattler et al. 20 Vols. Frankfurt: Roter Stern, 1975–2008.
H	*Hyperion*, Trans. Ross Benjamin. Brooklyn: Archipelago Books, 2008.
HF	*Hymns and Fragments*. Trans. Richard Sieburth. Princeton: Princeton University Press, 1984.
HS	*Hölderlin's Sophocles*. Trans. David Constantine. Newcastle upon Tyne: Blood Axe Books, 2001.

PF *Poems and Fragments*. Trans. Michael Hamburger. London: Anvil Press, 2004.

SA *Grosse Stuttgarter Ausgabe. Sämtliche Werke*. Ed. Friedrich Beissner. 8 Vols. Stuttgart: Kohlhammer, 1943–1985.

SPF *Selected Poems and Fragments*. Trans. Michael Hamburger. Harmondsworth: Penguin, 1998.

HEIDEGGER

BC *Basic Concepts*. Trans. Gary Aylesworth. Bloomington: Indiana University Press, 1993.

BT *Being and Time*. Trans. Joan Stambaugh. Albany: State University of New York Press, 1996.

CP *Contributions to Philosophy*. Trans. Parvis Emad and Kenneth Maly. Bloomington: Indiana University Press, 1999.

CPC *Country Path Conversations*. Trans. Bret Davis. Bloomington: Indiana University Press, 2010.

EdP *"Europa und die deutsche Philosophie."* In *Europa und die Philosophie*, ed. Hans-Helmuth Gander. Frankfurt: Klostermann, 1993.

EGT *Early Greek Thinking*. Trans. David F. Krell and Frank Capuzzi. San Francisco: Harper and Row, 1975.

EHP *Elucidations of Hölderlin's Poetry*. Trans. Keith Hoeller. New York: Humanity Books, 2000.

EM *Einführung in die Metaphysik*. Tübingen: Niemeyer, 1953.

EOT *The Essence of Truth*. Trans. Ted Sadler. New York: Continuum, 2002.

EP *The End of Philosophy*. Trans. Joan Stambaugh. New York: Harper and Row, 1973.

FCM *Fundamental Concepts of Metaphysics*. Tran. William McNeill and Nicholas Walker. Bloomington: Indiana University Press, 1995.

GA *Gesamtausgabe*. Frankfurt: Klostermann, 1975 ff.

GA 4 *Erläuterungen zu Hölderlins Dichtung*. Ed. Friedrich-Wilhelm von Herrmann. Frankfurt: Klostermann, 1981.

GA 5 *Holzwege*. Ed. Friedrich-Wilhelm von Herrmann. Frankfurt: Klostermann, 1977.

GA 7 *Vorträge und Aufsätze*. Ed. Friedrich-Wilhelm von Herrmann. Frankfurt: Klostermann, 2000.

GA 8 *Was heisst Denken?* Ed. Paola-Ludovika Coriando. Frankfurt: Klostermann, 2002.

GA 9 *Wegmarken*. Ed. Friedrich-Wilhelm von Herrmann. Frankfurt: Klostermann, 2004.

GA 11 *Identität und Differenz*. Ed. Friedrich-Wilhelm von Herrmann. Frankfurt: Klostermann, 2006.

GA 13 *Aus der Erfahrung des Denkens*. Ed. Hermann Heidegger. Frankfurt: Klostermann, 2002.

GA 16 *Reden und andere Zeugnisse eines Lebensweges*. Ed. Hermann Heidegger. Frankfurt: Klostermann, 2000.

GA 18 *Grundbegriffe der aristotelischen Philosophie*. Ed. Mark Michalski. Frankfurt: Klostermann, 2002.

GA 20 *Prolegomena zur Geschichte des Zeitbegriffes*. Ed. Petra Jaeger. Frankfurt: Klostermann, 1988.

GA 21 *Logik. Die Frage nach der Wahrheit*. Ed. Walter Biemel. Frankfurt: Klostermann, 1995.

GA 29/30 *Die Grundbegriffe der Metaphysik: Welt-Endlichkeit-Einsamkeit*. Ed. Friedrich-Wilhelm von Herrmann. Frankfurt: Klostermann, 1985.

GA 36/37 *Sein und Wahrheit*. Ed. Hartmut Tietjen. Frankfurt: Klostermann, 2001.

GA 39 *Hölderlins Hymne "Germanien"und "Der Rhein."* Ed. Susanne Ziegler. Frankfurt: Klostermann, 1989.

GA 43 *Nietzsche: Der Wille zur Macht als Kunst*. Ed. Bernd Heimbüchel. Frankfurt: Klostermann, 1985.

GA 46 *Zur Auslegung von Nietzsches II. Unzeitgemässer Betrachtung"Vom Nutzen und Nachteil der Historie für das Leben."* Ed. Hans-Joachim Friedrich. Frankfurt: Klostermann, 2003.

GA 47 *Nietzsches Lehre vom Willen zur Macht als Erkenntnis*. Ed. Eberhard Hanser. Frankfurt: Klostermann, 1989.

GA 48 *Nietzsche: Der europäische Nihilismus*. Frankfurt: Klostermann, 1986.

GA 50 *Nietzsches Metaphysik*. Ed. Petra Jaeger. Frankfurt: Klostermann, 1990.

GA 51 *Grundbegriffe*. Ed. Petra Jaeger. Frankfurt: Klostermann, 1991.

GA 52 *Hölderlins Hymne "Andenken."* Ed. Curd Ochwadt. Frankfurt: Klostermann, 1992.

GA 53 *Hölderlins Hymne "Der Ister."* Ed. Walter Biemel. Frankfurt: Klostermann, 1993.

GA 54 *Parmenides*. Ed. Manfred S. Frings. Frankfurt: Klostermann, 1992.

GA 55 *Heraklit.1. Der Anfang des abendländischen Denkens; 2. Logik. Heraklits Lehre des Logos*. Ed. Manfred S. Frings. Frankfurt: Klostermann, 1994.

GA 65 *Beiträge zur Philosophie*. Ed. Friedrich-Wilhelm von Herrmann. Frankfurt: Klostermann, 1989.

GA 66 *Besinnung*. Ed. Friedrich-Wilhelm von Herrmann. Frankfurt: Klostermann, 1997.

GA 75 *Zu Hölderlin-Griechenlandreisen*. Ed. Curd Ochwadt. Frankfurt: Klostermann, 2000.

GA 77 *Feldweg-Gespräche*. Ed. Ingrid Schüssler. Frankfurt: Klostermann, 1995.

GA 78 *Der Spruch des Anaximander*. Ed. Ingrid Schüssler. Frankfurt: Klostermann, 2010.

HCT *History of the Concept of Time*. Trans. Theodore Kisiel. Bloomington: Indiana University Press, 1985.

HHI *Hölderlins Hymn "The Ister."* Trans. William McNeill and Julia Davis. Bloomington: Indiana University Press, 1996.

IM *Introduction to Metaphysics*. Trans. Gregory Fried and Richard Polt. New Haven: Yale University Press, 2000.

M *Mindfulness*. Trans. Parvis Emad. New York: Continuum, 2006.

MLS *"Mein liebes Seelchen!": Briefe Martin Heideggers an seine Frau Elfride*. München: Deutsche Verlags-Anstalt, 2005.

N i *Nietzsche, Volume i: The Will to Power as Art*. Ed. David Krell. New York: Harper and Row, 1979.

N ii *Nietzsche, Volume ii: The Eternal Recurrence of the Same*. Ed. David Krell. New York: Harper and Row, 1984.

N iii *Nietzsche, Volume iii: The Will to Power as Knowledge and as Metaphysics*. Ed. David Krell. New York: Harper and Row, 1987.

N iv *Nietzsche, Volume iv: Nihilism*. Ed. David Krell. New York: Harper and Row, 1982.

P *Parmenides*. Trans. Andre Schuwer and Richard Rojcewicz. Bloomington: Indiana University Press, 1992.

PLT *Poetry, Language, Thought*. Trans. Albert Hofstadter. New York: Harper and Row, 1971.

PM *Pathmarks*. Trans. William McNeill. Cambridge: Cambridge University Press, 1998.

QCT *The Question concerning Technology*. Trans. William Lovitt. New York: Harper and Row, 1977.

SZ *Sein und Zeit*. Tübingen: Niemeyer, 1976.

WidP *Was ist das, die Philosophie?* Pfullingen: Neske, 1956.

WiP *What Is Philosophy?* Trans. Eva Brann. Annapolis: St. John's College Press, 1991.

WCT *What Is Called Thinking?* Trans. J. Glenn Gray. New York: Harper and Row, 1968.

ZS *Zollikoner Seminars: Protocols-Conversations-Letters*. Trans. Franz Mayr and Richard Askay. Evanston: Northwestern University Press, 2001.

ZSG *Zollikoner Seminare, Protokolle-Gespräche-Briefe*. Ed. Medard Boss. Frankfurt: Klostermann, 1987.

NIETZSCHE

BT *The Birth of Tragedy*. Trans. Ronald Speirs. Cambridge: Cambridge University Press, 1999.

GOA *Grossoktav Ausgabe*. 20 Bände. Ed. Elisabeth Förster-Nietzsche. Leipzig: Kröner, 1903 ff.

KGW *Werke. Kritische Gesamtausgabe*. Ed. Giorgio Colli and Mazzino Montinari. Berlin: de Gruyter, 1967ff.

KSA *Kritische Studienausgabe, Sämtliche Werke*. 15 Bände. Berlin: de Gruyter, 1988.

PPP *The Pre-Platonic Philosophers*. Trans. Greg Whitlock. Urbana: University of Illinois Press, 2001.

PTAG *Philosophy in the Tragic Age of the Greeks*. Trans. Marianne Cowan. Washington: Gateway, 1962.

UTM *Untimely Meditations*. Trans. R. J. Hollingdale. Cambridge: Cambridge University Press, 1983.

WP *The Will to Power*. Trans. Walter Kaufmann and R. J. Hollingdale. New York: Vintage, 1967.

CELAN

DG *Die Gedichte*. Ed. Barbara Wiedemann. Frankfurt: Suhrkamp, 2003.

GW *Gesammelte Werke*. Ed. Beda Allemann and Stefan Reichert. Frankfurt: Suhrkamp, 1986.

LD *Lightduress*. Trans. Pierre Joris. Los Angeles: Green Integer, 2005.

LP *Last Poems*. Trans. Katherine Washburn and Margaret Guillemin. San Francisco: North Point Press, 1986.

MSS *Mikrolithen sinds, Steinchen*. Ed. Barbara Wiedemann. Frankfurt: Suhrkamp, 2005.

PC/IS *Paul Celan/Ilana Shmueli Briefwechsel*. Ed. Ilana Shmueli. Frankfurt: Suhrkamp, 2004.

PC/FW *Paul Celan/Franz Wurm Briefwechsel*. Ed. Barbara Wiedemann. Frankfurt: Suhrkamp, 1995.

PCGL *Paul Celan/Gisele Celan-Lestrange. Briefwechsel*. Ed. Bertrand Badiou. Frankfurt: Suhrkamp, 2001.

PCS *Paul Celan Selections*. Ed. Pierre Joris. Los Angeles: University of California Press, 2005.

PPC *Poems of Paul Celan*. Trans. Michael Hamburger. New York: Persea Books, 2002.

SP *Snow Part*. Trans. Ian Fairley. New York: The Sheep Meadow Press, 2007.

SPP *Selected Poems and Prose of Paul Celan*. Trans. John Felstiner. New York: Norton, 2001.

TCA/LZ *Tübinger Celan Ausgabe. Lichtzwang*. Ed. Jürgen Wertheimer. Frankfurt: Suhrkamp, 2001.

TCA/M *Tübinger Celan Ausgabe. Meridian*. Ed. Bernhard Böschenstein and Heino Schmull. Frankfurt: Suhrkamp, 1999.

TCA/NR *Tübinger Celan Ausgabe. Niemandsrose*. Ed. Jürgen Wertheimer. Frankfurt: Suhrkamp, 1996.

TS *Threadsuns*. Trans. Pierre Joris. Los Angeles: Sun and Moon Press.

ACKNOWLEDGMENTS

The rendering of thanks exceeds the structure of debt, exchange, and repayment. The very gesture of thanking reaches out for what cannot be properly expressed since it extends beyond propriety. Some of the lines of acknowledgment intersect, however, in their institutional, professional, and personal spaces, making it difficult to give voice to what remains deeply felt. It is in this spirit that I offer thanks here.

I begin with a thought of remembrance: for my beloved Aunt Cathy, for Ray McCauley, Edgar Maier, and Paul Zeller, friends all, who will be dearly missed.

For their generous financial support I would like to thank the Earhart Foundation for enabling a research leave to Cambridge, Massachusetts, and the Fulbright Senior Scholar Program for an extended grant at the University of Tübingen, where Prof. Manfred Frank of the Philosophisches Seminar generously hosted my work. I would also like to thank the University of Texas-Dallas and Dean Dennis Kratz for granting me two SFDA leaves.

In Dallas, I want to thank my friends and colleagues in the DASEIN Seminar, who helped to organize the yearly North Texas Heidegger Symposium, especially my co-chair Rod Coltman as well as Robert Wood, Mark Thames, Luanne Frank, Peter Park, Michael Wilson, Andy Amato, Frank Garrett, Sigrid Koepke, Tom Douglas, Dale Wilkerson, and above all, John Loscerbo for his unfailing passion to think through the *Gesamtausgabe*. I also want to thank all the participants in our yearly Heidegger conference, especially Will McNeill, Holger Zaborowski, Robert Bernasconi, Bret Davis, Walter Brogan, and John Sallis for their willingness to share their work so freely. And a special thanks to the Teds—Ted Kisiel and Ted George—for reading this book in manuscript form and offering their insightful suggestions. I have learned much from all of you.

At SUNY Press I would like to thank Andrew Kenyon for his timely advice and encouragement and Laurie Searl and Anne Valentine for their helpful suggestions and professional expertise. Most of all, however, I would like to thank Dennis Schmidt for his interest in my work and for his thoughtful reflections on ethics and poetry, which have provided a model for all of us who write on Heidegger, Hölderlin, Celan, and the problem of language.

I wrote most of this book in Cambridge, Massachusetts, and Tübingen, Germany, where I came to feel at home through the generosity and friendship I experienced there again and again. In Cambridge, I appreciate the support and graciousness of Peter Gordon and Dan Dahlstrom for hosting my work. I also want to thank my friends there—John Scanlan, Bill Ellet, Alan Andres, Tehila Lieberman, Robert Mazzetta, and Elizabeth McCauley.

In Tübingen, I was blessed to be part of a wonderful group of friends who withstood all my persistent questions about *Fug, Fügung, Fuge, Gefüge*, and *Verfügung* with insight and humor, especially the members of our Tuesday evening Stammtisch. I also want to thank Christian Backer, Tina Schwarz, Ekki Kirsch, Georg Würzer, and Friederike Scholvin for their unstinting support, as well as Norbert Schuler of Bader Antiquariat. I would also like to thank Wolfgang Zwierzynski for his help in procuring books, but most of all for his infinite patience and wisdom. My time in Tübingen over the course of writing this book owes so much to Karin Bukenberger and Rolf Maier, whose friendship has meant the world to me. As Hölderlin expressed it, "Nie treff ich, wie ich wünsche, das Maas."

Above all, I want to thank my family for their love and support, my brother John and his wife Jane, my goddaughter Mary, my sister Linda and her husband Mario, and especially my daughter Hannah, and my wife Lucy. You have been amazing. Thank you for bringing forth the poetry of everyday life.

An earlier version of chapter 2, section vii, was published in *Philosophy Today* 50, no. 2 (Summer 2006): 143–55.

I want to thank W. W. Norton & Company for kindly granting permission to cite translations from John Felstiner, *Selected Poems and Prose of Paul Celan*.

INTRODUCTION

THINKING POETIC MEASURE

> Before you play with fire, whether it be to kindle or extinguish it, put out first the flames of presumption (*Vermessenheit*) which overestimates itself (*sich vermisst*) and takes poor measure because it forgets the essence of *legein*.
>
> —Martin Heidegger, EGT, 76/GA 7, 231

MEASURING THE POETIC MEASURE OF JUSTICE

In the "Concluding Remark" to his SS 1942 lectures on *Hölderlin's Hymn "The Ister,"* Heidegger rounds off his reflections on the essence of poetry with a paradoxical gesture. On the rhetorical note of closure he opens up a fundamental question that, despite its singular precedence, remained concealed in his reflections on the Ister. The Ister cannot, Heidegger claims, be interpreted as a poetic "symbol" or "image" pointing to "something else." Rather, as he sees it, "the essence of rivers can, from the outset, be expressed only from the poetic dwelling of human beings" (HHI, 166–67/GA 53, 204–205). Poetic dwelling, in turn, does not signify domestic housing, architectural building, or the securing of shelter; it denotes the fundamental character of human existence as an abiding in being. The usual way we pose this question, Heidegger tells us, must be abandoned if we are to enter into the question of dwelling poetically. "Poetry demands of us a transformation in our ways of thinking and experiencing, one that concerns being in its entirety." To heed the call of authentic poetic dwelling demands that "we must first altogether let go of the actuality of such actual things as providing our supposed measure of truth, so as to enter that free realm in which the poetic is." Yet, given the poverty of our current state of questioning and its entanglement in the network of actual things, how can we even begin such a transformation? As Heidegger formulates this problem: "If this measure of what is actual and of beings is invalid, then from where are we to take our measure?"

In the age of frantic measuring where the straightedge and the bevel were giving way to new computational techniques of cybernetic calculation, Heidegger remained attuned to the necessity of reflecting upon the originary sense of measure and its intimate connection to the possibility of poetic dwelling. Recalling Hölderlin's late poem "In lovely blueness," Heidegger poses again the question that the poet raised:

Is there a measure on earth?

And he answers immediately and decisively:

There is none—

> This sounds like a token of hopelessness and despair. And yet it names something else and points to something else, provided we dwell poetically upon the earth . . . If we merely attempt, on our own authority, to set or seize upon the measure, then it becomes measureless and disintegrates into nothingness. If we merely remain thoughtless and without the wakefulness of a searching intimation, then once again no measure will show itself (HHI, 167/GA 53, 205).

In what follows I want to take up this Heideggerian-Hölderlinian question about the relation of measure to poetry and to poetic dwelling as a way of rethinking the problem of justice. My hope here is to engage the works of two philosophical poets who stand as the bookends of modernity: Friedrich Hölderlin (1770–1843) and Paul Celan (1920–1970). As part of my approach I try to offer close textual readings of poems from each that I see as defining and expressing some of the crucial problems of German philosophical thought in the twentieth century: tensions between the native and the foreign, the proper and the strange, *das Eigene* and *das Fremde*. At the center of this hermeneutic engagement with Hölderlin and Celan stands the conversation with Martin Heidegger about the meaning of poetic dwelling as a measure for a nonsubjective form of *ethos*. Ethics is possible—in the sense of poetic dwelling—only insofar as we genuinely dwell, an insight that Heidegger draws from his reading of Hölderlin. Our proper home is language, and the poet speaks bpth to and from our condition of homelessness. The poet acknowledges that we are strangely not at home in language and, in his poetizing, addresses this strange destiny as what is proper to us. At the same time, the poet acknowledges that we need to reclaim our lost home in being by carefully attending to the resonances of the poetic word as a way to find our way back home. Poetry cultivates an *ethos* of dwelling, an *ethos* of the ethicality of dwelling even as it takes the measure of our lack of just such an *ethos*. As Heidegger will express it, "Poetry is an originary kind of letting-dwell (*Wohnenlassen*)" (PLT, 227/GA 7, 206). It opens us to the hermeneutic wonder of language and its potential for both soaring transcendence and doubling ambiguity, but it also helps in attuning us to the ethical struggle for sense amid the senselessness of the modern condition. It is precisely as a response to such senselessness that Celan turns to poetry.

For Celan, poetry speaks to the homelessness of the Jewish dead, it houses the ashes of those murdered in extermination camps, attempting to provide a site for their burial. Yet as Celan's poetry so often shows us, the act of (re)collecting these scattered ashes (in both memory and in the poem) proves oftentimes impossible, as impossible as reclaiming the justice denied them in life. In the face of such impossibility Celan's famous Meridian speech exhorts us to "remain mindful" of the strange imbalance between what is native and foreign in German letters and in German history. As he frames this problem he asserts that "the poem has always hoped to speak . . . on behalf of the *strange* (*fremder*)—no, I can no longer use this word here—to speak *on behalf of an Other*—who knows, perhaps on behalf of a *wholly Other*" (GW III, 196). As a poetry of this Other, Celan's verse draws on a notion of the ethical that will both reinscribe and disrupt Heidegger's reflections on *ethos* as dwelling in an abode. A good deal of what follows can be read as a displaced conversation between Heidegger and Celan on the meaning of poetic dwelling as the measure of our human abode. If, as Heidegger claims, "ethics ponders the abode of the human being" (PM, 271/GA 9, 356), then Celan's poetry can be termed "ethical" for it thinks the lack of this abode for the *Ostjude*, for the exiled refugees of Central European power politics, for the unburied victims of the camps. Yet the way in which Heidegger and Celan approach this form of ethics as the abode or *Aufenthalt* of the human will be marked by profound difference. From his native Swabian homeland, Heidegger will turn to his fellow Swabian Hölderlin as a way of thinking the essence of poetry, going so far as to claim: "The poet's vocation is homecoming" (EHP, 47/GA 4, 28). But for the *Ostjude* Celan, denied a homeland by the logic of political exclusion, what emerges from this encounter with Heidegger's writing on Hölderlin is the sense of the very lack of having an abode. Against this shelterless existence without a homeland, Celan will come to craft an ethics of alterity for the Jew in exile. Hence, as Celan ponders Heidegger's notion of the home and his privileging of the proper against the foreign, he will think it in terms of a "reversal—the foreign as the proper—that which is Jewish"/ "Umkehr—das Fremde als das Eigene—Jüdisches" (TCA/M, 127).

In the chapters that follow we will engage this fateful juxtaposition of *das Fremde* and *das Eigene* as a way of thinking through a philosophical poetics of justice that attempts to loosen it from the grips of the metaphysics of the subject and its egological constitution of justice as a legal-moral measure.

But what is measure? And how are we to come to terms with measuring? Simply put, *Was heisst Messen?* (GA 7, 200). What is, or rather, what calls for(th) measuring? What does it mean to think measure? To think a poetic measure? And how might we come to think the poetic measure of justice? I raise these questions because I find in Heidegger's work a way of thinking about measure that finds its claim in the possibility of a nonmetaphysical way of dwelling that takes its inspiration from the poetry of Friedrich Hölderlin. In his 1951 essay ". . . Poetically Dwells the Human Being," Heidegger offers an engaged reading of Hölderlin's poem "In lovely blueness" as a way of thinking about poetic measure. As Heidegger puts it, "In poetry (*Dichten*) there essentially occurs (*ereignet sich*) what all measuring (*Messen*) is in the ground of its being. . . . Poetizing is, understood in the strict sense of the word, measure-taking (*Maß-nahme*) through which the human being first receives the measure for the expanse of its being" (PLT, 221–22/GA 7, 200). Such a measure can never be fixed as a standard for rules or directives; it does not allow itself to be measured by the matrices of number and calculation. Poetic measure, as the "taking" of measure (*Maß-nahme*), "does not consist in a clutching or any other kind of grasping, but rather is a letting-come of that-which-is-to-be-allotted (*in einem Kommen-lassen des Zu-Gemessenen*)" (PLT, 224/GA 7, 203). Poetic measure-taking is, then, less a "taking" than a *releasing* or a *letting-come* of that which cannot be thought in advance: of that which Schelling calls "the unprethinkable" (*das Unvordenkliche*).[1] In this sense, poetry takes the measure of that which cannot be taken measure of; it is incommensurable with any of the common standards of measure (Latin: *mensura*). In the very immeasurability of such measure the poet lets go of any egological gauges for the measure to be taken and opens himself to the event-character of being as that which conceals itself in withholding or withdrawal. It is in terms of this measure that Heidegger will put forward his own reading of Hölderlin:

> No German poet has ever achieved such distance from his own ego as that distance that determines Hölderlin's hymnal poetry. That is the real reason why we of today, who despite all "community" remain metaphysically, that is, historically entangled in subjectivity, have such difficulty in bringing the right kind of hearing to encounter the word of this poetry. What has for a long time hindered modern, contemporary human beings, who think in terms of self-consciousness and subjectivity, from hearing this poetry is

> simply this: The fact that Hölderlin poetizes purely from out of that which, in itself, essentially prevails (*west*) as that which is to be poetized. When Hölderlin poetizes the essence of the poet, he poetizes relations that do not have their ground in the "subjectivity" of human beings. (HHI, 165/GA 53, 203)

Poetic measure attunes itself to what cannot be thought in advance, to that which has no ground in subjectivity, to what is unknown and hidden. Such a measure does not reside *in* or *upon* the earth nor in the realm of the human but, rather, traverses the span of the human being's dwelling *between* earth and sky. In this "between" the human being dwells. By taking measure of such dwelling we come into the proximity or nearness (*Nähe*) of our being: "Only insofar as the human being takes the measure of (*ver-misst*) its dwelling in this way is it capable of *being* commensurate (*gemäß*) with its essence (*Wesen*)" (PLT, 221, 227/GA 7, 199, 206). Heidegger is well aware that this measure-taking is difficult and unusual. He variously terms it "strange" (*seltsam*), "alien" (*fremd*), "unknown" (*unbekannt*), and "mysterious" (*geheimnisvoll*). Poetry measures what is absent, what withdraws, what recoils from being measured. It measures the withholding power of language and the strange, foreign element of the invisible and the unthinkable. Poetic measure-taking is marked by a temporality of remembrance (*Andenken*) and waiting (*Warten*), a temporality of absence that "takes the measure for the architectonic, for the structural enjoining (*Baugefüge*) of dwelling." To release the self to this enjoining of time's mysterious order, to give oneself over to the event-character of being as a self-manifesting concealing, is to dwell in the space of the "between" that marks the dimensions of earth and sky. Hence, Heidegger can write: "Before anything else, poetizing lets human dwelling come into (*einläßt*) its essence. Poetizing is originary dwelling as a letting-dwell."

Yet this poetic measure is nothing that stands as a rule or standard outside of dwelling, nothing that can be applied to dwelling as an external criterion. Rather, the measure of dwelling is a *metron* of the unknown, the absential, the concealed, and the withheld.[2] In his Heraclitus lectures of SS 1944, Heidegger reflects on measure, claiming that "the essence of *metron* is the expanse (*die Weite*), the open (*das Offene*), the self-extending, self-expanding clearing (*Lichtung*)" (GA 55, 170). It is a *metron* that exceeds the limits of any calculable measuring, a *metron* whose measure Heidegger thinks not as distance, depth, height, or amplitude, but as our very relation to being. In this sense, Heidegger will rethink poetic dwelling as the taking of measure that gauges the essence (*Wesen*) of the human being—*Wesen* understood here not as a fixed, absolute "essence," but in its verbal sense as an event or happening ("essencing"), as the self-manifesting, self-concealing "happening of the truth of beyng" (CP, 202/GA 65, 288). Here the "essence" of the human being is understood in its Greek sense as *ethos*, which Heidegger will translate as *Aufenthalt*—sojourn, stay, residence, dwelling, abode. In the "Letter on Humanism" Heidegger will think the "*Wesensaufenthalt des Menschen*" ("the essential abode of the human being") as *ethos*, but not as "ethics" or "ontology" (PM, 271/GA 9, 357). Abjuring the term *ethics* as an impoverished discourse that has become caught up in the entanglements of modern technological enframing, Heidegger will instead ponder the problems of dwelling and poetic measure, claiming that "*only* this measure [the measure-taking of poetizing] gauges (*er-mißt*) the essence of the human being" (PLT, 223/GA 7, 202).

Poetry—especially the poetry of Hölderlin (whom Heidegger calls "our greatest poet")—brings us into proximity with the gods and with the distance of the gods' proximity (GA 39, 5).[3] Poetry offers hints (*Winke*) and insights into language, opening us to the concealed presence of being's reigning power in the ordinary, everyday phrases of our spoken dialects, disclosing the world to us in ways that resituate us in our accustomed haunts. In so doing, poetry takes the measure of the world—and therewith the measure of human being. Heidegger goes so far as to say that "poetizing first brings the human being onto (*auf*) the earth and toward (*zu*) it and in this way brings it into dwelling" (PLT, 218/GA 7, 196). That means that poetizing opens and shapes a way of being for humans as they inhabit the world in all its dimensions. But this measuring finds the human being as incommensurate with the measure of its own being. In its very haunts, in the very habitat that the human being inhabits, it is haunted by a sense of its lack of sense or meaning (*Sinn*). As Heidegger succinctly puts it, "That which is proper (*Eigenheit*) to the human being lies in this—that the human being does not belong to itself."[4] Heidegger's claim here should not, however, be understood as an existential pronouncement about the self-alienation of the human being. Rather, Heidegger discloses a more fundamental sense of being "alien" or "other" that he traces back to the tragic situation of Sophocles's *Antigone* where the human being is understood as *deinos*—the awesome, aw(e)ful being whose uncanny abilities yield strange and terrible wonders. The human being is alien to itself as part of its "singularly counter-turning character" in the way that "everything that is, is essentially permeated (*durchwest*) by its counter-essence (*Gegenwesen*)" (HHI, 68, 52/GA 53, 83, 64).

This sense of being strangely unsettled in the very settlements of our dwelling, of being utterly haunted in the haunts of our habitat, extends beyond any ontic question about domestic residence. It constitutes, rather, an interrogation of the very limits and possibilities of human existence since, for Heidegger, our existence is marked by a profound homelessness that is of ontological provenance. We are, he tells us, unique among beings in that we are not at home in being: "The human being alone can be called by the name 'the uncanny' (*der Unheimliche*), the un-homely one" (HHI, 69/GA 53, 84). But it is precisely this sense of not-being-at-home (*Un-heimlichkeit*) that remains concealed to modern humanity. At home in the technical world of computation, reckoning, and calculative thinking, we become habituated to the excess of large-scale proportion (*Ausmaß*) and "the properly dangerous configuration of measurelessness (*Maßlosigkeit*)" (HHI, 70/GA 53, 86). In so doing, we "overstep the limits of the homely, precisely in the direction of the uncanny" (IM, 161/EM, 116). In both his 1935 and 1942 lectures Heidegger will think such measureless excess in terms of Greek tragedy—especially Hölderlin's translation of the first choral ode of *Antigone*—and in Hölderlin's translation of *hybris* as *Vermessenheit* or "recklessness," the recklessness that comes from an excess of reckoning.[5] Both Oedipus and Antigone come to function as exemplary figures of such *Vermessenheit* in that they each experience the primordial homelessness of the human being in the uncanniest (*unheimlichste*) ways. As he comes to think the measure of such measurelessness, Heidegger will turn to Hölderlin's readings of Greek tragedy since only a *poetic* form of thinking strikes him as fitted for the task of thinking the measure of an essential human dwelling. And it is precisely to this question of "fit"—what Heidegger will variously think as *Fug, Gefüge, Fügung, Verfügung*—that I want to turn. In what ways does the human being "fit" in the world? How might the poetic reflection on dwelling be thought in terms of this fit? And how might we begin to ponder what is both fitting and unfitting about the human attempt to dwell in and against the poetic measure of being? Tragedy raises just such questions in its reflections on justice. Yet, as we shall see, Heidegger will reject the traditional discourse about justice as always already caught up in the moral-juridical metaphysics of Western thinking. Leaping back to the premetaphysical world of Anaximander and Heraclitus, Heidegger will think time itself as *dike*—not "justice" but "fittingness"(*Fug*).[6] He will even go so far as to write: "Being is fittingness that enjoins (*fügender Fug*): *dike*" (IM, 171/EM, 123). In other words, being is so essentially conjoined in the fit of *dike* that any human initiative to transgress its liminal horizons will be met with a countervailing limit. This is the lesson of Antigone and Oedipus that Heidegger would draw on in *Introduction to Metaphysics*: against the limits of the limit—made manifest in death—no human insurgency can prevail. For what comes to limit in Heidegger's thinking of a nonmoral, nonjuridical *dike* is nothing other than the limits of the human being against being itself. "Justice," in this sense, is less the standard set by any kind of human measure than it is being's own measure against which human beings must adjust. Justice as adjustment to being, as fitting-into the fit of *dike*, points to a realm of balance and equipoise that happens "beyond good and evil" in a way that cannot be configured by the figurations of human will. This pre-Socratic *dike* named by Anaximander and Heraclitus names something other than human justice; it thinks, rather, the poetic, world-forming jointure of discord and concord, strife and harmony, that eludes human control and comprehension. It names that which is "fitting" and measures its fittingness not by any human standards, but as the revealing/concealing play of the openness of what Heidegger calls *Ereignis*. This "event of appropriation" thinks being's claim (*Anspruch*) upon the human being as one that happens in/through language (*Sprache*)—especially the poetic language of poets such as Hölderlin and Sophocles.

HEIDEGGER'S POETIC MEASURE: AN ETHICS OF HAUNTING

In attempting to think the poetic measure of dwelling as *ethos*, Heidegger takes up the question of the strangeness of the human being to herself, of the unsettling and awesome dimension that both befits our tragic situation even as it shows us at moments how unfit we are to accede to the strange jointure of *physis*. My intention is to pose this question of the strangeness of human dwelling (*ethos*) by pondering the strange, uncanny language of Hölderlin and Celan, two German poets whose work is intimately connected to Heidegger. In the work of these two poets we find the doubled, contradictory possibilities of poetic dwelling thought against the very limits of strangeness and incalculability. For Hölderlin, this will take the form of a poetic meditation on tragedy as a discourse that sets into relation what is proper to the home as one's own (*das Eigene*) *and* what is strange, foreign, and other (*das Fremde*). As the "native stranger," Oedipus comes to embody this "furious excess (*Übermass*)" of "ever-contending (*immer widerstreitende*)" contrarieties that rend his search for a singular identity into the multiform shapes of monstrous polarities (SA V, 198, 201). As Hölderlin will read it, tragedy comes to embrace the impossible oppositions of a world that is enigmatic and marked by irreconcilability. Within such a world, tragedy provokes us by laying bare the very loss of measure that characterizes the recklessness of the human being who has forfeited its metric for dwelling. If modern metaphysics, armed with its Cartesian metric of control and calculation, presents a world where human beings strive to gain mastery and hegemony over beings, then Hölderlin's tragic poetry points to the foundering of such *hybris* as a form of *Vermessenheit*, a frantic measuring that has lost its measuredness. Such poetry leads us to confront difficult problems and decisions that emerge for those beings, like ourselves, who dwell at the limits of ambiguity and uncertainty, problems that have traditionally been called "ethical." In this sense, Hölderlin's writings, much like Heidegger's, literally resituate traditional problems of ethics at the site of a strange kind of *ethos*—understood as the "dwelling place," "abode," "site," "sojourn," or "stay" (*Aufenthalt*) of the human being upon the earth. In "The Rhine," Hölderlin poetizes this finitude of the human being as a form of dwelling within

> . . . the bounds
> Which God at birth assigned
> To him for his term and site (*Aufenthalt*). (SPF, 202–203)

As he attempts to articulate a nonmetaphysical language of poetic dwelling, Heidegger will take up Hölderlin's term *Aufenthalt* and think it in conjunction with Heraclitus's word about *ethos* as "the open region in which the human being dwells" (GA 9, 354–57; GA 39, 273–75). Moreover, in texts such as the "Letter on Humanism" and "The Verdict of Anaximander," both written in 1946, he will think such a possibility precisely at a moment of historical catastrophe. In the wake of Germany's incalculable loss of both human life and native habitat, Heidegger will think *ethos* in terms of its openness to a poetic form of dwelling. At the same time, he will resolutely lay bare this site as one that is also open to a monstrous inhabiting that might devastate any hopes for abiding in the home. As part of this selfsame effort, Heidegger will also take up a confrontation with the metaphysical tradition of justice by attempting to retranslate *dike* not through the Latin term *justitia*, or the German concept of *Gerechtigkeit*, but as "Fug"—that which is fitting or what befits our proper way of dwelling. What Heidegger undertakes to think in these translations is an untranslatable possibility of what cannot be named in the lexicon of ethics and justice. In casting aside "ethics," however, as the residue of a metaphysical stance toward beings, Heidegger does not somehow become "unethical." Instead, he will resituate those concerns that are typically classified under the discipline of ethics in a much broader region that will variously be named *ethos*, "originary ethics," *dike*, "fittingness," and "jointure." What pervades such a discourse and its possible translation is something that exceeds both the framework of humanism and the moral reckonings of an ethical calculus of good and evil.[7] In the "Letter on Humanism," Heidegger embraces a Heraclitean vision of *ethos* as a reciprocal belonging together of *Seyn* and *Dasein*, of being and the human being, whereby thinking abandons its erstwhile role as arbiter of values/measures and comes to a place where "it lets beings—be" (PM, 272/GA 9, 358). Here, ethics is no longer to be thought as constituting solely that realm governing relationships among human beings or between the human being and God. Rather, ethics is to be thought in an originary way as a modality of being's own way of holding (*halten*) us in its jointure as the order and habit of being itself—an ontological ethics rather than an ontic one. In this ethicality of ethics marked by the *ethos* of *Gelassenheit*, human beings will have been released from the cybernetic metaphysics of grasping and control that holds them in its thrall. And it is here in the realm of poetic dwelling that, I would argue, we can begin to see how powerfully attuned to ethical questions Heidegger's work truly is.

As Jean-Luc Nancy writes, "Only those who have read Heidegger blindly, or not at all, could think him a stranger to ethical preoccupations."[8] Heidegger will, following Nietzsche, break with the metaphysical tradition of good and evil that lies at the heart of the Judeo-Christian tradition. But he will also distance himself from the Kantian notion of a deontological ethics of obligation grounded in the subject. Thinking the ethicality of ethics will move Heidegger to deconstruct the idea of subjectivity back to the fundamental event of being (*Ereignis*) as the very disclosure of beings that appropriates us to its singular situatedness. Here, "ethics" will not be understood as the practice of "applying" principles, but as that which happens in the way being manifests itself. Within Heidegger's thought, "being displays its own ethicality," as François Raffoul so poignantly expresses it.[9] That means that Heidegger's reflection on the ethicality of ethics moves away from any egological enclosure within the subject and toward the open expanse of being as an event of truth that both reveals this openness, even as it veils this very revelation. On this reading, *ethos* as *Aufenthalt*, abode, sojourn, residence might appear to have the sense of a fixed dwelling "place." Yet, from its etymological roots in the verb *halten*, *Aufenthalt* indicates something much more than a place; it is also to be understood as a "holding" (*halten*) "up" (*auf*), a "holding-back" (*ent-halten*), or "with-holding" (*vor-enthalten*) that happens as the movement and temporal dynamic of being. *Halten*, from its medieval High German roots in *haltan*, denotes *hüten* and *bewahren* (to shelter or preserve) back to *Hirt* (shepherd)—so that we might understand Heidegger's pronouncement about the human being as the "shepherd of being" as being intimately bound up in his *Aufenthalt*—the proper *ethos* of holding and being held in the *Zuspiel* of being. *Aufenthalt*, then, might be understood as the site where the human being is held up for a while and in this whiling-abiding-staying is exposed to the self-manifesting and self-withholding of being as a temporal movement. This is why Heidegger will focus on Hölderlin's river hymns as having such an intimate relation to *Aufenthalt* since in their very movement they "determine the dwelling place of human beings upon the earth" (HHI, 20/GA 53, 23).

To think *Aufenthalt* in this way as poetic dwelling means to think it as a sojourning-in-withholding; it means a comportment (*Verhalten*) of self-restraint (*Sichverhalten*) in which we are held up in the withholding movement of being (CPC, 118–19/GA 77, 182–83). Here it is not the poet who is to be held as the measure, but being's way of holding us up in the withheld promise of its coming-to-be. Being is the measure, not "a" being—not God or the gods or law or principle or "ethics." In Heidegger's words: "The relationship of the human being to what gives a measure is a fundamental relationship to what is" (ZS, 100/ZSG, 130). To think this measure poetically is to think it as *ethos*—as a way of what Heidegger calls a "correspondence to the being of beings" (*eine Entsprechung zum Sein des Seienden*).[10] This involves responding to a call (*Zuspruch*) from being that calls us to what is properly our own (*das Eigene*)—and yet, as Hölderlin and Sophocles so powerfully remind us, what is proper to us is not our property, but something improper that eludes us in a way that is haunting. An ethics *of* being—in both senses of the genitive—would thus be an ethics not of a "substance," but of a calling to the task of dwelling in the openness of the event of being, an event that appropriates us through its claim (*Anspruch*). This is nothing other than "re/sponsibility"—a responding to the claim that being makes upon us. As Raffoul puts it, "Such original responsibility (response, correspondence, attunement to being) represents the essence of man."[11]

This is why ethics as the *Anspruch* (claim) of being can only come as a *Zuspruch* (appeal/calling) of language (*Sprache*) and not as a set of rules or directives. Ethics begins where the case does not fit the rule. It starts in uncertainty and aporia and opens us up to the incalculability of the decision. As Derrida will claim, "A decision always takes place beyond calculation."[12] And it is this incalculability that haunts ethics, that marks the site of our *Aufenthalt* as the unhomely, the improper, the strange, and the alien. At the very core of what is our own we are inhabited by a strange otherness that turns us away from our habits and habitudes toward the site of the inhabitual and monstrous. Such monstrousness haunts us in our haunts, threatening to dislodge us from our lodgings. Yet in this haunting visitation we are paradoxically opened to a realm of crisis and undecidability that jars us from the routinized, slumberous habits of our daily existence. Jean-Luc Nancy terms such an inhabitual *ethos* of dwelling "an ethics of haunting" and traces such haunting back to its etymological roots in the whole series of expressions clustered around the term *home*.

> Now what haunts (*hante*) is, according to its accepted etymological origins, what inhabits or occupies (*habite*) or, on a more knowing etymological reading, what returns to the stable, to the hearth, to the home. *Haunt* is from the same family as *Heim*. The proximity of the imperative might well be the *Un-heimlichkeit* that haunts our thinking, a disturbing peculiarity that disturbs only because it is so close, so immediate in its estrangement. But to return to the

> familiar abode is still to return to the *ethos*. The stakes here are none other than those of an ethics, therefore—not in the sense of a science or discipline, however, or in the sense of a moral sense or sentiment, but in the sense, precisely, of a haunting.[13]

To attend to this haunting of one's home, to follow the traces of an absential visitation (*Heimsuchung*) back to an abode that is uncanny (*unheimlich*), means to think at the limit of human possibility. Such an *ethos* abides in the traces of "something domestic that cannot be domesticated." Nancy recognizes in this uncanniness a dimension where ethics ceases to be something about rules to be applied and instead comes to haunt us as a responsibility that exceeds the measure of the human. Here "ethics"—understood as originary ethics that "ponders the abode of the human being"—is not a worldview, a value judgment, a norm, or a cultural principle, but the very ethicality of being itself (PM, 171/GA 9, 356). In this rendering of a non-egological ethics, being is understood as an event, an event that is at play in being's appropriation of us. Given that being is incalculable or unprethinkable (*unvordenklich*), a gift of the *es gibt* ("there is/it gives"), we can never get back behind this event to something more originary than the event itself. Hence, Heidegger's problem with "ethics" is that it does not remain open to the withdrawal of the event. It does not abide in the immeasurable singularity of this withdrawal, but strives instead to place the event "under" the rule or the category. For him the very desire for an ethics is marked by the technological strategy of calculating the measure of human action in advance so as to be able to "apply" its principles for the future.[14] Such an ethics, carried out within the calculative reckoning of *das Gestell*, closes off the openness of the event by circumscribing it within the measure of human estimation. But Heidegger's notion of originary ethics as a mode and measure of poetic dwelling attempts to twist free of the cybernetic conception of the ethical by rethinking our fundamental relationship to language.

Language is what is most proper to the human being—and yet, precisely *as* this most proper, it is at the same time that which is strangest and most foreign. As Heidegger writes in "The Letter on Humanism," "Language is the house of being" (PM, 239/GA9, 313). Still, the human being dwells within this house as if a stranger, where what is "ontically nearest is ontologically farthest" from it (BT, 12/SZ, 16).[15] Within the reigning *Gestell* of technological enframing, language has been literally dis-placed from the heart of humanity's dwelling place, devolving into an instrument for the production, delivery, and measurement of all oral and written discourse as "information." In viewing language as this thingly instrument, we are turned away from the fundamental event of being that happens in and through language. What transpires through the dominance of this calculative understanding of language is a leveling and formalizing of being's polytropic ways of presencing. This instrumental language literally in-forms beings by rendering them uni-form so that there can no longer be anything singular. Everything now con-forms with a standard of universal measurement. Yet how are we to overcome such a bleak prospect? For Heidegger, there is no hope for "overcoming" the technological epoch of *das Gestell* since any stratagem modeled on overcoming is fated to fall back into the selfsame structure of cybernetical calculation that informs it. At best, Heidegger thinks, we can only initiate a kind of "recovery" (*Verwindung*) from such a calculative approach to language that would eventuate in a "twisting free" (*Herausdrehung*) or "wresting free" (*Entwindung*) of it (GA 6.2, 330–36; GA 7, 77–78; GA 6.1, 304; GA 78, 175–78).[16] Yet transforming our relation to language means that "we must first turn back to the place where we already properly abide (*eigentlich aufhalten*)" (GA 12, 179, 177). This requires "finding in the proximity of the poetic experience with the word a possibility for a *thinking* experience with language," since this proximity "pervades everywhere our sojourn (*Aufenthalt*) upon this earth." Heidegger was convinced that "no human calculation-fabrication can, from out of or through itself alone, bring about a turn in the present state of the world."[17] Nonetheless, he claims, poetry, in league with thinking, could help to situate us in the proximity of such a turn by turning us to hidden possibilities that lay concealed amidst our contemporary relation to language. As Heidegger expresses it:

> Hölderlin's poetry is, for us, a fate. It waits for mortals to correspond (*entsprechen*) to it. This correspondence leads to the path of a turning that enters into the nearness of the gods that have fled, i.e., in the space of their flight, a flight that spares us.
>
> Yet how shall we recognize all of this and retain (*behalten*) it? In that we heed Hölderlin's poetry. (GA 4, 195)

Human beings can only come into this correspondence if they attend to the words of the poet. Only then can they dwell in nearness to the gods. "It remains necessary, therefore, to prepare the sojourn (*den Aufenthalt*) in this nearness." This can happen only if we "fatefully correspond to the fate that is Hölderlin's poetry."

What Heidegger privileges in this Hölderlinian *Aufenthalt* upon the earth corresponds to the ethicality of being as an attunement to the openness of an event that appropriates us (*Ereignis*). It is this openness, which Hölderlin terms "das Offene" (the Open), that comes to shape the relation between what is proper to us (*das Eigene*) and what continues to be strange and foreign within our propriety. In Hölderlin's poetry this constellation of issues comes to language in exemplary fashion in his elegy "Bread and Wine," where, he writes:

> By day and by night we're urged on by a sacred fire that
> Impels us to set out. So come! Come behold the Open (*das Offene*)
> Where we may seek what is ours (*Eigenes*), distant, remote, though it be!
> One thing is sure even now: at noon or reaching towards midnight
> Whether early or late, always a measure endures (*immer bestehet ein Maas*)
> Common to all, though his own to each one is also allotted
> Each coming and going according to his reach. (SPF, 152–53; translation altered)

In this poetic rendering of the Open that finds a measure for all things while simultaneously heeding the singular measure of what is properly our own, Heidegger will find a nonmetaphysical hint for doing justice to beings, of properly thinking their poetic measure. Heideggerian justice means thinking the measure of beings according to the measure of being—but that, in turn, means thinking being as an event of withdrawal that shelters and conceals its measure from the static gaze of the present. Hence, poetic measure can never be grasped as a normative measure or standard (*Maßstab*), but instead needs to be attuned to the immeasurability of concealment (*a/letheia*), withdrawal (*Entzug*), and withholding (*Vorenthalt*). It is in heeding the draft (*Zug*) of this withdrawal (*Entzug*) that we are drawn into "the nearness of the claim (*Anspruch*)" of being (WCT, 8–9, 17/GA 8, 10–11, 19). To fit into the order of this withdrawal, to let ourselves be taken up in this claim, means to hold ourselves open to the appropriating event of being, to correspond to its way of self-withholding—a mode of comportment Heidegger will term *Gelassenheit*, a releasement of the egological structure of the will.[18] To correspond to (*entsprechen*) the appeal (*Zuspruch*) of being, however, is nothing less than a heeding of our responsibility, a heeding the call for a responsible comportment to this event as an event of withdrawal. For Heidegger this means thinking in an originary way Hölderlin's mourning lament for the gods who have fled. It means thinking the order of being as one marked by a proper allotment that accords with the assignment of a finite, temporal sojourn that fits with the jointure of being, a jointure that lets itself be thought of as *dike*—a justice that cannot be thought as justice, a justice in excess of the measure of human justice, a justice that claims us in our disjointed time, waiting for us to accede to that fit which is befitting.

HÖLDERLIN'S HERACLITEAN MEASURE

Hölderlin's "Bread and Wine" exhorts us to "behold the Open" in such a way that we recognize that what is proper to us is remote and foreign; it calls us to recognize that there is "always a measure [that] endures." Though "common to all," this measure belongs to each one of us in an ineradicably singular way, granting us an abode where we can properly dwell in our sojourn upon the earth. To dwell, however, is not to remain within the self-enclosed boundaries of a residence or domicile; it is to be exposed to the openness of what-is-coming (*das Kommende*), to the measureless possibilities of what cannot be calculated in advance.[19] And yet, at the same time, the sojourn is itself limited by the finite boundaries granted to us by being for our stay on earth. This, I would argue, is what Heidegger means when he writes: "Thinking builds upon the house of being, the house in which the jointure of being (*die Fuge des Seins*), in its destinal unfolding, enjoins (*verfügt*) the essence of the human being in each case to dwell in the truth of being" (PM, 272/GA 9, 358). To dwell is to be open to the excess (*Übermass*) of being that exceeds all beings, especially the human being. To belong to being, to be claimed by its call, is to be open to this excess in a way that heeds the measure of our finite dwelling. What the poetry of Hölderlin signifies for Heidegger is a measure-taking of the human dwelling place, of its sense as the *ethos* where we are open to the appropriative event of being as that which is coming. In "Poetically Dwells the Human Being," Heidegger contends that such measure-taking occurs most properly in poetry, a poetry that attunes itself to the "letting-come of what has been measured-out and apportioned (*Zu-Gemessenen*)" (PLT, 224/GA 7, 203). On this reading, poetic justice would consist in embracing an Anaximandran sense of justice as the proper apportioning of being in each and every case, an apportioning and allotment that gives each being its due measure without surmounting its singularity or subsuming it in a metaphysics of the whole. It would mean doing justice to being—as event, not as substance.

This kind of poetic justice would designate a kind of belonging to being that does not measure it in terms of the reigning set of relations that obtains in the world in which we dwell. Such a poetizing of justice would be in excess of the world, would not be enclosed within the configurations of values, worldviews, moral systems, juridical principles, customs, or habits. It would exceed such subjective enclosures in the direction of language itself as the call that is not simply "the call of conscience," but rather the call of being, calling us to properly attend to our ownmost possibilities of dwelling (PM, 260/GA 9, 342). This, for Heidegger, would characterize freedom in its deepest sense: "Being-open for a claim" (*Offensein für einen Anspruch*), the claim that being makes upon us and to which we are called to respond

(ZS, 217/ZSG, 272).[20] In responding to this call, the human being comes to itself by coming into the just allotment gifted to us as the appropriate dispensation in the event of appropriation (*Ereignis*).

As Jean-Luc Nancy puts it, "What is appropriate is defined by the measure proper to each existent *and* to the infinite, indefinitely open, circulating, and transforming community (or communication, contagion, contact) of all existences between them."[21] Such appropriateness defines the condition of justice, which he sees as what happens to human existence in its being exposed to the event of being, being ex-posed or expulsed from its egological enclosure toward the otherness, alterity, multiplicity, exteriority *of* being. Justice here comes to mean grasping the groundless coming out of nothing that characterizes the gift that *is* the world, a world that "is without models, without principle, and without given end, and that this is precisely *what* forms the justice and the meaning of a world."

Framed differently:

> Justice is thus the return to each existent its due according to its unique creation, singular in its coexistence with all other creations. The two measures are not separate: the singular property exists according to the singular trace that joins it to other properties. What distinguishes is also that which connects "with" and "together."

One finds resonances here of Heraclitus's fragment B 8—"The counter-thrust brings together (*sympheron*), and from tones at variance (*diapheronton*) comes perfect attunement (*harmonia*), and all things come to pass through conflict (*eris*)"—that Heidegger will translate in his Heraclitus lectures of SS 1944 as, "Faring-against [is] a bringing together and from out of setting-at-variance: the one radiant enjoining" (*Das Gegen-fahren ein Zusammenbringen und aus dem Auseinanderbringen die eine erstrahlende Fügung*) (GA 55, 145).[22] The jointure of *physis* enacts a harmonizing opposition that claims and enjoins (*verfügt*) us to dwell in the abode allotted to us. Heidegger comes back to this Heraclitean notion of justice as jointure (*Fuge*) in his discussion of originary ethics from "The Letter on Humanism," when he thinks it in relation to poetic dwelling:

> Thinking builds upon the house of being, the house in which the jointure (*Fuge*) of being, in its destinal unfolding, enjoins (*verfügt*) the essence of the human being in each case to dwell in the truth of being. (PM, 272/GA 9, 358)

In the Heraclitean play of conference and difference, *sympheromenon* and *diapheromenon*, Heidegger will point to an originary indication of the full phenomenological interplay of presencing and absencing, appearance and withdrawal that marks the pre-Socratic notion of truth as *aletheia*—un-concealment. Hölderlin's poetry, like the texts of Anaximander, Heraclitus, Parmenides, and Sophocles, points toward an originary sense of the openness of the human being within this event of playful concealment as revelation. What Hölderlin offers is a poetic measure for thinking the Heraclitean notion of *metron* as "the Open." In the Heraclitus lectures Heidegger affirms that "the fundamental meaning, i.e., the essence, of *metron* is the expanse (*die Weite*), the open (*das Offene*)" (GA 55, 170). Here, poetic measure is thought less as a normative standard than as a measure attuned to the immeasurability of being's withdrawal, of its play of *pres-ab-sence*.[23] To think this measure poetically is to gain an opening to a site for originary dwelling, an *Aufenthalt* or *ethos* that holds us open to the withholding event of being. In the draft (*Zug*) of this withdrawal (*Entzug*) stands the figure of Oedipus who is strangely at home in his loss of measure, marked by an excess of measure that sets him apart in an uncanny singularity. In his poem "In lovely blueness," Hölderlin expresses this Oedipal mark of excess by exclaiming:

> King Oedipus has an eye too many perhaps. (PF, 791)

Oedipus's excess or *hybris*—from the Greek verb *hybrizein* used to describe the wanton growth of plants running riot—sets him apart in multiple ways, not least of which is his bifurcated, conflicted, and ambiguous relation to the proper.[24] In the figure of Oedipal excess, the human being, as Hölderlin puts it, "incites itself to know more than it can bear or comprehend" (HS, 65/SA V, 198). "In the doubled-schismatic sojourn (*Aufenthalt*) of the human being," Heidegger claims, "presumption (*Vermessenheit*) comes to dominion" (GA 55, 326). As we inhabit the habitat allotted to us within being, we comport ourselves in a doubled ambiguity: strangers to ourselves, we lose the measure for a proper dwelling, forgetting being's measure as we get lost in the quotidian measures of habit and custom. To dwell in the uncustomary-inhabitual (*ungewöhnlich*) exile of Oedipus is to come to terms with the finitude of our sojourn, its destitution and displacement. Hölderlin thinks this displacement as belonging to our proper sense of dwelling. Indeed, he conceives of it as bound up with negotiating the tragic tension that shapes our fate as finite creatures who, unlike the deathless gods, must inevitably perish. The human sojourn, understood as the proper form of *ethos*, must attend to the just limits admeasured by *dike*. To live within these limits, to abide by the abode ordained as our proper dwelling, is to embrace a poetic *ethos* of limitation—of an *Aufenthalt* (*ethos*) marked by *Verhaltenheit* (restraint) (GA 45, 1–2; GA 65, 12–16, 33–36, 398–408).

While acknowledging the immeasurable distance of the gods to such a fate, Hölderlin calls upon the poet "to present the world in an attenuated or diminished measure (*im verringerten Maßstab*)," since he is mindful that there is no measure on this earth, no humanly scaled vision of justice that could do justice to the incalculable openness of being (SA V, 272).

For Hölderlin, the amplitude of this "diminished measure" will play itself out in the Heraclitean opposition between strife and harmony, emergence and expiration that shows itself as an "everlasting fire, kindled in measures and in measures going out" (Fragment B 30).[25] As Heidegger reads it, the taking of such a measure defines the task of the poet which, in its most essential sense, "is the measure-taking for the dwelling of the human being" (PLT, 224/GA 7, 202). Hölderlin will poetize this dwelling in a dialogue with the ancient Greeks, focusing upon the relation between what is foreign and what is proper. To properly dwell, Hölderlin wants to say, requires that we set out from our home and journey outward to encounter the foreign as an estranged possibility that holds forth the promise of a healing return. Dwelling, sojourning, requires journeying abroad in an Odyssean wandering that takes the form of a *nostos*—a return home that completes the spirit's journey toward self-knowledge. To become who we are requires an exposure to the other, an exposure that takes the form of a Hölderlinian law of history: authentic self-unfolding depends upon the foreign, the strange, the uncanny, the Other. "Poets must first be mariners," since it is only in voyaging upon strange seas that they come to a proper sense of self (EHP, 118/GA 4, 95). The measure of poetic dwelling thus becomes an encounter with the immeasurable openness of the foreign. In his essay on Hölderlin's "Remembrance," Heidegger writes:

> This is the law of poetry for future poets, and the fundamental law of the history that is to be grounded by them. The historicity of history has its essence in a return to what is proper to one (*in der Rückkehr zum Eigenen*), a return that could only be made as a journey outward into what is foreign (*als Ausfahrt in das Fremde*). (EHP, 118/GA 4, 95)

In his epistolary novel *Hyperion*, Hölderlin expresses this Heraclitean law in succinct terms: "The life of the world consists in the alternation of opening and closing, in departure and return to itself (*in Ausflug und in Rückkehr zu sich selbst*)" (H, 51/SA III, 38). This selfsame pattern of journey and return, *Ausflug* and *Rückkehr*, will shape all of Hölderlin's late hymns, functioning as a way of measuring the poetic possibilities of Pindaric self-knowledge. Hölderlin's own attempts at translating Pindar's odes will take the form of this model of journey and return, shaping his understanding of the relation between Germany and Greece expressed in his famous Böhlendorff letter. There, Hölderlin writes that the enigma of self-identity can only be properly addressed by entering into the ordeal of the foreign. Yet the name *Greece* here, as Dennis Schmidt reminds us, is not a historical destination, but "the name of the experience of an absence, of a sorrow once removed" that is marked by exile from, and mourning for, a possibility of dwelling poetically.[26] For Heidegger too, "Greece" would be thought of not as a geographical location, but as the site for an archaeology of poetic measure attuned to the Heraclitean experience of *ethos* as an originary ethics of dwelling. In his lectures of WS 1941/42, *Hölderlins Hymne 'Andenken,'* Heidegger will read the Hölderlinian journey into the foreign as bound up with the poet's "free sojourn" (*freien Aufenthalt*) in the proper, a sojourn he calls "the most difficult" (GA 52, 173). Yet for Heidegger the strangeness of the foreign, like the alterity of the other, is thought essentially only in and through the proper. As he puts it:

> Indeed to be able to freely use the most proper (*das Eigenste*), in order, first and foremost, to be able to learn the free use of the proper (*den freien Gebrauch des Eigenen*), requires a confrontation with the foreign (*dem Fremden*). Hence, spirit must venture into the foreign, not to get lost there and to neglect what is of the fatherland, but so that it can prepare itself in the foreign for the proper and make itself strong. . . .

Or as he formulates it later in these same lectures:

> The sojourn (*Aufenthalt*) in the foreign and the learning of the foreign—which is not for the sake of the foreign, but rather for the sake of the proper—demands that kind of persistence that no longer thinks of the proper. (GA 52, 123, 190)

And yet what remains fundamental to Heidegger as he thinks through the measure of this Hölderlinian law of history is the return home to what is properly one's own. That remains primary: "What is of the proper and its appropriation—that is the most difficult. Learning the foreign, however, that stands in the service of such appropriation (*Aneignung*)" (HHI, 124/GA 53, 154). What remains primary for Heidegger is less the journey outward for its own sake than the return homeward for the sake of coming back to the proper. The *ethos* of poetic dwelling that runs through Heidegger's meditations on Hölderlin is marked by a vision of "homecoming [as] the return into nearness to the origin (*die Rückkehr in die Nähe zum Ursprung*)" (EHP, 42/GA 4, 23). In his essay "The Trace of the Other," Levinas offers a powerful critique of Heidegger's reverie of homecoming, which he terms "the tautology of ipseity" where everything that is other, alien, foreign, "the *outside of me* is *for me*."[27] This inability to think the other in its otherness, rather than as an element in the self's pilgrimage homeward, is, Levinas claims, endemic to Western philosophy's reigning tendency from Parmenides through Hegel (and beyond) to privilege identity over difference. For Levinas, Heidegger's reading of Hölderlinian *Ausflug* and *Rückkehr* merely reprises the Odyssean myth of *nostos* as a return home to the self by way of the other, rather than as a journey outward into the foreign that abdicates the possibility of return. In this allergic reaction to the other, Heidegger (as Levinas reads him), continues "to affirm being as identical with itself" and represses the absolute exteriority of the foreign to the proper. Against Heidegger's Odyssean myth of homecoming, Levinas wishes to juxtapose the Abrahamic myth of exile, which he sees as a radical alternative to the isomorphic thinking of Western philosophy.

> *A work conceived radically is a movement of the same unto the other which never returns to the same*. To the myth of Ulysses returning to Ithaca, we wish to oppose the story of Abraham who leaves his fatherland forever for a yet unknown land and forbids his servant to even bring back his son to the point of departure.

Like Franz Rosenzweig, Levinas seeks to challenge the hegemony of Parmenidean identity and Odyssean homecoming as the legacy of the West and draw instead upon Hebraic sources for an Abrahamic *ethos* of exile and dispersion. In the Jewish experience of wandering and exodus each finds a way of privileging the alterity of the stranger "outside all enrootedness and all dwelling."[28] It is this experience of exteriority that Levinas sees as defining the rupture that forms the fault line of the Athens/Jerusalem (non)-conversation in Western thought. Here Levinas is, like Derrida, Celan, and Arendt, part of those for "whom immigration, dispersion, and the impossibility of integration make despair of any return."[29] Haunted by a profound mourning for the loss of the singular—of the singular dwelling, the singular life, the singular word of hope for a future whose unfolding was cut off at the root—Levinas and Derrida will vigorously oppose the philosophical movement toward totality and its totalizing, totalitarian imperatives. Resisting the drive to render ethics as something universal, applicable across all cases, both will affirm a way of thinking that comes to privilege justice over truth, ethics over ontology, the responsibility of care over the primordiality of essence, lack over plenitude, the theology of the cross over the theology of glory. In their rabbinic call for a "justice to come," for an "impossible justice" that resists becoming a static principle, Derrida and Levinas appeal to the ethical legacy of Jerusalem over the ontological legacy of Athens. It is this legacy of privileging justice over knowledge that will shape their thinking as a way of reclaiming the ethical significance of exile, absence, foreignness, and alterity in the face of Heidegger's privileging of homecoming and German dwelling. It is precisely this kind of critique that I wish to pursue later in my reading of the poetry of Paul Celan.

CELAN AND THE (IM)POSSIBILITY OF JUSTICE

The poems that I will look at closely in chapter 3 ("Tübingen, Jänner," "Todtnauberg," and the "Jerusalem Poems") all deal with the notion of geographical location and the realm of being-in and being-out-of place. All of these poems in their own way focus on the problem of "dwelling" and its impossibility in the shadow of the Shoah. Celan understood in a profound way Adorno's lament that "[d]welling, in its proper sense, is no longer possible."[30] His poems attempt to bring to language the limits of the unsayable, pushing against the boundaries of speech in an effort to mourn the numberless dead in the name of what Derrida would call a "justice of the impossible." These poems bring the German language to the strange and uncanny (*unheimlich*) limit that defines the proper relation to the homeland—or perhaps to the propriety of such a limit in the face of both the destruction of the homeland as an *Eigenes* and the homeland's destruction of the other as a *Fremdes*. Here, Celan would follow Levinas and Derrida in his unrelenting critique of Heideggerian totality and totalitarianism. In his private journal he would draft a devastating letter to Heidegger that he would never send, charging him "that you, through your comportment (*Haltung*) decidedly undermine the earnest will to responsibility in both the realms of the poetical (*Dichterische*) and, if I dare presume, the thinkerly (*Denkerische*)."[31]

As brutal and severe as Celan's critique may strike us, it gives voice to a long-standing uneasiness within continental thought to what Reiner Schürmann terms "the modern hegemonic phantasm" that reigns in modern philosophy—namely, philosophy's thetic tendency to bring all difference under the genus of a unifying singularity that is paradoxically a totality—be it water, *pneuma*, God, *Geist*, will to power, *Seyn*.[32] This philosophical desire for univocity, the univocal law of all being, betrays a longing for universality, completeness, totality that denies the inconvenience of factical experience in its fragmented, broken shards. The poetry of Celan affirms this irreducible singularity in its insistence on the uniqueness of the word, as well as the *Einmaligkeit* of the date.[33] In his celebrated "Meridian Speech," Celan will draw attention to such singularity in his claim that "the poem (*das Gedicht*) . . . remains mindful (*eingedenk*) of its dates."[34] In the relationship between *Dichten* and *Denken*, a relationship so highly prized by Heidegger, Celan comes to affirm the poetic dimension of the singular, the strange, the other, and the foreign that the poem privileges over philosophical totality. "The poem wants to reach an Other, it needs this Other," claims Celan. When Heidegger and Celan finally met at the philosopher's mountain retreat at Todtnauberg in the summer of 1967, the poet brought with him a deep ambivalence about engaging the former Nazi rector. After his public reading at the University of Freiburg he refused to have his photograph taken with Heidegger, yet he nonetheless accepted an invitation to go to his Hut in the Black Forest, symbol of Heidegger's renowned discourse about home, hearth, roots, and *Heimat*.[35] When he did arrive there with Heidegger the conversation was uneasy; a long car ride was marked by a painful breech of silence. A proposed *Wanderung* on the moors of Todtnauberg was interrupted by wet ground and poor weather conditions. Against this background, it is clear that the encounter with Heidegger was anything but an insignificant academic formality for Celan.[36] He had read Heidegger with great intensity since 1953 and his personal library contained thirty-three of Heidegger's works. Clearly, he was (as his poem "Todtnauberg" relates) seized by "a hope . . . / for a thinker's / (un-/delayed coming) / word / in the heart" (SPP, 314–15)—a word that, not surprisingly, never came.

Celan was convinced that "poems are gifts," gifts given to us by language, a language that in his eyes was threatened by the onslaught of technological and cybernetic modes of understanding. In a letter to a friend he writes, "There is no longer language (*Sprache*), no longer conversation (*Gespräch*)—no, it is information, systems of words with an exact specification of wavelengths for 'reception,' sterile *formal designing* tuned to the eyes of a complex."[37] In offering this critique of language Celan undoubtedly draws heavily on the work of the postwar Heidegger who, in various essays, lectures, and books, addressed many of these same issues—especially language's relationship to the homeland and those rooted in the German earth.[38] It is no mistake that Heidegger would address this primordial connection between language and the homeland, *Sprache und Heimat*, precisely in those texts by Friedrich Hölderlin and J. P. Hebel dealing with poetry and its relation to thinking (*Dichten und Denken*), texts that Heidegger read as focusing on the intimate connection between autochthonous dwelling in the Alemannic homeland and "the poetic being of fateful autochthonous language" (GA 13, 177). Celan too would come to understand cybernetics and the information-sciences as threats to the vitality of the German language, especially the language of poetry; but he would radically challenge Heidegger's fateful association of language with an all too provincial grasp of dwelling, homeland, *Volk*, earth, and dialect. Following Heidegger's reading of *ethos* as *Aufenthalt* ("dwelling") in "The Letter on Humanism," Celan would interpret language itself as *ethos*, as the place of dwelling for those without a homeland, those wandering exiles banished from the province and forced to live as expatriates expelled from the *patria* or "fatherland." As Celan came to express it, "language, especially in the poem, is *ethos—ethos* as fateful truth-projection (*Wahrheitsentwurf*)."[39] It is clear that the language employed here is unmistakably Heideggerian. Nonetheless, Celan will turn this language away from Heidegger's ontological project of *Seynsgeschichte* back toward an ethical awareness of the human being as a singular Thou who demands of me a recognition of her otherness. Denied access to the privileged *Feldweg* of autochthonous poetic rumination, Celan will rethink Heidegger's poetic abode of the homeland in terms of an *ethos* of/for those displaced and abandoned.

In the face of all the destruction and monstrous, *unheimlich* brutality wrought by the whole complex of NS-Deutsch and its "formal designing" of *topoi* of murder and extinction, Celan will speak of enduring the "answerlessness" of language, of having to "pass through frightful muting, through the thousand darknesses of deathbringing speech" in order to "orient myself, to find out where I was and where I was meant to go, to project [*entwerfen*] reality for myself" (CPP, 396/GW III, 186; translation altered). It is in this spirit that Celan speaks of writing poetry as a "despairing conversation" addressed to "a Thou [who] . . . brings along its otherness into this present" (CPP, 410/GW III, 198). As I will argue, the meeting with Heidegger at Todtnauberg will constitute just such a "despairing conversation" since Celan's hopes for "an earnest conversation" would be dashed by Heidegger's silence on the very *topos* of the National Socialist destruction of the Jews and of Heidegger's complicity therein.[40] In and through this despairing conversation with Heidegger—about poetry, about language, about the homeland and one's own in relation to the exiled and the foreign—Celan would try to confront what he believed Heidegger was unable to confront. And yet so much of Celan's poetic language draws from Heidegger, especially Heidegger's claim that "language is grounded in silence. Silence is the most concealed form of holding-the-measure (*Maß-halten*). It *holds* the measure, in that it first posits measures" (CP, 359/GA 65, 510; translation altered). In this shroud of language's silence, Heidegger would withdraw back into the sheltered abode of his Black Forest retreat, making any genuine *Gespräch* with Celan impossible. In attempting to address the impossible conditions for such an encounter, Celan would write his poem "Todtnauberg," a text marked by *aporia*, caesura, distance, and silence. In the first draft of the poem, which he excised from his final manuscript, Celan configured his encounter with Heidegger in words drawn from Hölderlin and from Heidegger's renowned essay

"Hölderlin and the Essence of Poetry" (1936). In this text Heidegger grants to the poet a founding role in the instauration of an other beginning in the life of a *Volk* and references Hölderlin's classic line from the early drafts to "Friedensfeier": "since we are a conversation / and able to hear from each other" (PF, 518–19). But Celan turns the poet's words against the thinker and writes, "*since we are a conversation* / on which / we choke / on which I choke / that thrust me out of myself, three times / four times."[41] And he does so precisely in the way he challenges both Heidegger's understanding of the role of language and the poet *and* in the way he reads Hölderlin.

Central to Heidegger's Hölderlin interpretation is the poet's letter to Casimir Ulrich Böhlendorff written in December 1801 on the eve of his journey to southern France. From the role it plays in several of his major writings we can see how Heidegger's whole relation to Hölderlin, poetry, language, the homeland, the Greeks (and their relation to the Germans) and the history of the West, is deeply invested in a reading of its significance.[42] This letter will become a focal point in the chapters that follow because in it I locate a fundamental relation between the native and the stranger, one's own (*das Eigene*) and the foreign (*das Fremde*) that will get played out in the three major figures of this book as the relation of Germany to Greece, modernity to antiquity, Athens to Jerusalem, Occident to Orient. For Heidegger, the foreigner, the stranger, the Jew, the Asiatic will all come to represent a threat to the homeland, constituting an "uncanny" (*unheimlich*) other who undermines the rooted dwelling of the homeland (*Heimat*). Yet Celan will challenge this way of reading the Böhlendorff letter's thematization of *das Eigene* and *das Fremde* and will raise questions that subvert Heidegger's understanding of the proper.

Part of what I want to try to unravel in this book is a way of navigating the perilous transition/translation between "ourselves" and the "foreign" that marks the discourse of twentieth-century German thought, a discourse imbricated in, and inseparable from, the names "Heidegger" and "Celan." In his own translations from ancient Greek—especially the poetry of Pindar and the tragedies of Sophocles—Hölderlin will attempt a poetology of the native and the stranger that brings into relief the tensions, caesuras, and aporias of poetry and philosophy, Greek and Hesperian, Athens and Jerusalem, ethics and ontology. In Hölderlin's work, I will argue, we can find traces of a nonmetaphysical, poetic *ethos* that strives to bring the native and the foreign into relation without subsuming them into a higher third term that "reconciles" them in a supersession while losing the tension that holds them together. In Hölderlin's texts I will try to locate a poetology of the *unheimlich* that is not generated by what Schürmann calls a "hegemonic phantasm" of totality, universality, identity, and a nostalgia for the purity of the singular origin. Rather, here we might be able to find sketches for what

Celan will paradoxically term "*FREMDE NÄHE*"—"strange nearness"—the uncanny sense of coming into one's own through the nearness of what is alien. Something of this paradoxical logic of opposition without subsumption under the metaphysical dream of *Versammlung*, assembly, gathering is captured in a passage from *Negative Dialectics* where Adorno writes:

> The reconciled condition would not be the philosophical imperialism of annexing the alien. Instead, its happiness would lie in the fact that the alien, in the proximity it is granted, remains what is distant and different, beyond the heterogeneous and beyond that which is one's own (*das Eigene*).[43]

When the Greek "other" becomes native in the German homeland, when "the Asiatic" is banished in the hope of a longed-for "preservation of the European *Völker*," when claims are put forth *ex cathedra* that "there is only *Greek* tragedy and no other besides it," then the power of Heraclitean *polemos* collapses into homology (EdP, 31; P, 90/GA 54, 134).[44] As an attempt to carry out that "despairing conversation" that was never held between Heidegger and Celan, I want to pose questions about the relation of native and foreign that go to the heart of the philosophical-poetic notion of *ethos* and dwelling posed by Heidegger in "The Letter on Humanism." But I want to frame these questions by virtue of a conversation about the role of Athens and Jerusalem and the way in which each tradition frames the question of *ethos* against its own notion of dwelling and exile respectively, and how each brings into question their differing notions of justice. One will be measured by *physis* itself as a cosmic play of contention and harmony (Anaximander, Heraclitus, Nietzsche, Heidegger) and the other will be thought as the incommensurable relation between a self and an other—what Levinas, writing in the wake of the unacknowledged Shoah, would term "the face of the other."[45] My reading will be determined by the conviction that Hölderlin's interpretation of the Greeks has much in common with the twentieth-century Jewish critique of ontology in Rosenzweig, Levinas, Derrida, and Celan—namely, that it sees in the Greeks' positive appropriation of the foreign a way of working through the metaphysics of totality-identity that dominates the work of Western philosophy from "Parmenides to Hegel," as Rosenzweig put it.[46] In tracing these themes through a reading of Greek tragedy and its aporetic understanding of justice, I hope to follow a thread of interpretation for a poetic form of justice that seeks to rethink the problem of *measure* in poetic terms as something wholly other than the Protagorean-Cartesian notion of a human measure. In this ungrounding of the subject as the fundament of measure, a new possibility of ethics emerges in its sense as a non-anthropocentric *ethos*.

As I undertake an interpretation of the problem of poetic measure in Hölderlin, Heidegger, and Celan, I try to think this in relation to questions about ethics and justice. In each chapter I try to focus on the work of the figure discussed. Hence, in chapter 1, I concentrate on the work of Hölderlin apart from a Heideggerian interpretation. There I offer close readings of three of Hölderlin's poems—"The Ister," "In lovely blueness," "Der Frieden"—as well as discuss "Patmos" and the famous Böhlendorff letter, focusing on the problem "das Eigene und das Fremde." As part of my focus, I try to show how Hölderlin's various texts—especially his translations of Pindar and Sophocles—constitute a way of understanding poetic dwelling in ethical terms derived from Greek tragedy, yet open to its alterity. Chapter 2 takes as its starting point the question that Heidegger raises in his "Letter on Humanism" about the relationship between ontology and ethics. Raising this question in 1946, just after the German defeat in World War II and the volatile situation brought about by the Nürnberg trials, Heidegger rethinks the question of ethics in terms of the pre-Socratic experience of "jointure," rather than "justice." In this chapter I offer close readings of both GA 46, *Zur Auslegung von Nietzsches II. Unzeitgemäßer Betrachtung* and of the 1946 essay "The Verdict of Anaximander," as well as discuss Heidegger's notion of *ethos* in his Aristotle lectures from the early 1920s and his Heraclitus lectures from 1943–44. In Chapter 3, I present a reading of some of Celan's most important poems, one that situates their poetic-philosophical questions against the work of Derrida, Levinas, and Blanchot. There I do close readings of "Tübingen, Jänner," "Todtnauberg," and six of his lesser-known "Jerusalem Poems" from *Zeitgehöhft* written months before his death. In Celan's attempts to juxtapose the Kabbalah against the poetry of Hölderlin and the philosophy of Heidegger, I engage Celan's poetology of place and displacement as a way of rethinking Heidegger's ethics of dwelling as the proper measure for what we might call the thinking of "justice."

ONE

THE HÖLDERLINIAN MEASURE OF POETIC JUSTICE

> Fate, it measures us perhaps with the span of being,
> so that it appears strange to us.
>
> —Rilke, *Sonnets to Orpheus*, II, 20

> The measure has a name: justice.
>
> —Jean-Luc Nancy, "On the Multiple Senses of Democracy"

"THE SIGNS OF THE TIMES": "PATMOS"

Poetry opens to us as an act of interpretation. The poet confronts the world in all its recalcitrance and attempts to render its possibilities in terms of the limits afforded the poet by the resources of language. For Hölderlin, poetry as *Dichtung* is fundamentally tied to *Deutung*, as he puts it in the last lines of "Patmos":

> . . . but what the Father
> Who reigns over all loves most
> Is that the solid letter (*Der veste Buchstabe*)
> Be given scrupulous care, and that which endures
> Be well interpreted (*gut/Gedeutet*) . . . (SPF, 242–43)

The poet's song offers a way for humans to negotiate the venerable distance between gods and mortals by providing an interpretive framework for their awe. The gods are, for mortals, both awe-full and awful: the gods fill us with awe at their power, distance, and glory even as our attempts at getting close to them often prove awful and threatening. Uncertainly, the poet dwells in the middle between gods and mortals mediating the distance that separates them, caught in the tension between being the voice that brings together a community and being the isolated and homeless wanderer in search of his homeland. To be a poet for Hölderlin, to take on the poet's task of approaching the divine, means to live in tension and ambivalence, ever balancing the poet's special calling with the human, all too human, presumption of hybristic knowledge. In Hölderlin's poetic interpretation, we venture to balance the middle against the ends, the present against the past and future, the human being against nature and the divine. Always the poet lies in the middle, the hermeneutic mediator who strives to interpret the overarching scheme of divine order for a humanity that has forgotten how to read the signs of the times.

In his office as interpreter of divine signs, the poet becomes a prophet, the one who—in its etymological sense—"speaks (*phasis*) before (*pro*)" something is known and through such speaking makes it known. But the Greek root *pha* "to declare, make known, say" also relates to *phan* "to bring to light, to show, to shine."[1] The poet, then, as the prophet who makes known to other members of the community that which is hidden, stands in the middle, or at the threshold, of darkness and light. And yet the poet is unable to bring the light to the darkness on his own. To arrogate such a claim for himself would be to exceed the boundaries of his office. The poet can only hope to call forth the light, to evoke its force and let it come of its own power. But he can never cross the boundary line between light and darkness, speech and silence, mortality and divinity. To do so would occasion a certain kind of self-destruction and annihilation. For the poet must always know how to honor the boundaries between speaking in the name of a god and striving to become as a god, between interpreting god's will and imposing his own will. In reading the signs of the god's will in the world around him, and by honoring the boundaries between the realm of the gods and the realm of mortals, the poet must balance the tension of nearness and distance even as he must negotiate a way of bringing them into proper relation. As Hölderlin put it in the opening lines of his 1803 hymn "Patmos":

> Near and
> Hard to grasp, the god.
> Yet where danger lies,
> Grows that which saves. (HF, 88–89)

In this much-cited verse, Hölderlin points to an essential problem for the poet: the difficulty of finding the proper balance between the desire for the unmediated nearness of divine presence *and* the fear and danger of being consumed by its overwhelming force. Caught between these two alternatives, the poet utters a warning about divine presence and an elegiac lament for divine absence. As the first stanza of "Patmos" indicates, the poet's attempt to negotiate the tension between nearness/distance and presence/absence will require him to take a journey from his own home across the chasm of the Alps to the source of divine/human contact in time and space: the ancient East. What is most difficult to grasp, the poet wants to say, is what lies closest to us. Understanding requires distance, the distance of a journey—and so the poet must journey between Alpine peaks and valleys, heights and abysses, across dangerous bridges guided by eagles. The eagles, emissaries of Zeus, help transport the poet on a flight eastward back to the source of the temporal-spatial *arche* of divine immanence in Asia Minor, the Ionian coast of pre-Socratic *harmonia*, the site of Heraclitus's *hen kai pan* of "All-Unity."[2] Because the poet's journey signifies more than a mere spiritual attempt at communion with the god who lies paradoxically near and far, Hölderlin speaks of it as "hard" in a double sense: communication with the divine is difficult and requires mediators/translators (eagles) even as it demands a transformation (spiritual/geographic) of the traveler's inner spirituality.

As the title indicates, "Patmos" is a poem about the ancient island of Patmos that lies close to the shores of Asia Minor (v. 46) yet distant from Hölderlin's own German or Hesperian homeland (v. 18–20). In the second stanza we learn that it is twilight, the time of transition/mediation from light to darkness as the poet begins his imaginative journey from west to east. But the spatial journey to Asia will also be enacted symbolically as a temporal one: across mountains, valleys, rivers, oceans, and continents the poet will be transported from modern Hesperia to ancient Hellas. As the poet reaches the shores of ancient Ionia he encounters, "in its radiance, surging / from the golden haze / with every surge of the sun" (v. 27–29), Asia. "Dazzled" by the sight (one thinks of Plato's Cave), the poet turns back toward the west and longs "to turn in" (*einzukehren*, v. 55) to the island of Patmos and its dark grotto. As with all of Hölderlin's poems, the symbolism is striking, the logic unclear, and the overall design puzzling. To further complicate matters, Hölderlin's spatial-temporal journey from Hesperia to Hellas and from modernity to antiquity will be reenacted in the very writing of the poem, which serves as a circuitous journey on an "eccentric path"—namely a path that veers off slightly from the center of its circular journey. Hölderlin takes over this notion of an "eccentric path" from the astronomer Johannes Kepler who, like Hölderlin, studied theology at the Stift in Tübingen. In Kepler's theory of the orbit of planets, the heliocentric vision of Copernicus does not adequately account for the irregular, uneven course through the heavens taken by planets and comets, which diverge as they come closer and move farther from their circular orbits. As with the planets, so too with human life, Hölderlin will claim. The eccentricity of human orbits/striving is not merely self-directed or controlled but, rather, belongs to a larger historical-ontological-cosmological structure from which the individual sets out and to which it returns. The deep structural interplay of these countervailing centrifugal and centripetal forces affect rivers and stars, individual human beings, and the course of civilizations.[3] What the writing of "Patmos" indicates, then, is that an understanding of human history requires that we follow the structural dynamics of Keplerian eccentricity. Kant himself believed that Kepler's attempts to provide laws for the irregular movements of the planets might be another sign for arriving at a law-ruled understanding of the irregularities and deviations of human behavior.[4] But where Kant sought to overcome the anomalies of eccentric astronomy by subsuming them under the regularity of historical laws, Hölderlin interpreted eccentricity as a structural characteristic of human history that eluded "law" even as it provided an overarching grasp of such history. Following the structural dynamics of the "eccentric path," the poetic composition of "Patmos" can be understood as an attempt to deal with the irregularities of a journey that proceeds outward from the homeland toward Asia and then involves a return back home that is interrupted by an interlude on the island of Patmos.[5] Yet even as the particularities shift in all their contingent variety, Hölderlin's poems consistently reenact this same eccentric movement away from unity with the sun (the Platonic center of all being) back toward dispersion, fragmentation, estrangement, abandonment, and exile. Whether it be the course of the Rhine that in its inception veers from its straight course northward toward its divine origin in the East ("The Rhine," vv. 16–31) or whether it involves the desires of the lover to merge fully with his beloved even as he is thwarted by melancholic parting and separation (H, 132–33/SA III, 99–103), Hölderlin's poetic compositions invariably enact the orbit of the eccentric path. "Nearness" and "distance" from God, as the opening of "Patmos" frames it, indicates an ever-recurring difficulty for the human being—but also for nations, cultures, races, and civilizations. Originary unity can never be experienced directly; it reveals itself to us only in and through the fragments of nature whose inner force reveals a constant struggle between unity and dispersion, nearness and distance, the centripetal and centrifugal. The eccentric path offers a model for an ever-recurring structural dynamic of human experience. As Hölderlin put in the penultimate preface to *Hyperion*:

> We all traverse an eccentric path and there is no other way possible from childhood to completion [of our life's course]. Blissful

> unity, being, in the singular sense of the word, is lost for us and we must lose it if we are to strive for and attain it. We tear ourselves loose from the peaceful *hen kai pan* of the world in order to bring it about through ourselves. We have fallen away from nature and what, if one can believe, was once One, now opposes itself and supremacy and servitude alternate on both sides. . . . To end that eternal conflict between our self and the world, to bring back the peace of all peace that is higher than all reason, to unite ourselves with nature in one boundless and infinite whole—that is the goal of all our striving. . . .
>
> But in no period of our existence does either our knowledge or our action arrive at a point where all conflict ends, where All is One; the particular route unites itself with the universal only in an infinite approximation [*Annäherung*]. (SA III, 236)

All beings follow an eccentric path, not only individuals; all nations, cultures, races, and civilizations undergo an eccentric course of approximation and withdrawal, of getting nearer to "the peaceful *hen kai pan* of the world" and falling back, eccentrically, into estrangement and separation from universal unity, harmony, and peace.[6] Like the errant trajectory of a comet that follows an elliptical path, so too nations and peoples traverse eccentric paths, sometimes getting closer to union with the sun, at other times spinning out away into dispersion and fragmentation.

Throughout *Hyperion* we get glimpses into the structure of Hölderlin's overall design for human existence: the pattern of a circuitous journey. From a naive, childlike unity with being at the *arche* or origin of human existence, the self journeys forth in an eccentric orbit through isolation and estrangement with the aim of returning back to the *arche*, now understood paradoxically as the *eschaton* itself. As Hyperion puts it in a letter to Bellarmin: "Once long ago the peoples set forth from the harmony of childhood; the harmony of spirits will usher in the beginning of a new world history" (SA III, 63). This circuitous journey of spirit configured in terms of an underlying structure for all being, an ontological poetics of *Ausflug* and *Rückkehr*—departure and return—will put its stamp on virtually all of Hölderlin's writings. Again, as Hyperion puts it, "The life of the world consists in an alternation between unfolding and impeding, between going forth and returning" (H, 51/SA III, 38).

In the very first stanza of "Patmos" we find the poet invoking the gods to provide him with both "innocent water" (so that he might sail to the island) and "wings" (v. 14) (so that he might fly over the abysses that obstruct his path), all in the hope that he might "cross over and return" (v. 15). This journey outward of crossing over to Asia and returning by way of Patmos indicates both a spatial-geographical journey by eagles (emissaries of the Father God/Zeus) and by the poet. But this movement of crossing-over and returning will structure the writing of the poem as well and will involve the poet in an imaginative engagement and self-reflection on the task of the poet himself. What is the poetic word? How does it figure in the ontological schema of departure and return? What is its role in the working out of the eccentric path? How might a self-reflective poem on the writing of poetry provide insight into the meaning of journeying forth and returning? Hölderlin's "Patmos" will provide a poetological account of the metaphysics of the circuitous journey even as it comes to confront the limits and boundaries of such a task. Essential to such an interpretation, and to my overall project of reading Hölderlin in terms of an ontological ethics of measure, balance, and justice, will be the framing of the opening question of "Patmos"—the distance/nearness paradox of gods and mortals. In this tension between being at home in the nearness of the divine and departing forth into what is strange, foreign, distant and other, Hölderlin will situate the *polemos* of being itself as a way of dwelling upon the earth and honoring nature as divine. As "Patmos" shows, to enter into this tension will be to mediate the terrain of nature and history into an eschatological vision of harmony between divine and mortal beings. A poet's task, the very conditions for poetic composition—what the German tradition names "poetology"—will involve for Hölderlin an understanding of ontology and eschatology. All involve a deeply poetic way of abiding the tension between *arche* and *eschaton*, origin and end, with an eye toward mediating the eternal and the historical through the holy word, the *logos* that the poet finds in the hidden recesses of nature that opens up poetology to the seer/prophet. But as in all of Hölderlin's writings, insight into divine nature lies in its details. Originary unity can never be experienced directly; it reveals itself to us only in the fragments of nature whose signs are left to be interpreted by those who know how to mediate the distance *between* a history that shows us only the signs of a god who has departed *and* a nature that is filled with his presence. In "Patmos" we are confronted with the reality and possibility of each.

Within Hölderlin's poetic geography, Patmos stands as an island of transition and passage between Greece and Asia. It lies "in the middle." But what constitutes a "middle"? And against what extremes can it be measured? Much of the poetic labor of "Patmos" will be directed at precisely these issues. In a hermeneutically self-conscious way, the poem enacts the work of mediating a middle as a geographical-philosophical-poetological site for rethinking the entire Western tradition. As the island where the exiled apostle John is supposed to have written the Book of Revelation, often called "The Book of Signs," Patmos becomes for Hölderlin a symbol for mediating the two realms of antiquity and modernity. In antiquity Patmos played almost no role at all; because of its poverty it became a place of banishment for outcasts and exiles.[7] Yet Hölderlin calls it "*gastfreundlich*" or "hospitable" (v. 61) because it offered refuge to St. John the Divine at the end of his life when he was shipwrecked, in exile, and still grieving the departure of Jesus. The poetic encoding here is layered and difficult precisely in these contrasting images of succor and suffering indicated in the fifth strophe. But what persists in all this poetic imagery is a vision of Patmos as a place at the crossroads between two extremes that will variously be defined as east and west, Greek and Christian, homeland and exile. Patmos serves as a place of dwelling in the middle, at the crossroads between extremes. For dwelling, understood in its Greek sense as *ethos* (*Aufenthalt*/sojourn) becomes for Hölderlin a way of dwelling in the middle between the extremes of estrangement from the home and dwelling in it, between distance and nearness.[8] So conceived, Patmos becomes the symbol for the possibility of a poetic *ethos* of dwelling, a poetic ontology of mediation and of hospitality that come together to form a Hölderlinian sense of poetic justice. In the details of poems such as "Patmos," "Der Frieden," "The Ister," and "In lovely blueness," I want to uncover a poetic sense of balance that for Hölderlin shapes not only the temporal sojourn of the human being, but extends to the very cycles of birth and decay that define both history and nature. In this way I want to raise questions about an ethics of human dwelling marked by a nonhuman measure to which the poet accedes, a measure found in the experience of withdrawal and absence.

As with the Evangelist, the poet finds on the island of Patmos refuge from his state of spiritual shipwreck. In his temporary sojourn on the hospitable island, he, like John, finds a site for healing the breach between a god who has departed and the followers he has left behind. If the island of Patmos provides the conditions for John to work through the mourning of his "departed friend" (v. 66) Jesus by writing the *Apocalypse*, it also provides the poet the site for an analogous form of *Trauerarbeit*: the writing of the poem "Patmos" as a way of mourning the departed god (*deus absconditus*) from the realm of history.[9] In attending to the holy word, the poet finds signs of god's presence even in his absence; in the "living images [that] grow green in the depths of mountains" (v. 120) as well as in "the sand and willows," the poet discerns the signs of divine nature, signs that he will mediate through the poetic word. It is in absence that presence makes itself felt; it is in default that the longing for abundance makes itself manifest.

The poet's imaginary journey in "Patmos" will bring him to the brink of a mediation of the god's distance, much as John's earlier sojourn on the island brought him ever closer to his departed friend. In this paradoxical relation of distance/nearness, the poet journeys forth (*fahren*) from his homeland by confronting the danger (*Gefahr*) of divine presence in an intimate way even as he recognizes the need for distance. By mediating the tension between distance and nearness, the poet (like the apostle) comes to grasp the paradox of divine manifestation. As Jean-Luc Marion puts it, the mystery of such manifestation is intimately tied to the god's withdrawal: "God never arrives more intimately than through the mediation of an envoi. . . . For God gives himself only within the distance that he keeps, and where he keeps us."[10] In this way Patmos itself becomes for both poet and evangelist a place of revelation for mediating the chasm between the divine and the human. As the place of the writing of the Book of Signs, that holy book revered by the Swabian Pietists as the *gnomon* for interpreting the modern age, Patmos functions as the site for revelation itself. As a theology student at the Tübingen Stift, Hölderlin studied the Book of Revelation and later read the commentaries of Johann Bengel (1687–1752), who prophesied the imminent coming of the Kingdom to Swabia.[11] For Bengel, John's *Book of Revelation* was the most important text in the *Bible* since it offered a sweeping vision of a divine plan for history as salvific promise of a new Advent, a *Heilsgeschichte* that would offer redemption from the spiritual estrangement of the present epoch by ushering in a Pentecostal age of peace and reconciliation.[12] In his early poem "Hymne an die Unsterblichkeit," Hölderlin, (echoing the apocalyptic vision of Bengel and his follower Friedrich Oetinger), speaks of an "eternal worldplan" (SA I, 116) and in one of the drafts for "Friedensfeier" announces: "Behold! It is the evening of time, the hour when the wanderers turn to a place of rest and stillness" (SA II, 699). "Patmos," "Friedensfeier," "Der Frieden," "Heimkunft," "Germanien" all share the Swabian pietists' yearning for an eschatological peace as the meaning and aim of human history.[13] And though Hölderlin's poetic vision will depart significantly from the pietists' religious orthodoxy (especially in its embrace of the political messianism of the French Revolution), it nonetheless will draw upon some deeply shared symbols and *topoi*. One that I especially want to draw upon is the notion of *gnomon* from Bengel's theological commentary. *Gnomon* in Greek (from the verb *gnorizo*, "to make known," and the noun *gnosis*, "knowledge") refers to the vertical plate of a sundial that casts a shadow which indicates the time of day.[14] It also can be translated as "interpreter," "the one who knows," or "judge." In common usage it came to signify a carpenter's instrument for determining angles (the "plumb-line"), a compass for geometricians, and a "level" for various kinds of measurement.[15] As the "set square" or "vertical rod" for measurement, the *gnomon* expressed a prominent feature of Greek orthogonality: "the correct relationship between vertical and horizontal."[16] In this understanding that uprightness mapped not only the relationship of the pin or pointer on the sundial to the shadow of the sun but, more significantly, the standing human body to the earth, the early Greeks came to define the *gnomon* as that which mediates earth and sky. As the *Richtmass* or "gauge"/"right measure" for all kinds of activities, the *gnomon* came to signify a principle of practical conduct, a standard by which to know, judge, and interpret a proper measure for human life. Beyond this, *gnomon* came to signify not only an instrument for marking the time of day but, as Diogenes Laertius relates, a way of indicating the fundamental turning points of the solar year in the solstice and equinox.[17] As an instrument of temporal measure in both an ephemeral and cosmic sense, *gnomon* becomes synonymous with a knowledge of turning points, of *Kehre* and *Umkehr*, so that Aeschylus can understand a *gnomon* as "an interpreter of divine utterances or prophecies (*thesphatoi*)" (*Agamemnon*, 1130). I want to understand Hölderlin's poetology as a reading of justice formed in the interplay between the *gnomon* as a deictical measure for turning points and as a mediator of oracular wisdom, a way for indicating the proper balance of human interpretation within the cosmic order. In Bengel's commentary, *gnomon* was defined as "an Index, in the sense of a *pointer* or indicator, as a sun-dial . . . to *point out* the full force of words and sentences in the New Testament."[18] Yet Bengel also grasped this deictical function of the *gnomon* metaphorically as a means for indicating the "right time" for the apocalypse on the sundial of history. In his own sweeping vision of a poetic philosophy of history, Hölderlin would transform Bengel's *gnomon* for his own poetic purposes. Bengel looked to the Bible as the ultimate source of gnomic wisdom and as the only sure *regula* for human conduct; yet Hölderlin did not find the leveling orthodoxy of such a narrow Swabian pietism at all appealing. His deep affinity with the early Greek tradition from Homer, Hesiod, Heraclitus, Pindar, the tragedians, and Plato taught him to honor the gods of Western history in all their forms and to worship Christ as the brother of Dionysus and Apollo. His philosophical engagement with Fichte, Kant, Herder, Schelling, and Hegel, his poetic debt to Klopstock, Schiller, and his contemporaries, all helped to form a deeply layered poetic *Geschichtstheologie* ("theology of history") that looked for a *gnomon* by which to measure the nearness/distance of the human being to the gods in order to interpret the "signs of the times." For Hölderlin, the poet as both interpreter and mediator of the turning point in Western history would be thought of as the *gnomon* for indicating the "right time" for revolutionary upheaval or *Umkehr*.

In this chapter I want to explore Hölderlin's poetic *Geschichtstheologie* because it seems to me that in its vision of modernity as an era in default, an age marked by the departure of the gods from human history ("Gottes Fehl," SPF, 82–83), we can find traces of a poetic measure that will deeply affect modern German thought—especially the works of Nietzsche, Heidegger, and Celan. Heidegger and Hölderlin both share this same Swabian pietist vision of history in terms of an eschatological *Heilsgeschichte* of *Ausflug* and *Rückkehr*, departure and return. Each will understand the whole course of Western history in terms inherited from the Swabian pietist typology that shapes the writings of Bengel and Oetinger. (One can find traces of this same eschatological vision in the *Geschichtsphilosophie* of Herder and Hegel as well.) In its most rudimentary form it grasps the creative force of history as a processual movement from East to West modeled on the path of the sun. Hence, Asia is dawn; Europe, dusk. The origins of human history lie in the East, "the land of morning" as the Germans call it, *Morgenland*, whereas the fulfillment and end of human history lies properly in the West, "the land of evening" or *Abendland*. As Hegel put it in his *Lectures on the Philosophy of World History*: "World history travels from east to west; for Europe is the absolute end of history, just as Asia is the beginning."[19] "The sun rises in the Orient . . . and by evening, man has constructed a building, an inner sun, the sun of his own consciousness." The very terms "Orient" and "Occident" from their Latin roots *oriri* (v., "to arise") and *occidere* (v., "to set" or "to fall") derive their meanings from the movement of the sun across the sky.[20] Little wonder then that Hölderlin should understand the course of human history as a "*Wanderung*" or "Journey"(SPF, 182–89) and interpret it in terms of how "it shifts from the Greek to the Hesperian" (ELT, 111/SA V, 267) where "Hesperia" (from the Greek *hespera*, "evening") comes to signify *Abendland*, the land of evening.[21]

These governing tropes of Orient and Occident, morning and evening, Hellas and Hesperia, will come to form a poetic theology of history marked by the experience of exile, loss, asylum, estrangement, and distance—in other words, the poetry of "Patmos." It is the experience of the god's distance that forms the epochal mood of mourning for the poet. But how are we to understand this mourning and what does it signify for Hölderlin's poetic theology (*Dichtertheologie*)? Moreover, how do the Johannine writings on revelation, prophecy, and the *parousia*, especially in the chiliastic form mediated by Bengel's notion of the *gnomon*, come to affect Hölderlin's reading of the Greeks? In the textual readings to come I will look at the paradoxical crossing of the Greek and Hesperian in Hölderlin's work as a way of exploring a poetic ethics of dwelling and an ethics of "hospitality," one that honors the tension between journeying and dwelling, the foreign and the native, self and other. I do so because it seems to me that in Hölderlin's diagnosis of the spiritual shipwreck of the modern *conditio humana* we can find hints and traces of a nonanthropological grounding of ethics that seeks a measure of the holy in *physis*, not metaphysics. Here, Hölderlin's poetry offers a way of thinking through the problem of distance/nearness as another kind of difference/identity without finding a resolution or *Aufhebung* of the metaphysics of presence/absence. On the contrary, Hölderlin's work embraces the tension between presence-absence by underscoring the positive role of limits, boundaries, and ambiguity in shaping human fate. In the lessons of Greek tragedy Hölderlin will confront the aporia at the boundary between the divine and the human. What the justice of the gods vouchsafes often exceeds human understanding. In turn, human beings often respond with an excess of their own, with what the Greeks call *hybris*—what in German is translated as *Anmassung* ("arrogance").[22] In this tragic condition of being "measureless," Hölderlin will situate his interpretation—not only of human excess, but of the whole sweep of world history as a narrative about the loss of measure. Within this narrative the modern epoch distinguishes itself as an age of excess, of a boldly Cartesian exuberance to make *physis* conform to our will, to transform human beings into becoming "the masters and possessors of nature."[23] But Hölderlin will seek to redress this imbalance by offering a tragic interpretation of Cartesian egology and attempting a mediation of the abyss that separates us from nearness to divine nature. In taking upon himself this poetic task of mediating the distance between gods and mortals, Hölderlin will attempt to find a poetic measure for measuring the spiritual measurelessness of the modern age, the Age of Night where the gods have fled. In his poem "Patmos" he offers a clue. At the very center of the fifteen-strophe hymn, in line 113 of a 226-line poem, he writes of "the coming again" (*wiederkommen*) of the god "when the time is right" (*zu rechter Zeit*). In this chialistic allusion to "the coming of the Lord" in the *parousia*, Hölderlin will express his hope for the return of measure to the earth. What his poetry expresses is a Pauline call to prepare ourselves for this *kairos*-event: "But of the times (*chronoi*) and seasons (*kairoi*) brethren, ye have no need that I write unto you. For yourselves know perfectly that the day of the Lord so cometh as a thief in the night" (I Thess. 5:1–2).

I want to look at Hölderlin's work, especially his river hymn "The Ister," his fragment "In lovely blueness," and his translations of Pindar and Sophocles as a way of showing how, under the expectation of a radical turn or *Umkehr* of/within time, Hölderlin seeks to develop a proper *ethos* for preparing the coming of the *parousia*. Clearly, Hölderlin's theological training will shape the way he poses his questions, but his sense of the coming of time is not merely Christological. Rather, he sees the signs of this coming revealed to him on his imaginary Patmos in the political events of his day: the French Revolution, the Peace of Luneville, the arrival of Napoleon. All of these historical occurrences stimulate his hopes for the formation of a new Swabian republic to extend north from the Swiss Alps all the way to the Swabian Alb. But beyond Hölderlin's dream of social and political revolution, I want to show how Hölderlin develops an ethics of poetic dwelling, a way of experiencing nature as *physis* that finds in the limit (*peras*) of this experience (*expeiri*) a measure for the human being's belonging to the holy.[24]

For Hölderlin, poetry, beyond all other forms of human expression, helps us find a Pindaric *gnomon*, a measure of wisdom for human conduct rooted in an experience of *physis* as "the holy." This poetological interpretation of *physis* will have ontological consequences for the work of Heidegger, as we will see later, even as it helps to form what, in our postmodern lexicon, we might call an ecological ethics of justice. Before I turn to a fuller reading of Hölderlin's poetry as an ethics of dwelling, however, I will need to explore his interpretation of the Greek-Hesperian dynamic in more depth. I will do so by turning to a reading of two short texts written between 1799–1801—the poem "Der Frieden" ("Peace") and the famous letter written in December of 1801 to Casimir Ulrich von Böhlendorff.

"THE EVENING OF TIME": "PEACE" (*DER FRIEDEN*)

Hölderlin experiences his own age as a time of advent, as an epoch not merely of transition or change, but as a fundamental turning or *Umkehr* (SA II, 878) in/of time. Especially in his poetry at the turn of the eighteenth century we can detect an underlying millennial attunement to the signs of "a coming revolution of ways of thinking and of imagining that will cause us to blush with shame at everything that's happened till now" (SA VI, 229). Within Hölderlin's poetic mythology, however, the *Umkehr* or "reversal" would involve a *Wiederkehr* or "return" of the gods. What was required to unify and transform the splintered race of Germans at the end of the old historical epoch was a poetic annunciation of the *parousia* at "the evening of time," a revelation that "the golden age of innocence is returning, the time of peace and freedom, that there is one joy, one place of rest upon the earth!" (SA III, 252). Accordingly, the task of the poet involved announcing this event of coming, the time when "the day of all days shall go forth" (SA VI, 185), to prepare his countrymen for its mediation. Caught "in the middle of time" (SPF, 194–95) or, rather, in the time "between the times" of the ancient Greek Day (in which gods and mortals lived in harmony and balance) and the millennial Day to Come (which would signify the return of the gods to earth), the poet called out in a godless Hesperian Night to reflect on the power of the departed gods, to offer them remembrance, as in an "Andenken." Juxtaposing an archaic longing for the Pindaric wisdom of Delphi ("Nothing in excess") with a revolutionary faith in Herder's notion of cultural-historical "rejuvenation" (*Verjüngung*) and palingenesis, Hölderlin attempts here a complex retrieval of the Greek achievement even as he sets it into confrontation (*Auseinandersetzung*) with his Hesperian vocation.[25] This crossing of the Greek and Hesperian will be experienced as both a return and a reversal, all in the name of "a categorical turning"

(HS, 68/SA V, 202), a radical, unconditional reversal of time that finds in the signs of the times a revelation of the coming day. As Hölderlin puts it in his fragment "Die Verjüngung": "the sunlight wakens in me joys that have passed" (SA II, 316).

One of the places where we can trace the outlines of this day-night-day typology as a categorical reversal in the age of Hesperian night is the poem "Der Frieden." Written in the late fall of 1799 under the shadow of the approaching century and the second coalition wars between French and German-Austrian-Russian armies, "Der Frieden" offers a poignant call for peace at the end of the long Hesperian night of godlessness. The "Peace" ode is structured triadically in fifteen strophes that are modeled on a Pindaric design.[26] The first six strophes present an account of war as a destructive, vengeful, and violent occurrence; the last six strophes offer a hopeful call for a coming peace. It is, however, in the middle three strophes that the poet turns to the *arche* of war, that great Heraclitean theme that is "father of all things" and that rules over all being from its very beginning.[27] In this ontological questioning of *polemos* as the originary ground of *physis*, Hölderlin will find a philosophy of strife and conflict that will help him to find unity, order, and purpose even in the contentious political struggles of the wars of the French Revolution.

Going back to his student essay "Parallele zwischen Salomons Sprüchwörtern und Hesiods *Werken und Tagen*" (1790), Hölderlin follows Hesiod in understanding *eris* (strife) as having a dual nature (SA IV, 176–88). On the one hand, as Hesiod puts it, *eris* "stirs up the evil of war [*polemos*] and conflict of battle"; on the other, she takes root in the earth and brings about prosperity by instilling in the human being a competitive eagerness "to work whenever he sees another prospering."[28] In the tension between these two realms, Hesiod—and Hölderlin—find an underlying dynamic for the unfolding of human history. In *Hyperion*, Hölderlin draws on the Heraclitean insight into *eris* and *polemos* as a way of understanding the Greek War for Independence that forms the background of the narrative. Whatever harmony is achieved happens through a reciprocally determining balance of conflicting forces that finds reconciliation only momentarily, never permanently (SA III, 163). Human existence follows an eccentric path that ever again diverges from the center of being even as it strives to draw nearer to it. In human life and in the life of nations, peace and reconciliation can only be achieved through strife, conflict, struggle, *polemos*, and *eris*. In this sense, war takes on the positive function of redressing the imbalances within an epoch by setting them into a necessary and cathartic form of confrontation. Hölderlin addresses this question of the cleansing function of war in the opening strophe of "Peace":

As if the ancient flood waters, which
in an other more
terrible, metamorphosed wrath were returning
again, to cleanse, since it was needed. (SA II, 6)

Through an analysis of the dense imagery of these opening lines we can perhaps better understand how Hölderlin situates the problem of war within his overall poetic theology of history and its vision of a coming *parousia*. In his allusions to the "ancient flood waters" and the "other more terrible, metamorphosed wrath" of Zeus, Hölderlin seeks to bring the ancient Greek myth of Deucalion told in Ovid's *Metamorphoses* (Bk I, vv. 262–415) to bear on his understanding of the situation in Europe at century's end. As Ovid relates, Deucalion was the son of Prometheus who, when Zeus wrathfully sent a flood to the earth during the Iron Age to destroy the human race for their transgressions against the gods, survived the flood and brought forth a new race. In Pindar's version of the myth, Deucalion becomes the father of the Greek peoples (Oly. IX, 43–55).[29] In Hölderlin's reappropriation of the myth, the coalition wars following the French Revolution are likewise "sent by Zeus" to cleanse and purify Europe for its *hybris* in overstepping the boundaries between mortals and gods. Moreover, like the original flood of Deucalion, they signal a radical turn in human history. From Hesiod's *Theogony*, Ovid's *Metamorphoses*, Vergil's "Fourth Ecologue," and the odes of Pindar, Hölderlin draws on the image of "the golden age" when mortals and gods lived in originary unity. With the passage of time, however, and the onset of human forgetfulness, human beings strove to set themselves in equal measure to the gods. Due to this excessive, hybristic overstepping of the boundaries between gods and mortals, human beings lost the innocence of unalienated oneness with divine being and fell into a state of estranged conflict. What each of these poets deemed necessary for a return to the golden age of unity was purity of heart and the unspoiled simplicity of childhood wonder, a disposition that Hölderlin found expressed in Rousseau's *Emile*.[30]

This whole poetic mythology of a golden age, when crossed with the chiliastic vision of Swabian pietism, comes together in Hölderlin to form a poetic theology of history modeled on the Heraclitean-Hesiodic principles of strife and conflict. If the archaic Greek "day" of unalienated harmony with nature had been superseded by the onset of Hesperian night that began with Christ's departure from the earth, then the signs of contemporary history promised to Hölderlin the coming of a new day and the return of peace to the world. Drawing upon Herder's "theory of organization" outlined in *God: Some Conversations*, Hölderlin envisioned a Neoplatonic cycle of *mone-proodos-epistrophe* (rest-procession-reversion) that followed his ontological poetics of *Ausflug* and *Rückkehr* (SA III, 63; SPF, 152–53, v. 54).[31] Everything in nature loses its originary balance (*mone*) as it goes forth from itself (*proodos*) only in the end to return to itself (*epistrophe*) via a circuitous journey back to the *arche*. From the childlike innocence of peace through the contentious struggles of war that cease and thereby usher in a renewed epoch of harmonious peace and balance, the movement of human life proceeds according to a circuitous, eccentric journey from its *arche* eccentrically outward and then back again. This poetic theology of day-night-day renewal, grounded in the purifying journey outward from the homeland, would, Hölderlin believed, ultimately bring us back home where we could dwell in greater proximity to the gods.

For Hölderlin, poetry in its deepest sense is homecoming. No matter how difficult the journey, no matter how much isolation, estrangement, conflict, and strife we encounter in our wanderings, there is ultimately a purpose in the crises and caesuras of our experience. But as "Der Frieden" shows, human beings fail to recognize this. Like Heraclitus, Hölderlin understands the poetic word as a *logos* spoken to those who are asleep and are not attuned to the signs of the times (Heraclitus, Fr. 1, Fr. 89).[32] In this sense, his poetry needs to be understood poetologically as an attempt to transform the understanding of poetic language through a philosophical reflection on its meaning. And, like Heraclitus, this entails for Hölderlin an understanding of poetic *logos* as being an interpretation of the *kosmos*—of *physis*, *nomos*, and *dike*. "Der Frieden" attempts just such a broad philosophical reading by offering a theodicy of history, a justification of the conflicts, strife, and violence of war in the age of night. As Hölderlin put it at the end of *Hyperion*: "Like lovers' quarrels are the dissonances of the world. Reconciliation is there even in the midst of strife [*mitten im Streit*] and all things that are parted find one another again" (H, 215/SA III, 160).

This cosmological interpretation of *eris* and *polemos* is expressed in the first six strophes of "Peace" where Hölderlin describes the tumult of the coalition wars in Switzerland and Italy in terms of the role played by the goddess Nemesis. Nemesis is the ancient Greek goddess of justified retribution, the daughter of Dike (Justice). In her role as "avenger" (v. 10) she brings on the "flood" of war to purify the nations. "The stern scales of Nemesis," as Pindar puts it (Pythian X, 44), balance out in an unrelenting and pitiless way the excess and transgressions of human impiety.[33] When *hybris* (*Anmassung*) and excess (*Übermaß*) bring mortals beyond their limits, Nemesis strikes to reassert balance and measure (*Maß*) once again. In Isthmian Ode V, Pindar offers this stern warning to those tempted to overstep their boundaries: "Do not seek to become Zeus! You have all there is, if a share of blessings should come to you. Mortal things befit mortals."[34] In "Peace," Hölderlin interprets Pindaric Nemesis as a counterbalancing force to such hybristic impiety, as she brings "needful" war to the Germans.[35] Addressing "holy Nemesis" (SA II, 391), the poet asks her:

> have the nations done you
> Penance enough for their luxuriant slumber?
> Who started it? Who brought us the curse? Not from
> Today nor yesterday does it spring, and those
> Who first lost the measure [*Das Maaß verloren*], our fathers,
> Knew it not, their spirit drove them. (PF, 166–69; translation altered)

Hölderlin's analysis of the coalition wars finds their causes less in the power politics of French, German, Austrian, or Russian aggression than in the eternal principles of *eris* and *polemos* found in Hesiod and Heraclitus. It is only amidst the wasteland and destruction of war that peace can take effect; only by experiencing in a productive way "the eternal conflict between our self and the world" can we achieve "the peace of all peace that is higher than all reason" (SA III, 236). How did human beings "lose the measure"? How did the process of historical decline begin? Hölderlin draws on two traditions for his answers—the archaic Greeks (Hesiod-Heraclitus-Pindar) and the modern Hesperians (Bengel-Herder-Rousseau). In cosmological terms, *physis* is ruled by limits and boundaries. Anaximander's insight that all things "must pass away according to necessity; for they must pay penalty and be judged for their injustice according to the ordinance of time" can be read as a moral dispensation of cosmic justice. But it also can be read as an ontological account of the *Gefüge* or "structure"/"jointure"/"just fitting" of beings where *Fug* serves as a German translation (as in Heidegger) for *dike* ("justice").[36] On this reading, "measure" is not something imposed from without by divine fiat, but lies within the very ligatures of being as part of the dispensation of energies that inexhaustible *physis* generates out of itself. No part of *physis*, not even the deathless sun, can serve as the originary source of measure since measure is not an entity or a being, but a phenomenological process; it does not exist external to this process as a standard or benchmark. Nor should measure be understood anthropologically in terms of "values" on a human scale; rather, Hölderlin, following his pre-Socratic sources, reads it ontologically as something written into the very grammar of being by *physis* itself. Hence, Heraclitus writes, "The sun will not transgress his measures (*metra*). If he does, the Erinys, ministers of Justice (*Dike*), will find him out" (Fr. 94).[37] Nemesis rules over all things as a way of countering transgressions and setting things back into their proper jointure. And it is this hidden jointure within being that rules over all things from their *arche* following the path of *polemos* as a polemology of being. This cosmological reading is given a mythic foundation in the work of Hesiod and Pindar. As Pindar tells it, the origins of human strife, war, and suffering lie in the ancient violation of the boundaries between mortals and gods perpetrated by the mythic figure Ixion. Driven by unrestrained *hybris* (*Übermaß*), Ixion attempts to seduce Hera and violate Zeus's marriage-bed. Moreover, as "the very first to bring upon mortals the stain of kindred blood" (Pindar, Pyth. II, 32–32), Ixion receives divine retribution, chained to a fiery wheel that rolls on perpetually in Hades.[38] Reflecting on the fate of Ixion, Pindar offers his poetic *gnome*: "It is ever right to mark the measure [*metron*] of all things in the limits of one's own station."

On Hölderlin's reading, Ixion is one of the originary Greek "fathers" who first "lost the measure" for mortals and helped draw upon them the counterbalancing force of *nemesis*. He functions as a mythological counterpart to the Hebrew Cain, the prototype of the intermediate period of human history when the gods' distance from mortals brings on the age of night.[39] Given the return in 1799 of "the ancient flood waters" (v. 1) of the archaic Greek era, Ixion's fate stands for Hölderlin as a mythic reminder of human excess and violation. As Hölderlin grasps it, Ixion's fate exemplifies an unbalanced form of subjectivity and willful singularity that serves as a source of estrangement from the gods. The whole process of human history during this period of *Götterferne* (distance of/from the gods) is marked by the tragic dominion of singularity, a singularity that refuses to acknowledge or remember its archaic roots in divine *physis*. Nowhere is this one-sided form of willful singularity better expressed than in the tragic figure of Sophocles's Oedipus. For Hölderlin, Oedipus in his manic search for his "own" identity violates the boundaries of nature, upsetting not only his own sense of balance, but the very balance of *physis* itself (patricide, incest, murder, impiety). In his attempts to mold Apollo's oracles to his own strategic planning and in his arrogant dismissal of the god's prophet (Teiresias), he exhibits an uncanny form of isomorphic leveling, of calculatively reducing all difference to a monstrous sameness with an eye toward control and subjugation. Like Ixion, Oedipus too has "lost the measure" and has become an icon of modern subjectivity in its distance from the gods. In his aorgic rage, Oedipus rends all sense of connection and integration with organic nature; in his rigidity and excess (*Übermaß*) he embraces only the extremes of his own choosing and, in so doing, both violates and forgets what lies in the "middle," the hermeneutic center of complexity.

Tragically driven to the extremes of measurement in his planning, calculation, and instrumental projection, Oedipus is in the end unable to find a measure, powerless to harness his unbounded will to power. In this he becomes for Hölderlin a symbol of modernity itself in its Cartesian form as the grounding subject pressing itself onward in its unending quest to subdue nature.[40] Within this Cartesian metaphysics of self-presence, "the human being gives beings their measure by determining independently and with reference to himself what ought to be permitted to pass as being. The standard of measure [*Maßgabe*] is the presumption of measure [*Anmassung*], through which man is grounded as *subjectum* in and as the midpoint [*Mitte*] of beings as a whole. However, we do well to heed the fact that the human being here is not the isolated egoistic I, but the 'subject,' which means that the human being is progressing toward a limitless representing and reckoning disclosure of being, . . . the discovery and conquest of the world" (Heidegger, N iv, 121/N II, 171).[41]

In his self-made identity as enlightened riddle-buster, armed with the tools of sophistic *mathesis*, Oedipus will offer a calculus of human fate and futurity that abandons the cryptic language of divine oracles for the instrumental language of political and psychological control. Oedipus's lack of attunement to the infinitely elusive and recalcitrant forms of human discourse, especially poetic discourse, is no mere idiosyncratic character trait. It represents nothing less than a fundamental inattention to the other, to the need for understanding limits. In this Oedipus comes to symbolize a modern form of subjectivity that lacks the measure for measure itself, a way of being and self-comportment that, for Hölderlin, comprise the very foundation of tragedy. Here tragic insight and Cartesian calculation reveal themselves as irreconcilably opposed, so much so that, as Dennis Schmidt has so incisively put it, "the conception of philosophy found in Descartes does not make the themes that tragedy represents necessary."[42] The whole early modern project of instrumental rationality that finds its apotheosis in the eighteenth-century Enlightenment erases the possibility of the tragic by subjecting all human difficulties to the project of therapeutic amelioration. Yet the figure of Oedipus remains for Hölderlin as a symbol of the tragic imbalance that persists between gods and mortals.

In one of the great ironies that only tragedy can properly reveal, Oedipus's relation to Apollo, the god of music, poetry, archery, medicine, and prophecy, shows how out of balance a human being can truly be. To honor Apollo is to honor the power of measure. In the measured pacing of musical and poetic meter, in the medical practice of moderate intervention, in the archer's attunement to the tautness and amplitude of the bow, in the interpreter's reception to the mystery and paradox of the oracle, lies the enigmatic riddle of Apolline wisdom. But Oedipus, of course, is unable to heed the lessons of Apollo's *metron*. When he visits the god's oracular shrine at Delphi to find an answer to his true parentage, he wildly misinterprets its message.[43] Instead, he claims that "Apollo sent [him] home again unhonoured in what [he] came to learn" (*Oedipus*, ll. 788–89).[44] Inscribed above that shrine were the two great precepts of archaic Greek ethics: *meden agan* ("nothing in excess," "*Nichts im Übermaß*") and *gnothi seauton* ("know thyself"). For this archaic Apolline tradition, self-knowledge or self-identity involved an acknowledgment of one's own limits, which required at the same time an awareness of the boundaries that separated gods and mortals. Distance and proximity to the gods were understood as the determining limits of human fate. To go beyond these liminal markers was to invite disaster and self-dissolution. Genuine and abiding self-knowledge meant that one understood the *metron* or measure of existence as honoring the boundaries of divine *physis*. This pre-Socratic ethical notion of measure (*metron*, *Maß*) as moderation (*metriotes*, *Mäßigung*) does not signify, however, "a resigned retreat from external pressure; it does not mean that one settles for less than one is worth. Nor does it involve false modesty or indicate petit-bourgeois cowardice in facing up to one's life-choices. . . . [Rather], moderation is a freely chosen self-limitation that emerges out of one's insight into the imperfection of the world and of human beings."[45] To cultivate moderation means to find deep meaning "in-the-middle," understood not as mediocrity but as what Aristotle terms *mesotes*—a "holding-the-middle" between two extremes, balancing the scales in homage to the metric balance of Apollo and the divine wisdom of symmetry (Aristotle, *Ethica Nicomachea* 1106a–1109b). Lacking all insight into the virtue of the hermeneutic middle, Oedipus blindly embraces the extremes of his own calculative designs. Armed with all the sophistical skills and resources of the fifth-century Greek enlightenment, Oedipus contrives with uncanny linguistic cunning to wrest from *physis* her hidden secrets. Nowhere in the play is this unmeasured comportment toward language as a "ready-to-hand" tool more powerfully expressed than in Oedipus's abrasive exchange with Apollo's prophet Teiresias. Resisting Oedipus's aorgic desire to discover the underlying causes of the plague raging in Thebes, Teiresias finally responds by uttering an enigmatic warning:

> Of themselves things will come, although I hide them
> and breathe no word of them.

Oedipus replies:

> Since they will come
> tell them to me. (*Oedipus*, ll. 341–42)[46]

Here, as elsewhere in the play, we find Oedipus's boundless impatience with a *physis* recalcitrant to Sophistic *logoi*. With a ferocity matched only by his brutal treatment of Laius and his retinue at the crossroads, Oedipus blindly forges ahead in his effort to put the hiddenness of *physis* into *logoi*, to direct truth into the frame of a language that can be manipulated. In doing so he comes to embody for Hölderlin the tragic extremity of enlightenment itself, its boundless ambition to demythologize the divine, to discover all that is hidden and indistinct, to render intelligible, hence controllable, all that is riddling, enigmatic, oracular. In this tragic imbalance between excessive rationality and the recalcitrance of nature that characterized the fifth-century enlightenment, Hölderlin comes to see the tragedy of the eighteenth-century Enlightenment as well. As with the age of Ixion, Hölderlin's own epoch had "lost" the Delphic measure of Apollo, the hermeneutic wisdom of keeping the middle course through the *agon* of opposed extremities and of finding therein a balance to mediate the distance between gods and mortals.

THE BÖHLENDORFF LOGIC

In the extremities of Oedipus's reach—in the tensions, oppositions, contrarieties, and crossings of all the Oedipal themes (gods/mortals, the language of *techne*/the language of prophecy, control/wildness, organic/aorgic, calculation/the incalculable)—Hölderlin finds the living principles for offering a new poetic *ethos*, a way of dwelling at the limit between the mortal and the divine. Here between earth and sky the limit is experienced less as a definitive border that terminates than as a threshold that mediates. In this sense, the limit is not understood as a boundary marker that demarcates for the project of building fortifications at the frontier, but, thought in its etymological sense as the Latin *limes*, Hölderlin's "limit" becomes a "passageway," "cross-path," or "crossroads" that holds together what is distant and separate, as at the *limen* or threshold of a house.[47] Thought within Hölderlin's poetic conception, the limit is that which sets into relation what is proper to the home as one's own *and* what is strange, foreign, and other. In his paradoxical fate as the "native stranger," the one who, by virtue of his uncanny transgressions of all limits, dwells as that most paradoxical, oxymoronic being of all—Oedipus is thought as the foreigner in his own homeland, the being estranged from his own being. In this tragic paradox of Oedipal self-estrangement, Hölderlin finds a model for the contorted liminality of modern German fate, existing at the threshold between absence and presence, withdrawal and arrival, the *deus absconditus* and the coming *parousia*. At the limit of night and day, dwelling "at the middle of time [*Mitte der Zeit*]" (PF, 496–97), Hölderlin grapples with the difficult problem of finding a proper measure for what is one's own in relation to the foreign. To fashion such an *ethos* becomes for him the poetological response to the limitless reach of modern Cartesian subjectivity in its enlightened form. There are few places in his work where the tensions, reversals, inversions, and paradoxes of this *ethos* come to such pointed expression as in a letter that he wrote to his friend, Casimir Ulrich von Böhlendorff, in December 1801.

The Böhlendorff letter offers in condensed form the outlines of Hölderlin's tragic interpretation of modernity as an age "at the limit." For him, this signifies an aesthetic-philosophical mediation of the modern age as an axial epoch of transition in the day-night-day schema of historical homecoming. What matters most to him poetologically is to experience the poet's task as a Pindaric attempt to open a space in the community for the arrival of the gods.

By uttering "the sacred word," the poet invokes the gods to come back to earth during the age of night to celebrate a new *hieros gamos* or "holy union" between gods and mortals—the theme of "Friedensfeier"—allowing them to dwell in harmony in a new age of cosmic justice (PF, 462–63). But Hölderlin is no mere utopian *Schwärmer*. In "As on a Holiday" he also warns of the dangers of an all too immediate union between mortals and gods in his allusion to the fate of Semele (PF, 464–65). As ever, Hölderlin strives to seek a balance between these two extremes, to find a Delphic measure in the "harmonious opposition [*harmonische Entgegensetzung*]" that he sees ruling over all being. To come to oneself, to find one's identity—for nations, epochs, races, and individuals—always involves an *agon* or contest between the native and the foreign, what is "one's own" and what is radically "other." Only by negotiating the tension between these opposites can one come to self-understanding. In his essay "The Ground of the *Empedocles*," Hölderlin expresses this tension by reflecting on the relation of nature and art. "The divine," Hölderlin claims, "rests in the middle [*in der Mitte*] between these two." He goes on to write:

> [I]n the middle lies the struggle, and the death of the individual, that moment when the organic lays down its selfhood, its particular existence, that had become an extreme, and the aorgic lays down its universality, not as at the start in an ideal mixture, but in a real highest struggle, in that the particular at its extreme must actively and increasingly universalize itself towards the extreme of the aorgic, must increasingly tear itself from the center, and the aorgic must increasingly concentrate itself towards the extreme of the particular and increasingly gain a center and become the most particular and increasingly gain a center and become the most particular of all, *where, then the organic which has become aorgic seems to find itself again and seems to return to itself, in that it supports itself upon the individuality of the aorgic, and the object, the aorgic, seems to find itself, in that, at the selfsame moment where it assumes individuality, it also finds the organic at the greatest extreme of the aorgic, so that in this moment*, IN THIS BIRTH OF THE GREATEST ENMITY THE GREATEST RECONCILIATION SEEMS TO BE REAL. (E&L, 262/ SA, 153–54)

In this paradoxical understanding of "the greatest enmity" as a condition yielding "the greatest reconciliation," we can uncover the hidden threads of Hölderlin's Böhlendorff logic.

Böhlendorff was a young poet friend of Hölderlin's who had sent him a copy of his recently published play, *Fernando oder die Kunstweihe*, a text that juxtaposed two contrasting styles: the poetry of sober distance and passionate nearness. Hölderlin writes back to his friend in terms that situate his play within the great questions of Hölderlin's own poetology.

> We learn nothing with greater difficulty than to freely use the national. And, I believe, that it is precisely the clarity of presentation which is so natural and original for us, as the fire of heaven is for the Greeks. That is why they will need to be surpassed in beautiful suffering, which you too have retained, rather than in the Homeric presence of spirit and gift of presentation.
>
> It sounds paradoxical. But I will say it yet again, and submit it to your test and your free employment, that in the progress of culture, the truly national becomes of limited advantage. That is why the Greeks are less masters of sacred pathos, because it is innate to them, whereas they excel in the gift of presentation from Homer onward, because this extraordinary man was sufficiently soulful to conquer (*erbeuten*) the Western *Junonian sobriety* for his Apollonian empire, and thereby to truly appropriate (*anzueignen*) the foreign.
>
> With us it is the reverse. That is why it is also so dangerous to abstract the rules of art exclusively from the excellence of Greece. I have labored on this long and now know that, with the exception of what for the Greeks and for us must be the highest, namely, to have a living relation and destiny, we must not bear any resemblance to them. But the ownmost (*das Eigene*) must be learned as well as the foreign (*das Fremde*). That is why the Greeks are unavoidable for us. Only we will not follow them in our own, our national, since, as said, the *free* use of *one's own* is most difficult. (BL, 165–66/SA VI, 425–26)

Hölderlin's focus on the question of "the national" and its free use, especially in the context of a discussion about German art and its relation to antiquity, points toward a reformulation of the question of tragedy and its relation to the Delphic measure. Hölderlin writes to Böhlendorff on the eve of a trip to Bordeaux that marks a caesura in his life; he has decided to leave his homeland and pursue yet another tutor's post. But, in his letter, his tone expresses the sense that he is going into exile:

> I am now full of parting. I have not wept for a long while. But it cost me bitter tears when I decided to leave my fatherland, perhaps forever. For what do I have that is more precious in the world? But they cannot make use of me. I am and must remain German, and even if the needs of the heart and for nourishment were to drive me to Tahiti.[48] (BL, 167/SA VI, 428)

At the limit of his exilic wandering, as he is about to cross over the border between Germany and France, Hölderlin reflects on the meaning of border crossing itself as a way of negotiating the distance/nearness of all his poetological concerns. These concerns are reflected for him in the meaning of Greek tragedy for German poetry, in the significance of ancient art for modern culture, in the thematics of journey and return for a poetic theology of history, and in the act of translation between all these realms. How do we negotiate the limit, border, boundary, and threshold of all these oppositions and imbalances? Where might we be able to locate such a limit? And what would be proper to the limitations of such a limit? In order to gain a sense of the depth of Hölderlin's concerns here, I would argue that understanding his notion of what is "proper" can be traced back to its etymological sense as *proprius* (L.), ("one's own," *das Eigene*) from *prope* ("near," *nah*), related to *propinquitas* ("nearness," "*Nähe*") in terms of what is most appropriate.[49] Hölderlin's juxtaposition of Greek "sacred pathos" and "Western Junonian sobriety" brings into confrontation the fundamental questions of his poetic philosophy of history as they relate to the problems of measure, balance, equilibrium, and cosmic justice that we have been examining.

Against the background of Hölderlin's yearning for a new *parousia*, understood as the Pentecostal appearance of the gods in the age of night, the Böhlendorff letter announces a bold rejection of Winckelmann's staid classicism as a model for German self-development. The chiasmic juxtaposition of Hellas and Hesperia that forms the basis of Hölderlin's interpretation challenges Winckelmann's Philhellenism in a double sense. First, it unqualifiedly rejects Winckelmann's mimetic ideal for German art—namely, that "the only way for us [Germans] to become great, and indeed—if this is possible—inimitable, is by imitating the ancients."[50] Second, if Winckelmann finds the highest measure of Greek art in the "noble simplicity and quiet grandeur" native to the Greeks, Hölderlin will invert this logic and see the great achievement of Greek art—its "gift of presentation"—as something not native, but foreign.[51] For him, Winckelmann's ideal is static and calcified; it turns Greek "form" into an absolute measure in itself. But Hölderlin understands measure—in aesthetics as in theology—as something liminal and in need of constant mediation and re-mediation. Hence, for him, what matters most in the German appropriation of Greek art is an attunement to what is "proper" in it, viz., what is ownmost. And this he finds not in Greek form or rules of art but in the Greeks' harnessing of their excessive passion, their "fire from heaven," through the exertion of a counterbalancing discipline that finds a new measure in the middle between extremes of what he terms aorgic nature and organic art. The point of such measured appropriation is not to imitate the greatness of the Greeks, but to unfold the potential for greatness in the Germans. Only if the Germans are able to "determine the Hesperian *orbis* in opposition to the *orbis* of the ancients" (SA II, 876), can Swabia hope to become the site for the future arrival of the gods. That is, only when the poet can genuinely mediate the distance between the ecstatic celebration of divine presence (futural, "Friedensfeier") and the sacred mourning of divine withdrawal (historical, "Patmos"), can the "*Umkehr der Zeit*" ("reversal in/of time") occur. But as always in Hölderlin, this *Umkehr* will be experienced as both a *Rückkehr* and a *Heimkehr*. That is, this "reversal" will be understood both as a "return" and a "homecoming." The Böhlendorff letter will lay down the formal grammar for these various forms of the *Kehre*.

The letter expresses two fundamental thoughts: (1) that the Greeks and Germans are different—and opposite; *and* (2) that the measure of the Greeks' greatness lay in their ability to strive against their own nature and to master that which is their opposite. Self-development, self-formation, *Bildung*, requires a "reversal" of one's inborn traits and an appropriation of foreign elements. To become German means to think the Greek in such a way that it loses its status as a classical, canonical measure in itself. Rather, what the Greeks teach us is that measure can only be achieved through an *agon* with one's own sense of identity, as a struggle with identity itself. Identity necessitates difference—something that can best be experienced via a journey outward from the homeland to confront the foreign. Just as the Greeks had to struggle with the "foreign"—i.e., Western Junonian sobriety—in order to come to themselves, so too the Germans will need to come to terms with their "foreign" element—viz., Greek sacred fire—for them to achieve their identity. As we have seen, however, this can only be gained in and through a reversal of the Greek achievement. As Hölderlin expresses in a letter to Schiller from June 1801, he hopes to be "especially useful" to young students who are interested in the Greeks "by freeing them from strict adherence to the Greek letter" (SA VI, 422).

To understand the differences between Greeks and Germans, and the reversal that Hölderlin deems so essential for each to achieve its proper identity, requires that we first come to grasp what he means by the phrase "the free use of the national." By "national," Hölderlin does not refer to a "nation-state" in our sense; rather, as Dennis Schmidt argues, "Hölderlin's sense of the word draws upon its roots in the Latin *nasci*, to be born, and as designating 'the collective of peoples born under the same sky and thus sharing the same destiny.'"[52] What is "national" designates "the ownmost," "the proper," what is "one's own." In the Greeks, Hölderlin wants to say, we Germans confront our own proper origin—but, through the logic of a chiasmic reversal, this proper origin is experienced as something foreign and strange. The path to one's own identity requires a turning (*Kehre*) that needs to be experienced both as a reversal (*Umkehr*) and a return (*Rückkehr*). One needs to journey abroad to understand the national so that the return homeward can provide a perspective of distance from the nearness and propinquity of the proper. In this act of distantiation lies the possibility and hope of poetic freedom. To freely *use* the national, then, means to traverse the boundaries of nations in an effort to come to another limit or border—that between gods and mortals. The poet attempts to exist at the threshold of such a limit, mediating not only his own experience of journeying but also, and more significantly, the experience of a national *Volk* in its journey through history. Hölderlin's journey to France becomes in this sense a figural reenactment of the world-historical journey that culture makes as it migrates from the ancient Mediterranean south in Hellas to the modern transalpine north in Hesperia.[53] Western Junonian sobriety, the clarity of representation, and the order and regularity of German culture confront Apollonian fire from heaven, the aorgic, and the sacred pathos of Greek culture in a historical struggle for self-determination and national identity. Deeply influenced by the historical theories of Herder and Baron von Riedesel on the progress of civilization from east to west, Hölderlin develops a poetic geography that finds in the notion of "*das Abendland*," "the Land of Evening," "Hesperia"—from the Greek *hesper*, evening—a new measure for cultural appropriation or *Aneignung*. On Hölderlin's reading, evening lies halfway between the brightness of the day and the darkness of the night; it is the time of transition, the time "between the times" in the eschatological language of Swabian Pietism.[54] The mythic language of rivers, mountains, landscapes, and locales that forms the poetic geography of Hölderlin's work becomes of "use" to the poet as he seeks to freely determine his own as well as his national identity.

According to the Böhlendorff logic of reversal and return, identity depends upon difference and harmony, even as unity depends upon strife. The confrontation—or *Auseinandersetzung*—between two extremes brings each of them into a determining relation; to define this conflict in terms of an either/or struggle for supremacy is to resort to the logic of extremes. As Hölderlin expressed it in his essays on Antigone and Oedipus, such extreme forms of self-definition lead to excess, or *Übermaß*, a stepping beyond the measure or limit. To violate the limit as measure initiates the counterforce of the tragic, a movement that threatens self-dissolution. But the very act of poetically configuring tragic fate into the form of aesthetic presentation signifies for Hölderlin a sobering countermovement to excess, *ekstasis*, and self-immolation. Homer, Sophocles, Pindar—all of these poets knew how to harness Greek sacred pathos in the "clarity of presentation." What Hölderlin proposes to his friend Böhlendorff as a remedy for the ills of German culture is a reverse of this: to overcome the excessive orderliness, regularity, and sobriety of their Junonian natures, the Germans need to cultivate Greek-Apollonian passion. Tragedy celebrates the contradictions of this juxtaposition/conjunction of pathos and sobriety in a way that balances them in a mediation of extremes. In-the-middle between the Greek extreme of *ekstasis* and the Hesperian extreme of rigid discipline, Hölderlin seeks a measure for the measurelessness of tragic destiny.

In his own writing Hölderlin had attempted to fashion just such a measure by composing a tragedy, "The Death of Empedocles," that focused on the *polemos* between the principle of rational organization (the *organic*) *and* the nonrational forces of nature and the divine (the *aorgic*). Empedocles is torn between his excessive inwardness (*Übermaß der Innigkeit*) and his desire to become one with the gods (ELT, 50/SA IV, 149). Caught in this tension between his desire for "boundless union" and his inner tropism toward "boundless separation," Empedocles winds up violating the boundaries that constitute and delimit the opposing spheres of the mortal and divine (ELT, 107/SA V, 201). Hölderlin attempted three separate versions of this tragedy, ultimately abandoning it after 1799 to devote himself fully to refashioning his odes and developing a new style—the hymns of the fatherland. Yet because of its state of cultural poverty, Hölderlin believed Germany was not yet ready to master the forms of Greek tragic presentation. To do so it would need to cultivate what was foreign to it—by following Pindar's gnomic injunction from the second Pythian ode "to become what you are," or in Hölderlin's German rendering: "*Werde welcher du bist erfahren*" (Become that which you have experienced) (SA V, 74).[55] For the Germans to become wholly themselves, to gain insight into their own nature, they would need to experience their inwardness from the distant realm of the archaic Greeks. Pindar's *gnome* about self-becoming, understood within its Greek context, involved an awareness of the double meaning of Apollo's Delphic oracle: self-knowledge required an understanding of limits against limitless excess. Only by measuring oneself against the measure set by Apollo could the human being come to self-awareness. Precisely in its insensitivity to such limits, Oedipus's violation of the oracle yielded a tragic fate. By representing Oedipus's excess in its transgressive form, Sophocles was able to express with balance, equanimity, and equilibrium the "national" character and fate of the ancient Greeks.

But Germany lacked genuine tragedy in Hölderlin's view because it had not yet achieved the self-knowledge implicit in the Delphic measure. As Hölderlin put it in his "Notes on *Antigone*," the Greeks' main inclination was the ability "to grasp themselves" (*sich fassen*), to temper heavenly fire—since "this was their weakness," this was what they lacked (ELT, 113–14/SA V, 269–70). The Germans' main tendency, by contrast, is their ability to "hit the mark," (*etwas treffen zu können*), to possess "technical skill" (*Geschick zu haben*), to find the controlled posture of self-restraint. This technical *Geschicklichkeit* or "skillfulness" serves as a way of compensating for the German condition of being *das Schicksalslose*—"the ones without a fate"—*dysmoron* in relation to *moira*.[56] To be able to write tragedy, Hölderlin believed, requires a cultural-national sense of fate, something that he thinks the Germans clearly lack. The fate of Hesperian culture is to be fateless. What the Böhlendorff letter strives to articulate, however, is a poetic vision of Western history that positions Germany at the border of a great turning from the godless night of modern fatelessness to a new day of a great coming via a return and retrieval of the opposite of Hesperian culture in archaic Greek thought. The light of Apollo's sun brings with it the Delphic measure for a new historical day in the turning of time.

THE *ETHOS* OF GUEST-FRIENDSHIP AND THE ORIENTAL "OTHER"

Hölderlin seeks to challenge the German propensity for regularity (*Regelmäßigkeit*) by exposing its excessive (*übermäßige*) character and by locating a new measure (*Maß*) for Hesperian culture in a retrieval and conquest of what is foreign to it. This constitutes what is appropriate (*angemessen*) for its proper Hesperian identity. In the Greek tragedies' exploration and exposure of *hybris* (*Anmassung*) as a stepping over the boundaries between gods and mortals and in the mortal striving to achieve immediacy with the gods, Hölderlin locates the measureless existence of tragic fate itself. But as much as Hölderlin preoccupied himself with the aesthetic character of Greek tragedy—its rules of pacing and representation, its counter-rhythmic ruptures and caesurae, its modulation and meters, its laws of poetic calculus (ELT, 101–16/SA V, 195–202, 265–72)—his ultimate question always concerned its possibilities for German self-development. For him, Greek culture held out the possibility of being a *gnomon* or *Richtmass* for German culture that would both indicate (in the sense of a phenomenological *deixis*) and "gauge" the "right measure" for the times, would help to show what was "fitting" or "proper."[57] This alone would "hit the mark." But opening up this possibility for Hesperian self-development, required, Hölderlin claimed, a wholesale rejection of Winckelmann's classicism by way of "a reaction against the positive animation of that which is dead through a genuinely reciprocal union of the two" (ELT, 40/SA IV, 222; translation altered). Winckelmann's claim "to seek the source itself and return to the beginning to find truth, pure and unmixed" struck Hölderlin as a deadening calcification of Greek art.[58] The Böhlendorff letter, the theoretical essays, but most of all the poems themselves show that Hölderlin wants to exploit Greek art for his own aims, thereby rendering the classical not as an ideal to be imitated but as one to be challenged, reversed, and transformed. In Peter Szondi's well-known formulation, "Hölderlin overcomes classicism without turning away from the classical."[59] But even this description does not go far enough. In the Böhlendorff letter Hölderlin claims that Homer was "sufficiently soulful to conquer the Western Junonian sobriety for his Apollonian empire and thereby to truly appropriate the foreign."[60] Genuine appropriation requires that one "conquers" (*erbeuten*) what is opposite and other. Hölderlin's use of the German term *erbeuten* here—"to capture," "to carry off *Beute*" or booty, plunder, spoils—indicates a very different mode of cultural appropriation than Winckelmann's "noble simplicity and tranquil grandeur." This cultural-historical myth of carrying off plunder that Hölderlin appropriates from Pindar's third Olympian ode—which recounts Heracles's originary founding of the Olympic games through his transalpine journey to carry off the cooling shade of an olive branch from the source of the Ister—will come to shape the way he configures the very history of Western civilization.[61]

On Hölderlin's reading, the West does not begin in Athens—or on the Ionian coast. The Greeks were an oriental people—"oriental" in its Latin etymological sense of *oriri*, "to arise," and *origo* "origin, source," hence *oriens* "the east," "the rising sun."[62] Rather than serving as the site for an originary founding of measure and truth as permanent or eternal ideals worthy of imitation, Hellas was itself a crossroads between East and West and needed to forge its own identity in conflict with the forces of each. What becomes decisive here in Hölderlin's understanding of the Greeks is "their way of taking on foreign natures and communicating themselves through them" (ELT, 152/SA VI, 432). Analogously, what becomes decisive for Hölderlin's interpretation of the Germans is his demand that they recognize the foreignness of the Greeks and forge their own identity in confrontation with this radically "other" Hellas. This version of Philhellenism breaks with the identity-metaphysics of Enlightenment cultural theory by stressing the utter alterity of the Greek world in its oriental origin. The upshot of such a radical thesis is that long before the divisive quarrels of Black Athena, Hölderlin will challenge the European fear of the Asiatic by positing an Asiatic origin for Greece and finding therein the key to German self-development. As Alexander Honold has so incisively argued, the cleaving of Greek culture from its African and Asian contexts was a Hellenistic invention brought on by the hegemonic policies of a Roman imperium bent on purifying Hellenism of all its "oriental" influences.[63] "This massive adaption of a Hellenism purified of its oriental elements stood . . . as a blockade between Europe and Asia" and provided the background for the Renaissance *topos* of a Greece that served as "the mythical origin of culture itself." Eighteenth-century Europe's sense of cultural identity came to be invested in such rigid demarcation, a demarcation that became formulaic until the challenges levied by Herder. But what is the significance of such an insight? And how does it help us in understanding Hölderlin's idiosyncratic version of German Philhellenism? Moreover, what does this augur for Hölderlin's attempts at finding a new Delphic measure for Hesperian culture? Long before Nietzsche made his own anticlassical form of Philhellenism the focus of his "untimely" or *unzeitgemäße* critique of German culture, Hölderlin attempted to disrupt the classical measure of Greek art by setting it against an untimely measure: the oriental sacred fire of Apollo rather than the tranquil serenity of Winckelmann's Apollo Belvedere. In doing so, Hölderlin set out to challenge the staid classicism of his contemporaries who found in the ancient Greeks merely a more archaic version of themselves and their cultural values. In all of his work from this period he boldly attempted to rattle the foundations of German identity by exposing its carefully protected sense of cultural homogeneity to the Böhlendorff logic of difference and contrariety. In a way that is radically *unzeitgemäß*—that is, measured according to a different trajectory of time—Hölderlin reframes the European myth of original identity by a circular return to an *arche* that undermines its own stability and singularity. In "The Journey" he will even posit an oriental *arche* for German settlement (SPF, 184–85) and retell the myth of Hesperian-Hellenic cultural exchange in such a way that reclaims the Pindaric binary exchange of *oikos/allotrios* (one's own/the other) as a new poetic *ethos* for modernity.

To dwell poetically upon the earth (PF, 788–89), to find therein one's genuine home, Hölderlin intimates, means to recognize the other as essential to self-identity. The alterity of the foreign brings us back to ourselves *if* we are able to undertake the difficult journey of exploration outward in a spirit of openness toward the "distance" and "difference" of that which is *fremd*, strange, or foreign. As the Böhlendorff letter intimates, "the *free* use of *one's own* is most difficult"; yet, as we saw in our reading of "Patmos," what is "difficult to grasp" (SPF, 230–31) is difficult precisely because of its nearness to the divine. Nearness and distance stand in an uncanny, enigmatic relation much as the native and the foreign. Moreover, for Hölderlin, the foreign is so "indispensable" precisely by virtue of its foreignness. Unlike Heidegger who feared the otherness of the Asiatic as threatening (EdP, 31), who grasped the *ethos* of poetic dwelling in the reaffirmation of the provincial, the native, and the narrowly "national," Hölderlin came to understand nationality as dependent upon the foreign even as he realized that to understand the German required the Greek and the Greek, in turn, required the Asiatic. Hence, journey, travel, wandering, exploration, migration, all become essential to the poet as a way of shaping national identity. In the Pindaric *ethos* of guest-friendship or *xenia*, Hölderlin locates the proper mode of reflection between self and other, one's own and the foreign, nearness and distance, Hesperian and Greek, mortals and gods. As an indictment of his own age and its cultural provinciality, Hölderlin asks: "If the life of the world consists in the alternation and exchange (*Wechsel*) of opening and closing, in departure and return to itself (*Ausflug und Rückkehr*), why should the heart of man not also?" (H, 51/SA III, 38; translation altered). In this persistent, recurring exchange between Germans and Greeks—and, in turn, between Greeks and the Oriental—Hölderlin situates an *ethos* of guest-friendship that reflects the archaic Greek measure of the festival as a way of honoring and welcoming the gods (SPF, 214–15). In the age of night, in the time of *Götterferne*, Hölderlin asks his fellow Germans to open themselves to a futural coming that requires the *ethos* of guest-friendship, a way of dwelling that he learns from the Greeks—not in imitation of them, however, but as a way of transforming Hesperian sobriety by confronting the power and danger of Apollonian fire. In his untimely critique of German classicism, Hölderlin hopes to find a proper measure for measuring the times—and time itself. But the path toward such an untimely self-transformation will lead Hölderlin on a difficult journey of chiasmic reversal, inversion, and counterturning, a Heraclitean path that finds in both the way up and the way down an identity-in-difference worthy of the Böhlendorff logic.[64] I want to follow the inverted path of such a journey by turning to a reading of Hölderlin's 1802–03 poem "Der Ister," written in the summer just after his return from France and a few months after the second Böhlendorff letter.[65] In this poem we can find the outlines for a Hölderlinian reading of exchange that will serve as an indication for a poetic *ethos* of dwelling at the limit between the foreign and one's own.

THE ISTER: THE ETHICAL MEASURE OF DWELLING

"The Ister" is a poem about directionality, about the flow of a river from its source to its mouth—and the poetic projection of a reversal of this course as a way of figurally uncovering its essential identity-in-difference. Hölderlin achieves this by imagining an inversion of the *natural* course of the river (its physical movement of water from west to east) by a chiasmic reading of its *cultural-historical* course (following Herder's fundamental law of historical development that all cultures move from east to west).[66] Hölderlin draws here upon a wide range of sources: Herder's penchant for employing the river and the notion of source (*Quelle*) as symbols for an overarching philosophy of history; Bengel's eschatological figuration of the *parousia* as a *Kehre*; Pindar's jarring and inverted use of poetic myth; Heraclitus's polemology of oppositional forces whose very unity lies in recursive difference; Hesiod's notion of the "boundary" or limit between Day and Night as that which provides a balance essential to a cosmic measure of justice; and Sophocles's interpretation of tragedy as a "border zone" between humanity and divinity held together by the polarity between excess and deficiency, a measure perilously close to the measureless.[67] As Jean-Pierre Vernant puts it, tragedy in this sense constitutes a sphere where "the human and divine levels are sufficiently distinct for them to be opposed while still appearing to be inseparable."[68] What Hölderlin seeks to bring into relation in this border zone between realms is the unifying power of *agon*, *eris*, and strife. In the liminal space between oppositional forces that forms the interstitial boundary and threshold of polarity itself, Hölderlin will locate a measure (*mensura*) for the incommensurable distance that separates the natural and the cultural, the divine and the human, the past and the future.

I want to read "The Ister" as a poem that seeks to orient Hesperian culture by placing it in an uncanny liminal relation to Greek culture precisely at the limit of the Orient itself—namely, the rising sun from the east that comes to define the land of the setting sun in the west. We can find this peculiar relation in the etymological kinship between the Latin *oriens*, *orientalis* (the rising sun, the East, oriental) and the Greek *ouron* (boundary-border-limit).[69] What emerges here at the crossing of the Greek and Hesperian is an ethics of poetic dwelling that honors the opposition of native and foreign so endemic to the Ister itself. Here, we can understand "The Ister" as a poem that seeks to negotiate the limits of the Oriental and the Occidental (Latin *occidens*—setting sun, west) as a way of reading the fate of Hesperia within the history of the West. Hölderlin's aim, I would argue, involves an attempt at presenting a new mythology of *Umkehr* or "reversal"—but not a traditional "*vaterländische Umkehr*" or "national reversal" posited by the older generation of Hölderlin scholars following Wilhelm Michel and Friedrich Beissner.[70] Rather, as I read it, the *Umkehr* will be imagined as a reversal of the course of a river as a way of reading the possibility of Greek-German relations through the logic of the Böhlendorff letter's "free use of the national." At the same time, Hölderlin's notion of reversal here draws on the language of Greek tragedy, especially that insight from Euripides's *Medea* (v. 410–11): "Flow backward to your sources, sacred rivers, / And let the world's greater order [*dika*] be reversed." What is at stake in "The Ister" is an order of cosmic justice whose balance and symmetry (*metron*) rest on the figure of reversal. The fate of the Occident hangs in the balance dependent on the métier of the Germans to find the measure of what is their own in the foreign source of archaic Hellas. Before I proceed with a reading of the poem, however, I would like to focus some attention on the whole problem of myth in Hölderlin's late poetry.

Myth, as Jean-Pierre Vernant writes, is marked by polysemy, ambiguity, contradiction, enigma.

> In the unfolding of its narrative and the selection of the semantic fields it uses, [myth] brings into play shifts, slides, tensions, and oscillations between the very terms that are distinguished or opposed in its categorical framework; it is as if, while being mutually exclusive, these terms at the same time in some way imply one another. Thus myth brings into operation a form of logic that we may describe, in contrast to the logic of non-contradiction of the philosophers, as a logic of the ambiguous, the equivocal, a logic of polarity . . . not the binary logic of yes and no, but a logic different from that of the *logos*.[71]

If we understand Hölderlin's Böhlendorff logic in Vernant's oxymoronic terms as a "mythic" form of "logic," a non-binary logic of reversal and inversion, of turning, *Wende*, and *Umkehr*, then perhaps we can better understand the opening lines of the poem as an orientation that finds the river's source not at its *Quelle* but, paradoxically, at the river's mouth, at its end rather than at its origin. Complicating this initiatory poetic gesture are a number of crossings and traversals that displace and destabilize a linear, diachronic logic of natural progression by positing a myth of regress and return. It is as if Hölderlin wants to say that "the free use of the national" does not lie there waiting for us at its source, but can only be recovered through the difficult journey of turning back to the source in a journey of return. To construct a Germany that might be ready for the possibility of a new coming, of a political-theological-poetological *parousia* that will transform the "all too patient" (v. 58) Germans into a *Volk* of genuine revolutionary action, Hölderlin will put forward a new myth of mediation between the old world and the new, between origin and end, archeology and eschatology. Already in "The Oldest System-Program of German Idealism" from 1796 (written with Schelling and Hegel), Hölderlin had put forth the call that "we need a new mythology" in an effort to enable the founding of a "new religion" (ELT, 155–56/SA IV, 299).[72] But if Hölderlin's call for a new mythology and a new religion is to be properly heard, then I think we need to understand it in a fundamental way as a "binding back" in its Latin sense of *religare* (from *ligare*, v. "to bind," whence "ligament")—a binding back of mortals and gods.[73] Within such a bold eschatological framework the poet's word serves as a *gnomon* to measure and mediate the proximity and distance of the German community to the gods. This selfsame paradox of nearness and distance that we saw at the outset of "Patmos" is read here as an impossible juxtaposition between the *immediate* (the Dionysian instantaneity of the "now"; the immediacy of fire) and the *mediate* (the poet's task as intermediary between mortals and gods). It is on this note of mediation that the poem's epiphany begins:

> Now come, fire!
> We are impatient
> To look upon Day,
> And when the trial
> Has passed through the knees
> One may perceive the cries in the wood. (SPF, 252–55)

The poem opens, traditionally enough, on a note of invocation. Like his ancient Greek predecessors, Homer, Hesiod, and Pindar, Hölderlin offers homage to the muses, those divine beings who help the poet bridge the distance between the profane realm of history and the sacred realm of nature. In this archaic tradition, Greek *poiesis* is understood as a kind of "making" (from the verb *poieo*, "to make, produce, create"), whereby it is the gods themselves who make the work of the poem and it is the poet who receives it.[74] In this sense the poem becomes an expression of *theophany*, a site or *topos* wherein the gods can make themselves manifest; the poet serves here as the mediator of such revelation.[75] Crossing his Swabian pietist reading of the *Book of Revelation* with a Pindaric attunement to the poetry of *theophany* (as a double genitive), Hölderlin performs the work of divine service—in opening he offers a prayer to the gods. But this is no typical prayer; by invoking fire—the "heavenly fire" of the Böhlendorff letter, Apollo's sun, Heraclitus's *logos*, Promethean *techne*—Hölderlin seeks to redress the imbalance in the cold, sober, Junonian temperament of the Germans by issuing a call for what is opposite to them, a call for what they lack. The poem begins at this threshold between deficiency and excess. But it also begins at another threshold—that between night and day at the threshold of dawn. Employing the first person plural, indicating the poet's belonging to a community or *Volk*, Hölderlin pronounces that "we are eager to look upon Day" (v. 2–3). Waiting through the dark and chilly Hesperian night, the night of godless absence, the poet longs for a sign of the heat- and light-bringing sun, the new era of the gods' return. Here again we find traces of Hölderlin's Swabian pietist and Herderian figuration of Western history as following the pattern of a day-night-day cycle of renewal and rebirth. In this historical figuration of the Ister as a river offering "a poetic view of history," Hölderlin will grasp its movement, flow, and direction in terms of the *topos* of German destiny, "especially insofar as it is different from the Greek" (SA VI, 438).

At the threshold of daybreak, anterior to the destiny to come, the poet invokes the sacred as a way of crossing the threshold. As Maurice Blanchot put it in "The 'Sacred' Speech of Hölderlin": "The Sacred is the day . . . but anterior to the day, and always anterior to itself; it is a before-day, a clarity before clarity to which we are closest when we grasp the dawning, the distance infinitely remote from daybreak."[76] In Blanchot's reading, poetry "bears witness to the awareness of an anterior power surpassing the gods as well as man." In other words, the poem is anterior to the poet; it anticipates (in the Latin etymological sense of *capere*, a "seizing" or "taking hold of," *ante*, "in advance") the poet by seizing him with a sacred force that enables him in the kairotic "now" of invocation (v. 1) to mediate anteriority and futurity, the anterior destiny of the Greeks and future destiny of the Germans.[77] But in keeping with a reading of his own time as an age of divine withdrawal and absence, Hölderlin understands such mediation as requiring a chiasmic reversal, a revolutionary *Umkehr* in/of time. What is absent are not only the gods, but a way of even measuring their absence. The "now" of poetic invocation not only calls upon the absent gods, it invokes time itself as *kairos*, as the "right time," the "fitting moment," for the appropriation of the truth of the gods. In keeping with Pindar's notion of *kairos* as the time of fulfillment, the moment wherein the poet is appropriated by the occasion itself and what it requires, Hölderlin's kairotic "now" comes upon the poet at the limit of time to allow him an entryway into his role as mediator. Moreover, it helps to form the limit and measure for his task of uttering the sacred word. As the controlling force of all *physis*, especially fire, the "*metron* is operative in all things; to perceive it is the highest form of *kairos*" (Pindar, Olympian XIII, 48) or, as Hölderlin put it in "Bread and Wine": "immer bestehet ein Maas"/ "always a measure exists" (SPF, 152–53). Hölderlin's poetic *kairos* here echoes the insight of Anaxarchus: "One must know the measure [*metron*] at the right time [*kairos*], for this is the boundary [*horos*] of wisdom."[78] *Kairos* presents to us the threshold opportunity, the moment that "mediates the near and the far, and all other oppositions," as Thomas Hubbard puts it in *The Pindaric Mind*.[79] Thought within this Pindaric context, Hölderlin's opening line reflects Pindar's understanding of poetry as achieving a balance or measure with all that is, of finding in the temporal particularity of a moment, its *Jeweiligkeit*, an *ethos* for proper dwelling. This constitutes Pindaric justice, finding the measure of the moment in all things, and in all things the measure of the moment. To speak of poetic justice in this sense is to locate both Pindar and Hölderlin within a tradition that finds the measure of ethics in *physis* rather than in *anthropos*. The poet's task for Hölderlin at the threshold of time (night/day), then, is to seek a measure for his epoch's measurelessness, a *mensura* that would be—in the sense of future anteriority—incommensurate with any present measures of Enlightenment-Cartesian philosophy.

To underscore this incommensurability of the night of godlessness with the yearning for the coming Day of Revelation, Hölderlin chooses to open his poem on a note of paradox. A river poem commences with fire. In good Heraclitean fashion Hölderlin undermines the Enlightenment affinity for enduring foundations by beginning with opposition rather than stability. At the very *arche* of the poem we face a countergesture of *an-arche* that challenges the thetic metaphysics of singular principles and eternal foundations. Fire and water do not lend themselves to easy mediation. Rather, in the *polemos* of their opposition at the *arche* we encounter the paradox of nearness and distance that will rule over (in the sense of *archein*) the entire poem. Fire and water, heat and coolness, will become major themes in Hölderlin's crafting of "The Ister" on the principles of his Böhlendorff logic. The divine fire of the Apollonian sun will need to be cooled by the waters of Junonian sobriety. Only by finding the proper measure between them can we begin to cultivate an *ethos* for learning how to dwell poetically upon the earth. In this Hölderlinian ethic of dwelling, the poem serves as a way of mediating the distance and calibrating the balance between extremes. Here, Hölderlin will find a Hesperian form of the Delphic measure: know yourself by knowing your limits. Nothing in excess; *Nichts im Übermaß*. Such a Hölderlinian ethic will attempt a recovery of the Pindaric *metron* that all being obeys the law of limit and measure.[80] "In all things there comes due measure [*metron*] and it is best to perceive the right moment [*kairos*] for it" (Pindar, Olympian XIII, 47–48). In this sense, Hölderlin's poetry offers an ontological reading of measure that finds its sources in the archaic Greeks, especially Pindar, Heraclitus, Empedocles, and Hesiod. Justice and measure cannot be grounded in the Enlightenment principles of autonomy, the rights of man, the calculus of reason, or cosmopolitan tolerance. Rather, these principles themselves must be understood within the scope of *physis* and the *Weltmaß* or "world measure" set by *moira* and *nemesis*.[81] What "The Ister" proposes is an ontological reading of history that recognizes the loss of measure in the godless night and offers a prayer of invocation and entreaty to help us find the right measure for dwelling. This Hölderlinian *ethos* will be operative in the very movement and measure of the Ister itself. By focusing on a close reading of the imagery we can get a sense of how Hölderlin's reading of measure will have consequences for understanding the world as an order of justice beyond human ken.

THE PINDARIC MEASURE

As the poem proceeds, Hölderlin alludes to "the trial [that] has passed through the knees" (v. 4–5), a difficult line that can be read in any number of ways. The "trial" (*Prüfung*) can refer to the trial of the German *Volk* as it comes to confront its task of preparing for the *parousia*; it can refer to the poet's own trial as he comes to terms with the task of mediation, but it can also allude to the river's trial as it moves slowly from its source to its mouth. In this context, then, the knee would refer to the southeasterly turn, bend, or curve of the Ister on its journey halfway through the Habsburg Empire.[82] This crossing of identity between the course of the river *and* the task of the poet is expressed in the very next lines:

> One may perceive the cries in the wood.
> But, as for us, we sing from the Indus,
> Arrived from afar, and
> from the Alpheus, long we
> Have sought adequacy to fate [*das Schickliche*]. (SPF, 254–55, translation altered)

Hölderlin's use of the term *fernangekommen* ("arrived from afar") can refer both to the river's geographical course and to the poet's imaginative historical journey—spatially, from the eastern source of the Indus (the river from which Dionysus comes, "The Poet's Vocation," vv. 2–3 SPF, 78–79) across Greece (the Alpheus runs from Olympia, home of the gods and site of the games celebrated in Pindar's epinician odes) to the source of the Ister. After his encounter with the farthest limit of the world (symbolized by the Indus), the poet can now turn back to his own Hesperian point of departure. To use the language of the Böhlendorff letter, only after journeying outward from his homeland, his native language, his historical epoch, to encounter the foreign at its extremest limit, can the poet "freely use the national," for only then can he truly measure his "adequacy to fate," *das Schickliche*. Hence, the poet can write: "Not without wings may one reach out for that which is nearest" (v. 11–12).

Within Hölderlin's poetological configurations, rivers create the space for "the life-giving" force that animates plants, animals, and human beings (v. 16–20). Following Herder's conviction that rivers are the source of civilization, Hölderlin will see the movement from the Indus across the Alpheus to the Ister as a kind of eagle's flight of civilization, much as he does in "Germania" (v. 42–48).[83] But rivers are, like poets, intermediaries between heaven and earth and in his translation of the Pindar fragment, "The Life-Giving," Hölderlin identifies "the spirit of a river" with the demigods, the centaurs, who likewise occupy a liminal space between the bestiality of nature and the divinity of the gods (PF, 720–21). Rivers set boundaries; they order space according to the force of *physis*. They offer a proper measure for negotiating the nearness/distance of mortals and gods. They provide direction and orientation. But they also traverse boundaries and provide passageway between distant realms. Rivers mark both settlement and transition; they help to form and found the *polis*, even as, in their physical movement, they offer the possibility of journeying away from the homeland. Mediating between source and mouth, *arche* and *parousia*, they offer a path of transition from the departed gods of archaic Greece to the coming gods of a futural Hesperia. In their coming (v. 43) and going (v. 42), progress and regress, Hölderlin finds an axis for mapping his poetic geography of Western history. The poem continues:

> This one, however, is called [*man nennet*] the Ister.
> Beautifully he dwells. The pillars foliage burns [*es brennet*],
> And stirs.

Reading the German text, one is struck by the unusual pattern of rhyming—*nennet*, *brennet*—that opens up the second stanza. It is as if Hölderlin wished to draw special attention to the link between "naming" as a poetic activity and the "burning" that characterizes divine fire. German poets, lulled by the sobriety of their Northern temperaments, will need to appropriate the energy of Apollo's sun if they are to achieve their artistic and national destiny. But beyond this, naming comes to signify for Hölderlin an important task of the poet. In his "Notes to Antigone," Hölderlin claims that "the sacred name under which the highest is made palpable or occurs may be altered" (ELT, 111/SA V, 267, translation altered). The gods become palpable for human being, Hölderlin wants to say, only in the Gestalt of poetic language. Hence, since the usual names for them have lost their power through the deadening repetition of usage, it falls upon the poet to transform their names by bringing them into the nearness of their originary manifestations in *physis*. Already in *Hyperion* Hölderlin had begun to explore the phenomenological possibilities of naming.[84] And later, in *The Death of Empedocles*, Hölderlin has Empedocles make a plea that we forget the old names of the gods and desist from using them until we learn once again to employ them with animating force (SA IV, 65–66). Names have a doubled nature. On the one hand, they offer recognition and familiarity; on the other, they calcify and deaden a thing by rendering it all too familiar. The poet must learn to use the name as a way of opening up the phenomenality of a thing that gets closed off by an all too habitual definition. Thus, instead of using the name "Zeus," Hölderlin will opt for the apellation "Father of

Time" or "Father of the Earth" (ELT, 112/SA V, 268; SPF, 228–29) and instead of the name "Gaia" he will invoke "Mother Earth" (SPF, 120–21). Will the gods hear an invocation if the names by which they are called have lost their sonority?

To approach the sacredness of a space inhabited by a god means to destructure its all too familiar name through a poetic nomination that will defamiliarize its sphere of entry and, through a new name, allow its numinous quality to appear. Names are incommensurable with phenomena; they cannot adequately express the power of divine *physis*. As Hölderlin so poetically formulated it at the end of his elegy "Homecoming": "*Es fehlen heilige Namen*" (We are "deficient in names that are holy") (SPF, 164–65). Hence, to summon the gods at the threshold of mediation between night and day to the river that joins the gods of Orient and Occident requires a renaming of the river Danube (*Donau*) with its ancient name "Ister," the Latin translation of the original Greek name for the river "Istros." Enciphered within this complex figuration of the Ister's name lies a poetic phenomenology of naming that occurs at the axis of intersection between Hellas and Hesperia explored in the Böhlendorff letter. The crossing at this axis, like the river-crossing alluded to in verses 11–14, will involve both a reversal and an exchange. The Romans employed two different names for the same river. They called the upper Danube "Danuvius" and the lower, "Ister."[85] But Hölderlin will see them as one and in renaming both the upper and lower Danube by a single name, "Ister," he will come to express a Heraclitean sense of identity-in-difference clustered around the phenomenon of naming. Now the spatial division of upper and lower regions will be unified in and through a temporal reversal back to the Greek originary experience of the river thought in conjunction with its Hesperian source. In other words, Hölderlin will find in the singular name "Ister" a way of unifying not only two distinct spatial regions, but also a way of unifying them temporally by finding an underlying kinship between ancient Greeks and modern Germans, a kinship whose unity and identity depends, paradoxically, on their radical difference. Hence, unlike the later use of this poetic configuration in Heidegger's 1942 Ister lectures where Greece and Germany are conjoined in an autochthonic bond of identity, Hölderlin will insist that apart from "a living relation and destiny," the Germans "must not share anything identical to them" (ELT, 150/SA VI, 426).[86]

Names provide identity, or at least attempt to do so, even when the designation of a name can render the person or thing multiple or plural. In the *Bacchae*, Euripides presents Dionysus as the polynomic god of multiplicity and fluidity, the native Greek who is designated "the Stranger" by Pentheus, the king who refuses to acknowledge Dionysus's name and by so doing learns, ironically, the meaning of his own name—"grief" (from the Greek word *penthos*). This selfsame kind of reversal in the tragic presentation of names also characterizes Sophocles's Oedipus who, as the native stranger, fails to uncover the hidden significance of his own name ("know foot"/"swollen foot").[87] Greek tragedy abounds in the portentous play between the named and the nameless as a way of manifesting the reversal of destiny for human beings. Something of this same play is at work in Hölderlin's line "one names this one however the Ister" ("*man nennet aber diesen den Ister*," v. 21) where the "one" doing the naming is nameless and anonymous (from Greek, *an*—without, and *onoma*—name). Moreover, Hölderlin reinforces this emphasis on anonymity in naming by punning on the Latin word *iste* ("this one") as a way of naming the Ister.[88] But what is the significance of this complex juxtaposition of anonymity and naming that Hölderlin so carefully crafts into the texture of his poem? Since naming has such a close connection with destiny in Greek tragedy, we can see how by renaming the Danube with its Greek name (via the Latin translation), or rather by reverting to its originary name, Hölderlin sets out to forge an authentic identity for the Germans by journeying against the flow of space and time. In this archetypal movement of *Ausflug* and *Rückkehr*, he hopes to achieve a poetic encounter with the foreign that will bring both the poet and his *Volk* into an awareness and experience of what is their own. To convert the Hesperians to their own destiny will require both a reversion and an inversion—such is the logic of Hölderlin's *Umkehr*: "the reversal [*Umkehr*] in all ways of perceiving things and of all forms," that occurs (or will occur) when "the Greek shifts to the Hesperian" (ELT, 114, 111/SA V, 271, 267).[89] In a self-consciously poetic way it is the (re)naming of the river that spurs the movement of this *Umkehr*.

Besides providing one with a historical identity and fate, names also serve the important function of setting things into relation. They separate the civilized from the wild, culture from nature, and the tamed from the untamed. In Hölderlin's use of the single name "Ister" there lies an overcoming of the bifurcated identity of the Danuvius/Ister that had broken the connection between the geographical-spatial source of the river in Hesperia and its historical-cultural "source" in ancient Hellas. In and through the name one defines the limits of the home and sets it against the world of the strange, hostile, and other—a relation that Pindar characterizes in the terms *oikos* and *allotrios*.[90] The *oikos* in Pindar refers to one's home, abode, or dwelling; but it can also refer to that which lies near.[91] *Allotrios*, by contrast, refers to what belongs to another, what is different, what is distant. As Thomas K. Hubbard explains it, *oikos* and *allotrios* refer to "what is properly one's own and what is foreign."[92] The proximity here to the language of the Böhlendorff letter is hardly coincidental. Hölderlin thought of the opposition/juxtaposition of this Pindaric dyad as essential for grasping the relationship between Germany and Greece and the question about "the free use of the national." One of the most prominent ways of deploying the *oikos/allotrios* theme in Pindar revolves around the whole issue of *xenia* or "hospitality" ("guest-friendship"). *Xenia* qualifies as a foundational *ethos* for aristocratic behavior in Pindar's poetry; it brings that which is distant, near and it renders that which is other and strange, familiar. *Xenia* initiates, through the exchange of gifts and hospitality, a reciprocal relationship between parties. As Émile Benveniste puts it in *Indo-European Language and Society*, *xenia* involves "a gift qua contractual prestation, imposed by the obligations of a pact, an alliance, a friendship, or a bond of hospitality; the obligation of the *xeinos* (guest), of the subjects towards their king or god and also the prestation of an alliance."[93] For Pindar the code of *xenia* serves as one of the important bastions of an aristocratic *ethos* that knows how to properly negotiate the complex and threatening realm of boundaries, limits, thresholds, and borders that separate and bring together what is of the home and what is foreign. But within Greek religion *xenia* involves more than social tact; it implicates the human being within a web of sacred relations to Zeus, god of strangers, guests, hosts, and the household.[94] Indeed, Pindar underscores the sacred boundary of *xenia* and of mortals' relationship to Zeus *xenios* in two of his epinician odes with references to the transgressions of Tantalus (Olympian I, 36–66) and Ixion (Pyth. II, 21–48), a relationship that Hölderlin draws out in his poems "As on a Holiday . . ." (SPF, 176–77, vv. 68–74) and "Der Frieden" (PF, 168–69, vv. 25–29).

Hölderlin will again draw on the *topos* of Pindaric *xenia* in verses 26–34 of "The Ister," when he recounts the story of Heracles's journey to "the shady springs of the Ister" to procure the olive branch placed on the head of the victors at the Olympic games, said to be founded by Heracles (Pindar, Olympian III, vv. 10–18).

> No wonder, therefore,
> I say, this river
> Invited Heracles,
> Distantly gleaming, down by Olympus,
> When he, to look for shadows,
> Came up from the sultry isthmus,
> For full of courage they were
> In that place, but, because of the spirits
> There's need of coolness too. (SPF, 254–55)

On Hölderlin's telling, Heracles's journey northward to the land of the Hyperboreans/Hesperians fulfills the cultural-historical destiny of the Greeks laid out in the Böhlendorff letter, for by procuring the olive branch, Heracles brings cooling shade to balance the sultry heat from the Greeks' Apollonian fire. Pindar had exploited this myth to explain the source of the Olympic games, the focus of his epinician or victory odes (from the Greek *epi*—upon + *nike*—victory), where the victory wreath was brought from a mythic land to celebrate the *agon*. But Hölderlin would alter his emphasis by focusing on the aesthetic and cultural significance of the olive branch as a symbol of Greek-Hesperian difference and exchange. For Hölderlin it is the Ister herself who extends an invitation to the hero to come as a guest-friend to her source and bring back something of the foreign, thus helping to set a measure for what is native. In this way the story of Heracles comes to serve as a determining myth at the very center of "The Ister," for it comes to instantiate the movement of journeying/migration with which the poem opened—the movement of the sun from east to west.

In the first stanza we saw that the birds' "cries in the wood" were the songs from the Indus that "arrived were afar" (*fernangekommen*), much as the sun itself. This parallel identification between birds/sun will be repeated in the second stanza around another composite word linked to the adjective *fern*—"*fernglänzend*." As in the first example, there is a self-conscious ambiguity in Hölderlin's use of the term—it can refer either to Heracles or the Ister as what is "distantly gleaming" (v. 29)—but now Heracles's movement is from south to north.

In describing the movement of Heracles's journey in such pointed terms, the poem seeks to highlight it as a determining measure for Greek-German relations. If the ancient hero journeyed north in search of coolness, Hölderlin seems to say, it is the task of the modern poet to journey southward in search of Apollonian fire. Only by a parallel, inverted exchange of guest-friendship between the two peoples and the two epochs can a proper measure for dwelling be established. This German measure would, like the *zweites Maß* ("second measure," v. 25), serve as a way of translating the differences between cultures as an essential part of cultural formation and identity. To be German then, for Hölderlin, means to journey forth from the provinces and to leave behind what is familiar; it means to enter into the realm of what is foreign, strange, and other, so that what is one's own can be cultivated in and through an encounter with alterity. Here in "The Ister" we can see how radically Hölderlin's notion of Germanness differs from that developed in Heidegger's 1934 radio address, "Creative Landscape: Why Do We Remain in the Provinces?"[95] If there Heidegger clings to the narrow myth of autochthony with its ideal of German cultural supremacy, Hölderlin will find in the broad myth of *xenia* a way of negotiating the boundaries and borders between Germania and her neighbors. The Heracles journey in "The Ister," reflects this sense of cultural exchange and reciprocity as essential to the founding and identity of a *Volk*. The Ister itself as a river traversing, yet binding, Germany and other peoples proposes a model for such an ideal. The centrality of this Heracles myth at the heart of the Ister only reconfirms this. Its story of cultural exchange in the olive branch as a gift of *xenia* would serve Hölderlin well. In his 1801 poem "The Migration" ("Die Wanderung"), Hölderlin would relate another myth of *xenia* situated at the Danube. There he tells the story of an eastward migration of early Swabians to the region around the Black Sea where, under an olive tree, they encountered an oriental race, referred to by the poet simply as "children of the sun" (SPF, 184–85, vv. 31–42). There on the banks of that sea the Greeks called *pontus euxeinos*—"the sea hospitable to strangers"—they "exchanged weapons" as well as "exchanged the word;" out of this archaic scene of cultural reciprocity they intermarried and produced a "race more beautiful / Than all who before or since have called themselves human" (v. 59–63)—the ancient Greeks. In this same spirit of *xenia,* the poet undertakes a second German journey eastward to extend an invitation of guest-friendship to "the Graces of Hellas" to come to modern Hesperia and extend their *euxenia* to the Germans. Clearly, the journey eastward through the Black Forest to the Black Sea, from the source of the Danube to its mouth serves as an inversion of the Heracles journey in "The Ister."[96] Each myth involves the crossing of a boundary that offers cultural exchange rather than transgression, guest-friendship rather than the clash of enemies. Nowhere is this mutually implicating, reciprocal interchange more poignantly expressed than in Hölderlin's description of the linguistic interchange between the Germans and Orientals on the shores of *Pontos euxeinos*:

> But when their garments had touched
> And none could comprehend
> The other's own speech (*Die eigene Rede des anderen*), a quarrel
> Might well have begun, if coolness had not fallen
> Upon them from the boughs. (SPF, 184–85, vv. 43–47)

In this notion of "*die eigene Rede des anderen,*" that mutually implicating double genitive whereby one's own speech becomes other, while the other's speech becomes one's own, Hölderlin finds the measure for that cultural exchange expressed in the Böhlendorff letter. Genuine cultural exchange aims not at mimetic reproduction or smooth unproblematic appropriation; rather, it demands that even when the other's language becomes our own, it remain other in its strangeness and alterity. Something of the paradox inherent in this relationship of sameness/otherness comes to language in the ambiguous German term "*eigentümlich*"—which can mean "that which is proper to one," "characteristic of one" but also "that which is strange," "peculiar," or "odd."

To be overcome by the foreign, to remain so open to its seductive appeal that one loses one's own language and cultural uniqueness, continued to pose a genuine threat to Hölderlin as he attempted to appropriate Greek Apollonian fire. For as we saw in our reading of "Patmos," the danger of proximity brings with it the possibility of self-dissolution. Hölderlin expressed something of these fears of loss in the opening lines of "Mnemosyne" (second draft):

> A sign we are, without meaning
> Without pain we are and have nearly
> Lost our language in a foreign land. (HF, 116–17)

What made the Greeks so strangely singular, so *eigentümlich*, as Hölderlin expressed it in a second letter to Böhlendorff, was "their openness to others, their way of taking on foreign characteristics and expressing themselves through them; that is the reason why they have their own individual character [*Eigentümlichindividuelles*]" (SA VI, 432).[97] On this reading, the Greeks came to their own cultural identity in the appropriation of foreign cultures. Again, unlike Heidegger who clung to the myth of a pure Greek *arche* untouched by foreign influence, Hölderlin viewed the Greeks as a syncretic *Volk* whose uniqueness grew out of its struggles and interchange with other peoples. The "free use of the national" here arises from the constant interaction with other national cultures and languages. But appropriation or *Aneignung* involves much more than imitation; it requires an *agonal* genius for conflict, strife, and cultural differentiation. Only in and through a separation and distinction from others, Hölderlin claimed, could the process of cultural appropriation be productive and lead a nation or an individual to fulfill the Pindaric injunction to "Become that which you have experienced" (Pyth. II, 72; SA V, 74).[98] In our own Hesperian age of divine withdrawal we can only come to ourselves by acknowledging our lack of destiny—our "being *dysmoron*," as Hölderlin put it in his "Notes on Antigone" (ELT, 114/ SA V, 270). To come to our destiny will require an *Umkehr* or "reversal" that finds in what is other, strange, and foreign the conditions for the possibility of dwelling poetically in our own native land. To fulfill our destiny as Germans, Hölderlin wants to say, will require an inversion of a Heraclean journey where we receive the gift of *xenia*—yet now not the shade from an olive branch, but rather the poetic fire of Apollo's sun.

Hölderlin will imagine just such a migration in the form of the Ister's own winding, meandering journey from Hesperia to Hellas. Now the historical destiny of the *Volk* and its *Umkehr* will be configured as the spatial-geographical destiny of the river, a theme that pervades all the river hymns. Here, the Ister will be experienced not merely as a local or national phenomenon, but as a mediating force in the encounter with the foreign through a Heraclitean reversal of its flow, direction, and orientation. Within such an optic, the river enacts through its natural movement the same task demanded of the Germans culturally: namely, the task of returning to its origin in Asia in an effort to mediate Greek sacred fire. As Hölderlin expresses it in the third stanza:

> Yet almost this river seems
> To travel backwards and
> I think it must come from
> The East.
> Much could
> Be said about this. And why does
> It cling to the mountains, straight? The other (*Der andere*)
> The Rhine, has gone away
> Sideways. Not for nothing rivers flow
> Through dry land. But how? A sign is needed
> Nothing else, plain and honest, so that
> Sun and moon it may bear in mind, inseparable. (SPF, 256–57, vv. 41–52)

Hölderlin writes here as if the genuine provenance or source of the Ister were in the East rather than in Hesperia, inverting the actual course of the river through an imagined reversal that has the river "travel[ing] backwards." He then adds "much could be said about this." And indeed much could. This poetic reversal of geography, when crossed with Herder's philosophy of history and Bengel's theology of the *parousia*, yields a law of historical destiny for Hölderlin that involves the same principles of appropriation/differentiation as expressed in Hölderlin's phrase "*die eigene Rede des anderen.*" In his attempts at understanding the movement from one's own language to the other's, in the impossible nexus of translating difference itself into a language of identity, Hölderlin locates that experience of the foreign that is so essential to entering into the experience of what is one's own. The proper must be appropriated, but how? What kind of an *Aneignung* must be carried out if we are to reclaim *das Eigene*? Hölderlin explores the poetic possibilities and limits of such a task. The relation of one's own to the foreign, he wants to say, reenacts the double genitive of language itself—of the genus constituted in and through the play of the heterogeneous and the homogeneous, of the other and the same. In a sense, this is the core of Hölderlin's poetological *ethos*, an openness to the other that exceeds the limits of the self and can not be reduced to mere self-identity. This *ethos* of letting oneself be appropriated by the other so that the self can appropriate what is one's own expresses something of the ethical meaning of limits and the limitless in the work of Emmanuel Levinas. Levinas recognizes the incommensurable distance between self and other, "the way in which the other presents himself, exceeding *the idea of the other in me*."[99] And he insists on acknowledging that "the relationship between the same and the other, my welcoming of the other, is the ultimate fact." "The Other measures me with a gaze incomparable to the gaze by which I discover him." In recognizing the chiasmic relation between self and other, where one's own language becomes other and the other's, one's own, Hölderlin brings into play the power of this Levinasian ethics of alterity. For what animates Hölderlin's figuration of reversal in "The Ister" is the insight that self-appropriation can never be achieved in Cartesian isolation, but must always involve the exchange and interplay of self *and* other. In the formulaic phrase from the Böhlendorff letter, "the ownmost must be learned as well as the foreign" (BL, 165/SA VI, 427). Or, to translate this into the *ethos* of the Ister hymn: the ownmost can only be learned *in* and *through* the foreign. The genesis of the self, like that of a nation, demands the Heraclitean play of heterogeneity and homogeneity, of *diapheromenon* and *sympheromenon*—the divergent and convergent. As Heraclitus expressed it: "The counter-thrust brings together [*sympheron*], and from tones at variance [*diapheronton*] comes perfect attunement [*harmonian*] and all things come to pass [*ginesthai*] through conflict [*erin*]."[100] What the Ister brings together across time and space (Swabians/Orientals, Black Forest/Black Sea), sets itself apart in the process of genuine cultural appropriation. That which comes together—in its etymological sense as con-ference—comes together precisely in and through the process of setting things apart (dif-ference). *Auseinandersetzung* as reciprocal determination, as the "placing" or "setting" (*setzen*) of things "apart-from-one-another" (*auseinander*) in order to achieve a genuine "confrontation," serves as the underlying principle not only of the Böhlendorff logic, but of all *physis*. Being here is understood as a just order that thrives on oppositional unity, a justice of strife and tension that finds harmony not in the end of conflict as cessation, but in the unfolding of strife itself. Like Heracles himself, that half-god whose struggles to mediate the boundary lines between gods and mortals led him to establish his pillars at the ends of the earth, the Ister too seeks a mediation of limits at the ends of Europe, the Black Sea. And it is in terms of these limits that Hölderlin will define his own role as mediator.

Caught between his *vocation* as the voice of his *Volk* and his *fate* as one of those poets who "live in the world like strangers (*Fremdlinge*) in their own (*eigenen*) house" (H, 165–66/SA III, 155), Hölderlin attempts to mediate the polarities of his world and to find in the poetic word a measure by which to balance them within the amplitude of a moment, thought of as the "right moment" or *kairos*. In this sense, Hölderlin's poetry attempts to initiate a Pindaric movement toward balancing the extreme possibilities of human action against the limits imposed on them by their own mortality and by the immortals. Hölderlinian anthropology reflects here Pindar's insight expressed in Pythian VIII (v. 95–96) about the ephemerality of the human being's place within being:

> Creatures of a day (*epameroi*, *Tagwesen*). What is a man?
> What is he not?
> A dream dreamt by a shadow is our mortal being.[101]

Only within the finitude of a moment measured against eternity, what Nietzsche in *Also Sprach Zarathustra* would call "the moment of vision" (*Augenblick*), can the human being come to dwell in the fullness of time. For Pindar, as for Hölderlin, time is like a river whose source and mouth stand in the dynamic tension of traversal; to be able to navigate the river requires a poetic insight into the ontological measure of *physis* itself (Olympian XIII, 48).

The Ister fulfills in its movement outward from the source a law of measure; it begins "all too patient" (v. 58) in an apparently passionless expression of its Western Junonian sobriety. Yet soon after it leaves its source in Donaueschingen and travels across the Swabian homeland, it encounters a "dry" bed (v. 50) at Tuttlingen that further undermines its directional push eastward. The Ister appears in this way to represent an excess of measure precisely in its sluggishness. The Rhine, however, as the poet describes it here, presents us with an inverse case—of starting out from its source in the Alps with an overabundance of passion and attempting desperately to go east before ultimately settling into its northwesterly course. In this inverted juxtaposition, a juxtaposition that crosses the vertical movement of the Rhine with the horizontal movement of the Ister, we can locate another expression of the Böhlendorff logic of appropriating one's own through the foreign. "The sign" of the river as "*schlecht und recht*" ("plain and simple," but also "upright," "straight" or "vertical") indicates a vertical axis intersecting the horizontal axis—and not simply the vertical hills of the Swabian Alb that guide the horizontal course of the river. Rather, this also indicates the intersection of "the heavenly" (v. 54) with mother Earth or "Herta" (v. 57) and the divine with the mortal. What is "right" (*recht*) is that these two realms be balanced against one another in proper measure, just as dry and wet, sun and moon, day and night find their proper equilibrium. The *gnomon* or index for such a measure, as "The Ister" attempts to show, lies both in the river's intersection with the earth and in the poet's mediation of "the Highest" (*des Höchsten*) (v. 56) with his own community. As the proper movement of the river appears to the poet as a backward-turning reversal of its original course, so too the historical movement of the *Volk*, to achieve its "proper" identity, must involve a *Rückkehr* as *Umkehr*, a return as a revolutionary reversal. By inverting Heracles's journey to the source of the Ister and the Ister's own journey from it source eastward, the poet seeks to create a poetic myth of return that will serve as a guiding trope for Hesperian history at the threshold of a new *Umkehr*. As in the "Patmos" hymn, "The Ister" attempts a mediation of eternity in the ephemeral by way of a journey eastward to an ancient site that had earlier served as a place of mediation. Time will be mediated as space, space will be measured by time. Poetic geography will intersect with a theology of history as a way of preparing for a new advent with Swabia as its site.

The poem ends on an enigmatic note, borrowing the form of a Pindaric *gnome*. That which is holy retains the character of a mystery, ever recalcitrant to the language of mastery and control:

> Yet [*aber*] what that one does, the river,
> Nobody knows. (SPF, 256–57)

Is Hölderlin alluding here to the emptying of the river at its end into the Black Sea? Is he recursively pointing back to its source in the Black Forest? Does the enigma have to do with the apparent reversal of the river's course? with its temporal mediation of Greek and Hesperian? with the chiasm of space and time, landscape and history, Heracles and Böhlendorff? If we follow the Pindaric links of myth, style, structure, and theme that pervade the Ister hymn in its various motifs—alternating between gnomic utterances and narrative description: the use of Heracles as a mediator of mortals/gods; the determining influence of *kairos*; the employment of a triadic structure of turn, counterturn, and return; the use of enjambment, caesura, and hard jointure; the concern for poetology; the embrace of limits; the attention to a Delphic measure—we come to grasp the end of the poem as a challenge to the romantic metaphysics of goal, resolution, *Aufhebung*, and climax. Like an oracle, the river provides signs of divine measure mediated in the banks and turns of its confusing course of apparent reversal and return. What the river offers to a *Volk* in harmony with its movements is a sense of orientation, a poetic map of mythic appropriation that can help it to find a *gnomon* for measuring its horizontal intersection on earth with the vertical axis of the heavens. To follow the words of Bengel: as "an index . . . the *Gnomon* points the way well enough. If you are wise, the text itself teaches you everything."[102] So too the river. Each serves as a *gnomon* for pointing the way.

Hölderlin's chiliastic vision of the *parousia*—so powerfully drawn out in "Patmos," "Bread and Wine," and "Celebration of Peace," (where he offers prayers to "the Heavenly who once were / Here and shall come again, come when the time is right {*kehren in richtiger Zeit*}," [SPF, 158–59])—pervades his late work. If one can speak of a "*vaterländische Umkehr*" or "turn to the national" in Hölderlin's late hymns, then it can only properly be understood as a turning that requires a confrontation with the ancient Greeks and an experience of the foreign in order to come to knowledge of one's own. If the river is enigmatic, then that merely reflects the enigma of *Auseinandersetzung* itself whereby transformation happens only in the encounter with the foreign, the alien, the other. Rivers mediate the strange and the familiar and, in so doing, they bring us nearer to the mystery of proximity itself as a proximity of distance. By mapping the Ister as the vein connecting the Greek to the Hesperian and the ancient to the modern, Hölderlin encounters the paradox of identity and difference that appears to him as so essential to finding a poetic measure for human existence.

HÖLDERLINIAN JUSTICE AND THE MEDIATION OF DIFFERENCE

In a late draft of "Bread and Wine," Hölderlin lays out once again the law of cultural exchange and migration that forms the poetic philosophy of history at work in the Ister hymn.

> Namely at home is the spirit
> Not in the beginning, not at the source. The homeland gnaws at him,
> The spirit loves the colony and courageous forgetting.
> Our flowers and the shade of our forests give joy
> To the one who languishes. The animating one was almost consumed by fire. (SA II,608)

Much as the Ister needs to run its course from the source to the mouth in order to mediate an identity between its upper and lower sections, so too the spirit needs to journey outward from its homeland into the foreign ("the colony") in order to come to itself. This migratory impulse "to cross over and return" ("Patmos" v. 15), to undertake an *Ausflug* to Asia via Greece and then to complete the *Rückkehr* back to Hesperia, would reign over all of Hölderlin's late work. Spirit too undertakes this journey as it moves from its oriental source in Asia across Ionia and the Aegean to mainland Greece and thence to Swabia with its hope for a new day of the gods' return to earth. It is in this sense that Hölderlin can write in "Bread and Wine"

> What of the children of God was foretold in the songs of the ancients,
> Look, we are it, ourselves; fruit of Hesperia it is! (SPF, 158–59)

In the polarity between homeland and colony, Hesperia and Hellas, Hölderlin maps a Heraclitean tension whereby what is at one with itself comes to unity and identity only through difference—*hen diapheron eauto*. Hölderlin's own life manifests itself as a constant struggle to find a measure between such extremes. After his own journey outward from Swabia to Bordeaux in the winter of 1802, Hölderlin returns home in a near bipolar state. He writes to Böhlendorff again in November of 1802:

> The violent element, the fire of heaven and the tranquility of the people, their life within nature, their restraint and contentment affected me continually and, as it is said of heroes, I can well say that Apollo has struck me. (ELT, 152/SA VI, 432; translation altered)

Crossing the border of his homeland, venturing westward over the Auvergne, Hölderlin takes upon himself an inverted Heraclean task: to find in the "colony" that which was lacking in the homeland. For Heracles, shade; for Hölderlin, Apollo's fire. Yet, as we have seen in so many of our readings thus far, the isomorphic character of the homogeneous is not blithely overcome by a simple turn to heterogeneity. Rather, as Pindar, Heraclitus, and Hesiod taught him, only in the struggle *between* identity and difference, homogeneity and heterogeneity, can one hope to find a measure to balance the extremities of polar opposition. Only in the agonal strife of genuine experience can the relation between "the shade of our forests" and "the animating one who was almost consumed by fire" find its equilibrium. We cannot simply appropriate the archaic Greek measure for our own. No abstract standard or *Maßstab* exists that can be carried off as Heraclean booty or plunder. To find a genuine measure for human dwelling, an *ethos* in its etymological sense, means to mediate archaic truth *with*, and *at*, the threshold of a moment—to find the *metron* in the *kairos* and to allow the *kairos* to find its proper *metron*. This Hölderlinian wisdom echoes the insight of Hesiod offered in *Works and Days*: "Carefully keep to due measure [*metron*]; what's fitting [*kairos*] in all things is best [*aristos*]."[103] As the principle of order underlying all phenomena, *metron* can never be a merely human standard of measurement. The measure for being in its ontological dimension is *physis* itself. In this inexhaustible, immeasurable processuality played out in the Anaximandran jointure of coming to presence and withdrawing into absence, *physis* finds its ordering principle, its *dike*.

If we can speak of Hölderlinian justice at all, then, perhaps we can think of it as the adjudication of an ontological strife between identity and difference, the disjunction that occurs in the phenomenon of jointure itself. Things that are in strife come together in the discord that occurs in accordance with all that is. In this Heraclitean understanding of being, justice comes to be understood as strife where "the old French root of the *jouste* (joust) continues to prevail in the adjustment. In the joust differences cross one another, and this crossing is their most intimate gathering. Where the differences meet is where the joust is."[104] Because he was so keenly attuned to the phenomenon of crossing—in all its senses as exchange, translation, reversal, migration, mediation, transgression—Hölderlin came to understand the poet's task as the honoring of boundaries, borders, limits, and dimensions. Here Pindar proved once again a wise teacher. In his Third Olympian ode, Pindar writes in praise of Theron of Akragas who has prevailed in a chariot race:

> So now Theron has come to the verge by his prowess
> And reaches from home (*oikothen*)
> To the Pillars of Herakles.
> What lies beyond may not be trodden
> By wise or unwise.
> I'll go no farther: I'd be a fool.[105]

To learn the proper measure of the human being requires of the poet a certain sense of equipoise, of learning to balance the familiarity of home with the furthermost reaches of the earth. "The Pillars of Herakles" demarcate the limits of the Greek world. To cross beyond them, the poet intimates, would be madness. Yet Greek tragedy offers a searing account of precisely such *hybris* or *Anmassung*, as the Germans translate it, a presumption that takes its measure only from itself. As Blanchot puts it, "Unmeasure is for the Greeks human; it expresses the audacity of the man who trusts to his own forces, whereas measure is divine."[106] Only human beings experience the kairological measure of the world; only human beings have a fate. Hence, when Hölderlin translates Pindar's notion of *kairos* with the German term *das Schickliche* (SA V, 67) or "the fateful" we can begin to lay bare a connection between measure and limit as between fate and mortality (FA 15, 202–203). By translating Pindar's poetic motif of journey and return into his own *Dichtertheologie* of *Ausflug* and *Rückkehr*, Hölderlin takes upon himself the task of finding a proper measure for poetic dwelling in the German homeland. As Albrecht Seifert has persuasively argued, this pattern of journey and return shapes almost all the hymns.[107] For Seifert this pattern takes the form of an imagined poetic journey modeled on the poetic forms of Pindar's epinician odes. Hölderlin does not simply "borrow" Pindar's style and thematics, however; he varies it according to his own poetological concerns about the native and the foreign in the relationship between ancient Hellas and modern Hesperia. For example, Pindar's odes start from a particular subject/event (an athletic victory) and then move toward a universal theme (*hybris*, *nemesis*) by way of an excursus into the realm of myth (Ixion, Heracles) and then come back again to the particular "yielding a type of identity to both, an actual representation of the universal in the particular."[108] By comparison, Hölderlin's poems make this same journey outward from the particular to the universal and then back again—in spatial and temporal ways—but whereas for Pindar myth functions as the middle-term in the poetic movement from journey to return, for Hölderlin it is the poetic excursus into Greek antiquity that helps to shape the poem's pattern of journey and return.[109] In a decisive way, the poem itself—for both Pindar and Hölderlin—helps to mediate the distance between what lies near at hand and what is distant. The jarring effect of Hölderlin's all too literal style of translating the Pindaric odes—the strange word-combinations; the unusual employment of Greek enclitics to effect abrupt transitions; the elaborate preludes/proems; the metrical, syntactical, and compositional structure of the hymns; the sudden introduction of the *gnome* as *Weisheitsspruch* (a wisdom-dictum); the hard jointure and enjambments that fracture continuity and create the effect of fragmentary incompletion; the rejection of climax and closure as poetic strategies for ending the poem; the abrupt interjection of first person narration; the use of praise and remembrance as fundamental ways of poetic attunement to the holy; the irregular, syncopated rhythms that come near to prose—all lead him to find a language for that which can not be said and yet which might allow a revelation or *Offenbarung* (*apokalypsis*) to take place.[110]

In his insightful study, *Hölderlin and the Dynamics of Translation*, Charlie Louth argues:

> Hölderlin's poetics may be understood as a continual effort to determine "das Lebendige," and this consists in finding a precise relation of language in which manifestation is possible. Translation provides an analog of this process: a form has to be found in which the Greek poem can be conveyed. Part of what is conveyed is the incommensurability of Greek and German. But that revelation of incommensurability is itself a form of expression: the German's brokenness is witness to something beyond itself, to something it cannot sustain. In that sense the Pindar translation foreshadows the stance of Hölderlin's great poetry; not as its beginnings, but as a fully developed prior instance.[111]

In the incommensurable relation between Greek and German, source and colony, the poet stands as the translator/mediator of the abyssal distance between the near and the far. *Physis*, inexhaustible and ever-recurring in its cosmic roundelay of conference and difference, reveals its divinity to mortals only in the mediations of natural processes that the poet can attempt to translate into a language of ineffable distance. The effect of this fundamental insight into the incommensurability of being and language would be to push Hölderlin to the limit of saying the holy word. The aim of his efforts would be to translate Pindaric forms and motifs into his own Hesperian epoch of the age of night.

One of the last of Hölderlin's surviving poems, "In lovely blueness" attempts to provide a post-Christian reflection on Pindaric measure. In the blueness of the sky, in the self-manifesting of *physis* as the revelation or *Offenbarung* of the divine, Hölderlin relates his own poetic reticence to trod "what lies beyond." Instead, he clings to the measured awareness that it is the poet's task to "depict the world in a diminished measure" (*die Welt im verringerten Maßstab darstell[en]*) (SA V, 272). "In lovely blueness" approaches the question of measure from the measureless distance of human beings from the gods and provides a poetic *gnomon* for the task of thinking the measure of justice. In this next section I want to offer a close reading of this poem that reflects on the poetological concept of ethics that lies at the heart of Hölderlin, one that helped Heidegger to form his own thinkerly notion of dwelling poetically upon the earth.

THE MEASURE OF THE INCOMMENSURABLE: "IN LOVELY BLUENESS"

In "Bread and Wine" Hölderlin writes,

> Day-long, night-long we're urged on by a fire that's divine.
> Urged to set forth. So come, then! Let us look upon what is
>   open (*das Offene*),
> Where we may seek what is ours (*Eigenes*), distant, remote
>   though it be!
> One thing is sure even now: whether at noon
> Or approaching midnight, always a measure (*Maß*) exists,
> Common to all, yet to each something of its own (*eignes*) is
>   also allotted (SPF, 152–53; translation altered)

In the tension between the day-long and the night-long, noon and midnight, one's own and the foreign, Hölderlin attests to the belonging-together of opposites in a unity beyond their ken. "Always a measure exists," he affirms, yet wherein does the amplitude of such measure lie? In the Protagorean gauge of the *anthropos* as the measure of all things? In a Cartesian securing of subjectivity as the ground and essential fundament for all measurement, including the measure of measure itself? In the Enlightenment designation of the human being as a new Prometheus set to wrest the secrets of *physis* from the fortress of the gods? Where does Hölderlin find the measure that always exists?

The late poem "In lovely blueness" attempts to address the question of measure, which for Hölderlin is not an anthropological question, but an ontological one. To speak of "the measure of man," "the measure of the human being" is already to be implicated in the world of appropriation and possession, the realm of *Aneignung* and *das Eigene* (one's own)—that which, in grammatical terms, belongs to the realm of the genitive case. To speak of the measure of the human being in these terms is to acknowledge the role of the double genitive. This means recognizing that the possession of the object by the subject as well as the belonging of the subject to the object transpires in a way that exceeds each, occurring in a mutually implicating, bilateral conjunction of opposites beyond mere volition or control. I belong to tradition as much as tradition belongs to me. Or rather, in my attempts to appropriate tradition for myself, I am appropriated by tradition in ways I cannot foresee or direct. To speak of the measure of the human being as a double genitive, then, means to recognize that in our attempt to arrogate the measure of all things solely to the human being we push against the limits of arrogation defined by "arrogance" (L. *arrogare*, v., "to claim"). Rather than asserting that the realm of measure belongs to the human being, Hölderlin seeks to show how it is the human being who belongs to measure. "In lovely blueness" offers a commentary on this question of ontological measure.

One of the crucial questions of this late poem (said to be written circa 1808, two years after Hölderlin's confinement in the Autenrieth Clinic in Tübingen) concerns the relationship between human beings and the gods precisely as a question of poetic dwelling (BA 12, 22–24). How are human beings to dwell in the age of night, in the epoch of transition between divine withdrawal and the coming *parousia*? How are they to find a measure for gauging the boundaries and limits between mortals and gods that enables such dwelling to take place? And what kind of measure would be fitting for such an endeavor? Before proceeding to an interpretation of the poem itself, I would like to briefly consider an ode from Pindar (Nemean VI, 1–7) that addresses this question in terms of a fundamental paradox—of the affinity and yet radical difference between human beings and the gods.

> There is one race of men, one race of gods
> Yet from one mother we both take our breath.
> The difference

is in the allotment
of all power,
    for the one is nothing
while the bronze sky exists forever,
a sure abode.
    And yet, somehow
we resemble the immortals,
whether in greatness of mind
or nature, though we know not
to what measure
day by day and in the watches of the night
    fate has written that we should run.[112]

For Pindar the relationship between human beings and the gods is always defined in terms of limits and boundaries. While the gods may traverse such boundaries and raise mortals above the reigning human station in luck, grace, victory, wealth, and happiness, human beings can never escape the mortality of their fate, which serves as an inalterable limit upon human achievement. The gods never die; human beings, on the other hand, must contend with death as an ever-present feature of mortal fate (Olympian II, 30–31). And yet in the teeth of such awareness Pindar nonetheless celebrates the excellence (*arete*) that he finds in human nobility, courage, and perseverance. There are times, Pindar grants, when our striving hits the mark and raises us to such stature among our peers that we almost reach the gods. Such experiences are governed throughout by the gods' dispensation of grace within a circumscribed moment that brings together the forces of chance, luck, effort, skill, composure, and coincidence. Within this confluence of contending forces that meet in the *kairos* moment, the poet preserves the ephemerality of victory in words that seek to render it eternal. And yet throughout both the victor's performance and the poet's celebration of it there remains the element of uncertainty. We can never know what fate has in store for us. Always we remain wanderers on a journey whose end often appears in sight and yet always withdraws from view just as we get near to it. At the end of Nemean Ode XI, Pindar sets into opposition these competing strains of human limits and the illimitable:

. . . destiny leads our mortal race.
As for that which comes from Zeus, no clear sign
attends men, but all the same we embark on ambitious projects
and yearn for many accomplishments, for our bodies are
  enthralled
to shameless hope, and the streams of foreknowledge lie far off.

> One must seek due measure [*metron*] of gains;
> too painful is the madness of unattained desires. (v. 42–48)[113]

Between the gods and human beings there is affinity and alterity, identity and difference. The measure of such difference lies in the way we are measured in and against our proximity to, and our distance from, that which exceeds our grasp. Our very manner of dwelling upon the earth, beneath "the bronze sky [that] exists forever," depends upon our skill in negotiating this distance as the liminal condition for the very possibility of such dwelling. For Hölderlin, poetry itself is what enables the measure of this distance to shape the dwelling place. If we abide by the limit imposed by such a measure, biding our time in securing our abode, then the calling to which we are bidden—namely, to dwell within the limits (fate, mortality, *hybris*, *nemesis*, *dike*) imposed by such a measure—may forebode something proper, something that we can call our "own" (*das Eigene*). But if we extend the reach of our grasp beyond its limit, into a realm where entry is forbidden—the realm of the gods, the heavenly, Apollonian fire—then we risk losing our abode and becoming foreigners, eternal wanderers, strangers even in the homeland, like Oedipus the "poor stranger [*Fremdling*] in Greece," as Hölderlin describes him in "In lovely blueness . . ." (PF, 793; SA II, 374).[114]

The poem opens with an oxymoronic image: the "blossoming" of a church steeple whose metallic roof reflects the sun and from whose windows there emerges the sound of church bells. At a number of points in the opening lines Hölderlin juxtaposes nature ("blossom"-ing, "the crying of swallows," the "trees of the wood") with culture (metal roof, steeple, sheets of tin, the sound of church bells, the weathercock, windows) attempting thereby to set each into a specific relation to the presence of "lovely blueness" that gathers it in its form as a phenomenological manifestation of that which is. At the same time, Hölderlin sets into motion another contrast: that between the height/altitude of the sun, steeple, weathercock and the descent of a person who "comes down those steps" (I, 5). In all of these difficult contrasts and oppositions Hölderlin seeks a poetic grammar for manifesting the difference between the self-manifestation of nature as *physis* and the constructed forms of culture (through *techne*) that allow such manifestations to be understood. What unites each sphere in its difference is manifestation itself or, to speak in the language of Swabian pietism, "revelation" (*Offenbarung*). To say that steeples "blossom" is to grant them the power of self-manifestation. Yet, we might ask, to what extent does the human being manifest the divine? How are we to think of the relationship between mortality and immortality as a way of navigating the distance between the two? "In lovely blueness" offers a vertiginous account of these questions by constantly moving back and forth between the highest possibilities afforded by the sky (the dwelling place of the gods) and the boundaries imposed by our attachments to the earth (the dwelling place of mortals). In what sense can we find a connection, a line of affinity or relation between the vertical life of the immortals and the horizontal life of us mortals? And to what task is poetry called to relate them?

In the poem's opening image of "lovely blueness" we come back to a complex symbol alluded to in Hölderlin's "Greece," written just a few years earlier. There Hölderlin writes:

> O you voices of fate, you ways of the wanderer!
> For amid the blue (*Blau*) of the school,
> From afar, amid the uproar of heaven
> Rings out like the blackbirds' song
> The clouds happy mood, well
> Tempered by the existence of God (*Daseyn Gottes*), the
> thunderstorm.
> And calls, like looking out, for
> Immortality and heroes;
> Memories are many. Where ringing out
> On it, as on the calf's hide,
> The earth, proceeding from devastations, temptations of the
> saints,
> For at the beginning the work is shaped,
> Pursues great laws, and knowledge
> And tenderness and the width of heaven, all wrapping, later
> becoming
> Visible, sing clouds of song.
> For firmly fixed is the navel
> Of Earth. For captive in banks of grass are
> The flame and the common
> Elements. But above, all reflection, lives Aether. But silver
> On pure days
> Is light. (SPF, 316–19, vv. 1–21)

In "Greece" Hölderlin brings into play many of the same poetological themes as in "In lovely blueness . . .": the dyadic tension between earth and sky, between the purity of Aether and the captivity of earthly elements, between revelation ("becoming visible" vv. 14–15) and concealment (God's "face conceals itself [*verberget sich*] from knowing"). God's *Daseyn*, here manifested in thunderstorms—as in "As on a Holiday . . ." (vv. 39, 56)—mediates itself in and through the clouds. By serving as the *topos* of divine revelation, the heavens become the "school" wherein the blueness of the skies serves to educate human beings in the ways of the gods. "Blue" here, as in medieval theology, takes on the significance of divine wisdom.[115] To dwell in lovely blueness is to dwell as if our dwelling were a way of nearing the possibility of divine wisdom, a form of wisdom that "conceals itself from knowing," that resists the calculation of knowledge and measurement and that holds forth the hope of achieving a *Verbindung* or union with the gods that might merit the name of *Dasein*. Yet such union does not come of its own. All of the conditions for experiencing such union are in place under the vault of the sky and the light of the sun. But the human being must be in the proper position to receive such revelation. "Nature lies open" before us ("Greece," v. 34); though, as Hölderlin warns, God "limits unmeasured paces" (*Ungemessene Schritte/ Begränzt*) (vv. 40–41).

In the first stanza of "In lovely blueness . . . ," Hölderlin presents the conditions for the possibility of human nearness to the divine. To even hope to enter into such nearness requires that we undergo a *katabasis*, a purifying journey of descent from the church tower—from whose windows the bells sound the music that brings together gods and mortals much as the blue sky gathers the manifold of sun, wind, light, and sound.[116] *Physis* manifests itself in diversity. And yet when the spirit is earnest (I, 11) and can achieve a stillness and a detachment (I, 5–6), a simplicity (I, 11) and a purity of heart (I, 17, 21; II, 7, 17), it may commune with the holy (I, 12). To do so is to find in the interiority of poetic attunement, in the experience of *Untergang* (going-under, descent, *katabasis*), a certain comportment of humility and moderation that teaches the poet about limits, thresholds, borders, and measures. Only within the finite limits of human singularity can the poet approach the infinite totality of all being. Borrowing an image from the language of Swabian pietism, Hölderlin refers to the poet as a figure who is *abgesondert* (I, 7): "set apart," "detached," from the bustle of human activity, someone who by undergoing the experience of spiritual descent can achieve a "still life."[117] In the withdrawal and *Absonderung* from the world, in the detachment that Eckhart termed *Abgeschiedenheit*, the poet finds a form of spiritual attunement that brings into relation the universal and the singular. The human desire for contact with the divine can prove deadly, as Hölderlin made all too clear in "As on a holiday . . ." with his references to Semele's destruction by Zeus (SPF, 174–75, vv. 51–53)—or in his poem "Greece" where he relates how "air and time cover / The terrible one, so that not too much a man / With prayers shall love him" (SPF, 318–19, vv. 28–32). Throughout "In lovely blueness . . ." Hölderlin sets union and detachment into a relation of "harmonious opposition" where each attempts to bring the other into a measured balance of stillness and enjoining (*Fügung*). The human longing for immediacy (with the divine) must be mediated by the divine manifestations of nature. The return of the gods to the earth in the age of night must be prepared in advance by poets who can find the traces of the gods' paradoxical presence-in-absence in the lovely blueness that gathers all the forms of nature's beauty (sound, light, color, and tone) into the stillness of figural harmony. *Physis* alone can hold together the oppositional elements of earth and sky in a harmony of contrasts; it is the poet's task to mediate such opposition in a way that brings the human element into proximity with the divine. In Hölderlin's poetology, "Greece" is the name of the highest achievement of unity between human beings and nature that the West has ever known—hence, it serves as the name of a possibility for Hesperia's future. Remembrance of the Greek achievement remains a crucial form of enunciating the path of Hesperian union with the gods who are to come. But why did the gods depart? And how might an awareness of the Greek achievement be crucial for Hesperian destiny in an age of the gods' absence?

Hölderlin touches upon these questions in one of his late fragments ". . . *Meinest du es solle gehen*." There he writes:

> do you think
> Things will go
> As they once did? They wanted to found
> A kingdom of art. But in the process
> Neglected what was native [*das Vaterländische*]
> To them, and Greece, most beautiful of all,
> Perished [*ging zu Grunde*] miserably.
> The case is certainly
> Different now. (HF, 164–65; translation altered)

Echoing the logic of the Böhlendorff letter, here Hölderlin presents an account of Greek art that sees its decline in the neglect of *das Eigene* and in the unmeasured appropriation of all too much "Junonian sobriety." The gods took flight from Greece precisely because Greek artists and philosophers became estranged from the native element of their own culture, expending all their energy in the pursuit of what was foreign to them. In their eagerness to journey outward from the homeland to embrace the "colonies," they succumbed to a paralyzing forgetfulness of their own source (*Quelle*) and beginning (*Anfang*) (SA II, 608). In the transitional epoch of the age of night, Hölderlin hopes to achieve a poetic *anamnesis*, a remembrance and recollection of the Greeks' errors of excess, of *Übermaß*, of surpassing the proper measure, in an effort to prepare a "guest house" (*Gasthaus*) for the return of the gods (SA II, 582). If only the Germans can come to understand how to appropriate the foreign without losing their connection to what is native, they might be able to bring forth a Hesperian form of *Gastfreun-*

dlichkeit or "hospitality" to rival Pindaric *xenia* and welcome back the gods of antiquity to a new day of festal worship and peace. Yet before that day can come, Hölderlin believes, it is imperative that Hesperian culture learn the proper measure for achieving what, in letters to Wilmans (1803) and Seckendorf (1804), he calls "a solid balance" ("*veste[s] Gleichgewicht*") or a "good balance" (SA VI, 436–37). The question of balance, long the focus of Hölderlin's poetological essays on meter, tragedy, and lawful calculation, as well as his *Hyperion* (SA III, 77; SA IV, 228; SA V, 196, 265, 266, 269, 272), would now be framed as a question about "the poetic view of history and the architectonics of the skies, especially our nation's insofar as it is different from the Greeks" (SA VI, 437). "In lovely blueness . . ." lays out in triadic form the struggles to achieve such balance and the tragic consequences that unfold when "in earnest spirit" (I, 11) the human being exceeds its limits and, like Hercules, undertakes "to clash with god" (*mit Gott zu streiten*) (III, 11).

After laying out his account of "lovely blueness" as the divine manifestation of balance that orders and organizes earth and sky, mortals and gods, Hölderlin then turns to the question of measure and the role of poetry in taking the measure of measure. As he attempts to limn the figure of the human in all its sculptural plasticity (*Bildsamkeit*) (I, 6), Hölderlin confronts a fundamental paradox: the very resemblance (I, 14) of mortals to the gods that Renaissance art depicted in the trope of the *imago dei* betrays at the same time an impossible distance between the perishable human form and the imperishability of the divine. And yet as Jean-Luc Marion claims in *The Idol and Distance*, it is precisely such distance that makes possible the nearness of the divine and the mortal. As Marion puts it, "The intimacy of man with the divine *grows* with the gap that distinguishes them, far from diminishing it. The withdrawal of the divine would perhaps constitute its ultimate form of revelation."[118] It is in the absence of the gods that their presence makes itself visible—not as "presence" but as the trace of their presence in images that reflect the divine light of phenomenological revelation. In the lovely blueness of the sky, in the sculptural plasticity of the human form, in the poetic words whose curves and contours reveal the outlines of the enigmatic wonder of divine presence that refuses to be encapsulated in written form, the gods reveal themselves as present by their absence. "The architectonics of the skies," hidden from view except to the poet, finds its structural integrity reflected back in the spires and steeples of the church whose metal roof stands out from the blue and foregrounds it, much as the human form foregrounds the divine.

In the architectural detail of each—church and human form—the poet finds a symmetry that puts separate spheres into relation, offering a way of understanding what is distant through the foregrounding presence of what lies near. Here, the effect of this architectural ordering of sky and earth brings together the incorporeal realm of the divine and the corporeal *Bildsamkeit* of the human to form a symmetrical balance of harmonious opposition.

In this same fashion, we can understand the architectonics of "In lovely blueness," its construction in three parts modeled on the poetic architecture of Pindar's triadic form, as another way that Hölderlin presents the problem of mortal estrangement from, yet unity with, the divine.[119] For in the dynamic of the poem—as it moves from the first stanza to the second and from the second to the third—we experience the parallel movement of elevation and descent set up in the first few lines. From an opening scene (I, 1–10) of apparent unity and integration of all being, including the human being, the poet moves toward a warning that though these images are both "simple" and "holy," "often one is afraid to describe them" (I, 11–12). But why? Because as radically *unheimlich* or uncanny, they threaten the human being with the immeasurable presence of the divine, much as Semele discovered. This experience of awe—in both its senses as awe-some and aw-ful—will come to fuller expression in the second and third sections of the poem.

The promise of the opening lines (with their images of architectural symmetry uniting the blue skies, the church tower, and the human being) will be imperiled by the very movements of ascent and descent, transcendence and limitation, that form the vertical-horizontal relations of mortals and gods. In the next two sections of the poem Hölderlin will show us that this symmetry is tenuous and fraught with danger and the threat of dissolution. What confronts the poet here is the same question that he addresses in "Der Frieden"—namely, the loss of measure (PF, 168–69, v. 23), that thematic arc of rise and fall, victory and defeat that shaped Pindar's epinician odes and the forms of Greek tragedy. Little wonder then that this poem too should end with a reference to a tragic *gnome*. Here, as in so many of Hölderlin's poems, the yearning for unity and totality, for oneness with the lovely blue of the opening line, remains unfulfilled. Ever does the sense of completion and integration elude the poet. "In lovely blueness" follows this Pindaric arc of rise and fall between the bliss (*olbos*) of grace/joy (*charis*) and the destructive excess of *hybris* (Pyth. XI, 50–58). The "Highest" for Hölderlin needs to be mediated with an understanding of measure. "In lovely blueness" reflects the insights that Hölderlin gleaned from his reading of Pindar, expressed in his commentary on Pindar's Fragment "The Highest":

> The immediate, strictly speaking, is impossible for mortals, as for immortals; the god must differentiate between different worlds, measured according to his nature, because heavenly goodness, for its

> own sake, must be holy, unmixed. The human being, as knowing, must also differentiate between different worlds, because knowledge is only possible through opposition. That is why the immediate, strictly speaking, is impossible for mortals, as for immortals. But strict mediacy is the law. (PF, 712–13; translation altered)

How to find the measure? How to achieve a strict mediacy in relation to the divine? How to approach the divine in such a way that the human being grasps the *unheimlich* question of measure? Having raised some of the essential questions that shape the construction of "In lovely blueness," let us return to our reading of the poem itself.

At the end of the first stanza Hölderlin raises his own questions about the proper relation between mortals and gods, questions that help him define the position of the poet:

> May, when life is all hardship, may a man look up and say: I too would like to resemble thee? Yes. As long as kindliness, which is pure, remains in his heart not unhappily a man may measure (*misset*) himself with the divinity. Is God unknown? Is he manifest (*offenbar*) as the sky? This rather I believe. It is the measure of man. Full with what is our due, yet poetically, dwells the human being on this earth (*Voll Verdienst, doch dichterisch, wohnet der Mensch auf dieser Erde*). (I, 14–20; PF, 788–89; translation altered)

In this description of human *Verdienst*—usually translated as "merit"—Hölderlin lays out his interpretation of poetic justice. What in Latin is defined by Cicero and the Stoics as *merita*, a concept that serves as the basis of the Renaissance ideal of *dignitas hominis*, will be rethought by Hölderlin as *Verdienst*.[120] Framed from within an understanding of poetic measure, *Verdienst* signifies "that which is our due"—due measure in Hesiod's sense of that which is granted us by the seasons, the fluctuating cycles of nature that the farmer and the sailor must abide if they are to weather the hardships afforded by *physis*. Only those skilled in reading the signs of nature and of the times are able to thrive in this process of receiving due measure. Hence, when Hölderlin writes of the "measure of the human being," he draws on this Hesiodic notion of due measure as having a relation to the gods, a notion he also finds in Pindar. But the text here is enigmatic, to say the least. What is this "it" (I, 19) that constitutes the measure of the human being? In German, Hölderlin expresses this relation between measure and human being in the genitive case: "*Des Menschen Maaß ist's*," literally: "of (the) human being measure it is." To express this more properly, one might perhaps insert a comma so that the sentence would read: "of the human being, measure it is." But even here the perennial issue of Hölderlinian word order and syntax arises. In his attempts to write a Hesperian poem modeled on the Greek and yet uniquely its own, Hölderlin was quite self-conscious of the jarring effect that his enigmatic word order would produce in his German readers. The very recuperation of Pindaric enjambments, paratactic constructions, chiasms, hard jointure, and the *Abbruchsformel* of suddenly introducing breaks or radical shifts in narrative form, were undertaken to produce an *Entfremdungseffekt* ("the effect of alienation"). Here, readers were forced to grapple with the interpretive enigma of the poem, much as one might with an oracular pronouncement from Delphi. The poetic disruption and discontinuity became a function of the pressing need to find order and balance. Again, here in the poem's formal architectonic we find another instantiation of harmonic opposition where the effect of foreign Greek forms on native German readers would serve as a poetic excursus of the same *Ausflug* and *Rückkehr* thematic that we saw earlier in "Patmos" and "The Ister." But the irregular word order served another function as well in that it blurred the very question of genitive possession: To whom did measure belong? To which genus was it generic? To gods? To mortals? To each or both? And could one move back and forth between the genera?

Taking his cue from Pindar's Sixth Nemean Ode (v. 1–7), Hölderlin uncovers a deep affinity between gods and humans who, in their *Bildsamkeit*, come to embody the *imago dei* of *Genesis* I, 26–27. And yet through his word order and the paratactical constructions of his sentences that set the two side-by-side yet effect a fundamental distance (and difference), Hölderlin sets up a tense, difficult, and strained relation between them. What emerges from this paratactical conjunction of mortal and divine is a jarring philosophical and ethical disjunction of each from its opposite. Human beings may compare themselves with gods—but only if their hearts remain "pure," purity here connoting the same revelatory quality as the purity of blueness, the purity of a comet, the purity of children, but also the Pietist notion of a pure heart (II, 16–17). Such purity remains the precondition for measure in all its forms. Yet Hölderlin does not posit the human being as the measure. Rather, he sees the human being as the one who is measured—and who receives his measure from/by the gods. To dwell poetically upon the earth, to have an abode or *ethos* that abides, means to find in the relation of earth and sky an incommensurable *mensura* or "measure" that sets a limit to the boundless yearning of the human being to direct and hold dominion over its own fate. To challenge this dominion involves for Hölderlin not merely a momentary dissatisfaction with a specific cultural program or attitude; it involves, rather, the calling into question of the whole history of the West, especially the history of its genesis and inception in the Greeks. "In lovely blueness" seeks to deconstruct the idea of a pure Greek measure or standard for Western art and philosophy generated in Winckelmann and German romanticism. But it also seeks to challenge the Cartesian-Enlightenment notion of a self-generated human measure in the autonomy of reason. The archaic Greek tradition teaches Hölderlin that the Delphic measure of limits and boundaries always involves oracular enigma and hermeneutical dexterity. "Measure" can never constitute a factically given standard by which to direct earthly phenomena into the frame of Cartesian certitude. Rather, measure resists formulation and establishment; it can only emerge *in* and *as* a relation. For Hölderlin, the human relation to measure needs to be grasped, above all, in terms of the human relation (*Bezug*) to the gods' withdrawal (*Entzug*) from the earth.

The second stanza then opens with a fateful question, followed by a definitive answer and an enigmatic excursion:

> Is there a measure on earth? There is none. (*Gibt es auf Erden ein Maß? Es gibt keines.*) For never the Creator's worlds constrict the course of thunder. A flower too is beautiful, because it blooms under the sun. Often in life the eye finds beings that would be more beautiful to name than flowers. Oh! Well I know it! For to bleed both in body and heart and wholly cease to be, does that please God? Yet the soul, it is my belief, must remain pure, else the eagle with songs of praise and the voice of so many birds reach as far as the Almighty. It is the essence, the form it is. (II, 1–9; PF, 788–91; translation altered)

Measure does not exist "on" the earth, nor "in" it, nor "of" it. Indeed, measure does not arise from human measurement at all. This much the poet deigns to tell us. But then he journeys forth on an excursus into thunder, flowers that bloom, an eagle, and the voice of birds—*topoi* that he paratactically juxtaposes with the eye, the soul, the heart, the body, the act of naming, and the problems of form and essence. What might such a complex of themes denote—or is this, as some have speculated, simply the incoherence of a man on the verge of madness? Perhaps by attempting to connect these images with the conclusion of the first stanza and the notions of "that which is our due" and "poetic dwelling" we might perhaps find a way back to the problem of poetic measure that we have explored in a range of Hölderlin's texts.

Just as nothing upon the earth can constrict the course of Zeus's thunder, so too the human being cannot hope to control the force of divine measure. Flowers bloom under the sun (II, 3)—much as church towers do (I, 1). Each receives the creative force of divine *physis* as its generating principle—and "the eye" (of the poet, of the pure soul [II, 6]) takes this in, even as it finds beings even more beautiful to name than flowers. And yet in its project of naming, classifying, and measuring, the eye can go too far; it can succumb to the ocular excess so endemic to human perception. This tension between exceeding the measure and falling short of it, between finding one's center in the midst of being and losing one's way in the pursuit of beings, constitutes the harmonic opposition of "In lovely blueness." Like the poet himself, we are caught in the immoderate rhythm of the back and forth between union with divine *physis* and estrangement from it, between being at home in the world and being a stranger even in our own home. At the heart of the poem's thematic concerns we find this ever-present tension that constitutes the poetic measure of human dwelling. The poet identifies with "the beautiful brook" (II, 9) that flows on as "clear as the eye of divinity"; but from his own eyes flow tears of suffering. He imagines that he would like to be a comet because comets "blossom with fire" and are pure; yet he offers a Pindaric *gnome* to balance this excessive hope, exclaiming: "To desire more than this is to venture beyond human measure" (II, 18–19). A beautiful virgin must wreathe her head with myrtle, but myrtle is what the Hesperians lack; it is only found in Greece (II, 21–23). In the virgin's deficiency we can find the cultural deficit of Hesperian existence (*Wesen*)—its lack of Greek fire, its spiritual neglect of *Gefühl* (feeling) and its need to complete the cycle of cultural exchange and transformation outlined in the Böhlendorff letter.

In the third stanza this tension is heightened even more. As in the last stanza of "As on a Holiday . . . ," where the poet suffers the fate of Tantalus and is "cast down" into the abyss as "the false priest . . . to sing . . . the warning song," here he confronts the fear of dissolution as well. The mortal dangers of excess, of *Übermaß*, of transgressing the limit, confront him as his tragic fate. As in "Der Frieden," the "loss of measure" (PF, 168–69, v. 27) strikes him as "the curse" afflicting human beings as they seek their dwelling place upon the earth.

There are times, the poet seems to say, when the human being has earned (*verdient*) the praise of the gods, when its soul remains pure (II, 6–7) and its spirit earnest (II, 20) as it achieves "the serenity of virtue" (II, 19). Within this moment the human being comes close to fulfilling its destiny, to achieving that state of purity that brings it near to the divinity granted it in the dispensation of the *imago dei*. When the human being has thus rendered its service (*Dienst leistet*) to the gods, it stands *Voll Verdienst*, filled with a readiness to receive its due (I, 19–20; II, 19), having found a proper measure for dwelling upon the earth in poetic communion with the divine.[121] But the promise of such communion is far from secure. The image of the human being is beset with a deficit all its own. We are not only creatures of merit and serenity; we are also beings who endure the sufferance of an ontological destitution that marks us alone of all beings. We are beings who suffer, beings who—because we reach too far—are without a center, adrift and destitute, strangers within the world and strangers to ourselves. And though at times we do reflect the image of god, at the same time we also resemble that most pitiable of all creatures, King Oedipus, whose "sufferings seem indescribable, unspeakable, inexpressible" (III, 4–5). Caught in this contradiction between the contending possibilities of unity with the gods and estrangement from them and from ourselves, we make our way through the world in default of our proper dwelling, lacking both *ethos* and measure, wanderers without destination, strangers without a homeland. In this figure of Oedipal estrangement, Hölderlin finds an image of the *anthropos* in radical disjunction with the reigning Enlightenment understanding of the human being as the freely determining, autonomous rational being, ever in pursuit of truth. Hölderlinian ethics, if we can speak in such a way, will be constituted precisely in terms of this disjunction, as a way of human dwelling that honors the power of withdrawal, absence, and the self-differentiating oneness of both a Heraclitean and Sophoclean vision of difference as unity.

"In lovely blueness" offers a tragic interpretation of human subjectivity that rejects the Cartesian confidence of instrumental rationality for an archaic Greek notion of the Delphic measure. When we look at the third stanza we can see how deeply this tragic reading affects the dynamic of the entire poem. Here, the poet recognizes that Oedipus's fate was determined by his overstepping of limits. In his attempts at controlling the outcome of oracles, forcing Teiresias to speak, and threatening both Creon and the herdsman, we see not merely a character flaw or a psychological imbalance. Rather, we become witnesses to a figure who, in his boundless quest for knowledge, violates the very limits that define the human sphere between the world of nature and the realm of the gods. Oedipus is the one whose own insight into the riddle of the Sphinx proves tragically incommensurable with his ability to see the meaning of his own name, which harbors a clue to his irreconcilable identity as stranger/native, son/husband, *tyrannos/basileus*, the one who both solves the riddle and remains a riddle to himself.[122] This Oedipus reaches too far; his yearning for the truth is immeasurable, as will be his suffering. He has, as Hölderlin so poetically puts it, "one eye too many" (III, 3–4). This compulsion to seek out the truth at any cost, beyond all limit and measure, will mark Oedipus as the figure who embodies the doubled, ambiguous legacy of all Enlightenment culture, its wonderful insight and terrible blindness. In his relentless pursuit of knowledge, Oedipus shows himself as the one who is both *ungeheuer* and *deinos*, the one who both inspires monstrous awe and is monstrously awful.[123] No creature that walks upon the earth, beneath the lovely blueness of the sky, is more aw(e) ful than the human being.

In his "Notes to Oedipus" (1803), Hölderlin offers his own assessment of Oedipus as the one whose "wondrously furious curiosity of knowledge has torn through its barriers and now, as though intoxicated in its lordly harmonious form . . . incites itself to know more than it can bear or comprehend" (HS, 65/SA V, 198; translation altered). Bereft of balance, "Oedipus interprets the message from the oracle *too infinitely*"; engaged in a "despairing struggle to come to himself, the degrading, almost shameless striving to be master of himself, the foolishly wild pursuit of a consciousness," Oedipus winds up embodying the monstrousness of his own bifurcated identity. Precisely here in the fissuring of identity, in the radical disjunction between his preeminent insight and his frightful blindness, Hölderlin locates the essence of tragedy:

> Tragedy consists chiefly in this: that the monstrousness (*das Ungeheuere*) of the pairing of God and the human being and the boundless coming together in anger of the powers of Nature and the human being's innermost heart, is grasped in the boundless union's purifying itself (*sich reiniget*) through boundless separation. *Tes physeos grammateus en ton kalamon apobrechon eunoun*. (He was *physis*' scribe, dipping the well-disposed pen.) (HS, 67/SA V, 201; translation altered)[124]

In a poem whose opening image of lovely blueness holds out the possibility of a "boundless union" between gods and mortals, Hölderlin comes in the end to confront the reality of the "boundless separation" that carries with it the burdensome legacy of human suffering. Near the very end of "In lovely blueness," Hölderlin returns to confront the doubled relationship between gods and mortals embodied in Oedipus's fate. There, he catalogues the sufferings of Herakles and the Dioscuri (Castor and Pollux) and remarks:

> To clash with God, like Herakles, that is suffering [*Leiden*]. . . . But this is also suffering, when a man is covered with freckles (*Sommerflecken*), to be wholly covered with stains (*Flecken*)! The beautiful sun does that: for it draws all things out. (PF, 790–91; translation altered)

This poetic conjunction of stains and suffering, *Flecken* and *Leiden*, that Hölderlin alights upon here, finds its echo in his own translation of *Oedipus Tyrannus*. Near the end of the play, just after Oedipus blinds himself, the chorus poses a fateful question to him:

> O you who have done such staggering (*gewaltiges*) deeds! How could you dare to so stain (*beflecken*) your eyes? Which *daimon* drove you to it?

And Oedipus responds:

> Apollo, Apollo it was, friends
> Who consummated such misery.
> Here, my, my sorrows (*Leiden*). (SA V, 185, vv. 1350–52)

Both *Oedipus Tyrannus* and *Oedipus at Colonus* contain numerous references to stains, spots, blemishes, and other marks of defilement and *miasma* that are linked both to Oedipus's suffering and to his fate.[125] In translating one of the opening scenes of *Oedipus Tyrannus*, Hölderlin employs the word *Reinigung* (*katharmo*) or "purification;" later he translates *miasmatus* as "*Schandfleck*" ("stain of desecration") and *miastori* as "*ein Fleck*" ("a stain") (SA V, 133, v. 247; 137, v. 357). These references to "freckles" from "In lovely blueness" that constitute "stains" upon the human body brought on by the summer sun (III, 14–15), have a deep affinity with the *kelis* and *miasma* references in Hölderlin's Oedipus translation and notes written just a few years before.

We human beings are, like Oedipus, "stained" by the sun, symbol of Apollo's divine fire, the source of unity for all life, the cosmic force that brings together the blueness of heaven and the metallic church steeple on earth. And yet, in spite of this vision of oneness and union that pervades the opening of the poem, the human form remains tragically estranged from this divine source, unable to fully realize the latent potential of its being made in the image of god. To achieve this union, the poet wants to say, requires of us that we remain "pure" of heart. And yet even as we approach the heavenly power of the sun, we suffer the affliction of its all too powerful rays and become stained with the mark of Oedipus: the *Fleck* of mortality that drives us on inexorably to overstep the limits of our fate. We succumb to this Oedipal affliction "as when a poor man laments that there is something he lacks (*dass ihm etwas fehle*)" (III, 18–19). Like Oedipus, Hölderlin intimates, what we lack is measure. All too preoccupied with overcompensating for our mortal incommensurability with the immortals, we dwell in a state of default, wanderers in the never-ending night of divine absence, "until God's default helps" ("*bis Gottes Fehl hilft*") (SPF, 82–83). This is our double legacy that cuts at "the innermost heart of the human being" (HS, 67/SA V, 271), that marks our tragic condition upon the earth: we are both pure and stained—pure in our staining, stained in our purity.

Oedipus stands as the determining figure in the third stanza of "In lovely blueness . . ." because in his struggles to reconcile purity and stain, consecration and defilement, he embodies the irreconcilability of inward contradiction that marks the human condition as tragic. In our inability to balance our boundless desire for divine union with our boundless desire for autonomy and separation (*Absonderung*), we fall back into the pattern of Oedipal excess and transgression that Sophocles portrayed as the *paradeigma* of human existence (OT, 1193). Hölderlin writes that Oedipus struck "beyond the measure" (*über die Maas*) (SA V, 180)—and it is precisely in relation to measure that he thinks the excess of the tragic.

"Is there a measure on earth?" Hölderlin responds: "no"—because no human limit can constrain the thunder (or divine rays) of the gods. "Is God unknown?" Yes, Hölderlin affirms in his fragment "*Was ist Gott?* . . . ,"

> . . . Unknown, and yet
> Full of qualities is the face
> Of heaven with him. . . . (PF, 614–15)

As soon as Hölderlin provides what we might naively call "answers" to these questions, his poetry recedes back into the enigmatic realm of ambiguity, scission, riddle, and poetic concealment. In doing so, he reclaims the power of Sophoclean tragedy for posing the questions of the human being. As the French classicist Jean-Pierre Vernant puts it: "Tragedy . . . carefully emphasizes distance. . . . [I]t never provides a solution that could eliminate conflicts either by reconciling them or by stepping beyond the oppositions. And this tension that is never totally accepted nor entirely obliterated makes tragedy into a questioning to which there can be no answers. In a tragic perspective, man and human action are seen, not as things that can be defined or described, but as problems. They are presented as riddles whose double meanings can never be pinned down or exhausted."[126] The problem of tragedy for Hölderlin involves, in its deepest sense, the problem of just measure. Neither human being nor god can provide the measure; the measure remains inscrutable, sphinxlike, and elusive. The question of measure resists appropriation and arrogation; to reduce it to a "standard" (*Maßstab*), a "measurement" (*Abmessung*), or a "gauge" (*Richtmaß*) would be arrogant (*anmassend*) and presumptuous (*vermessen*). Measure emerges in the interface of confrontation and engagement. It comes to presence in the reciprocal roundelay of earth, sky, mortals, and gods "in lovely blueness," the self-manifestation (*phainesthai*) of their mutually interpenetrating realms in a gathering (*logos*) at a threshold where, as the last line of the poem expresses it, "Life is death and death a kind of life" (III, 20). At the border of mortality, that enigmatic limit that refuses to be swept up in the Enlightenment project of calibration and reckoning, Hölderlin comes upon a horizon for reciprocal joining or *Fügung* that offers the poetic possibility of measure. To dwell at the limit of such a measure, balanced between the excess of union and the default of separation, would be to come into a strange proximity to the divine, the proximity of distance that renders the native, alien and the alien, one's own. To accept this order of withdrawal and estrangement as essentially conjoined with our own form of poetic dwelling would constitute a kind of justice for Hölderlin. This Hölderlinian justice acknowledges the powerful role that *physis* plays in the disjunction of presence and absence that accompanies every emergence into being.

In the gathering of earth and sky, mortals and gods, that comes to presence in the lovely blueness above the church steeple, Hölderlin finds the traces of god's absence that reveal themselves as a concealed offering or gift. Here, in a realm suffused with contradiction and paradox, Hölderlin (like Sophocles, Pindar, and Hesiod before him) finds the enigmatic order of Zeus, god of the skies, and his son Apollo, god of the sun. The blueness above him stands as an oracle with no clear sign of how to interpret its inscrutable message. If we take upon ourselves the *Übermaß* of Oedipus and attempt to render its signs intelligible through our willful direction and control, we will remain tethered to a world of suffering. But no program of cybernetical management or therapeutic engineering can redress the imbalances of fate that shape the mortal condition. As the Greek tragedians taught him, human life presents itself as a furious parade of vicissitudes and upheavals, a riddling periodicity of progress and regress, journey and return, without impregnable security or refuge. And yet to those who, like Hesiod's farmer in *Works and Days*, can endure the storms of adversity and find in the rhythmic cycles of nature the signs of divine order, there lies the hope of a "seasonable" measure (*Works and Days*, vv. 306–307).[127]

To dwell poetically upon the earth for Hölderlin is to find an *ethos* that balances joy and suffering, life and death, excess and deficit, one that knows how to both seize upon, and be seized by, due season, proportion, and right measure. As Hesiod expressed it, "Carefully keep to due measure (*metra*); what's fitting (*kairos*) in all things is best" (*Works and Days*, v. 694).[128] In this ethic of balance and measure Hölderlin locates the factical situation of human being caught in the temporality of its world and the mortality of its fate, *topoi* that Heidegger will take up as he explores the deeply enigmatic problems of justice. In the teeth of these limits that form the horizon of human existence, the gods offer only the enigma of the oracle. But, as at Delphi, the Apollonian order of the gods always proclaims to those mortals who will but listen—"Always a measure exists" (SPF, 152–53).

TWO

HEIDEGGERIAN "JUSTICE" AS *DIKE*

A new *justice* is needed!

—Friedrich Nietzsche, *The Gay Science*

What does Hölderlin's poetry say? Its word is: the holy. This word speaks of the flight of the gods. It says that the gods who have fled protect us, until we are inclined and capable of dwelling in nearness to them. The place of nearness is what is proper to the homeland. And so it remains necessary to prepare a sojourn (*Aufenthalt*) in this nearness.

—Martin Heidegger, EHP, 224/GA 4, 195

THE STRANGENESS OF JUSTICE

It is a strange thing to talk about justice. Strange in that the very notion of justice speaks to the strangeness of the human being as that being who—in Sophocles's words from the choral ode in *Antigone* and in Hölderlin's translation of them—exceeds all other beings in strangeness. Justice is the strange preoccupation of that estranged being who occupies the place of justice's departure and withdrawal. But justice is also strange in its etymological sense—from the old French word *estrange* and from the Latin, *extraneus*, from *extra*, that is, "without," "on the outside," "not included in," "beyond"—or that which is foreign, unconnected, alien (from Latin *alius*, "the other"). To speak of justice in this way is to speak of the other, the extra, the strange, and the foreign. In its strictest sense, justice is what is "extraneous" as that which lies outside or beyond what belongs to us; with justice, it is always a question of the "other." As Derrida reminds us, justice lies outside of and beyond law, even against law, as that which remains for us less a theme than a question. As something heterotropic, incalculable, and recalcitrant to law, justice resists being collapsed into anything legal—even as it calls out for legal redress of that which is in question. For Derrida, rendering justice exposes us to the incalculable excess and overflow of a time beyond history, of "a day belonging no longer to history, a quasi-messianic day" that is "infinitely foreign and heterogeneous at its source."[1] Here, justice resists coming to presence for the sake of a justice to come and never becomes present to itself or gathers to itself in a present all that remains—and persists in remaining—alien, other, heterogeneous, and perhaps even extraneous. Such a justice never collapses the other into a gathering of its possibilities, into a belonging-together of that which is separate and distinct. It never succeeds in gathering the heterogeneous into a homogeneity that reaffirms the reigning order of the day, but instead insists on the vigilant resistance to conformity, conservatism, and the reaffirmation of presence as the essence of anything we could term "justice." On the contrary, Derrida insists, justice resists repetition since it is never available as something "present" to be repeated. Justice is "the experience of an aporia," "the experience of the impossible"—or rather—as Derrida puts it, "Justice would be the experience of what we are unable to experience." To attempt to think the question of justice, then, brings us to the limit of thinking the im/possible against, beyond, and on the other side of, what manifests itself in the possibilities of the present.

I begin my reading of Heideggerian *dike* with a discussion of Derridean justice because it seems to me that Derrida's reading opens up an approach to the question of justice that touches on the issue of a justice beyond, other than, or extraneous to law, right, order, and *nomos*. Such an approach, I believe, helps us to situate Heidegger's insight that justice *is* strange—but not only as what is extraneous. Rather, Heidegger will think justice in a strange way by refusing to think it as justice at all, going so far as to abjure any positive references to the German word for justice—*Gerechtigkeit*—and instead insisting on thinking it from its ancient Greek sources in a lexicon whose meaning stretches the limits of both Greek and German usage. Writing in 1946, Heidegger holds fast to his conviction that, given the prevailing historical circumstances in Germany, it is no longer possible to speak of "justice"—a word that he thinks has already been so deeply co-opted by the machinations of a political, economic, legal, and moral order that it has become a codeword for affirming the occupation forces' imposition of Allied military rule upon the German homeland. In the teeth of such an Allied occupation, which sought to reassert "the rule of law" and institute the retribution of justice in a nation whose leaders sat accused of "crimes against humanity," Heidegger will dare to rethink what we could ever mean by "justice" even as he deconstructs its legal and moral edifice back down to its roots in a way of philosophy itself. On this reading, justice will be thought of not as a form of *techne* applicable to what we would call law or ethics, but as another name for *physis*. Responding to the judicial verdicts handed down by the Allied tribunal at Nürnberg, Heidegger will rethink the prevailing *Gerede* about the inner conjunction of ethical responsibility and the retribution of justice that defined the Nürnberg proceedings. Instead, he will find in the dislodging of justice from ethics a way of thinking through the contemporary plight of Germany in terms of a nonmetaphysical reading of ethics and justice in language derived from poetic thinking and tragedy. On the basis of this disjunction, I want to venture a reading of Heidegger's notion of justice by looking at two important texts dealing with this question: his seminar from WS 1938/39, *Zur Auslegung von Nietzsches II. Unzeitgemäßer Betrachtung* (GA 46), and his 1946 essay "Der Spruch des Anaximander" (GA 5, 321–73; GA 78).

As Heidegger thinks it, the word *justice* both names and refrains from naming a legal and ethical claim upon the human subject that measures human action against the limit of the strange and unorthodox. Legal and ethical justice rein in what is aberrant and anomalous, making it fall in line with the *nomos*. And yet, for Heidegger, justice is less the province of *nomos*-law-convention-usage than it is of *physis* understood as "being." In Heidegger's sense, justice names something that cannot be named—or, in Blanchot's words, it "simply names the unnameable of the name."[2] Justice exceeds law, exceeds the ethical sphere of action and responsibility, exceeds the very nameability of the conventional name "justice." Hence, Heidegger will refrain from speaking that name and instead will attempt to translate himself back into the archaic Greek experience of *dike*, so that he can translate it again—and in a decisively different way. But such a translation does not merely aim at "naming" justice or *Gerechtigkeit* with another name—order or *Fug*—as if some alternative translation could more properly name that which resists naming. On the contrary, Heidegger insists, "our thinking must first, before translating (*vor der Übersetzung*), be translated to (*übersetzt*) what is said in Greek" (EGT, 19/GA 5, 328). Only then can the *Spruch* of Anaximander be a verdict that "might preserve the translation from arbitrariness." Such an *Über-setztung* or "carrying-across" from the beginning to the end of philosophy enables the earliest *Spruch* of the tradition to claim us in its *Anspruch* as those latecomers who dwell in the shadow of a turning whose possibility still exceeds the name of what can be named in "justice."

Precisely because it exceeds this name, Heidegger cannot name it. When he does, finally, turn his attention to thinking the (im)possibility of justice, he reflects on its absence, not its presence, and comes to think of *dike* in terms of all that is *adikias*. Only by way of its absence, an absence that marks the totality of all that is present (*das All des Anwesenden*, EGT,

40/GA 5, 354), does Heidegger presume to translate what remains palimpsestically enshrouded by the concealment of legal and ethical inscription. In Anaximander's *Spruch* all being is thought in terms of presencing. Yet presencing itself, Heidegger claims, needs to be understood in two ways: first, as the lingering-awhile of what is presently present (i.e., of that which comes-to-be yet passes away and comes to acceptance of this whiling as its fundamental way of being). Secondly, however, he speaks of presence as a persisting lingering-awhile that embraces continual perdurance, a stubborn inclination to persist in hanging on, a willful resistance to the inevitability of passing-away that emerges as a presumptuous (*anspruchsvoll*) "craving to persist" (EGT, 45–46/GA 5, 339). This "insurrection (*Aufstand*) on behalf of sheer endurance" Heidegger interprets as a "disjunction" (*Un-Fug*) between presencing's implacable withdrawal into absence and its "rebellious whiling . . . that insists upon sheer continuance" (EGT, 43/GA 5, 356). Here presencing comes to presence in opposition to the jointure of the while, even as this disjunctive resistance (precisely as disjunctive) gives jointure.

But what does all this strange language about the strangeness of *dike*, jointure, and *Fug* come to? How are we to make sense of the labyrinth of withdrawal and coming to presence that is the articulated jointure of Anaximander's *Spruch* and Heidegger's response to its *Anspruch*? And given the power of the claim (*Anpruch*) of this saying/verdict (*Spruch*) upon us, how are we to *behave* in the wake of this insight into the tragic disorder of being as that which is ever ordered in a way that never fully comes to presence? Heidegger's discussion of presence and absence here constitutes a way of raising again the fundamental question about German *Dasein* that he raised in SS 1932 in his Plato lectures: "How can *aletheia* once again become history for us?" (EOT, 89/GA 34, 123). How can we come to a fundamental experience of that which speaks in the Greek word *aletheia* so that we might reappropriate it in a more primordial way? This "question of whether *aletheia* is to remain merely something from the past or rather become history (for us)," would be reformulated in 1946 as a question about the verdict of Anaximander and the truth-saying power of *dike*. In Heidegger's view, Anaximander's verdict about *dike* held within itself the resources to resist appropriation by the contemporary language of "justice" and "ethics" that everywhere pervaded German national discourse in "Year Zero." Against the legal-juridical-ethical language of his contemporaries, Heidegger reframes the tragic situation of 1946 as a question about how to find a proper place of dwelling in the midst of a widespread German diaspora. Moreover, in reflecting on this historical crisis, Heidegger thinks it as an oppositional tension and contention within *aletheia* marked by the movement of concealing and unconcealing, a movement that characterized the early Greek relation between tragedy and justice (*dike*). To free *dike* from its anthropomorphic encasing within the philosophical divisions of physics-logic-ethics and to grant it its own status as a master term for *Seyn* itself in its aletheic presencing/absencing becomes for Heidegger a way to resituate human dwelling within the poetic-philosophical experience of tragedy. For, as Heidegger puts it, "The possibility and necessity of tragedy itself has its single source in the conflictual essence of *aletheia*" (P, 90/GA 54, 134). Before he could open up a space for such dwelling, however, Heidegger needed to dislodge the language of justice from its place at the center of national discourse—something that could only be achieved by way of *de-structuring* the metaphysical presuppositions that underlay its conceptual power. In the sections that follow, I want to look at Heidegger's strange reading of justice in his interpretation of Anaximander, Hölderlin, and Nietzsche. In so doing I want to think justice in a nonhuman register as an "event" that has much to do with the possibility of poetic dwelling.

THE HISTORY OF BEING AND THE QUESTION OF JUSTICE

One of the singular achievements of Heidegger's Nietzsche lectures, delivered from 1936–1944, is their complex refashioning of the history of metaphysics as a history of being, what Heidegger terms "Seynsgeschichte."[3] Going back to *Being and Time* and even earlier, Heidegger had understood his work in terms of "the task of a destructuring of the history of ontology" (BT, 17/SZ, 19). But after his fundamental confrontation with Hölderlin, Nietzsche, and the pre-Socratics during the 1930s against the background of political-ontological revolution, Heidegger approached his task differently. Beginning at least with his seminal essay, "On the Essence of Truth" (1930), Heidegger came to understand the history of philosophy as determinative for the history of the West as a story about the transformation of the essence of truth as *aletheia*. What emerges from such a history is the understanding of truth as the dynamic tension within being itself of concealment and revelation, a play of *polemos* between that which shows itself in beings and that which cleaves to its hidden ground in being. Now what begins to characterize Heidegger's work in this period is a move away from the anthropomorphic question about the "meaning of being" (*die Frage nach dem Sinn des Seins*) that dominated *Being and Time* (SZ, 1–6) and a turn toward the more fundamental ontological question concerning "the truth of being" (PM, 256 / GA 9, 336). As part of this complex move or "turn" (*Kehre*) whose full character takes two decades to unfold, Heidegger will lay forth a reading of truth as an "appropriating event" (*Ereignis*) that grants to *Dasein* its own place in history that comes into its ownness not in human history, but rather only in the history of being. "History is the history of *being*," Heidegger proclaims in SS 1939 (N iii, 182/GA 47, 294). Throughout the

Nietzsche lectures Heidegger will offer different iterations of this history from Plato's interpretation of truth as *idea*, the medieval doctrine of truth as *adequatio*, to Descartes's notion of truth as self-certainty through Kant's notion of truth as transcendental knowledge as well as in Nietzsche's idea of truth as eternal recurrence of the same. All of these different versions of truth within the history of being constitute for Heidegger different ways of thinking truth as "enduring presence" (*beständige Anwesenheit*), a characterization that Heidegger defines as the fundamental trait of the metaphysics of the modern age.

As Heidegger begins to work through the deeply metaphysical implications of his earlier *Daseinsanalytik*, he comes to rethink both the meaning of the "Da" and his analysis of time in terms of historicity. Now Heidegger comes to understand the "Da" of *Sein* as much broader than the *human* horizon of being; indeed he sees it as "the appropriating event" of being itself, as the coming-to-be of truth in and as history, understood as the history of being. As Heidegger puts it in his notebooks from the late thirties: "The Da—(there-ness) as strife between world and earth."[4] That is, the "Da" of historical being—what Heidegger would later term "the clearing" (*die Lichtung*)—comes to manifest itself only in the strife and tension between the sheltering, concealing force of earth (the chthonic) and the manifesting, revealing force of world (the human realm of production and *techne*).[5] It is this tension and strife between revelation and concealment, a strife that is not merely that between beings but of/within being itself, that Heidegger comes to understand as the essential conflict between truth and its counteressence, untruth. Following Heraclitus's insight that "*Polemos* is the father of all and the king of all" (Diels Fragment 53), Heidegger puts forward a reading of the history of being as an ongoing *polemos* of/within truth as *a/letheia*.[6] This play between concealment and unconcealment happens as an originary occurrence that appropriates the human being to the event of being. As Heidegger will not tire of reminding his listeners, this event of truth does not occur within the locus of human judgment (the *logos apophantikos* of *Being and Time*, secs. 7 and 44) as an agreement between consciousness and its object; rather, the truth of being happens as an event of disclosure that grants the presencing of beings to the human being even as it withdraws in the sheltering event of concealment.

On Heidegger's reading, this history of being will be marked by the early Greek interpretation of beings in terms of their presence (*Anwesenheit*), an interpretation that from Plato and Aristotle became decisive for the entire history of philosophy as metaphysics. By deciding in favor of that which opens itself to ocular observation—a privileging that is etymologically present in the Greek word for theory, *theorein*, which designates "a looking at" or "viewing"—Greek metaphysics concealed the originary force of concealment itself in the coming to presence of truth. The history of being, rewritten by Heidegger as the history of truth, would come to be marked by this oblivion of the lethic dimension of *a/letheia*. But this interpretation of being in terms of its "constant presence" (*beständige Anwesenheit*) whether as *idea* (Plato), *ousia* (Aristotle), *ens creatum* (medieval scholastics), *res extensa* (Descartes), transcendental object (Kant), or "life" (Nietzsche), only succeeds in covering over the originary play/strife of concealment/unconcealment that Heraclitus understood as the original movement of being itself. Given this history of oblivion, Heidegger contends, we have been overcome by a nihilism that is not merely cultural or ideological, but that exceeds the dimension of mere *Weltanschauung* or generational malaise, to become an ontological feature of modernity itself. Not only have *we* forgotten being, but *being* has abandoned us. We are confronted by an epochal danger that threatens not only human beings, but the possibility of the earth's very being. In the lurking danger of nuclear war, environmental catastrophe, population explosions, and the erasure of boundaries between the natural and the artificial we find indications of the hidden possibilities of a technological mode of revelation that brings to completion an epoch of truth's being. What is at stake for Heidegger in the narration and recitation of this epochal history is nothing less than the future of the earth.

To narrate this overarching history of being in ways that would not succumb to the Hegelian metaphysics of historical *telos* and Prussian triumphalism, Heidegger begins to offer different versions of his eschatological interpretation of Western history. In *Contributions to Philosophy* (1936–38) he experiments with a new language of "originary thinking" that will adopt a tone of reticence and reserve to communicate the possibility of a "turning" (*Kehre*) in/of history under the name of *Ereignis*: the "event of a non-metaphysical appropriation" of human being (*Dasein*) by being (*Seyn*) that initiates a "clearing" (*Lichtung*) for the occurrence of the truth of being (GA 65, 55–60; 33–35; 11; 347–59). Against the logic of assertion and correspondence that dominated the Western conception of truth from Aristotle through the neo-Kantians, Heidegger attempts to recall the hidden possibilities of another kind of thinking that lies within the Western tradition, a thinking marked by reserve, silence, and poetic attunement. Through thoughtful engagement with the philosophical texts of Anaximander, Heraclitus, and Parmenides, as well as with the poetic texts of Sophocles, Pindar, Hölderlin, and Hebel, Heidegger hopes to deconstruct the metaphysical edifice of the Aristotelian notion of truth and to begin cultivating the ground for the possibility of a new kind of thinking. Such thinking might, he hopes, provide "the inceptive condition for the self-unfolding possibility of an originary—poetic—naming of being" (GA 65, 36). At the same time as he conducts this very private experiment with a new kind of language in his notebooks for *Contributions*, Heidegger delivers his public lectures on Nietzsche. Each needs to be read against the other as different forms for carrying out a rethinking of his earlier interpretation of the question of being in terms of a fundamental-ontological analytic of *Dasein*. What now emerges is an overarching narrative of the history of being that will shape all of Heidegger's work over the next thirty years. Heidegger will present this history in different ways, changing the optic of his analysis from politics to art, to poetry, and from technology to architecture. Moreover, he will offer different iterations of this history under such names as "the topology of being," *das Gestell* (Enframing), *das Geschick* (destining), "the principle of reason," the fourfold, and nihilism, cultivating a baffling new lexicon of *Besinnung, Ereignis, Gelassenheit, Lichtung, Machenschaft, Seyn, Unverborgenheit, Verwindung*, and *Zuspiel* (to list only a few).

As World War II ends and Heidegger is brought before a de-Nazification commission in Freiburg to account for his activities as rector and his support for the Hitler regime, he must now confront in a very public way deep criticisms about the fundamental meaning of his philosophical work. Most damaging among these criticisms is the judgment of his former friend Karl Jaspers, who writes a letter to the Freiburg commission in late December 1945 claiming that "Heidegger's way of thinking appears to me as unfree, dictatorial, and incommunicative in its essence."[7] In the fall of 1946 after a nervous breakdown and a bout of severe depression, Heidegger begins his rehabilitation (in all its various senses) by writing three important essays that address, in an indirect yet unmistakable way, the accusations levied against him by his accusers. These essays—"The Verdict of Anaximander," "The Letter on Humanism," and "Why Poets?"—I will argue, constitute Heidegger's inimitable response to those questions posed by his accusers concerning his "behavior" (*Verhalten*) during the National Socialist years. In the various missives, dossiers, and reports from the de-Nazification proceedings, there emerges a scathing indictment of Heidegger in terms of his ethical responsibility for his actions as rector as well as for his writings and philosophical views. And it is precisely in relation to questions of ethics, responsibility, and behavior that Heidegger would frame his response. What emerges in these texts is a deeply thoughtful engagement with the personal charges of the de-Nazification commission rethought as questions dealing with the history of being, questions of how to comport ourselves in "a destitute time" beset by "homelessness," "devastation," "the abyss of being," "terror," "the atomic bomb," and "the destiny of the world's night" (PLT, 91, 97, 116, 142 / GA 9, 269, 275, 294, 320). The eschatological history of being that Heidegger worked out in his readings of the pre-Socratics, Nietzsche, and Hölderlin from 1934–1945 would now be reframed to address the specific historical situation of Germany at the end of the war and Heidegger's role therein. To put it simply, these essays offer an eschatology of history as an autobiographical reflection on contemporary events. That is, at the very moment of a "*Stunde null*" (a "zero hour") in German history, Heidegger answers charges about his political past by reconfiguring them as questions about the history of being.

In this chapter I want to look more carefully at Heidegger's notion of justice against the background of his overarching history of being. But I also want to situate this reading of justice within Heidegger's own history and attempt to interpret it against the charged political events of postwar Germany to which it constituted a critical response. Heidegger develops his reading of justice in his confrontation or *Auseinandersetzung* with the traditional interpretations of the Anaximander fragment that he believed had dominated the history of metaphysics. Going back to the textual emendations offered by Aristotle's pupil Theophrastus, Heidegger claims, Anaximander's notion of *dike* was subjected to a legal and moral interpretation that occluded its original meaning. In 1946 Heidegger attempts via a close textual reading of this fragment to reclaim the nonmetaphysical sense of *dike* against the Aristotelian-Christian metaphysics of justice that pervades all moral and legal thinking since that time. "The Verdict of Anaximander" reads the original notion of *dike* not as "justice" in its moral or juridical sense, but as the cosmic play of strife in being between the coming-to-presence and withdrawal-into-absence of beings. Such a reading shifts the focus from the anthropomorphic measure of *Dasein* to the ontological measure of *Seyn*. Accordingly, Heidegger will reject the explicit focus on ethics, moral behavior, and political-legal justice in the essay and reconfigure these topics as reflections on the destiny of the West in "an epoch of errancy [*Irre*]" (EGT, 27/GA 5, 338). Underlying this deferral of ethics is a rhetorical strategy familiar to readers of Heidegger's occasional essays—namely, the practice of paralepsis (of making one's point by an act of indirection, that is, of not discussing ethics even as one discusses it). In the "Letter on Humanism" (also written in the fall of 1946), however, Heidegger will expressly take up the question of ethics and then only by way of denying its viability in the age of nihilistic thinking.

The "Letter on Humanism" marks an important moment in Heidegger's attempt to raise the question of justice, even though the topic of justice will never be directly addressed. Instead, Heidegger focuses his attention there on the question of "the truth of being" in relation to human beings within the history of being. As part of his attempt to think the truth of being as "the humanity of *homo humanus* . . . but without humanism in the metaphysical sense," Heidegger poses a decisive question: "But if *humanitas* must be viewed as so essential to the thinking of being, must not 'ontology' therefore be supplemented by 'ethics'?" (PM, 268/GA 9, 352). The "Letter on Humanism" decisively rejects any supplementary connection between ontology and ethics, claiming rather that "it becomes necessary to ponder whether what can be designated by both terms still remains near [*nah*] and proper [*gemäß*] to what is assigned to thinking, which as such has to think above all the truth of being" (PM, 269/GA 9, 353–54). For Heidegger, "ethics" as a regional ontology devoted to cultivating "rules" and "directives" that will be binding in advance for all human action signals nothing less than the nihilistic character of modern technology. In its unbridled will to measure [*messen*] and calculate what is proper [*gemäß*] to human action, ethics moves within the sphere of mere reckoning and machination, failing to bring the human being near to the truth of being. Such ethics remains an all too clear representation of an underlying crisis in Western thinking that signals the very homelessness of human being upon the earth. Against this ontological condition of homelessness, Heidegger will ponder the historical homelessness of Germany in 1946 by rethinking the human sphere of calculative ethics as Heraclitean *ethos*—namely, as the historical "abode" or "dwelling place" of humanity. But this historical phrasing of the question of ethics in terms of dwelling and abode did not suddenly emerge out of the historical crisis of defeat and despair that beset German culture in the wake of World War II. Its roots go back to the series of lecture courses that Heidegger held on Hölderlin, Nietzsche, and the pre-Socratics from WS 1934/35 on through the end of the war.

In this chapter, I want to trace Heidegger's concern for questions of ethics against his overarching narrative of a history of being and attempt to grasp it in terms of his perplexing reading of justice. I see this juxtaposition of justice and ethics as critical to Heidegger's project, even as I will acknowledge that Heidegger never explicitly develops a reading of ethics and justice as belonging together in an essential way. Before I begin to lay out my reading of this difficult question, however, I would like to raise a number of problems that I believe merit our attention. Foremost among these concerns is the question of justice itself. Justice is never explicitly addressed by Heidegger as a main focus for his history of being. Yet in 1946 as he comes to terms with questions concerning his own responsibility in the de-Nazification hearings and with questions concerning the fate of a defeated Germany, Heidegger takes up the question of justice in his reflections on the Anaximander Fragment. This extended reflection on the problem of justice continues the preliminary work Heidegger had done on Nietzsche and the pre-Socratics in his Freiburg lectures from 1936–1944. When Heidegger raises the question of justice he always thinks it from within the truth of being as another way of asking about the order, arrangement, and fit (*Fug*) of beings and not as an inquiry about normative behavior or legal-moral adjudication. All the way back to the *Introduction to Metaphysics* (1935), where he translated the notion of *dike* as *Fug* rather than as *Gerechtigkeit*, Heidegger would claim: "Being as *dike* is the key to beings in their conjunction (*Gefüge*)" (IM, 177/EM, 127). And a year later, in "The Will to Power as Art," he would write that "[k]nowledge of *dike*, of the articulating laws (*Fügungsgesetzen*) of the being of beings, is philosophy" (N i, 166/GA 43, 204). From these early pronouncements about *dike* we can see how Heidegger wished to think ontologically about the problems of *dike*, *Fug*, and *Fügung*. We will have to look more carefully at this translation of *dike* as *Fug* rather than as *Gerechtigkeit* to truly grasp what is at stake here for Heidegger in the difference between ontological order (*Fug*) and moral-juridical justice (GA 39, 126; GA 51, 119–20).

In all of these attempts Heidegger never explicitly draws a connection between ethics and justice, seeing in the very project of ethical-legal justice the same metaphysical impulses as those underlying Plato's *Republic* where "*dike* slips into the twilight zone of morality" (N i, 166/GA 43, 204).[8] And yet, in late 1946 as Heidegger writes "The Verdict of Anaximander" and "The Letter on Humanism," he will take up the issues of *dike* and of ethics, although without ever relating them directly to one another. This reluctance to confront the underlying resonance between justice and ethics is hardly fortuitous, I will argue, since it bespeaks an even deeper reticence on Heidegger's part to proffer any plan or order for directing human action or behavior. We can only raise the question of ethics, Heidegger will claim, when we have first thought through "the humanity of homo humanus" in relation to "the truth of being, but without humanism in the metaphysical sense" (PM, 268/GA 9, 352). But since we are immersed within the frame (*Gestell*) of a technological thinking that defines beings as "standing reserve" (*Bestand*) there for the needs and projects of human beings, we fail to think the dynamic temporality of the human being in its experiences and practices. Instead, we detach ethics from its lived experiential context and produce it as a kind of calculative technological measure, a set of rules and principles that will set up "standards" (*Maßstäbe*) for human behavior that will be binding in advance. But all of this ethical thinking merely winds up detaching us from our specific historical situation by attempting to provide a universal set of principles that will govern human relations. As with much of the technological project of universalizing-calculative thinking, ethics fails because it detaches us from our specific historical grounds and uproots us from the earth. Until we can reframe the Hölderlinian question of our proper belonging to the earth, that is, until we can rethink the question of what it means to be human, we will never be able to properly raise the question of ethics and its relationship to justice.

Hence, in "The Letter on Humanism" Heidegger first directs his attention to deconstructing the metaphysical edifice of humanism and its anthropology of "man" as "the rational animal," before addressing the possibility of an ethics.

> More essential than instituting rules is that human beings find the way to their abode [*Aufenthalt*] in the truth [*Wahrheit*] of being. This abode first yields [*gewährt*] the experience of something we can hold on to [*das Haltbare*]. The truth of being offers a hold [*den Halt*] for all conduct [*Verhalten*]. (PM, 274/GA 9, 361)

For Heidegger, the question of ethics as a philosophical discipline capable of dispensing normative principles of conduct and behavior is nothing but the expression of a technological will to nihilism. We cannot properly put forward an ethics in the epoch of technicity because we still think of the human being within the *Gestell* of metaphysical humanism and conceive ethics as if it were an achievement of subjectivity. Only when we rethink the question of *human* being in relation to the truth of being—and that means deconstructing the metaphysical notions of "truth" and "essence"—can we hope to understand the profound and abiding link between ethics and justice. This means that we can no longer think truth as an accomplishment of consciousness that corresponds with being (*adequatio*), nor conceive of essence as a permanent substratum (*ousia*) that constitutes the "inner nature" of the human being. Rather, Heidegger enjoins us to open ourselves to the event-character of truth and to the *ek-static* temporality of human ek-sistence that "stands outside" itself and recognizes the primordial claim that being has upon us long before we are able to take up our claims upon being. As Heidegger puts it in "The Letter on Humanism": "Ek-sistence thoughtfully dwells in the house of being" (PM, 274/GA 9, 362).

If we continue to think of ethics within the technological grip of planning and calculation—namely as "applied" ethics, business ethics, medical ethics, and the like—then, Heidegger tells us, we will be unable to find an originary relation between ethics and justice. Only when we come to terms with the poverty of contemporary technological thinking, when we recognize that we lack the proper language (*logos*) for conceiving the problem, the proper attunement (*pathos*) to its call, and the proper relation (*ethos*) to earth as a place for dwelling will we be able to even express the tragic incommensurability of human ethics and the truth of being. Clearly, Heidegger never does utter an extended reading of justice in terms of ethics and yet I want to argue that, despite this, Heidegger's postwar writing intimately concerns their relation. Ethics and justice remain metaphysical signatures for two realms of inquiry that are cut off from their primordial ground in archaic Greek experience. However, by abjuring "ethics" and attempting to think *ethos* as a form of poetic dwelling that gets measured by the heavens and not by human "values," Heidegger begins to find a way to think justice as the very jointure (*Fuge*) of being that balances the contending strife of all beings. Such an attempt signifies nothing less than the rethinking of the relationship between *Dasein* and *Sein*, between the temporal-spatial opening of human dwelling and the hidden play of being's concealment/revelation. The possibility of recovering such an *ethos*, Heidegger contends, lies in reclaiming the power of poetic thinking, especially the power of Greek tragedy. Tragedy belongs to the question of ethics in that it speaks to the issue of human dwelling and understands that such dwelling is uncanny, *unheimlich*, at odds with our notion of being-at-home upon the earth. We are homeless beings, adrift in the world of human machination, unsure of our boundaries and limits beneath the heavens against the unyielding limit of death. Having forgotten our place within the overarching order of being, estranged from our own sense of being, we experience the homelessness of the world night, cut off from the realm of what is holy. Like Hölderlin before him, Heidegger comes to understand the human being in the shadow of the Greek tragedians as that singularly estranged being who confronts the homelessness of his own destiny, cut off from the gods who have fled, wandering aimlessly in the darkness and nihilism of the world's night.

DWELLING AMIDST THE RUINS: *ETHOS*, ORIGINARY ETHICS, AND THE ABODE OF HUMAN BEING

In the "Letter on Humanism" Heidegger attempts to rethink ethics by starting from the ground of being rather than from the measure of the human being. In one sense, we could proffer a devastating critique of Heidegger's motives here by situating them against the whole background of the de-Nazification proceedings that threatened Heidegger's academic livelihood and the loss of his pension, library, and home.[9] And one could, I believe, make a strong case that the timing and focus of the essay was meant to favorably shift the official French reception of his work precisely at the moment when he was facing questions of his personal responsibility for the National Socialist disaster.[10] And yet, in another sense, this essay can be read as the authentic culmination of many of Heidegger's own concerns about ethics, justice, personal responsibility, and political crisis that had been germinating in the years before Germany's experience of devastation in 1945–46. In the "Letter," Heidegger revisits some of the essential ground of this period with brief allusions to "the tragedies of Sophocles," "Aristotle's lectures on 'ethics,'" a "saying of Heraclitus," and "the world-historical thinking of Hölderlin," themes that he had addressed in greater depth in his Freiburg lectures (PM, 258, 269/GA 9, 339, 354).[11] All of these themes are thought together in this essay as a way of responding to the French philosopher Jean

Beaufret's question about the compatibility of ethics and ontology within Heidegger's work.

As Heidegger sees it, the very discourse about humanism remains mired in the metaphysics of subjectivity with its emphasis on "values," "-isms," and a certain narrow conception of "thinking" in terms of *theoria* and of "action" in terms of *praxis*. Against this discourse Heidegger pursues a rethinking of *logos* not as "logic," "science," or "*ratio*," but as the language of poetic attunement. His aim here is to free thinking from its technical interpretation as *theoria* and to reclaim its originary form as a thinking that is "propriated by being [*vom Sein ereignet*], belongs to being" (PM, 241/GA 9, 316). A thinking that is attuned to its belonging to being no longer thinks "ethics" in terms of values, especially the values of humanism. Rather, it attempts to understand the region of ethicality as that which exceeds the human and can never be made to correspond with the human, all too human, realm of ethical judgment and normative behavior. In introducing this term *originary ethics*, Heidegger ventures to uncover its underlying kinship with the primordial Greek notion of *ethos* as "dwelling" and "abode." What animates Heidegger's concern here is his conviction—precisely in 1946—that the task of thinking can never be followed by placing "action" in the service of a transhistorical ideal of ethical behavior (PM, 239/GA 9, 313). Only a thinking that can grasp ethics primordially as what belongs to being as *dike* (not ethical-legal "justice" but the "jointure" and "configuration" of being itself) can properly follow the dynamic movements and dispensations of being within its different historical epochs. As "The Letter on Humanism" makes all too clear, however, the present age lacks precisely such thinking and remains caught up as ever in a moral calculus of good and evil that measures all beings against the humanistic values of Platonic and Pauline justice/righteousness (*dikaisyne*). Against this background, I want to situate Heidegger's essay within its historical context and show how it can be read as a well-timed assault against the prevalence and direction of such thinking.

As Heidegger prepared to write his essay in the fall of 1946, the Nürnberg Trials had just ended. On October 16, 1946, the Allied military tribunal handed down death sentences against prominent Nazi leaders for what they carefully termed "crimes against humanity."[12] In the midst of the ruins and wreckage of cities destroyed by the Allied bombings, the German people were now having to face difficult questions about their shared guilt and responsibility for the destruction that lay everywhere around them. Caught in the temporality of that moment, scrambling to recover from the devastation of loss and the Nürnberg appeal for retributive "justice," the German people were forced to "come to terms with the past," against the failed projections of the National Socialist future expressed in its orgiastic dream of a "Thousand Year Reich."[13] In this moment of contradiction, esteemed writers such as Thomas Mann and Friedrich Meinecke looked to Germany's rich cultural heritage for sources of humanistic values to counter the effects of the recent Nazi past.[14] Both believed that if the German people committed themselves to their roots in Weimar classicism, they might overcome the moral destruction of the Nazi years. In his 1946 book, *The German Catastrophe*, Meinecke exhorted his fellow survivors to cultivate their inner German spirit by forming Goethe study groups and preoccupying themselves with "the noblest music and poetry" of Bach, Beethoven, and Schiller.[15] In this climate of earnest cultural reflection where writers sought to find Germany's moral compass through a recovery of its humanist values, Heidegger turned his attention to writing an essay on the bankruptcy of humanist discourse.

One could easily read Heidegger's "Letter on Humanism" cynically as the strategic attempt of an embattled ex-Nazi academic to exonerate himself from any responsibility or guilt for the German catastrophe. Certainly Theodor Adorno read it that way, insisting that Heidegger's jargon of authentic "being" shifted responsibility away from *Dasein*, providing an ontological alibi for those who wished to free themselves from the charges of collaboration.[16] But Heidegger's "Letter" was not merely an ideological defense of his personal conduct during the NS years; it also provided an opening into the new thematics of Heidegger's decade-long reflections on the being-question. In this way, the "Letter" tries to imagine a German future that breaks with its humanist past and turns to Hölderlin rather than the Weimar classicists for a pathway out of the devastation. Framed as a critique of Sartre's existential humanism with its Marxist assumptions about the estrangement of human beings, Heidegger's essay rethinks the fashionable language of French existentialism by reconsidering the ontological significance of ek-sistence for an understanding of ethics and justice.

For Heidegger, the understanding of human being as "ek-sistence"—our "*standing out* into the truth of being"—offers a way of rethinking the metaphysical definition of the human being as the *animal rationale*.[17] Here, "existence" is no longer thought as medieval *actualitas*, Kantian "actuality," or Hegelian "absolute subjectivity" (PM, 248/GA 9, 325). Rather, Heidegger thinks it as "the ecstatic relation to the clearing of being [*die Lichtung des Seins*]" (PM, 249/GA 9, 327). What defines the human being is not any interiorized "essence"—thought as an egological core beneath the threshold of everyday activity—but its dynamic movement of being "outside" (*ek*) itself in its *relation* to being. On this reading, *Dasein* signifies less an enclosure of "selfhood" that defines itself among beings than an *ekstatic* being-outside-itself that is ever underway, ever ahead of itself, and whose departure remains tied to its worldly dwelling. *Dasein* "happens" as an event that never ceases to happen (except in death); its very happening occurs in and through the temporal ekstases of "having been" (*Gewesenheit*)—"making present" (*Gegenwärtigen*)—"coming-toward" (*Zukunft*) that Heidegger developed in *Being and Time* (BT, 299–303/SZ, 326–29). *Dasein* comes toward itself, paradoxically, in its standing-outside itself—an interpretation that goes back to the etymological roots of *ekstasis* in its Greek sense of "standing" (*stasis*)-"out" + (*ek-*)-from.

But if Heidegger's understanding of *ekstasis* in the 1920s was still too overdetermined by an anthropocentric understanding of the "da" of *Sein*, by 1946 he had come to underscore the genuinely ontocentric meaning of *Dasein* as the "clearing" of being. In the spatial-temporal nexus of possibilities, contingencies, projections, and foreclosures that is the care-driven movement of *Dasein*, Heidegger comes to stress the event-character of truth as *Lichtung*: the "clearing" for the playful *polemos* of light and darkness, revelation and concealment that constitutes the truth of being as *aletheia*. In the openness of the clearing, in the luminosity of the "da," understood as an event of appropriation (*Ereignis*), Heidegger gives equiprimordial significance to the *lethic* dimension of being and comes to stress the truth of being (*Sein*) rather than, as in *Being and Time*, the truth of *Dasein* (BT, 202–203/SZ, 220–21). Here, in a radical break with Cartesian-Husserlian egology, Heidegger rejects human consciousness as the site or *topos* of truth and comes to stress the *Lichtung* of being as an event that appropriates *Dasein* for its own way of appearing. In *Contributions to Philosophy* Heidegger enacts a turning within his thinking about *Dasein* that will be rooted in the turning of *Dasein* itself from "correctness to openness" and from Cartesian certitude as the mark of truth to an understanding of *Dasein* as an "event" (*Ereignis*). As Heidegger puts it, "*Dasein* has its origin in the event of appropriation [*Ereignis*] and its turn [*Kehre*]." This means that "*Dasein* is the mediating-opening and in this way sheltering 'between' [*Zwischen*]—between the arrival and flight of the gods and the human being who is rooted in this 'between'" (GA 65, 31). To come to an attunement of this event-character of *Dasein* requires what Heidegger terms "reservedness" (*Verhaltenheit*). This new fundamental attunement to beings—akin to what Heidegger would later term "releasement" (*Gelassenheit*)—"no longer begins with the human being as subject" but rather "is conceived according to the measure of *Da-sein* [*da-seinsmässig*] . . . in which the human being in its every comportment [*Verhalten*] and way of relating [*Verhaltenheit*] [to beings] holds itself [*hält sich*] within the realm of the clearing of being [*die Lichtung des Seyns*]" (GA 65, 489–90).

"The Letter on Humanism" thinks this new comportment (*Verhalten*) toward beings in terms of the etymological play of language thought as *Halt-Haltung-Verhalten-Verhältnis-Verhaltenheit-Aufenthalt*. Going back to his WS 1929/30 lectures, *Fundamental Concepts of Metaphysics* and his 1930 essay "On the Essence of Truth," Heidegger had underscored the connection between comportment and ek-sistence, suggesting that our existential situation is marked by a radical freedom and openness to beings that allows us to encounter them within a matrix of possibilities and relations. In our standing "in" this openness (*Inständigkeit*), we stand outside ourselves (*ek-sist*) in the matrix that constitutes the "there" (da) of being (*Sein*) (PM, 149–50/GA 9, 195–96). And it is precisely this openness of comportment that characterizes our being as human beings. In this we are fundamentally different than animals who, wholly driven by instinct and drive, never come to stand outside themselves in a free relation and thus never attain a "stance" (*Haltung*) nor achieve a way of "holding oneself" (*Sichhalten*) in the dynamic tension of a moment—the place of standing (*stasis*)—so as to be able to negotiate the dynamic play of the three ek-stases of time (FCM, 237–38, 274/GA 29/30, 345–46, 397–98).[18] And yet despite *Dasein*'s "freedom" and "resolutely open bearing [*Verhältnis*]," ultimately Heidegger claims, "the human being clings to [*hält sich*] what is customary and controllable even where ultimate matters are concerned" (PM, 149/GA 9, 194). In other words, in the teeth of our radical openness and freedom we shut ourselves off to the phenomenological play of possibilities by holding ourselves (*Sichhalten*) in a certain relation (*Verhältnis*) to things in a bearing (*Haltung*) that seeks to overcome the vacillating caprices of existence by seizing upon that which is stable and can provide a "hold" (*das Halt*) for what is "permanent" (*das Haltbare*). For Heidegger, however, such attempts to take one's "directives (*Anweisungen*) from the sphere of customary, readily available intentions and needs" only succeeds in further concealing the concealment of being's play within the world (PM, 149/GA 9, 195).

In the early Heidegger this whole discourse of *Verhalten*, *Verhältnis*, *das Halt*, and *das Haltbare* focused on *Dasein*'s sense of assuming a "bearing" (*Verhalten*) and of "holding itself" (*Sichhalten*) within the sway of beings. In other words, it articulated a discourse about "holding" where *Dasein* held itself in its openness. But after Heidegger's extended engagement with Hölderlin, Nietzsche, and the pre-Socratics during the 1930s–'40s, it is no longer *Dasein* who "holds" open the moment of engagement with beings. Rather, what now emerges is a rethinking of the language of *Halt*—and *Halten*—where *Dasein* is the one "held." Here, *Dasein* is held open in the propriative event of being's manifestation, a manifestation that manifests as a "holding-back" (*ent-halten*) and "withholding" (*vor-enthalten*). Here, being holds itself back or conceals itself precisely in its showing or revealing itself in the temporal moment that holds us. Time holds us within its compass. As we attain greater mastery over realms of being through our technical expertise and cybernetic calculations, holding things before our virtual gaze in a *Haltung* of control and dominion, we remain held as ever between the having-been (*Gewesenheit*) of our birth and the coming-toward (*Zu-Kunft*) us of our death (SZ, 325–29). In this fateful whiling where we are "held" (*enthalten*) "up" (*auf*), we find our "halting" place or "abode" (*Aufenthalt*) within being. This "human sojourn [*Aufenthalt*] between earth and sky, between birth and death, between joy and pain, between work and word" serves as the *topos* wherein we are held, the place that determines all our attempts at holding ourselves forth, of lingering with things, of coming to dwell in the mortal space "between" animal and god (GA 16, 537). This kind of dwelling, understood as our *Aufenthalt* upon the earth, becomes for Heidegger an essential way of rethinking ethics apart from any anthropological subjectivity and toward Heraclitus's and Anaximander's notion of the overarching order of being itself thought as *dike*: *Fug*, not *Gerechtigheit*; order, not justice. This order is not, however, fixed or eternal but emerges in/as the singular, *jeweilig*, temporally particular event (*Ereignis*) of reciprocal appropriation in which *Dasein* participates, though does not control.

On Heidegger's reading, we do not find our abode, our halting place in being, by mastering beings through machination (*Machenschaft*) or dominion (*Herrschaft*), nor by having beings standing ready at our disposal (*Verfügung*) (GA 65, 126–34; GA 48, 180–92). Rather, only when we stand within the jointure (*Fuge*) of beings with a *Haltung* or comportment of restraint (*Verhaltenheit*) that does not arrogate the measure of things to *Dasein*, but lets *Dasein* be measured by being itself, can we become attuned to the sojourn (*Aufenthalt*) of truth upon the earth. As Heidegger puts it in "What Are Poets For?":

> What threatens the human being in its essence is the view that [the] carrying out of production lets itself be ventured without danger. . . . As if given the essential relation to the whole of beings in which the human being is placed through its technological mode of willing, it were still possible to find a separate abode [*Aufenthalt*] in some residence on the side that would alter us more than a temporary escape into forms of self-deception, among which also belong the flight to the Greek gods. (PLT, 116–17/GA 5, 294; translation altered)

Going back to its etymological roots in the verb "*halten*," which means "to hold," "to retain," "to keep," *Aufenthalt* connotes the temporal sense of "remaining" (*Bleiben*), "lingering" (*Verweilen*), "pausing" (*Stillhalten*), or "staying" (*sich aufhalten*).[19] But it also derives from the middle-high German term *haltan* which is related to the verbs *hüten* ("to guard, protect, watch over, take care of") and *weiden* ("to tend a flock"). Closely connected to this whole family of terms deriving from *halten* is the German noun *Held* ("hero"), which originally referred to someone who "held" his ground in a skirmish, and the term *Hirt* ("shepherd") which connoted someone who held his post during the assault of wolves or robbers. Heidegger's famous allusion to the human being's status as "the shepherd of being [*der Hirt des Seins*]" in "The Letter on Humanism" preserves this original connection between "guarding" (*Hüten*) and "shepherding" [*Hirten*] (PM, 252/GA 9, 330–31). Conversely, however, Heidegger will often employ the term *Aufenthalt* to point toward the dynamic-kinetic character of human existence as a "journey" (*Wanderung*), specifically the journey from birth to death (GA 16, 537). Journeying, Heidegger claims, "remains the principle characteristic of dwelling (*Wohnen*)," which is why *Aufenthalt* takes on the meaning of a "sojourn"—a brief or temporary stay or halt where one takes up residence. Our dwelling upon the earth is marked by a finitude that, as Pindar puts it, renders us as "creatures of a day" (Gk. *epameroi*—from *hemera* "day;" Latin *diurnus* "of a day"—the Latin root for "sojourn").[20] To dwell is to be held in an abode where we stay and linger (from the Old English word *bidan*—"to stay, to remain"), where we abide the transience of our temporary sojourn between our coming into the world and our departure.[21] We abide in being, biding our time as we stand out into the truth of being. As the abode where we come to care for and shelter beings, even as we are cared for and sheltered by being, *Aufenthalt* speaks to the possibility of our dwelling upon the earth.

In the "Letter," Heidegger will attempt to reclaim this ecstatic, open, kinetic sense of dwelling by thinking it in terms of the archaic Greek notion of *ethos*. It is in terms of this primordial sense of *ethos* that he will offer an indictment of "ethics" as a way of thinking through the problem of human responsibility to the shepherding of beings. It is through his translation of Heraclitus's Fragment 119—*ethos anthropoi daimon*—that, Heidegger claims, "the essence of *ethos* immediately comes to light" (PM, 269/GA 9, 354). The standard way of translating this fragment, "A man's character is his *daimon*," strikes Heidegger as caught up in the anthropological metaphysics of modernity that thinks "ethics" as a separate discipline focusing on human "character." Yet, according to Heidegger, in its original Greek sense,

> *Ethos* means abode [*Aufenthalt*], dwelling place. The word names the open region in which the human being dwells. The open region of his abode lets what pertains to the essence of the human being, and what in thus arriving resides [*sich aufhält*] in nearness to him, appear. The abode of the human being contains [*enthält*] and preserves [*bewahrt*] the advent of what belongs to the human being in his essence. According to Heraclitus' phrase this is *daimon*, the god. The fragment says: the human being dwells, insofar as he is a human being, in the nearness of god. (PM, 269/GA 9, 354)

To dwell in nearness (*Nähe*) to the gods is to exist as if even "in the sphere of the familiar [*Geheueren*], *einai theous*, it is the case that 'the gods come to presence [*anwest*]'" (PM, 270/GA 9, 355). We need an abode that is habitually familiar (*geheuer*), one marked by the habitudes of the place we inhabit, if we are ever to come into nearness with the unfamiliar (*Ungeheuer*). Only as beings who have a home can we come into the realm of homelessness. Such homelessness, Heidegger insists, is not the result of the world war, the devastation of cities, or the political-economic collapse of the European banks (PLT, 161/GA 7, 163). It is the manifestation of the sending or *Geschick* of being in the age of what he calls "the world's night" (PLT, 91/GA 5, 269). Following Hölderlin's poetic notion of "the default of god" (*Gottes Fehl*) (PF, 236), Heidegger comes to grasp homelessness as "the abandonment of beings by being" that shows itself in "the symptom of the oblivion of being" (PM, 258/GA 9, 339). Given the epochal triumph of technology as the dominant form for revealing being, our very modes of building, dwelling, and thinking have taken on the character of the *Gestell* in terms of its ever-expanding demand for production, stockpiling, and consumption. Because of technology's privileging of presence as the only realm of truth, modernity has become oblivious to the lethic dimension of *aletheia*. As a result, we have lost all sense for the hidden power of the absential, the withdrawn, the unfamiliar. Going back to his discussions of Sophocles's *Antigone* in SS 1935 and SS 1942, Heidegger had offered a reading of the homelessness of human beings in terms of the unfamiliar (*ungeheuer*) by rethinking it as the uncanny or un-homely (*unheimlich*). In *Introduction to Metaphysics* he writes that "[f]or the poet, the assault of *techne* against *dike* is the happening through which human beings become homeless. When one is put out of the home in this way, the home first discloses itself as such" (IM, 178/EM, 127). In other words, our own relation to the home first manifests itself through our homelessness. As we dwell in our abode in the midst of beings, we come to a sense of how utterly alien our home has become for us. The character of human being is tinged by this tragic insight that we are not at home within being even though we are all too familiar with beings. This incommensurable distance between human being and being is a mark of our uncanny legacy as the uncanniest of beings. To speak the language of Sophocles's choral ode, "There is much that is uncanny (*deina*) yet nothing is uncannier (*deinoteron*) than the human being."[22]

Our manifold use of *techne* undermines our ability to dwell in nearness to being not because *techne* harbors within itself any destructive capacities, but rather because in its destinal form as enframing it serves to reveal being only in terms of beings that are present to us as objects. This epochal transformation of the truth of being from the pre-Socratic experience of *aletheia* to the modern project of enframing occurs as "the assault of *techne* against *dike*" where *dike* is understood as the order of being itself in its *polemos*. Here, Heidegger insists, "Being as *dike* is the key to beings in their structure" (IM, 177–78/EM, 127). This Heraclitean understanding of *dike* needs to be thought in terms of homelessness precisely insofar as it relates to the problem of human dwelling. How does dwelling relate to *dike*? to *ethos*? And how are we to think of the question of justice in relation to ethics at the nexus of human dwelling?

Heidegger provides some clues to thinking through these questions in the way he will take up the problem of dwelling in his reading of Heraclitus and Hölderlin.[23] But he will also reflect on the issue of justice in his Nietzsche lectures, reflections that we will take up later in this chapter. In his Heraclitus course from SS 1944 he will characterize the human being as that being who distinguishes himself from other beings not through his possession of *logos*—Aristotle's definition of the human being as the animal who has speech, *zoon logon echon* (*Politics*, 1253)—but in his belonging to *ethos*. As Heidegger puts it, "*anthropos zoon ethos echon*: the human being is that living being whose ownmost distinguishing character is *ethos*" (GA 55, 217).

> *Ethos* means dwelling (*Wohnung*), abode (*Aufenthalt*). We say: the dwelling of the human being, his abode in the midst of beings as a whole. *Episteme ethike*—"Ethics"—thought here broadly and essentially, seeks to understand how the human being in this abode restrains itself (*sich hält*) in relation to beings and in this way maintains and holds itself (*sich selbst behält und hält*). *Ethos* is the comportment (*Haltung*) in all the conduct (*Verhalten*) of this abode (*Aufenthalt*) in the midst of beings. "Ethics" does not concern the human being as an isolated object among other objects; rather, it considers the human being in view of its relation to beings as a whole and it considers beings as a whole in view of their relation to the human being. In a certain way, then, the human being stands in the middle of beings as a whole without, however, being the middle itself. (GA 55, 214)

Here we can see how Heidegger will develop a sense of *ethos* that breaks with Cartesian anthropocentrism and will focus attention back upon being itself and upon our ethical capacity to dwell in the midst of beings not as the center or measure thereof, but as the guardian, shepherd, and neighbor of being (PM, 239, 252, 261/GA 9, 313, 331, 342). In this primordial Greek sense, *ethos* designates the primacy of dwelling as that which opens up the possibility of our nearness to being, a nearness that is marked not by proximity in a spatial sense but as nearness to the *polemos* within being. Such a *polemos* manifests itself in the uncanny tension between mortality and divinity that characterizes our sojourn from birth to death. It is this sense of an ethics of dwelling as a critique of subjective values, norms, rules, and directives that pervades "The Letter on Humanism." Until we can deconstruct the metaphysical edifice of this humanistic definition of human being, Heidegger avers, we will remain homeless and without a genuine abode in being. Hence, Heidegger can write in 1946 that "[i]f the name 'ethics,' in keeping with the basic meaning of the word *ethos*, should now say that ethics ponders the abode of the human being, then that thinking which thinks the truth of being or the primordial element of the human being, as one who ek-sists, is in itself originary ethics" (PM, 271/GA 9, 356).

This form of "originary ethics" does not derive from the values or judgments of human beings but comes to us as a dispensation (*Schickung*) of being that propriates (*ereignet*) us to the order of being thought in Anaximander's and Heraclitus's sense as *dike* (PM, 256/GA 9, 336). To trace the conjunction of *dike* and *ethos* in Heidegger's thought, however, is not simply to bring together the realms of dwelling, dispensation, ek-sistence, propriation, and truth in a unified reading. On the contrary, it is to read *dike* as a fundamental word in Heidegger's lexicon that will serve as a master term for thinking the reciprocal relation of being and human being in the wake of the *Kehre*. Before turning to an extended reading of Anaximander, Nietzsche, and Hölderlin, however, I would like to briefly trace Heidegger's notion of *ethos* back to his early Marburg lectures where he situates *ethos* in relation to *logos* by way of a reflection on Aristotle's *Rhetoric*. There, Heidegger offers a reading of the human being as the one in search of an appropriate *ethos*—an *ethos* that authentically serves as a way to connect one's factical life to the hidden dimension of being covered over by habitual routine and familiarity.

ARISTOTELIAN *ETHOS* BEFORE THE *KEHRE*

In one sense we can perceive a real divergence in Heidegger's interpretation of *ethos* from his early Aristotle lectures of 1923–24 to the "Letter on Humanism" from 1946. As we have already seen, in the later period Heidegger will read *ethos* in terms of the fundamental significance of human dwelling as "abode," "dwelling place," and as the realm of the "familiar," thought within the horizon of the truth of being. Such a reading will attempt a nonmetaphysical interpretation of ethics that breaks with the Kantian notion of a self-regulating, autonomous subject who serves as the transcendental ground for all thought, judgment, and behavior. Rejecting all notions of ethics as a normative-regulative realm of rule making and imperatives, Heidegger's notion of *ethos* will, rather, seek to privilege our fundamental belonging to the order of being itself and not the distinctly human sphere of action that will serve as a model and measure for ordering beings in an ethical system.

We could also, of course, superficially view this as a fundamental break with the early Heidegger's understanding of *ethos* in the Aristotle lectures in terms of "character," and personal "comportment." That is, we could see it as a movement away from the *Dasein*-centered focus of Heidegger's fundamental ontology in the 1920s toward the *seynsgeschichtliche* reading of destiny and *Geschick* that emerges in the wake of the so-called *Kehre*. And while this general account serves as a reliable description of the shift in Heidegger's thought, it obscures a fundamental connection between the early Heidegger's Aristotelian reading of *ethos* and his later Sophoclean-Heraclitean interpretation. For in those early lectures we can find the beginnings of a radical hermeneutics of everyday life that understands *ethos* not simply as "moral character," but as both the "where" and the "how" of human existence as ek-static, as an originary "standing out" into the phenomenological play of being that appropriates us to its kinetic-dynamic movement in and through the temporally particular (*jeweilige*) situation into which we are thrown (SZ, 61–62; 135–37). In these incidental phenomena, Heidegger will argue, being shows itself, makes itself visible, manifests its primordial character, as a self-showing concealing that opens up to us as a place of "dwelling together with beings in the world" (*Sichaufhaltens bei dem innerweltlichen Seienden*). In this space of self-showing, *Dasein* comes to itself by coming out-of-itself—and nowhere does this happen as primordially as in the realm of language.

In the summer semester of 1924, three years before the publication of *Being and Time*, Heidegger develops such a reading of language in a course that focuses on the public character of speech in Aristotle's *Rhetoric*. Language becomes so important here for Heidegger in that it provides a ground for the being of human beings as they are appropriated by the concrete, practical matters of discourse that arise in the course of a life led in the Greek *polis*. Rhetoric is, in this sense, "the interpretation of concrete *Dasein*, the hermeneutics of *Dasein* itself" (GA 18, 110). In the everyday interactions of citizens within the polis—in the public square, in the assembly, in the law courts, at religious and civic festivals, at public funerals, and in the performance of tragic art works—we find the various modes of human speech manifesting themselves in the rhetorical forms of exhortation, consolation, persuasion, and deliberation. Here, language addresses itself not to the epistemological verification of the truth or falsity of a particular state of affairs, but to forming a mood of reception to effect a future course of action. And it is in this practical, concrete sphere of listening and reflecting that Heidegger will find the basis for a rhetorical ontology of everyday life, what later in *Being and Time* he will transform into a reading of "being-in," *In-sein*, and *Inständigkeit* (SZ, 130–34). We are "in" language in the sense that through our practical, everyday concerns and care for the world, we are "taken in by" (*benommen*) the world, we come to ourselves only through an ek-static standing-in the openness of time that language opens up to us (SZ, 61). Already in SS 1925 Heidegger put it this way:

> "In" comes from *innan*, which means to dwell [*wohnen*], *habitare*; "ann" means: I am accustomed [*gewohnt*], I am familiar with, I take care of something—the Latin *colo* in the sense of *habito* and *diligo*. Dwelling is also taken here as taking care of something in intimate familiarity, being-involved-with [*Sein-bei*] . . . "I am" thus amounts to saying, I dwell, I abide [*halte mich auf*] in the world as with something familiar. Being as in-being and "I am" means dwelling with . . . and "in" primarily does not signify anything spatial at all but means primarily *being familiar with*. (HCT, 158/GA 20, 213)

For the Heidegger of the early Marburg years (1923–27) one of the primary ways of nonspatial dwelling, abiding, and being-familiar-with for human beings occurs in language—and it is in this sense that he turns to Aristotle's *Rhetoric*.

The grounding question of Heidegger's inquiry concerns the primordial relation between being and truth. "Does truth really find its ground in judgment (*logos*) or has it been uprooted from a more native soil [*Bodenständigkeit*]?"[24] As Heidegger reads him, Aristotle finds the originary ground of *logos* not in judgment as a cognitive faculty for establishing a reliable conformity between human observations and being, but in an understanding that directs itself at the practical concerns of everyday life. This distinction between a *logos* of judgment and a *logos* of understanding would later get formulated in the language of *Being and Time* as a distinction between an "apophantic as," which distinguishes between the "true" and the "false" in terms of knowledge, and a "hermeneutical as" that directs its focus on interpreting the existential concerns of human beings (wishes, requests, imperatives, advice, exhortations, consolations, etc.) that do not neatly fall into the categories "true" or "false." It is this hermeneutical understanding of *logos* as the everyday realm of speech wherein *Dasein* genuinely dwells, abides, and comes to form its habits, cares, and concerns, that Heidegger finds the phenomenological meaning of Aristotle's *Rhetoric*. *Logos* in this sense constitutes the existential situation in which we find our bearings and attunement, what Heidegger terms our "dis-position" (*Befindlichkeit*): how we "find ourselves" positioned and disposed.[25] Aristotle's *Rhetoric*, then, is not a textbook about speechmaking but a hermeneutics of everyday life. As Heidegger expresses it in the very first lectures of his SS 1924 course, "The being-in-the-world of the human being is fundamentally determined by speaking"; "It is the fundamental way of life's being, that is, of being-in-a-world" (GA 18, 18, 21). Traditional notions of rhetoric have lost this intimate connection between language and being and have turned rhetoric into a formal academic discipline. In so doing, they have lost "the originary sense of rhetoric" as a hermeneutics of existence itself (GA 18, 110). But Heidegger strives to remind us that "the human being is a living being that has its authentic *Dasein* in conversation and discourse. The Greeks existed in discourse. The rhetor is the one who has authentic power over *Dasein*" (GA 18, 108). "Only when we can make this foundation of Greek *Dasein* present to ourselves, will we understand that the Greek definition of the human being as *zoon logon echon* is neither a fabrication nor an accident but, rather, shows how the Greek fundamentally sees his *Dasein*" (GA 18, 110).

The standard translation of Aristotle's *zoon logon echon* reads: "The human being is the animal who has speech" (*Politics*, 1253a9). Heidegger, however, will rethink the metaphysics of "having" in SS 1924 by turning to a phenomenological analysis of the Greek notion of *ousia* (which Aristotle defines in the *Metaphysics* 1017 b23–26 as "being"): "*Ousia*, according to the common meaning signifies 'property,' 'possession,' 'goods and chattels' (*Hab und Gut*), 'presence' (*Anwesen*)" (GA 18, 24). This standard approach to *ousia* sees it as what is there at our disposal (*verfügbar*). But, as Theodore Kisiel so persuasively argues,

> In placing *ousia* first in his philological analysis, Heidegger is here inaugurating his own lifelong project of replacing it, displacing the ousiological elements of "being as having" and habit operative in the Greek fixation on the real estate of an eternal, everlasting world. He wants instead to translate these ousiological insights of Greek *Da-sein* into the kairological language of a German *Da-sein* that never possesses itself but is always dispossessed, thrown into the world temporarily, in this temporal situation never constant and static, but ever ec-static, that is, underway in its project toward life, and death.[26]

Given *Dasein*'s habitual tendency to inhabit the practical world of domestic life with its goods and property (*Habe*, from L. *habere*, Gk., *echein*—"to have"), Heidegger wants to underscore the fact that Aristotle's ontology of *ousia*—essence—substance has its roots in the practical world of dwelling. In this world of habitual practice, *Dasein* in-habits a shared realm of language, custom, tradition, and history that places it into a world that is not of its making. As Heidegger would later put it in *Being and Time*, *Dasein* is "thrown" into a world of possibilities that constitute its there-being with a shared sense of being-with or *Mitsein* (SZ, 135–37; GA 18, 49–50). Indeed, as Heidegger puts it, there is an equiprimordiality between "being-with-one-another" and *logos* that shapes the life of the human being in the *polis* (GA 18, 62–64). Greek *Dasein* is a *Dasein* whose *ousia*—essence—"having" comes not from the self-grounding autonomy of a Cartesian-Fichtean ego, but from the language-community of the *polis*. Here, *Dasein*'s possibilities for existence are not self-generated, but are rooted in the speech-world of public life. In other words, Greek being-in-the-world can be characterized as a middle-voiced happening of language whereby Greek *Dasein* "has" language (*logon echon*) even as it is "had" by language in a way that powerfully shapes its possibilities of "be-having."[27]

For the Greeks this practically directed, shared world of care, concern, and possibility led them to privilege *logos* as the fundamental determination of *Dasein*. Out of this context Aristotle formulated both his *Rhetoric* and his *Nicomachean Ethics*, which focused on five ways in which the soul arrives at truth or whereby it is habituated to "true-ing" (*aletheuein*) (*NE*, 1139b). In Book Six of the *Ethics* Aristotle breaks down these habits (*hexeis*) of the soul's "true-ing" into *three* realms: (1) the two *theoretical* habits that deal with things that are necessary, universal, and incapable of variation he terms *episteme* (knowledge based on principles [*archai*] and causes [*aitiai*], i.e., scientific knowledge) and *sophia* (wisdom, the highest form of knowledge, of things eternal, *philosophia*); (2) the two *practical* habits that deal with things that can be otherwise and are ever subject to variation, chance, and temporal circumstance he calls *techne* (knowing how to get around in the way of producing things) and *phronesis* (circumspective insight into the situational context of human actions); and (3) the fifth habit, *nous* (pure beholding, *Vernehmen*—whence *Vernunft*, reason) which negotiates and discursively deliberates about the relation of the other four habits of true-ing, those that Aristotle calls dia-noetic virtues (*NE*, 1139 a-b).[28] *Nous* actualizes itself in *logos*, points us to the "there" in our concrete dealings with beings and helps us to deliberate our proper course of action within the situation from out of which and toward which our present concerns tend. For Heidegger, it is precisely as a way of negotiating the various choices and possibilities of action within the everyday world of the *polis* in which we are imbricated, that the *Rhetoric* needs to be read.

Even here in his early Aristotle lectures Heidegger is attuned to the pretheoretical, factical situation of *Dasein* as it attempts to gain access to the originary phenomenon of life as ecstatic existence out into the openness of truth. Much as earlier in his WS 1920–21 lectures on "The Phenomenology of Religious Life" where he interprets Paul's "First Letter to the Thessalonians" as a call to conscience to enact the possibility of the Lord's Coming (*parousia*), in his lectures on Aristotle's *Rhetoric* Heidegger turns to an analysis of *logos* as a way of persuading its hearers to effect/enact authentic decisions about their personal fate and their communal destiny. Each set of lectures rethinks traditional ethics by avoiding the realm of moral exhortation and emphasizing instead the need to cultivate habits of the soul (*psyche*) that do not become repetitive and static, but instead attempt to situate these habits in ever new and emerging contexts by negotiating the terrain of practical action in and through deliberative choice. Heidegger will here dispossess himself of the notion of ethics as a habitual possession of the soul and instead come to privilege phronetic wisdom as the highest phenomenological virtue since again and again it turns us back to the original sources of our action in an interrogation that forces us to continually rethink our relation to all that we think we possess.

The fundamental message of the early Heidegger repeats Aristotle's famous claim from the *Metaphysics* that "being is not a genus"—but it does so in a radically phenomenological way (*Meta.* 998622; SZ, 3). That is, the early Heidegger's whole project is one of constantly reiterating, reinscribing, recontextualizing the temporality of being in its ecstatic forms for *Dasein*. Simply put, "being" (*Sein*) is never "there" for us as substance, idea, or entity (*Seiendes*); rather, it resists any definitive or essential form and reveals itself only in the temporally particular (*jeweilig*) contexts or situations that simultaneously conceal its way of manifesting itself. The truth of being happens not as orthotic agreement between a subjective judgment and an objective state of affairs, but as *a/letheia*: the play of presence-absence that characterizes every coming-to-be as a withdrawal, a retreat into oblivion, a passing-away. Within the context of our discussion about ethics, this notion of truth will be situated in Aristotle's understanding of rhetoric as a way of showing how truth becomes a matter of "dwelling" in language, a way of situating speech within the temporal context of a practical situation, its *kairos*. In this temporally particular, kairological context, language performs the phenomenological action of directing being away from any generic realm toward its concrete, practical situatedness in crisis, decision, and fate. Language happens here not as mere theoretical exposition about "being"; it happens, rather, as "mood" and it is through this analysis of mood that Heidegger will read Aristotle's *Rhetoric*.

By the term *mood* (*Stimmung*) Heidegger intends not a psychological analysis of our quotidian affects but an ontological-rhetorical account of the unique, ever-changing temporal contexts within which we find ourselves in our disposition/attunement (*Befindlichkeit*). Rhetoric speaks to these moods, highlighting their kairological significance and rooting speech in the moods that constitute our habits, familiar practices, and fundamental dwelling place within the world. "Being," in this sense, means "being-in," understood as the existential situatedness of *Dasein* within language, community, history, and destiny. We interpret, understand, and act within a specific life-situation. Hence, against the Cartesian view of consciousness as that which approaches a thing, a matter, a *Sache* in an immediate and direct way without the intervention of external influences, Heidegger underscores how we come to a *Sache* through the language, speech, and discourse (*logos*) of our inhabited world that habituates us to our own sense of how we "have" things. It is there that we dwell, abide, and come to ourselves in the ordinary language available to us. But as Heidegger (following Aristotle) notes, this everyday language has the tendency of falling into idle talk; it gains a foothold in the *polis* by covering over the difficult issues of fate, mortality, and authentic commitment by seizing on *Dasein*'s inclination to engage in chatter, gossip, and cliché. Aristotle understood, however, that a gifted rhetor could draw on the native folk wisdom of the *polis*, on a *gnome* or maxim from its sages and poets, in an effort to mobilize a community to revisit its sources and reclaim them through an authentic reappropriation of their originary meaning within the present moment. Although *Dasein* is always already possessed of this possibility to dwell-in-the-truth-of-being (Aristotle's five modes of *aletheuein*), it often succumbs to its inertial habits of covering over this possibility by dispensing its energy in "reading the newspaper" and becoming "entangled" (*verfängt*) in the garrulous chatter of pseudo-knowledge and sophistication (GA 18, 108). Hence, Heidegger will speak of the sophists' dominance in ancient Athens as an example of the same cultural decadence and ruin that he sees afflicting Weimar Germany in the 1920s. Against this process of cultural decay, Aristotle's *Rhetoric* stands for Heidegger as an authentic countermovement to sophistic speech that attempts to win back the originary ground of *logos* by reflecting on its capacity to uncover the hidden, originary source of rhetoric in the moods and temporal situations of factical existence.

Aristotle will underline three fundamental forms of rhetoric that attempt to persuade and shape public beliefs and provide assurances for its listeners by winning over their confidence through communicative skill and rhetorical force. He terms these three modes of persuasion "*pisteis*" or "trusts"/"confidences" in that they inspire faith (from L. *fides*) in the speaker, the speech, and the argument. As Aristotle puts it:

> Of the *pisteis* provided through speech there are three species: the first depends upon the character (*ethos*) of the speaker, the second upon disposing the listener into a certain frame of mind, the third upon the argument (*logos*) itself by showing or appearing to show something. . . . (There is persuasion) a) through character (*ethos*) whenever the speech is spoken in such a way as to make the speaker worthy of confidence; b) through the hearers when they are led to feel emotion (*pathos*) by the speech; for we do not give the same judgment when grieved and rejoicing or when being friendly and hostile— . . . c) through the arguments (*logoi*) when we show the

truth or the apparent truth from whatever is persuasive in each case. (*Rhet.* 1356a)[29]

In this rhetorical situation of "speaking-with-one-another as being-with-one-another," Aristotle shows the formally indicative power of speech to direct its listeners toward a specific situational context (*kairos*) for action.[30] Here, *logos* will be grasped as a mode of uncovering the hidden sources for *Dasein's* authentic engagement with its ownmost possibilities, a way of rooting and grounding *Dasein* in a resolute openness to the truth of being. In this attitude or comportment (*Haltung*) where *Dasein* holds itself (*sich halten*) open for the truth of being, Heidegger touches on something that will prefigure his understanding of *Ereignis* and originary ethics.

In this early period, however, Heidegger will still focus on a *Dasein*-centered interpretation of truth and come to understand the three modes of persuasion from this perspective. *Logos* as "argument" can take the form of *doxa*, the common world of opinion that defines "an average being-with-one-another" (GA 18, 151). On the other hand, it can also provide the philosopher with a way of moving human beings from indifference (*apatheia*) to resoluteness and decision. *Pathos*—in its form as the frame of mind of the speaker and the mood and movedness of the audience—becomes then for Heidegger, "the 'dis-position' [*Befindlichkeit*] of the listeners" in the "temporally particular situation of things and the way one stands to them" (GA 18, 163). Within this same context Heidegger comes to understand *ethos* not merely as the "character" of the speaker, but his "*Haltung*," the habitual way he holds himself within his inhabited world, what the later Heidegger would term "dwelling." *Ethos* here stands for both the resolve and conviction of the speaker as well as for his ability to attune the fundamental *pathos* of his audience in such a way that they are "held" (*halt*) captive in the present moment, that their very sense of dwelling draws on both their sense of belonging to a shared tradition in the past and to a shared communal destiny in the future. Clearly, these issues would become decisive for Heidegger when he ventured forth into the tangled world of German politics in 1933. But even in 1923–24 he would draw on the meaning of Greek rhetoric for an understanding of German politics in his analysis of the Ruhr crisis and of Schlageter's call of conscience.[31] In its office as the practical habit of true-ing that directs itself at the temporally particular situation of *Dasein*'s dwelling, *philosophia* becomes for Heidegger a rhetoric of everyday habits and habitations, of a *logos* that disposes us in such a way that it "has" us as much as we "have" it. This rhetorically attuned *logos* finds the meaning of being (*Seinssinn*) not in our possession of a universal measure for all contexts, but in the dispersed, fragmented moments that come to us as parts that need to be joined together in a whole whose unity is ever-changing within the temporal dynamic of factical life. Here the speaker's task becomes one of holding (*halten*) together the matter (*Sache*) in its living form through his resolute comportment (*Haltung*) and being able to work through the merely partial appearances of a problem/situation so as to get at its genuine *kairos* (GA 18, 175–76).

By disclosing the world to us in all its manifest forms and appearances, speech (*logos*) helps to attune us in a practical, pretheoretical way to the temporality of being that everywhere forms our life-world, our existence, our sense of dwelling. In his reading of Aristotle's *Rhetoric*, Heidegger roots *logos* in the basic factical movement of life itself and aligns it with *pathos* and *ethos* as equiprimordial forms of *Dasein*'s being-in-the-world. *Pathos*, as attunement, disposition, *Befindlichkeit* discloses us to our own possibilities for being in the midst of beings; it enables our sense of dwelling, our *ethos*. As William McNeill so perceptively observes,

> By contrast with Greek ontology, for which the world is disclosed by the *theoria* of philosophy and science, the primary disclosure of the presencing of a world is, on Heidegger's account, accomplished not by contemplative or philosophical knowledge, but by a fundamental *pathos* or attunement (*Befindlichkeit*); and such *pathos* is fundamental in attuning, in advance of any explicit deliberative or discursive understanding, the way in which we are held in the presencing of the moment—in short, in attuning our entire *ethos*.[32]

This insight, that *ethos*, *pathos*, and *logos* are not qualities or faculties that reside "in" human consciousness or Cartesian egoicity, but are ways of being "in" the world, ways of attuning ourselves and uncovering structures of being whose origins lie not in human accomplishment but in the self-manifestation of being's poetic world-forming, will become crucial in shaping Heidegger's notion of ethics and justice. Early in his career, Heidegger would come to understand *Dasein* as the temporal opening for being's self-manifestation in the world. As an open site in the midst of beings, *Dasein* inhabits a web of imbrications and entanglements that intersect the dwelling places of its generation, its community, its nation, and its epoch. In this sense, it dwells in the world. This dwelling, understood in terms of Aristotle's notion of *ethos* as a resolute openness to a shared communal situation, will become decisive for Heidegger's later sense of originary ethics. *Ethos* here will not be thought of as a static, permanent kind of moral character, but as a structure or way of being's self-manifesting that opens itself *to* us and in which we participate. In his lectures from WS 1925/26 on "Logic: the Question Concerning Truth," Heidegger will define *ethos* as "the self-having or be-having (*Sichgehaben*) self-comportment (*Sichver-*

halten) of the human being to other human beings and to itself. . . . In the *episteme ethike* the human being is understood as a being who, as it were, takes charge of its own being" (GA 21, 1–2). In this early iteration *ethos* will be understood, like *pathos* and *logos*, in terms of an interpretation of the meaning of being that has its center in *Dasein*. Even as he rejects the decalogic understanding of ethics as commandments, imperatives, or rules for human behavior, Heidegger still thinks of *ethos* primarily in terms of the habits and habitats of the human being. *Ethos* is still defined as a mode of rhetorical persuasion. But as he moves away from a *Dasein*-centered analysis of language (*logos*) and mood (*pathos*), toward an awareness of the event of being itself in its destinal sendings (*Geschick*), Heidegger will come to grasp *ethos* not as "self-having," as he did in WS 1925/26, but as a middle-voiced "being-had" by what Theodore Kisiel terms a "be-having."[33] In this rethinking of *ethos* in and through "the turn" in/of being (*Seyn*), Heidegger will no longer think of *Dasein* as the one who performs the *logos* as an act of persuasion. Rather, for him *logos* will be understood as the performance itself of being's way of self-showing. *Logos* here will have lost its subjective connotations as what belongs to speech, reason, or argument; rather, Heidegger will think of it in Heraclitus's sense as "the eternal structure of the world as it manifests itself in discourse."[34]

In the "Letter on Humanism," Heidegger attempts to think through a Heraclitean version of *ethos* as a reciprocal belonging together of *Seyn* and *Dasein*, of being and thinking, whereby thinking abandons its erstwhile role as arbiter of values and measures (in its form as metaphysics) and comes to a place where "it lets being-be" (PM, 272/GA 9, 358). In this new comportment where it "lets that toward which it goes comes toward it," thinking is appropriated by the truth of being and comes to find therein its proper abode—as *ethos* (PM, 272/GA 9, 358). To "think" means here to dwell in the midst of beings, to find one's abode in abiding the event of being whereby thinking loses its status as a possession of *Dasein* and becomes appropriated by the truth of being, becomes in a sense its possession; or, to put it differently, it becomes possessed by the truth of being. Here "true-ing" is no longer an achievement of *Dasein* but a happening or sending of *Seyn*. Hence, Heidegger can translate *ethos* in 1946 as "Aufenthalt" (dwelling, "abode"—but also "sojourn" and "stay") since he thinks it in a Heraclitean way as a "lingering—namely the 'dwelling' of the human being in the midst of beings as a whole. What is essential in this *ethos* as lingering is the way that the human being holds onto beings and thereby maintains itself (*sich behält*) and holds itself (*sich hält*) and lets itself be held (*sich halten läßt*)" (GA 55, 206). This middle-voiced phenomenology of holding and being-held in the *Aufenthalt* of human being upon the earth would come together for Heidegger in terms of a Heraclitean *ethos* of dwelling that would rethink the relationship of human beings to the earth. Now ethics would no longer be thought in Kantian terms as the relationship between human beings or between a human being and god. Rather, ethics would be thought in an originary way as a modality of being's own way of holding us in its jointure as the order and habit of being itself. In the discourse of the pre-Socratics, such an order would be thought as *dike*—not "justice" in human terms, but a poetic, world-forming jointure of discord and concord, strife and harmony that eludes human control and understanding. To think justice in this sense, Heidegger deems it essential to think a new relation between *ethos-logos-pathos* that is not confined to the traditional modes of rhetoric as they are configured in human speech and understanding. Rather, Heidegger envisions a nonmetaphysical form of thinking that is marked by the *ethos* of what he terms *Gelassenheit*—a letting-be of the cybernetic metaphysics of grasping and control that holds human beings in its thrall.

Before we turn to a more engaged analysis of *Gelassenheit* and of the pre-Socratic notion of *dike*, however, we will need to more properly understand Heidegger's relation to ethics as a philosophical discipline.

ETHICS-PHYSICS-LOGIC

When Jean Beaufret approached Heidegger in the fall of 1946 to pose the question of how "to determine precisely the relation of ontology to a possible ethics," Heidegger responded by deconstructing the metaphysical premises that lay at the root of such a formulation. The question presumes, Heidegger claimed, that we already know what we mean by the terms *ontology* and *ethics*—as if the foundational opposition of *Sein* and *Sollen* (being and the ought) laid down by Kant were already in place before any inquiry might begin. This Kantian schism between the "is" and the "ought," fact and value, ontology and ethics follows from a metaphysical dualism between a theoretical and practical reason (logic) that focuses on physics and ethics respectively.[35] For Heidegger, the metaphysical substrate upon which all of these divisions are founded goes back to the work of Plato and Aristotle who transformed "thinking" into "metaphysics" (GA 55, 235). As Kant put it in his *Groundwork of the Metaphysics of Morals*: "Ancient Greek philosophy divides itself into three sciences: *Physics*, *Ethics*, and *Logic*. This division is perfectly in keeping with the nature of the matter."[36] Heidegger will take up this historical division of thinking into the metaphysical partitions of physics-logic-ethics by way of a deconstructive retrieval of its historical ground in Greek philosophy. There, Heidegger will attempt to show how this tripartite division carried out in Platonic-Aristotelian metaphysics will serve to block all access to the originary ground of physics-ethics-logic in pre-Socratic thinking. Beginning with his *Introduction to Metaphysics* lectures

(1935), Heidegger will offer an account of the history of philosophy that narrates the onset of this occlusion in Plato and Aristotle and its rigidification in medieval philosophy and in the thinking of Descartes, Kant, and Hegel.

What transpires in this history is a "narrowing" of the rich philosophical language of the pre-Socratics into the thetic and technical vocabulary of disciplinary thinking (IM, 17–18/EM, 13). After Plato, *physis-logos-ethos* no longer function as names that explore the equiprimordial unity of being as a self-generating gatheredness that gives itself to human being. Rather, with the onset of Greek metaphysics, the emergence of physics-logic-ethics as disciplines comes to mark an anthropocentric turn within the history of being that begins to measure beings by the stance or *Haltung* of human beings. In the process, the possibility of finding a home within being, of experiencing the openness of *Dasein* as a site for a resting place or abode (*Aufenthalt*) amidst beings, begins to lose its footing. As Heidegger puts it,

> But this narrowing of *physis* in the direction of the "physical" did not happen in the way that we picture it today. We oppose to the physical, the "psychical,". . . . But all this, for the Greeks continues even later to belong to *physis*. As a counterphenomenon there arose what the Greeks call *thesis*, positing, ordinance, or *nomos*, law, rule in the sense of mores. But this is not what is moral (*das Moralische*) but instead what concerns mores (*das Sittenhafte*), that which rests on the commitment of freedom and the assignment of tradition; it is that which concerns a free comportment (*Verhaltung*) and *attitude* (*Haltung*), the shaping of the historical being of humanity, *ethos*, which under the influence of morality (*Moral*) was then degraded to the ethical (*Ethischen*). (IM, 17–18/EM, 13)

Yet Heidegger would steadfastly maintain that this degradation of *ethos* into ethics, much as the narrowing of *physis* into physics and the demise of *logos* into logic would shatter the originary unity of their essential unfolding and instead would cultivate the theoretical division of being into different areas of science that would later find its grounding in Kant's transcendental subject. What would be forgotten in this centuries-long self-assertion of metaphysics would be Heraclitus's gnomic insight about the unity and identity of *physis* and *logos* that found expression in the *polemos* of being as the event of true-ing that appropriates *Dasein* (IM, 138–40/EM, 100–101). In the *Introduction to Metaphysics*, Heidegger had not yet thought the originary belonging-together of *ethos* into this Heraclitean configuration. But in his later Heraclitus lectures from SS 1944, he would do so in a way that situated *ethos* in terms of the event of human dwelling. Here, he would come to the insight that, in their originary form, physics-logic-ethics all addressed the question of the totality of beings, but that even here, at this early point, what was never addressed was the originary question about being as the hidden unity of beings. There, he writes, "[*Logos*] is the originary gathering [*Versammlung*] that preserves [*wahrend*] the whole of beings, being. *Logos* is *legon*, the gathering that unifies, withholds (*einbehaltend*), and grants a dwelling (*aufenthaltsgewährend*) for the whole of beings" (GA 55, 337). The truth of being will be understood here not as a proposition of "logic," but as an event that grants unity to human beings and being, *Dasein* and *Seyn*. Here, truth is understood not as a possession of *Dasein*, but rather in such a way that truth possesses *Dasein*. Hence, Heidegger can understand truth as an event wherein *Dasein* does not inhabit the truth, truth inhabits *Dasein*.

Thought in a Heraclitean way, *ethos* then becomes a name for the unity of being that appropriates the human being, a name for being's middle-voiced "having" of us, not of our propositional "having" of being. As this equiprimordial unity of being, *logos* will be understood as the eternal order of being as a self-gathering gatheredness. In the same way *physis* will be understood here as the self-emergent bringing-forth of beings into disclosure as an unhiddenness that hides its middle-voiced happening. To offer a Heideggerian variation on Heraclitus's Fragment B123: *physis* loves to hide its hiding. In this same way, *ethos* will be experienced as the letting-be of the order of *physis* as a gathering (*logos*) of all beings. Together, these three realms of experience will be understood as the jointure (*dike*) of being itself (*physis*) in its gatheredness (*logos*), as the place where the human being is appropriated by being in its dwelling place (*ethos-Aufenthalt*). To think being in this equiprimordial sense means to understand *dike* in Heraclitus's way as the eternal order/jointure of all that is, its "justice"—but not in human terms as a moral-juridical judgment that has to do with human values. Rather, *dike* will be thought here as the balance of tensions and oppositions, the jointure set into place in and through the *polemos* of beings. On this reading, *dike* will come to be understood as having a close affinity with *ethos*, but not in the sense that justice has a deep connection with ethics. Rather, following Heraclitus, Heidegger's *ethos* will name the place of dwelling that enables human appropriation/having by being, a dwelling place where those who adopt a *Haltung* of *Gelassenheit* can let the place of dwelling (*Aufenthalt*) between emergent *physis* and its decline come into jointure. This understanding of *dike* becomes for Heidegger not the name of a legal or moral realm of justice or a place of human judgment; on the contrary, it names nothing less than the order of being within which human beings try to find their dwelling. *Dike* here "names the essence of being with reference to the essentially appropriate articulation (*wesens-mässigen Fügung*) of all beings" (N i, 156/GA 43, 204). It is this nonmetaphysical understanding of *dike* in its kinship with *ethos*, that realm of ethicality that cannot be defined or limited by the human, that Heidegger will try to articulate in the fall of 1946 when he begins to write the "Letter on Humanism" and his Anaximander essay. Heidegger will refuse to speak of either "justice" or "ethics" in their ordinary sense because for him what is imagined by the Greeks in the terms *dike* and *ethos* denotes a realm of being that exceeds the limits of the human, that points to an order of articulation/jointure that cannot be captured in either the philosophical questions of ethics or justice or in the broader metaphysical divisions of physics-logic-ethics. In thinking through this critique of ethics and justice, however, Heidegger does not simply reflect on the historical difference between pre-Socratic philosophy and the metaphysical tradition that followed. What he puts into language here is nothing less than a fundamental critique of the *epoch* of modernity as that age that is "held (*echein*) upon (*epi*)" the values of the human that cannot think jointure in its essential frame. In the wake of postwar ruin and devastation that lay everywhere around him in Freiburg in 1946, he poses the question: Do we have a home upon this earth? Yet Heidegger will not think through the question of homelessness in a merely historical way; on the contrary, he will grasp it as an ontological question about the place of human beings within the fourfold of being constituted by earth and sky, gods and humans. Having lost the measure for a possible sense of *dike* as a conjuncture of being and human being, Heidegger claims, we have at the same time lost our sense of being at home in being, of dwelling in the event of being's conjuncture with *Dasein*. Homeless and without a resting place we sojourn upon the earth in search of conjuncture. Unable to let *physis*' law of whiling unfold, we seek rather to permanentize our stay upon the earth as we deny the limits (*pera*) of our finitude. Willful in our self-assertion, we seek through *techne* to extend these limits into the limitless (*apeiron*), mistaking beings for being, reducing *physis* to entities, unable to abide the mercurial whiling of being. In the historical moment of fall 1946 the contingencies of this insight will be thought through the catastrophe of homelessness that besets the German nation in its historical sojourn through the crisis of World War II.

ANAXIMANDER'S *DIKE* AND THE QUESTION OF JUSTICE

One of the most prescient of Heidegger's insights regarding the historical confluence of justice and ethics in the modern world would be framed in his reflections on the pre-Socratic philosopher Anaximander, whose work had been covered over and occluded by the Platonic-Aristotelian and Roman understanding of ethics and *iustitia* that, on Heidegger's reading, had helped to shape the destiny of the West. Writing at a moment of historical collapse—"*die Stunde Null*" (zero hour) of German history—Heidegger attempts to think through the crisis of modernity in the West via a reflection on the earliest philosophical text that emerges within that tradition. In this sense, Heidegger attempts to think the end of Western history by attempting to retrieve its beginning. In the language of the pre-Socratics themselves, he essays an eschatology of the West by way of an archeology (*eschaton* Gk.: last, end; *arche* Gk.: origin, beginning). He poses his problem this way:

> Can the Anaximander fragment, from a historical and chronological distance of two thousand five hundred years, still say something to us? . . . Are we latecomers in a history now racing towards its end, an end which in its increasingly sterile order of uniformity brings everything to an end? Or does there lie concealed in the historical and chronological remoteness of the fragment the historic proximity (*Nähe*) of something unsaid, something that will speak out in times to come?
>
> Do we stand in the very twilight of the most monstrous transformation our planet has ever undergone, the twilight of that epoch in which earth itself hangs suspended? Do we confront the evening of a night which heralds another Dawn? Are we to strike off on a journey to this historic region of earth's evening? Is the land of evening only now emerging? Will this land of evening overwhelm Occident and Orient alike, transcending whatever is merely European to become the location of a new, more primordially fated history? Are we men of today already "Western" in a sense that first crystallizes in the course of our passage into the world's night? (EGT, 16–17/GA 5, 325–26)

To pose the question of the end of history—or what Heidegger terms "the eschatology of being"—is to take up the traditional question of theodicy: that is, the justification of history through divine justice, the justice (*dike*) of the gods (*theoi*). But Heidegger's discussion of *dike* has a different source and purpose. What he seeks to deconstruct is the very notion of *dike* as modeled on anything like a human view of justice in either its legal or moral sense. Yet that was precisely the reigning model of interpretation in Anaximander studies that shaped the whole discussion in the Germany of Heidegger's day. Hermann Diels, the renowned editor of *Die Fragmente der Vorsokratiker*, viewed Anaximander as a poet-philosopher still caught up in a mystical vision of the cosmos, a view shared by another prominent historian of philosophy, Karl Joel, who likewise noted "how strong poetic fantasy and mysticism play a part in Anaximander."[37] For both Diels and

Joel, Anaximander's mystical-poetic temperament clearly predated genuine philosophical reflections upon the cosmos, a view that Heidegger saw as wholly implicated in the metaphysical dualisms of rationality/irrationality that defined the post-Cartesian world.

What Heidegger found even more problematic in these so-called poetic interpretations of Anaximander, however, was the tendency to read the fragment metaphorically as a projection of an anthropomorphic notion of justice onto the cosmos. Three prominent German classicists of Heidegger's generation all contributed to this style of reading. In his highly influential study *Paideia*, Werner Jaeger claimed that Anaximander's "notion of *dike* is the beginning of the process of projecting the human world of the *polis* onto the *kosmos*."[38] Another well-known classicist, Hermann Fränkel, followed Jaeger's claim that in conceiving of *dike* Anaximander applied the language of human law and justice to the realm of *physis*, arguing, "Anaximander transfers (*überträgt*) the idea of law onto the processes of the cosmos. Here a problem that originally had been only of a social and religious nature is extended in a grandiose fashion."[39] Moreover, the philologist Walther Kranz would likewise affirm this same notion that the Anaximander fragment "compares for the first time in the Greek language the human form of body and soul with the *kosmos*."[40] This view, that the idea of "justice" in the cosmos was really a kind of metaphorical translation or *Übertragung* (as Fränkel put it) of social-political-religious notions into the realm of nature, became for Heidegger a powerful sign of the metaphysical poverty of modern thought in its attempt to think the archaic Greek notions of *dike* and *ethos*.

In Heidegger's eyes, such thinking only served to entrap the originary phenomena of *physis* and/or *logos* from emerging in the event of truth. Instead, they were taken up within the already familiar realms of the physical-logical-ethical that came to be "enclosed within the boundaries of particular disciplines" (EGT, 21/GA 5, 331). Within such boundaries the words of Anaximander's fragment were thoughtlessly ordered into existing categories without ever genuinely questioning their ground or meaning. On Heidegger's retelling, this leveling process had already begun with Aristotle's student Theophrastus, a fourth-century BCE doxographer whose lost work *Physikon Doxai* was used in the sixth century CE by Simplicius as the basis for the Anaximander fragment that survives today.[41] But Heidegger seeks to get behind the metaphysical determinations in these doxographical transmissions of the original fragment—not in an effort to achieve an even more pristine kind of philological research than Diels or Jaeger, but as a way of coming into dialogue with the equiprimordial unity of *physis-logos-ethos* before their division into the disciplines of physics-logic-ethics. This equiprimordial event of being signifies for Heidegger nothing less than the original happening of truth as *aletheia*, an event that stands in intimate proximity with Anaximander's attempt to think of *physis* in terms of *dike*. The history of metaphysics constitutes the programmatic forgetting of this originary bond between *physis* and *dike*, a bond that takes place long before the formulation of "ethics" and "justice" as separate spheres of inquiry. In attempting to think "originary ethics," as he does in the "Letter on Humanism," Heidegger struggles to find a fitting language for the strange event of appropriation that takes up the question of being as a meditation on the phenomenology of truth. To think in this way is, for Heidegger, a thinking of *dike* as that which exceeds justice and ethics, as that which cannot properly be thought in the standard translations of *dike* as *Gerechtigkeit* ("justice") and *ethos* as *Ethik* ("ethics"). In the *Parmenides* lectures of WS 1942/43 Heidegger will grope toward such an insight, attempting to think "the assigned temporal span of [our] earthly sojourn [*Aufenthalt*]" in terms of "the human being's emerging into order and his standing within [*Innestehen*] order [*Fug*] or *dike*, which is orderliness [*Fügsamkeit*], *dikaisyne*" (P, 93/GA 54, 137). This translation of *dike* as *Fug*/order, which Heidegger began in his translation of Sophocles's first choral ode from *Antigone* in SS 1935, would break with the whole Roman occlusion of Greek equiprimordiality that found its way into the Latin vocabulary of justice (*iustitia*) and ethics (*moralis*) that determined Western conceptions of law and morality. But, as Heidegger insisted, "*iustitia* has a wholly different ground of essence than that of *dike*, which arises from [*west*] *aletheia*" (P, 40/GA 54, 59).

Standing at what he considered to be a decisive moment in the history of the West—viz., Germany's fate in the fall of 1946—Heidegger looked back over the long history of oblivion and occlusion that had sequestered Anaximander's fateful language of *dike* within the juridical-moral terms of human experience and found that the traces of Platonic-Aristotelian metaphysics, Roman justice, Christian morality and the subject-philosophy of Descartes, Kant, and Hegel had prevented contemporary Germans from experiencing the primordial oneness of *physis-logos-ethos* as the order of *dike*. Instead, what he perceived as the originary oneness of the truth of being as an event of appropriating human being to the site of being's manifestation, its dwelling place (*Aufenthalt*/*ethos*), had been covered over and forgotten—and nowhere was this more powerfully inscribed in the work of German philosophy than in the writing of Nietzsche. Going back to his early lectures on *The Pre-Platonic Philosophers* and *Philosophy in the Tragic Age of the Greeks* (both from 1873), Nietzsche persisted in interpreting the Anaximander fragment in moral terms. In an entry from an early notebook he writes: "Anaximander—passing-away and coming-to-be in nature interpreted morally as guilt and punishment" (KSA 8, 106). And in *Philosophy in the Tragic Age of the Greeks*, he claims, "Anaximander was no longer dealing with the question of the origin of this world in a purely physical way. Rather, when he saw in the multiplicity of things that have come-to-be a sum of injustices that must be atoned for, he grasped with bold fingers the tangle of the profoundest problem in ethics. He was the first Greek to do so" (PTAG, 48/KSA 1, 820). Moreover, in a late note from 1888, Nietzsche adds:

> Since Plato philosophy has been dominated by morality. Even in his predecessors, moral interpretations play a decisive role (with Anaximander, the persisting of all things as punishment for their emancipation from pure being; with Heraclitus, the regularity of phenomena as witness to the moral-legal character of the whole world of becoming). (WP, 222/KSA 12, 259)

All of these sweeping attempts to read the fragments of the pre-Socratics in moral terms struck Heidegger as clear signs of Nietzsche's metaphysical entrapment in value-philosophy, which persisted in understanding *dike* and *ethos* in terms of an "anthropomorphic metaphor" that reduced the emergence and perishing of *physis* to human terms (KSA 1, 818). In the sections that follow I would like to pursue Heidegger's reading of Anaximander as a way of exploring his nonmetaphysical notion of originary ethics and its proximity to the Anaximandran-Heraclitean notion of *dike*. But, before I do so, we will first need to consider the whole background to Heidegger's first interpretations of *dike* in his reading of Heraclitus and of Nietzsche's "Second Untimely Meditation," which raised the question of justice in terms of the legal-moral traditions of Western philosophy. It was these early encounters with Nietzsche from the late 1930s that helped to convince Heidegger of the centrality of *dike* for understanding the history of the West, of coming to the notion that "knowledge of *dike*, of the laws articulating the being of beings, [*den Fügungsgesetzen des Seins des Seienden*]" constituted the very basis of philosophy (N i, 166/NI, 194).

NIETZSCHE, HERACLITUS, AND JUSTICE

One of Heidegger's recurring motifs was the attempt to explore an alternative notion of justice that would offer a way of dismantling the Western edifice of ethics by rethinking "justice" as that very structure of being within and against which all beings are measured. In this other myth of justice, one taken up by Heraclitus (in Diels Fragment 94), Heidegger sought a way of thinking justice against justice itself, in terms that did not lend themselves to being translated into the pregiven forms of ethical injunctions. In order to recall this other myth of justice, I want in this section to look at Heidegger's interpretation of the Heraclitean concept of *dike* read against the Nietzschean concept of *Gerechtigkeit*. Unlike Nietzsche, Heidegger will abjure the traditional German translation of *dike* as *Gerechtigkeit* or "justice" and translate it instead as *Fug* or "fugal conjointure"—a kind of organizing matrix that brings all beings together contrapuntally within the fugal structure of being. In the Nietzsche lectures (1936–1944), Heidegger will present a concise version of his sweeping history of metaphysics from the pre-Socratics through Nietzsche, organized around his notion of subjectivity as a measure for beings in their truth. This selfsame topic, thought through the problem of justice as a defining characteristic of the "essence of truth," will constitute for Heidegger one of the essential questions of Nietzsche's metaphysics and, beyond that, one of the crucial chapters in the Western understanding of truth. As Heidegger puts it, "To think beings as a whole in their truth and to think *the truth in them*—that is metaphysics. 'Justice' [*Gerechtigkeit*] is here the metaphysical name for the essence of truth, for the way in which the essence of truth must be understood at the end of Western metaphysics" (N iii, 141/N II, 637). In this section I would like to take up this Heideggerian directive of thinking the history of metaphysics in relation to the problem of truth and justice by looking more closely at Heidegger's interpretation of Nietzsche—specifically, his seminar notes from WS 1938/39, *Zur Auslegung von Nietzsches II. Unzeitgemäßer Betrachtung* (GA 46). I want to focus on this discussion of Nietzsche's second *Untimely Meditation* because in it Heidegger will explicitly take up the question of *Gerechtigkeit* in detail, something he neglects to do in *Introduction to Metaphysics* in his discussion of Heraclitean and Sophoclean *dike*. Part of what I want to consider is how Heidegger's interpretation of Nietzschean *Gerechtigkeit* will be juxtaposed against Heidegger's own reading of Heraclitean *dike* and how Heidegger will refuse to translate *dike* as *Gerechtigkeit* precisely because of the way he reads Nietzsche–or, more properly, because of the way he views Nietzsche's own reading (that is, *mis*reading) of Heraclitus. I want to situate Heraclitus between Heidegger and Nietzsche as a way of understanding two very different ways of reading the history of philosophy from the early Greeks down to the modern epoch. In this confrontation or *Auseinandersetzung* between these two thinkers over the notion of Heraclitean justice as *dike*—and its translation into German as *Gerechtigkeit* or *Fug* respectively—I want to locate a profound contest, struggle, or *agon* between Heidegger and Nietzsche over the "proper" way to read Heraclitus and, through him, "to do justice" to the power of early Greek thinking as a way of entering into confrontation with the history of the West and the nihilistic epoch of modernity.

Heraclitus stands "between" Heidegger and Nietzsche, then, as that thinker against whom one must measure the problem of justice, thought as a problem of translation. In terms of their knowledge of Greek, clearly Nietzsche had the advantage, being rigorously trained as a classical philologist and grammarian. But despite this apparent disadvantage, measured from the realm of philological *Wissenschaft*, Heidegger would claim that it was precisely in the realm of translation from the Greek that Nietzsche would be at a metaphysical disadvantage since he would thoughtlessly translate *dike* as "Gerechtigkeit." In "The Verdict of Anaximander," Heidegger would point to Nietzsche's all too timely translation of Anaximander from his 1873 book *Philosophy in the Tragic Age of the Greeks*. And in his WS 1938/39 seminar Heidegger would draw out his critique of Nietzsche's concept of justice as something built on the scaffolding of a metaphysics of "life" (*Leben*). In thinking life as the measure for being as becoming, Heidegger argues, Nietzsche will embrace the deeply metaphysical determinations of contemporary *Lebensphilosophie*. In this sense, Nietzsche's conception of life will be measured (*gemessen*) by the measure (*Maß-stab*) of the times (*zeitgemäß*). In keeping with the *zeitgemäße* metaphysics of his epoch, evident in Diels's translation of *dike* as *Gerechtigkeit*, Nietzsche will think of justice from a wholly *anthropological* perspective.[42] That is, (following Descartes) he will posit "man"—in his capacity as the self-determining subject who secures certitude as the new measure of truth—"as the measure of all things" (N iv, 122/N II, 172).

Against what he sees as Nietzsche's glorification of a metaphysics measured in accordance with the times (*zeitgemäß*), Heidegger will insist on reading Nietzsche against himself and attempt to find a way of thinking through the timely, all too timely, dimension of Nietzsche's philosophy to uncover an "untimely" (*unzeitgemäße*) possibility of originary thinking. This he finds in Heraclitus's experience of being as a cosmological principle of constant balancing in, through, and against the contentious opposition of beings in contrapuntal harmony. Heraclitus expressed this as the countervailing/prevailing play of *sympheromenon* and *diapheromenon* (*sich mit sich Zusammen- und Auseinander-bringen*) (GA 55, 147). Heidegger was keenly attuned to the productive possibilities for thinking that could be retrieved from beneath the palimpsest of Heraclitean doxography–and despite his frequent criticisms of Nietzsche (and of Nietzsche's metaphysical interpretation of Heraclitus), he understood that without his groundbreaking work such a retrieval would not be possible. At one point in his WS 1938/39 seminar, he remarks, "It is *decisive* that Nietzsche reverted back to Heraclitus at all and saw a connection between *dike* and *dokeonta* ["what shows itself"]. But this does not mean that Nietzsche simply gleaned his thoughts from Heraclitus" (GA 46, 196).[43] Even if "Heraclitus [was] *his* [Nietzsche's] philosopher," Heidegger maintains that "*between them lay the whole history of Western metaphysics*."

As he begins to offer his own fundamental history of Western metaphysics as an overarching narrative concerning the essence of truth, Heidegger will come to position Heraclitus "between" Nietzsche and himself as a way of recuperating the originary, untimely possibilities of a non-anthropological account of Western destiny. This will entail overturning the traditional reading of Nietzsche as an anti-Cartesian philosopher of the body and of vitality, of *Leib* and *Leben*, who rejects the calcifications of the bloodless *cogito* for the Heraclitean dance of becoming and of *physis* as cosmic *Spiel*. Nietzsche himself would position his own thinking in this way, writing in his *Nachlass*: "That the world is a kind of divine play, beyond good and evil—for that I have as predecessors Vedanta philosophy and Heraclitus" (KSA XI, 201). Nonetheless, Heidegger would contest this reading, claiming that, in his embrace of *Leben* as valuation and of will to power as justice, Nietzsche rejected the very Heraclitean principles that he sought to advocate. In doing so, Nietzsche succeeded in completing the Cartesian project of modernity as the securing and measuring of truth through the boundless will of the human subject. Hence, despite the dominant interpretation of Nietzsche as a philosopher of *physis* who finds the measure of being in a Heraclitean balance of strife and *polemos*, Heidegger will view Nietzsche as a proponent of *nomos*. That is, he will read Nietzsche as a thinker who takes "man" as the measure of being in the sense of anthropological subjectivity. "Life" for Nietzsche comes to mean "presence" (*Anwesen*), "subsistence" (*Bestehen*), "permanence" (*Beständigkeit*) (N iii, 85/N I, 571). It will be grasped as a kind of "permanentizing of becoming into presence" (N iii, 150/N I, 648). Hence, Heidegger will insist that despite Nietzsche's open embrace of *Werden* as the playful dance of *physis*, he will nonetheless cling to an interpretation of becoming as what is fixed, permanent, and "established in representing [*Vorstellen*] and securing [*Sicherstellen*]" (N iv, 131/N II, 184). Here, Heidegger will claim, "Nietzsche adopts Descartes' fundamental position completely" (N iv, 132/N II, 184).

Justice and the Problem of Truth

Heidegger's account of Nietzsche's covert, but fundamental, Cartesianism is well-known to readers of his Nietzsche lectures from the 1930s and '40s, lectures that provide the scaffolding for his sweeping history of Western metaphysics. But what has not received much attention, I would argue, is the way Heidegger will read this history from within the tradition of justice—and just what such a reading signifies for his own attempts at rethinking "the essence of truth" within the history of being. Why does Heidegger seize upon the topic of justice as essential for his project and for the history of being? On what grounds does he decide to privilege justice as a lever by which to raise again the question of truth? In what sense does the Nietzschean conception of justice offer a measure by which to think of being as *physis*? And how does Nietzsche's framing of the question of justice in this way through his *Auseinandersetzung* with the early Greeks, especially Heraclitus, Parmenides, and the tragedians, come to shape Heidegger's own interpretation of the pre-Socratic dawn? Here, I would like to address these questions by considering Heidegger's interpretation of Nietzsche's second Untimely Meditation "On the Uses and Disadvantages of History for Life."

In this seminar, Heidegger will come to consider a wide range of issues from Nietzsche's early writings—from his reflections on animality, life, biologism, the status of scientific knowledge, the horizon of values, historicity, and the problem of culture. But the focal point for his reflections will be Nietzsche's interpretation of justice. This singular focus on the topic of justice is remarkable given Heidegger's own admission that apart from the "On the Uses and Disadvantages of History" essay and a few later notebook entries, "Nietzsche is otherwise silent on the subject of justice" (QCT, 91/GA 5, 246). Still, Heidegger will acknowledge that "the thought of justice already dominates Nietzsche's thinking in his early years" and that during the period of *Zarathustra*, justice remains a decisive topic even though "in his last years, Nietzsche is completely silent about [it]." And yet, Heidegger will claim:

> Nowhere is the slightest attempt to be found to bring the thought of justice into an articulated connection with the essence of truth. Nietzsche never does this explicitly and in terms of the first foundations of his thinking. . . . Everything depends on our grasping justice in *Nietzsche's* sense . . . [and yet] Nietzsche is of no help to us here because he was unable to discern the historical roots of the metaphysical question of truth in general, and those of his own decisions in particular. (N iii, 137–38/N I, 632–34)

Here and in his WS 1938/39 seminar, Heidegger will set out to think through the unthought consequences of Nietzschean justice by turning Nietzsche's own work against him, even as he measures it against the measure of Nietzsche's own time, making it genuinely *unzeitgemäß*. In his remarks from the seminar, Heidegger will once again draw on his insight from SS 1935, "Introduction to Metaphysics," about the untimeliness of philosophy. "Every philosophy is untimely (in the sense of being measured against its own time), that is, every essential philosophy thinks 'against' the epoch . . . as a disclosure of its essence and as a decision about its future" (GA 46, 105; IM, 9/GA 40, 10). Heidegger then goes on to ask: "To what extent was Nietzsche's philosophy as a whole *un*timely in an essential sense? To what extent was it perhaps all too timely?" As he considers the overall structure of the essay and offers a section-by-section reading, Heidegger will take up a discussion about Nietzsche's three species of history—

monumental, antiquarian, and critical—as well as reflecting on the problem of remembrance and forgetting. All of this Heidegger will bring together as a way of rethinking Nietzsche's primary question about the "use" and "disadvantage" of history for life. Where Nietzsche thinks this question from within the question-frame of scientific knowledge or from the perspective of a Wagnerian-Schopenhaueran philosophy of art and culture, Heidegger will dismiss it as falling within the reigning metaphysics of the epoch. The same can be said about Heidegger's reading of Nietzschean biologism and his *lebensphilosophische* pronouncements about animality, the body, psychology, personality, and happiness. It is only when he takes up Nietzsche's discussion of justice—understood as *Gerechtigkeit*—that Heidegger will find the essentially "untimely" thematic in Nietzsche's thought.

As Heidegger will not tire from reminding his Freiburg listeners, Nietzsche's concept of "'justice' is meant neither in its Christian sense as something 'moral' nor as something juridical" (GA 46, 176).[44] On the contrary, Nietzsche will reject the standard nostrums concerning justice from "Christian, humanistic, Enlightenment, bourgeois, and socialist morality" (N iii, 244/N II: 325). As he turns his attention to the prevailing scientific culture of the nineteenth century and its idolization of "objective" knowledge, especially in the field of the historical sciences, Nietzsche will offer a devastating critique of historical scholars as "a race of eunuchs" who seek to objectively re-present the past "*wie es eigentlich gewesen ist*" (UTM, 84/KSA I, 281). Turning toward the scientific praxis of historians who seek to do "justice" to the past by rendering objective accounts of it, Nietzsche will ask: "Does modern man on account of his well-known historical objectivity have the right [*Recht*] to call himself strong, that is to say *just* [*gerecht*], and just in a higher degree than men of other ages? Is it true that this objectivity originates in an enhanced need and demand for justice [*Gerechtigkeit*]? Or is it an effect of quite different causes and only appears to originate in a desire for justice? Does it perhaps seduce one to a harmful—because all too flattering—prejudice as to the virtues of modern man?" (UTM, 88/KSA I, 285). Nietzsche will respond to these questions by quickly dismissing "historical objectivity" and "aesthetic detachment" as harmful to life and as impediments to the strong individual's decision to judge only in accordance with that which enhances life. Why does one need to be just to everything that has ever existed? What significance could such judgment have? And what gives one the right to judge? Nietzsche claims that only those who stand "'higher' than he who is to be judged," have a right (*Recht*) to judge (UTM, 93, 91/KSA I, 293, 290). Such judges measure the value of the past not according to canons of objectivity, but according to their own sense of resolve toward the past as something that calls one to perform "at least some high and great deed." Hence, for Nietzsche, "objectivity and justice have nothing to do with one another."

In 1873, at the same time he was working on the second *Untimely Meditation*, Nietzsche was also composing both his essay "On Truth and Lie in an Extra-Moral Sense" and his book *Philosophy in the Tragic Age of the Greeks*. In his preliminary discussion of Nietzsche's critique of objectivity, Heidegger will point out that in these works Nietzsche will reject the usual correspondence of objectivity with truth and of truth with morality. In Nietzsche's "extra-moral" reading of justice, Heidegger will claim, we can find traces of a Heraclitean strain, one that can be read in and through the concept of justice as *dike* (GA 46, 175, 211, 330, 343).[45] On this reading, Nietzsche's "higher" justice then is an "extra-moral" concept that measures what is "just" not according to what is *zeitgemäß*, or with an attitude of "justice" toward the past, but as the "creation and positing of a new standard of value [*Wertmaß-stabs*]." This is the highest virtue for Nietzsche—again, not in a Christian sense, but as Homeric *arete* (GA 46, 177). For what justice requires of the human being is the will to strength, to affirmation of life, and to instantiating a reversal of the Platonic-Christian interpretation of justice as a moral virtue by affirming the virtue of extra-moral *Wert-und Maß-setzung*—that is, value-estimation and the positing of a new standard of measure for humanity that is "beyond good and evil" (GA 46, 178). Heidegger will concede that here Nietzsche's thought of justice already shows itself in these early works from 1873 as being tied to Heraclitus. As he will put it, "Nietzsche's thought of a higher justice from the time of the *Untimely Meditations* is the hidden center from which his thinking radiates—hidden especially from Nietzsche himself" (GA 46, 211). Moreover, Heidegger will set out to reveal what he calls "the hidden essence [*Wesen*]" of Nietzschean justice—which he then interprets as "the truth of beings as such and as a whole insofar as being [*Sein*] is the will to power as unconditional subjectivity" (GA 50, 83).

In order to uncover "the hidden essence" of justice, Heidegger will offer a reading of Nietzsche's second *Untimely Meditation* (section six) which deals with the scientific ideals of historicist scholarship, particularly its focus on truth, objectivity, and the relationship between knowledge and life. Within this question-frame concerning "the essence of objectivity and the essence of truth," Heidegger will ask: "*Why and in which way* within the context of the question concerning the objectivity of science (especially history) is Nietzsche led to consider justice–and what does that mean?" (GA 46, 168). Nietzsche himself would insist on defining "justice as the highest representative of life itself" (KSA 11, 141; GA 46, 142, 182, 185, 335, 372). In this sense, justice comes to signify the dominant will to posit the highest values, to judge life itself in accordance with the measure of *physis* as self-emergent coming to presence. But Heidegger will see something other than a Heraclitean affirmation of life as "werdende" *physis*; he will, rather, detect in Nietzsche's use of language the underlying structure of a Cartesian attitude toward being that configures truth as *representation* or *Vorgestelltheit*. By *Vorgestelltheit*, Heidegger means that stance toward being "where the human being [comports itself] as 'subject'—that is, representation happens through *him* as the re-presenting 'I' and 'We' in general which is the standard [*Maßgebende*] for beingness—subjectivity" (GA 46, 143). More succinctly stated, "*justice* is the title for the dominance of the subject (of life in its vitality), that is, of beings as such and as a whole."

In a striking way here Heidegger's reconfiguration of Nietzsche's second *Untimely Meditation* exposes its hidden metaphysical scaffolding. Hence, if Nietzsche himself can argue that by privileging *Leben* over *Wissenschaft* and justice over objectivity he succeeds in overcoming the Cartesian demand for certitude and a methodologically secure notion of truth, Heidegger will claim that this merely masks a concealed Cartesian metaphysics of early modern representational thinking in its essential form. On Heidegger's reading, Nietzsche's vision of "higher justice" does not stand as an assault on the objectivity of science and history but, rather, affirms their metaphysical hegemony. As he sees it, Nietzsche will systematically configure justice in and against the reigning interpretation of truth that guides the work of the sciences in the nineteenth century. This scientific worldview, committed to the fundamentals of subject-object thinking, will constitute truth as "correctness" (*Richtigkeit*) of representation where correctness is understood as "*anmessendes Sichrichten nach*" ("a presumptive form of measuring that adjusts itself to" what is already given). Wherever truth is configured as *Anmessung*, *Richtigkeit*, correctness, or objectivity—whether from the perspective of "idea," "consciousness," "spirit," "will," or "body"—it still takes the form of the metaphysical principle of "agreement" by a judgment (subject) with its object. In essence, this is but another form of the medieval understanding of truth as *adequatio intellectus ad rem*. And, for Heidegger, Nietzsche's conception of justice falls within this chapter in the history of the essence of truth: "That the truth question comes at all under the heading of 'a higher justice' is decisive for all modern thinking, including our own time" (GA 46, 158).

The Ambiguity of Truth and Justice in Nietzsche's Thinking

Given Heidegger's devastating critique of Nietzschean justice as itself part of the Cartesian history of truth in Western metaphysics, we might expect him to dismiss the very topic and possibility of justice as itself immediately caught in the pincers of modern *techne* and its metaphysics of the subject. But Heidegger wants to salvage something from Nietzsche's audacious attempt to think justice in relation to truth in its "extra-moral sense." Accordingly, Heidegger will seek to resurrect the Heraclitean notion of justice as *dike*, the cosmic ordering of *physis* as the *Auseinandersetzung* of beings in polemical unity, as a possible *Verwindung* (*convalescence*) from modernist metaphysics.[46] Heidegger did not have to look far for the roots of such a *Verwindung*. They could, with a bit of hermeneutic exertion, be drawn from Nietzsche's early work of the 1870s where he developed a nuanced reading of Heraclitean *dike* as *polemos*—the law of the becoming of all things through the balance of strife and counterstrife. Such a vision of *dike* did not locate justice in subjective-anthropological "judgment" but in the cosmological sphere of conflict. As Nietzsche put it in one of his Heraclitus lectures: "Every individual struggles as if he alone were justified [*berechtigt*] yet an infinitely certain measure [*Maß*] of just judgment decides where victory rules." *Dike* in this sense is less a human judgment than "the immanent lawfulness in the decision of the contest," which comes from being itself (KGW II, 4, 272). Hence, for Nietzsche, Heraclitean *logos* manifests itself in the gathering of beings as *physis* through a ceaseless process of countervailing strife, "the game that time—as *aeon*—plays with itself" (PTAG, 62/KGW III, 2, 324). This non-anthropocentric rendering of *dike* is expressed by Heraclitus in Fragment 102 (Diels): "Human beings take some things as just [*dikai*, *gerecht*] and others as unjust [*adika*, *ungerecht*], but for the gods all things are beautiful, and good, and just."[47] Nietzsche will give voice to this same Heraclitean notion of justice in the *Birth of Tragedy*, holding "All that exists is just [*gerecht*] and unjust [*ungerecht*] and equally justified [*berechtigt*] in both respects" (BT, 51/KSA 1, 71).

In his later work Nietzsche will attempt a Heraclitean affirmation of life in the form of Zarathustra's doctrine of the eternal return of the same in yet another "extra-moral" interpretation of being. But Heidegger will have serious reservations about such a project. Even while he acknowledges this extra-moral dimension of Nietzsche's work and its affinity with the Heraclitean notion of *dike*, Heidegger will point to two pressing concerns in Nietzsche's interpretation that keep him from genuinely opening up the question of being. The first problem, Heidegger claims, is one of translation. The second problem for Heidegger concerns the fundamental ambiguity in Nietzsche's concept of justice, which leads to a contradiction.

Translation and Etymology: Dike, Justitia, Gerechtigkeit

With his rendering of Heraclitean *dike* as "Gerechtigkeit," Nietzsche will, on Heidegger's reading, succumb to the whole rhetorical tradition of *Recht* ("law," "right," "privilege") thought of as *Richtigkeit* ("correctness"). That is, he will think of Heraclitean *dike* within the metaphysics of representational thinking that posits justice as what is "correct" (*richtig, zurecht*) or what constitutes "ein Sichrichten nach" ("an adjusting to" what is there present)—in the sense of "doing justice to" what is (*einer Sache gerecht werden*). For the Nietzsche of the second *Untimely Meditation*, this will be expressed in the language of *Gerechtigkeit* since the task of the nineteenth-century historian is to do justice to the past—that is, to be "objective." But Nietzsche quickly dismisses such a notion as "hostile and dangerous to life" (UTM, 83, 94/KSA I, 279, 294). His vitalist approach to history demands that the excess (*Übermaß*) of historical learning be measured by a new standard (*Maß-stab*): that of doing justice not to the past but to the present and future. Only as "an architect of the future" who knows the present can one do "right" by the past. Yet this Nietzschean notion of "measuring" oneself against the past and future, Heidegger claims, betrays a predilection for the Latin understanding of truth as *rectus* as "keeping straight," "heading straight along," and being "correct."[48] Out of this Latin cluster of terms with close etymological roots we find *rego*: "to rule" or "govern"; *regula*: to set a "pattern," "rule," or "example"; *regio*: "a boundary line" or "region"; as well as *reor*: "to reckon" or "think"; and *ratio*: "reason." "The 'taking as true' of *ratio*, of *reor*, becomes a far-reaching and anticipatory security. *Ratio* becomes counting, calculating [*Rechnung*], calculus. *Ratio* is a self-adjustment to what is correct [*das Sicheinrichten auf das Richtige*]" (P, 50, 48/GA 54, 74, 71). In English we find the resonances of this Latin metaphysical tradition of *rectus* in terms such as "correct," "direct," "erect," "rectitude," and "rector"; in German—*Richtigkeit, Richtung, aufrecht, Aufrichtigkeit*, and *Rektor*.

As Heidegger will maintain, this Latin tradition of defining thinking in terms of *reor, ratio*, and *rectus* will usher in a distinctive chapter in the history of truth as *veritas*, where "*verum* is the remaining constant, the upright [*Aufrechte*], that which is directed to what is superior because it is directing from above [*das nach oben Gerichtete, weil von oben her Richtende*]. *Verum* is *rectum* (*regere*, "the regime"), the right [*das Rechte*], *justum*." Here, "*veritas* is then *rectitudo*, 'correctness' [*Richtigkeit*]." In this complex etymological pirouette from *rectus* and *justitia* by way of *Richtigkeit* and *Gerechtigkeit*, Heidegger will lay out the whole structure of the history of Western metaphysics within which he will place the Nietzschean conception of justice. As he puts it:

> The essence of truth in the modern period is determined on the basis of certainty, correctness, being just, justice [*der Rechtheit, des Gerechtseins, und der Gerechtigkeit*]. . . . [In] Nietzsche's thought, where the metaphysics of the Occident reaches its peak, the essence of truth is founded on certitude and justice. Even for Nietzsche the

> true is the right [*das Richtige*], that which is directed [*richtet*] by what is real in order to adjust itself to it [*sich ihm gemäss einzurichten*] and make itself secure in it. The basic feature of reality is the "will to power." All correctness must be adjusted in terms of the will to power. Correspondence to what the will to power utters is the just, i.e., justice. (P, 52/GA 54, 77).

As Heidegger will claim, Nietzschean justice expresses nothing less than the Roman metaphysics of imperial dominion and hegemony, the metaphysics of "self-assertion" (*das Sich-behaupten*) that culminates in the will to power. Here, the Nietzschean demand that all judgments be measured by the standard of what affirms "life"—that is, what is either of "use" to or a "disadvantage" for life—reveals itself to Heidegger as a metaphysics of subjective valuation. Life in this sense becomes literally the *status quo*—"the state in which something stands," "the standard" (*Maß-stab*) that, in the epoch of *Machenschaft*, becomes standardization. Because Nietzsche thinks justice on the basis of Roman *veritas*, *rectitudo*, and *justitia*, and because he thinks truth within the metaphysics of self-assertion and dominion where "*justum*, as understood in Latin, is 'to-be-in-the-right' [*im Recht seins*] and 'to have a right' [*Recht-habens*]," he cannot finally experience "the primordial essence of truth" expressed in Heraclitus's notion of *dike* (P, 40, 54/GA 54, 59, 79). As Heidegger will continually emphasize, "*justitia* has a wholly different ground of essence than that of *dike*, which essentially unfolds [*west*] as *aletheia*." For this reason, Heidegger will come to see Nietzsche's decision to translate *dike* as *Gerechtigkeit*—thought in terms of *justitia*—as signifying something more than a questionable philological judgment about the appropriateness of word equivalents. It becomes decisive, rather, as a signature moment in the history of truth for the West.[49]

Ambiguity and Contradiction in Nietzsche's Second Untimely Meditation

By the time of the Parmenides lectures in WS 1942/43, Heidegger had become convinced that "the metaphysics of Nietzsche, whom we like to consider the modern rediscoverer of ancient Greece, sees the Greek 'world' exclusively in a Roman way, i.e., in a way at once modern and un-Greek" (P, 43/GA 54, 63). Everything that characterizes the "modern age"—the dominance of the subject, representational thinking, the nihilism of technology, the interpretation of beings measured against the compass of justice—"is founded on the event [*Ereignis*] of the Romanizing of Greece." In WS 1938/39, however, Heidegger still held out some hope that Nietzsche's reflections on justice might provide a way for initiating what, in *Beiträge zur Philosophie*, he will call a "crossing to the other beginning" (*Übergang zum anderen Anfang*) (GA 65, 176). "To grasp Nietzsche as the end of Western metaphysics," Heidegger claims, "is not a historiographical determination about what lies behind us." It is, rather, "the historical onset of the future of Western thinking." In the seminar on the second *Untimely Meditation*, Heidegger will attempt a de-structuring (*Destruktion*) of Nietzsche's interpretation of justice that sees it as being complicit in the Cartesian history of truth. But, at the same time, he will attempt a retrieval (*Wiederholung*) of the Heraclitean, extra-moral strands of Nietzschean justice that he deems essential for the work of crossing to the other beginning. Instead of irretrievably relegating Nietzschean justice to pure Cartesianism, Heidegger will see it as "ambiguous" and "contradictory" and in need of originary retrieval.

As Heidegger will concede, "Nietzsche's thought of justice arises from his reflection [*Besinnung*] on pre-Platonic philosophy and is already articulated by Heraclitus" (GA 46, 343). But even in his extra-moral reading of Heraclitus's Fragment 52—"the world [*aeon*] is a child playing a board game"—we confront two contradictory demands: the demand on the subject to hold being fast as something stable, secure, certain, *and* the demand to overcome this subjectivity.[50] In *Philosophy in the Tragic Age of the Greeks*, Nietzsche will interpret the world in wholly nonsubjective terms as *aeon*—not simply as "time" but as "the force of life," a Heraclitean "ever-living fire" of "coming-to-be and passing away, structuring and destroying without any moral reckoning [*Zurechnung*] in eternally equal innocence. . . . Now and again the child throws its toy away; but soon it takes it up once more through innocent whim. But as soon as it builds, it joins things together, conjoins [*fügt*] them and measures them according to the inner ordering of lawfulness [*gesetzmässig*]" (KGW III, 2, 324–25). And, in his lectures on *The Pre-Platonic Philosophers*, Nietzsche will interpret the *aeon* as a game marked by harmony in strife where "this opposition of different characteristics, directed by justice, can only be grasped as an aesthetic phenomenon. This is a purely aesthetic way of viewing the world. The moral tendency to view the whole teleologically is just as strongly excluded, for the child that is the cosmos does not act according to ends and purposes, but only according to an immanent *dike*" (KGW II, 4, 278). Nietzsche's interpretation of *dike* here as the nonsubjective, immanent force of lawfulness that balances the countervailing forces of being in the cosmic play of consonance/dissonance and of *sympheromenon/diapheromenon* cannot, however, be read in isolation. It needs to be set off against the wholly subjective rendering of justice as "virtue," and as the life-measuring standard (*Maß-stab*) that rules over Nietzsche's work.

In Nietzsche's 1873 essay, "On Truth and Lies in an Extra-Moral Sense," Heidegger detects a subject-object metaphysics of adequation tethered to the binary logic of truth as both objectively constructed *Wissenschaft* and subjectively confected illusion. On the one hand, truth is recognized as what is fixed, permanent, binding; on the other hand, it is celebrated as a convenient fiction, an arbitrary designation made within a language community to understand truth as a "moveable host of metaphors, metonymies, and anthropomorphisms" (KSA 1, 880). And it is precisely due to its position as an anthropomorphic designation that Heidegger will interpret Nietzsche's doctrine of truth as wholly subjective. Here, he will claim, "truth arises out of the agreement of advantage and apportionment respectively; it arises, therefore, out of *justice*—and this in the sense of a distribution that evens things out and gives to each his own" (GA 46, 141–42, 138). On this reading, "Justice is the name for the dominance of the subject." Hence, even as Nietzsche thinks justice in a Heraclitean manner as "the conjunction in the relationship between truth 'and' life that conjoins [*fügt*] them," he will also affirm, as he does in his notebooks of 1873, that "it is wholly on the basis of the subjective that we are human" (KSA 7, 627). Because of this bifurcation between cosmic justice as *dike* and human justice as subjective valuation, "Justice itself is caught in the ambiguity of [Nietzsche's concept of] life." In one sense, life is conceived as "the legislation of law as such (life = beings as a whole)"—what Nietzsche would term "the immanent lawfulness [*Gesetzmäßigkeit*]" of life—understood as the cosmos (GA 46, 138; KGW II, 4, 272). In another sense, however, life is grasped as a "virtue" of the human being (life = being in its human form)—measured according to the standards of a subject.

By translating "becoming" (*Werden*) as "life" (*Leben*), Nietzsche succumbed to the Cartesian impulse to measure what is against the propositions of the *ego cogito*. And yet, Heidegger will claim, "despite his opposition to Descartes, he merely substitutes *vivo* in place of the *cogito* and in so doing raises the subject in its predominance to the last." In Nietzsche's ambiguous relationship to life—as both Heraclitean game and as Cartesian project—a "fundamental occurrence hides itself: the forgetfulness of being in the sense of no longer being able to transpose oneself into a relation with being and with the truth of being as the essential ground of human being" (GA 46, 83). This appears to Heidegger as the most essential question in the Nietzschean translation of Heraclitean *dike* as *Gerechtigkeit*. Despite his extra-moral interpretation of justice, "Nietzsche never asked in an originary way about the fundamental presupposition of morality itself—namely, 'metaphysics,' i.e., the determination of beings as such and as a whole, of truth, and of the human being" (GA 46, 178). In the end, then, Nietzsche's conception of justice winds up justifying the subjectivism of the *ego vivo* even as it brings it to completion in the *Machenschaft* of the human being. On the basis of this reading of Nietzschean *Gerechtigkeit*, Heidegger will pose the question that remained "unthought" in Nietzsche's work: "the decision concerning metaphysics" as the history of *Seyn* and of "the grounding of the truth of being [*Seyn*]" (GA 46, 218, 221). On the basis of this question, which Nietzsche never posed, not even in his reflections on Heraclitean justice, Heidegger will attempt to lay the groundwork for the "crossing" [*Übergang*] from the first beginning of *dike* to the other beginning of what is impossible to translate either in the language of "justice" or that of "*Gerechtigkeit*." It is against this limit of the untranslatable possibility of what lies concealed in the Heraclitean notion of *dike* that Heidegger will lay out his reading of Nietzsche.

The Untranslatable Possibility of Dike

It was Nietzsche himself who raised the issue of the "limit" as a philosophical problem—both in *Philosophy in the Tragic Age of the Greeks* with his notion of a "*Grenzstein*" or "boundary stone" and in the second *Untimely Meditation* with his discussion of the *Horizont* or "horizon" of life.[51] In both these texts, Nietzsche will point to the necessity of setting limits on the boundless possibilities that confront the self. One has to be able "to determine the limit" ("*die Grenze bestimmen*") at which the past does not overwhelm the present; for this, one needs to possess what Nietzsche calls "the plastic power" of creatively embodying the possibilities of the tradition while simultaneously knowing how to delimit their influence. In this delicate art of balancing what is healthful and noxious, what is of advantage and disadvantage to life, Nietzsche will locate the problem of justice. (Later, in *Thus Spoke Zarathustra*, this art of judicious balancing will emerge in the fate of the tightrope dancer.) Justice, in this sense, involves knowing one's limits and possessing the strength to understand the precarious equilibrium of existence between the cosmos and the polis, the world of being and the world of human being. Nietzsche characterizes this equilibrium in *Untimely Meditations* as learning how "to organize the chaos" from out of the endless possibilities provided by history. As his model Nietzsche chose the early Greeks as those able to master themselves and organize the chaos around them by heeding the oracular wisdom of Delphi:

> [T]he god of Delphi cries to you his oracle: "Know thyself." It is a hard saying: for that god "neither conceals, nor reveals, but only indicates," as Heraclitus has said. What does he indicate to you? (UTM, 122/KSA 1, 333)

In Heraclitus's oracular wisdom of *physis* as eternal "play in necessity" according to "the law of becoming" through strife, tension, struggle, and oppositional equilibrium, Nietzsche uncovers an interpretation of justice that *indicates* to him a "horizon" by which to measure human life. As he thinks through the Nietzschean question of limit and measure against the oracular wisdom of Heraclitus, Heidegger will point to what he perceives as the most fundamental problem in Nietzsche's reading: the problem of measure itself. As Heidegger puts it, for Nietzsche "horizon" means: "the limitation, restriction, securing, and fixation of 'life.' Here horizon is not so much *gefügemässig* [measured by the jointure (of being)] as it is *lebensmässig* [measured by life]" (GA 46, 137). Nietzsche's notion of measuring life is in the end, according to Heidegger, a measuring by life in its subjective form, a measuring that misses the Heraclitean insight into the primordial essence of *dike*. In this sense, horizon will be thought in a subjective way as "perspective," as something ocular and fixed; but there is here "a more originary and essential configuration of human being (in *Dasein*) that Nietzsche can see as little as all metaphysics before him" (N iii, 87/N I, 574).

Heidegger would find in this Nietzschean reading of horizon a limit that was wholly anthropological and determined by the metaphysics of Cartesian self-positing—but now measured by the self as *ego vivo* rather than as *ego cogito*. The balance or equilibrium found by Nietzsche's artistic genius was not that of the cosmos itself, but that of a self-legislating, autonomous subject. What Nietzsche ultimately failed to think in his notion of horizonal life-measure was its essential relation to Heraclitean *dike*—thought not as "*lebensmässige Gerechtigkeit*" (a measure of justice provided by life) but as what is "*gefügemässig*" (a measure by the jointure of being). Heraclitus's vision of the world as playful jointure, of an oppositional equipoise of conjuncture and disjuncture unfolding in the image of the bow and the lyre (Fragment 51) comes to expression in Heidegger as "the foundational conjointure [*das Grundgefüge*] of world and of humans" (GA 46, 344).[52] Thought from this Heraclitean perspective, horizon (*horismos*) is not a limit that human beings impose on *physis* to stabilize the chaos of becoming; it is, rather, a jointure granted by *physis* itself that sets limits to human being (N iii, 88/N I, 576). Hence, Heidegger will risk translating *dike* as *Fug*—in the sense of "what is fitting," that which, when it is joined together (*gefügt*), "fits." "*Dike*, as the enjoining structure [*das fügende Gefüge*] . . . essentially unfolds as being [*als Sein west*]" (IM, 177/GA 40, 175).[53] Justice in this sense is less the standard set by any kind of human measure than it is being's own measure against which human beings try to adjust. Justice as adjustment to being constitutes tragic wisdom in a Sophoclean sense. But it is precisely this understanding of justice as adjustment that is lost on Antigone, Creon, and Oedipus as well as on the later technicians of planetary *Machenschaft*.

What Heidegger seeks to think here in his *Auseinandersetzung* with Nietzsche is a way of thinking the hidden, essential meaning of *dike* in its non-anthropomorphic sense. This involves for him a recognition that there is a limit that emerges from out of *physis* itself that is not equivalent to the limits imposed on *physis* by the will; rather, it exceeds them and does so in a way that overwhelms the human subject and renders his planning and calculation as nothing. What *dike* points to is a realm of balance and equipoise that happens "beyond good and evil," beyond the "boundary stone" of the human horizon, a realm *between* being and human being that enjoins them in a way that cannot be configured by the figurations of human will. What is fitting is that we fit in at all. We do not make the fit; we accede to it.

What comes to language in Heidegger's barely articulated possibility of an originary ethics is the meaning of *dike* thought of as *Fug*, rather than as *Gerechtigkeit*. For the question of ethics can only be posed, Heidegger will claim, in relation to the originary sway of *dike* as the Heraclitean jointure of what is both in and out of joint. Against this Heraclitean landscape, Heidegger locates the crux of modernity's nihilism in its disjunction between being and human beings accomplished in the metaphysical predominance of the subject as *cogito*, *Bewusstsein*, *Geist*, *Leben*, and *Wille zur Macht*. This disjunction between being and human beings lies at the root of the homelessness that prevails in the age of technology. Within this disjunction itself, however, there lies hidden an untranslatable possibility of conjointure, or *Fug*, that barely comes to language in the translation of *dike*. Heidegger never really develops a full-scale reading of *dike* nor does he turn to justice as an explicit theme, except in a few of the Nietzsche lectures from the late thirties and early forties and in his Anaximander essay from 1946. "Justice" is not a master term in the lexicon of the late Heidegger like *Ereignis*, *Lichtung*, *Gelassenheit*, or *Gestell*. Yet this is not because it was not crucial for his thinking. On the contrary, I would argue that what Heidegger tries to bring to language in the translation of *dike* as *Fug*, *Gefüge*, *Fügung*, and *Un-fug* is an originary ethics in a genuinely extra-moral sense, something that Nietzsche, in his refusal "to experience the jointure [*Gefüge*] of the differentiation of being and beings as enjoined by being," could only express as mere "justice" (N iv, 182/N II, 240). To find one's place in the world among beings, to fit in with the overarching order of jointure, to ad*just* to the overarching power of *physis*, that would be to experience the limits of a justice whose name can only be expressed as what is still in need of thinking. To think against this limit and to let the limit shape the horizon of one's thinking—this is what Nietzsche could not think, thinking as he did within the horizon of anthropomorphic justice. What justice demands, however, is that thinking be carried on originally and in fugal counterpoint to what lets itself be thought of as originary ethics, a thinking that Heidegger takes up in his 1946 essay on Anaximander.

DIKE AND ORIGINARY ETHICS

Heidegger's interpretation of the Anaximander fragment, the first text of the Western philosophical tradition, stands as one of the most difficult and labyrinthine texts in his corpus. In it he attempts an enactment of a new form of thinking, a nonmetaphysical form of originary ethics as a thinking of/as *dike*—not "justice" in a juridical-moral sense but the name of a realm of unity of being and beings that, as a "fitting order," preserves the *polemos* at work between them. This order does not reflect a human order in the *polis* but first makes such an ordering possible, provides the site for the historical dwelling place of human beings upon the earth as they sojourn (*sich aufhalten*) between birth and death, emergence and perishing. In this sense, *dike* functions as the "fit" or "jointure" of beings in an eternal *polemos* between presence and absence, coming-to-be and passing-away, emergence and withdrawal that gives itself to the earth ("*es gibt*") even as it shelters such giving in its rescission.[54] In an effort to think such an order that does not have the human being (or its substitute, e.g., God, idea, "nature," et al.) at its center, Heidegger turns to the earliest fragments of the Greek tradition. Yet in no sense does Heidegger attempt a philological reading or an intellectual-historical one. Rather, what animates Heidegger's concerns is the crisis of the present, the nihilistic condition of sheer destruction and devastation that pervades Germany in late fall 1946. Within this historical moment the Anaximander fragment speaks to Heidegger as a way of negotiating the ethical bankruptcy and judicial chaos that he sees in the wake of the Allied bombing missions, the NS concentration camps, the moral righteousness of the Nürnberg Trials, and the military occupation of his homeland (and his own house).[55]

Because of their fragmentary nature, the writings of Anaximander, Heraclitus, and Parmenides appear to him as forays into originary thinking that were cut off at their roots by the sweeping power of Platonic-Aristotelian metaphysics. Through the work of doxographers such as Theophrastus, Diogenes, Hippolytus, and Simplicius, these earliest indications of thinking became encased in the disciplinary frames of physics-logic-ethics without any inner belonging to the ordering of a nonmetaphysical *dike*. In an effort to revive and cultivate this originary form of thinking within the historical crisis of the present, Heidegger seeks to engage the language of these fragments in a daring and radical way so as to free them from the encasements of philological correctness and calculation. To do so will involve him in a struggle to complete Hegel's notion of "the end of philosophy" by turning instead to the power of "thinking" (*Denken*) which, for Heidegger, is not a faculty of mind or a calculative ability to discern causes or grounds.[56] Rather, as he explains it in "The Anaximander Fragment," "thinking is poetizing (*Dichten*) and indeed more than one kind of poetizing, more than poetry and song. Thinking of being is the originary way of poetizing" (EGT, 19/GA 5, 328). This kind of thinking that challenges all technological forms of reckoning, planning, calculation, and projection, lays claim to that human being who dwells at the limit between what allows itself to be said and what denies expression. As Heidegger puts it, "The poetizing essence of thinking preserves (*verwahrt*) the sway of the truth (*Wahrheit*) of being" (EGT, 19/GA 5, 329). By attempting a translation of the Anaximander fragment, then, Heidegger aims not only at uncovering the hidden language of an archaic saying but at recollecting a forgotten *ethos*, a *Haltung* or comportment toward the world of thinking as a way of dwelling "in" the truth of being. In this sense, the task of translating the Anaximander fragment becomes itself a kind of ethics, a way of enabling the "crossing over" (*übersetzen*) from the first beginning to the other beginning by virtue of an attunement to a forgotten form of poetic thinking. Heidegger's exercise in translation here takes on an axial status, then, as a way of enabling a turn in/of thinking by letting ourselves be reclaimed by the truth of being that lay hidden in the enigmatic words of an ancient thinker. To bring about such a turn or, rather, to place ourselves in a position so that we might be genuinely appropriated in such a turning, becomes for Heidegger the focus of his postwar writings.

Left to our own devices we would not be able to engineer such a shift since any genuine insight into poetic thinking first requires that we let go of all calculative strategies of control, including the practice of rigorous philological science. Before embarking on such a venture, Heidegger exhorts his readers to let their thinking "be translated to what is said in Greek. Thoughtful translation to what comes to language in this fragment" would then constitute "a leap (*Sprung*) over an abyss (*Graben*)," an abyss that is not merely historical or linguistic but involves the basic metaphysical structures of all our thinking (EGT, 19/GA 5, 329). Going back to Aristotle's *Metaphysics*, which defined *physis* as "nature" and *ousia* as "substance," Western philosophy came to constitute itself through four determining structures: (1) the metaphysics of presence, (2) the metaphysics of substance, (3) the principle of noncontradiction, (4) the principle of causality.[57] All of the philological labors of the doxographical tradition that informed the work of German philologists had been shaped in critical ways by these fundamental principles, principles that rendered Anaximander's saying as a primitive utterance about the nature of the cosmos that lacked scientific foundation. Heidegger sought to read Anaximander's fragment as a palimpsest, however, and to consider how the metaphysical habits of doxographical-scholarly research had occluded any genuine access to its originary language, preventing us from any thoughtful encounter with its meaning. Heidegger's aim here was not an attempt at an historical recovery of what Anaximander "really said," but a way of indicating how it might be read as part of a "new, more primordially fated history" (EGT, 17/GA 5, 326). *Dike* belonged to that history in its incipient form. Yet in order to experience something akin to what Anaximander thought in his primordial rendering of *dike* as the order of being itself—the constant turning and counterturning of *physis* in its emergence and withdrawal, its self-gathering (*legein*) and self-dispersal, its letting itself be seen in the dwelling (*ethos*) of mortals—required that we come to experience thinking in a new way. Above all it required a nonmetaphysical *ethos* of letting be and releasing ourselves from the structures of calculative thinking that defined the modern practice of philosophy. In this way, the enigmatic and recalcitrant language of Anaximander might serve as a lever to raise the question about the viability of philosophy as a way of thinking in an age beset by destruction, loss, devastation, and collapse, even as it might also provide the hope of a new kind of genesis in the midst of the rubble brought on by the bombings and tank assaults.

GENESIS-PHTHORA-DIKE

Part of what I am trying to bring together in my focus on 1946 as a crucial year in Heidegger's thinking is the influence of pre-Socratic thinking and its confluence of themes relating to *ethos* as dwelling and *dike* as the groundless grounding that orders being into beings as it grants a limit to the flux and reflux of beings in and as time. How can we think time as kairological temporality in the factical life-world of 1946? How might Aristotle's notion of *ethos* as a temporally particular (*jeweilig*) experience of habitual dwelling help us to situate ourselves within the distinctive temporality and historicity of German practical life in 1946? How can such an experience of time open us to the possibility of our appropriation to/by a charged moment (*kairos*) of practical existence? And how might the thinking of *dike* from out of the historical world of Anaximander help us to come to understand such an *ethos* in terms of an originary ethics of dwelling that would prepare the way for a trans/lation or "crossing over" (*über/setzen*) to the other beginning? In raising these questions, I want to situate Heidegger's Anaximander essay against the whole middle-voiced retrieval of *physis-logos-ethos* that preoccupied us in our discussion of originary ethics in "The Letter on Humanism." For in attempting a Hölderlinian form of translation—that is, translation not as a retrieval of a fixed meaning within an ancient text but as a way of preparing the possibility of a futural German homecoming—Heidegger succeeded in transforming his reflections on the fragment of Anaximander into a kind of untimely meditation on the meaning of justice in the postwar world.

Given the timely, all too timely, effect of the Nürnberg Trials on German culture in 1946—eleven defendants were condemned to death in late October as a way of bringing to public consciousness the issues of war guilt and the planning of the Final Solution—Heidegger's decision to take up the question of "justice" by way of a reflection on the origins of the Greek notion of *dike* can hardly be considered a coincidence.[58] The whole pageant of Allied retribution and punishment, of "paying penalty to one another for their recklessness," struck Heidegger as an exercise in metaphysical nihilism with the introduction of the "rule of law" according to a victor's justice. His Hölderlinian vision of a National Socialist future had been destroyed by the Allied bombings and tank assaults that led to his retreat from Freiburg in December 1944. The Allied occupation had brought with it the "return" of the rule of law, but the legal and moral consequences of such a move, to say nothing of their political effect, appeared to Heidegger as the mere continuation of NS machination (*Machenschaft*) caught in the frame of the *Gestell* that was everywhere leveling modern existence in the epoch of technology.[59] Against this background, the essay on Anaximander constitutes an assault against the triumph of the "victor's justice" achieved at Nürnberg even as it offers a profound critique of all calculative planning, administration, and enforcement. We can perhaps hear something of these political overtones in the very title of the essay—"Der Spruch des Anaximanders"—which needs to be read as a double genitive. The "Spruch" or "saying" of Anaximander is also "Anaximander's saying," a saying that gives voice to how an ontological reading of Anaximander's language (*Sprache*) "makes a claim upon" us (*uns in Anspruch nimmt*). What this saying claims, however, is not simply its saying but also its "verdict"—(*Spruch*). In an age where an Allied court's verdict offered a moral-legal judgment on German *Dasein*, Heidegger counters with a nonlegal "verdict" about the fate of the West thought through the jointure of a German justice under erasure. In the forgotten language of Anaximander, Heidegger unearths here a way of thinking the contemporary watchwords of "catastrophe" and "birth" within the problematic of "justice" in a nonmetaphysical idiom, one that harbors a deep-rooted reaction against both the "democratic" and "Socialist" values of the Allied victors. In his recitation of Anaximander's pregnant terms *genesis* (birth, emergence, coming-to-be) and *phthora* (decline, catastrophe, passing away), Heidegger reconfigures the political landscape of German defeat and finds the proper *ethos* of/for the defeated: letting-be (*Gelassenheit*), a way of being attuned to the epochal process of history (*Geschichte*) as a destiny (*Geschick*) that shapes the catastrophe of the moment within the unfolding of being. This comportment, *Haltung, ethos* of letting oneself be open for the future even through the decline of the present was concretely expressed by Heidegger in a letter to his wife in April 1945 just weeks before the German collapse. He writes from Burg Wildenstein, where he is staying temporarily after being driven out of Freiburg: "I think that I have found the right course for the transition [that awaits us]. What appears essential to me is not that one survives, but rather that possibilities for a future are preserved [*bewahrt*]. Mere gestures, one way or another, signify nothing" (MLS, 235–36). Amidst the detritus of catastrophe, waiting for the possibilities of a German future to come to genesis, Heidegger reflects on the genesis of Western thinking in Anaximander as a way of preparing a dwelling place (*ethos*) for the event of being—Hölderlin's *parousia*—to appropriate the temporality of the *kairos* into the "eschatology of being" (EGT, 18/GA 5, 327).

This commitment to the future was hardly a new theme for Heidegger in the fall of 1946. His earlier public speeches as rector of Freiburg University had been epideictic exercises in the political ontology of a German future, ones that depended above all on "recovering the original Greek essence of science for our *Dasein*" (GA 16, 109). As his hopes for a National Socialist recovery of such a future faded, however, Heidegger came to see how deeply implicated National Socialism was in the machination (*Machenschaft*) of nihilistic dominion over beings. And yet, through the devastation of the war and the loss of his hopes, and after overcoming his debilitating depression at the clinic in Badenweiler in early 1946, Heidegger would emerge with his faith in the future intact. Only now the mood would be tempered by a new resolve for *Gelassenheit*, a letting-go of his overtly political hopes for a more subdued commitment to a Graeco-German vision of historical destiny. As he put in the Anaximander essay,

> If we stubbornly insist on thinking Greek thought in Greek fashion it is by no means because we intend to sketch a historical [*historische*] portrait of Greek antiquity. . . . Rather, our sole aim is to reach what wants to come to language [*Sprache*] in such a dialogue [*Zwiesprache*], provided it comes of its own accord. And this is that same which in different ways destinally [*geschicklich*] concerns the Greeks and us. It is that which brings the dawn of thinking into the destiny [*Geschick*] of the West, the land of evening. Only in virtue of this destiny do the Greeks become Greeks in the historical [*geschichtlichen*] sense. (EGT, 25/GA 5, 336; translation altered)

What both Greece and Germany share, unlike the other Latinized nations of Western Europe, is an attunement to thinking's place in the *Geschick* of the West as the land of evening. Anaximander represented the dawn of such a *Geschick*, even if, oxymoronically, his thought came to presence as the dawn of this evening. In his distinction between the historiological (*historisch*) meaning of Greek antiquity (i.e., its scientific-historiographical significance) and its historical (*geschichtlich*) sense for Germans (as "the immanent historicity of life itself," "the history that we ourselves are"), Heidegger finds an opening for the destiny or *Geschick* of the West (GA 56–57, 119; GA 9, 5).[60] In this sense, the Anaximander essay of 1946 stands as an exercise in a thinking attuned to language in a poetic sense, attuned to the inevitable loss and dehiscence of all translation. Attuning himself to the archaic language of Anaximander, especially his notion of *dike*, Heidegger hopes to think the decisive break of 1945–46 in European history as a moment of transition or *Übergang* in the history of thinking. If others around him focus their energies on the historical (*historisch*) work of retribution and punishment (Nürnberg Trials) or on forming supposedly "new" structures of world government (the United Nations) as a way of transforming the history of the West, Heidegger will interpret all these timely (*zeitgemäß*) phenomena as indices of the forgetting of being. Against such reifying historical expressions, Heidegger will attune himself to the enigmatic language of Anaximander as a way of rethinking the history (*Geschichte*) of the West in terms of the destiny (*Geschick*) of being. Within such a reading, "the decisive turn in the destiny of being" will be interpreted as a problem of translation. Following from this focus on thinking as translating the truth of being, Heidegger's translation of *dike* in 1946 risks the destiny of the West not on the Allied interpretation of a victors' justice, but on the thoughtful encounter with the earliest word for being—*dike*.[61] Yet how does Heidegger's notion of *dike*—thought through the palimpsest of translations afforded by the Latin term *iustitia* and the German term *Gerechtigkeit* (from *Recht*, Latin *rectus*, "straight," "cor-rect")—offer an insight into the *Geschick* of being?[62] In what sense does the archaic language of Anaximander offer a possibility of interpreting the history of the West against this history of moral-legal "justice" in a way that affords a profound connection between the historical situation of German in 1945–46 and a nonmetaphysical interpretation of justice as the truth (*aletheia*) of being? And how can we carry through the leap (*Sprung*) over the abyss that separates us from the language and destinal experience of Anaximander in such a way that we can preserve (*bewahren*) the truth (*aletheia/Wahrheit*) of being (EGT, 19/GA 5, 329)? As he begins to consider such questions Heidegger stresses how necessary it is to translate the *experience* of thinking that first made such language possible and that allowed Anaximander to frame his interpretation of the aletheic process of revelation and concealment. For this he turns to a parsing of the early Greek words *genesis* and *phthora*.

At the outset of "The Anaximander Fragment" Heidegger offers two different translations of the fragment, the first by Nietzsche:

> Whence things have their origin, there they must also pass away according to necessity; for they must pay penalty and be judged for their injustice, according to the ordinance of time. [*Woher die Dinge ihre Entstehung haben, dahin müssen sie auch zu Grunde gehen, nach der Ungerechtigkeiten gerichtet werden, gemäß der Ordnung der Zeit.*]

And the second by Diels:

> But where things have their origin, there too their passing away occurs according to necessity; for they pay recompense and penalty to one another for their recklessness, according to firmly established time. [*Woraus aber die Dinge das Entstehen haben, dahin geht auch ihr Vergehen nach der Notwendigkeit; denn sie zahlen einander Strafe und Buße für ihre Ruchlosigkeit nach der festgesetzten Zeit.*] (EGT, 13/GA 5, 321)

As he considers the palimpsestic inscriptions on the fragment carried out by Theophrastus, Simplicius, and their Christian successors, Heidegger turns first to the philological history of the text. Basing his reading on the philological labors of John Burnet, Heidegger claims that the first fourteen words of the fragment and the last five words are redactions of the original text.[63] The first section seems to him "much more Aristotelian in structure and tone than archaic," while the second section "betrays the same characteristic lateness" as the first. The only "immediate, genuine words of Anaximander" remain these:

> *Kata to chreon didonai gar auta diken kai tisin allelois tes adikias. . . .* according to necessity; for they pay one another recompense and penalty for their injustice. (EGT, 29–30/GA 5, 341)

Even as he puts forward his truncated reading of Anaximander, one that retrieves only a fragment of the fragment, Heidegger does not simply reject out of hand the language of these redacted texts. While he considers them to be "secondary testimony," nonetheless he claims that they "demand that we understand precisely these words *genesis* and *phthora* as they are thought in Greek, whether they be preconceptual words or Platonic-Aristotelian conceptual terms" (EGT, 30/GA 5, 341).

Deconstructing the conceptual lexicon of Platonic-Aristotelian metaphysics, and with it the philosophical division of experience into logic-physics-ethics, Heidegger rejects the simple counterpositioning of *genesis* as "development" and *phthora* as "regression" or "wasting away." Instead, he thinks *genesis* and *phthora* as countervailing possibilities of the selfsame manifesting of *physis* from concealment into unconcealment and from unconcealment into concealment. As Heidegger explains it,

> *Genesis* is coming forward and arriving [*Hervor- und An-kommen*] in unconcealment. *Phthora* means the departure and descent [*hinweg- und ab-gehen*] into concealment of what has arrived there out of unconcealment. The coming forward into . . . and the departure to . . . *become present* within unconcealment between what is concealed and what is unconcealed. They initiate the arrival and departure of whatever has arrived. (EGT, 30/GA 5, 342)

What emerges in Heidegger's reading is the originary belonging together of *logos-physis-ethos* in the play of being. That is, Heidegger will think "being" here as the gathering (*legein*) of all that emerges into presence (*physis*) as an emerging that is at the same a passing away, a passing-away-as-emerging that happens as the lingering or sojourn (*ethos*) of beings upon the earth, what he terms their "whiling" (*das Weilen*). Within the finite limits of existence granted to them by *physis*, beings rebel against the possibility of their perishing by clinging to their singular perdurance, denying mortality with the thought of eternal presence. What comes to language here in Anaximander's naming of *genesis* and *phthora* is an experience of being as a unified *polemos* between emergence and withdrawal held together in its temporal limits by the granting of time as/by being. What arises, perishes—and out of this perishing there arises the limit of all that can arise. And yet Heidegger will not think of this process as one of cyclical "becoming" against a fixed and static "being." Rather, he will think the unity of arising-perishing as being's way of self-manifesting, a self-manifesting that is—at the same time—a self-concealing. In this sense he understands Anaximander's experience of *genesis/phthora* as the play of *aletheia* itself—of the lethic hiding of being that emerges with and against (a) being's coming-to-presence (*physis*). Heidegger attempts to express something of this unity in his lectures from SS 1941 where he claims:

> Everything gathers itself together to say one thing: that from out of which emergence [*Hervorgehen*] properly belongs to [*eigne*] temporally particular presence [*dem jeweilig Anwesenden*] is the same as that back into which elusion [*Entgängis*] emerges, *ginesthai*. . . . [T]he former, from out of which emergence comes to presence [*wese*], is precisely *this latter one*, away into which evading (*Entgehen*) comes to presence. (BC, 91/GA 51, 106; translation altered)

Here we can see how, for Heidegger, coming-to-presence and withdrawal are not two separate phenomena divided by a temporal distance of whiling; rather, they come together in the selfsame happening of being as a coming-to-be that is simultaneously a going-away. Yet this unity is sundered in the conceptual thinking that places the human being at the center of this phenomenon and makes its "truth" dependent upon human apprehension. Within this metaphysical perspective being is thought as that which is *present* before the subject in a form that is stable and constant. We can find traces of this metaphysics of standing presence in the etymology of presence as that which "is" (from *esse*, v. Latin "to be") "before" (*prae*) us.[64] But the early Greeks, Heidegger tells us, experienced being as an *event* of truth, the happening of coming forth and going away as *a-letheia*, un-concealing/concealing. As he puts it, "As it reveals itself in beings, being withdraws" (EGT, 26/GA 5, 337). Within metaphysics, "being" is stable presence, whereas "becoming" is transitory change within beings, the coming and departing that happens to a "substance." For Heidegger, however, "If becoming *is*, then we must think being so essentially that it does not simply include becoming in some vacuous conceptual manner, but rather in such a way that being sustains and stamps the essence of becoming (*genesis-phthora*) in a way that is measured in accordance with being [*seinsmaßig*]" (EGT, 31/GA 5, 343; translation altered).

If within traditional metaphysics Heraclitus's interpretation of *physis* signifies "becoming" against the Platonic *idea* of eternal "being," for Heidegger the Anaximander fragment stands before such distinctions. What comes to language in the fragment is the Greek middle-voiced understanding of *genesis* as *ginesthai*, the coming-to-be of being in a space between the active and passive voices of subject-object metaphysics. In this intransitive happening marked by preconceptual ambiguity, there is no clear "agent" or "recipient" of an action; rather, there is activity that reciprocally appropriates what, in the language of metaphysics, we continue to designate by the terms *subject* and *object*. *Ginesthai* in this sense refers to the event-character of being, its self-reflexive, self-generating movement that appropriates beings and is appropriated by them in and through the movement of appropriation itself. Charles Scott has underscored the importance of this middle-voiced dimension in understanding Heidegger's reading of the Anaximander fragment. For Scott, *ginesthai* "says catastrophe (or passing away, withdrawing from appearance, ruin) comes to be in the coming to be, in the origin, of things. The middle-voiced *ginesthai* says that with the arising of things, nonarising also arises. Heidegger underscores the aporetic intimacy of arising and passing away when he says that that from which things arise also gives rise to their passing away. . . . The whence that gives coming to be gives, in the giving, passing away. Arising and withdrawing are of the self-enactment of origin. As coming to be comes to be, passing away, strangely, also comes to be."[65] Within this middle-voiced phenomenology of event, *ginesthai* points to the simultaneity of arising/passing away as what always already happens in the origin, as the very order of being that is anterior to the finitude, mortality, catastrophe that marks the *genesis/phthora* of beings. In simpler terms, catastrophe is not what happens "after" genesis as a kind of decline that follows upon the ripeness of birth. Rather, catastrophe is written into birthing itself as that which shows the emergence of life while hiding the giving/granting of death. Catastrophe happens in emergence as its very order or way of happening.

This Anaximandran middle-voiced understanding of *genesis* as *ginesthai* will prove decisive for Heidegger's interpretation of ethics and justice within the Western tradition. For when Heidegger comes to think the totality of beings in Anaximander he will think it in terms of a middle-voiced reading of *dike* as the order of being that orders beings: "Ordering orders [*Verfügung verfügt*] that which we call and have just called beings into being in which they are in each case only and ever beings" (BC, 95/GA 51, 111; translation altered). *Dike* for Heidegger, then, will not be understood as a form of justice accomplished through human action or volition, but will be interpreted as the middle-voiced ordering of beings by being or simply (beings') ordering order (through being). On this reading, *dike* is anterior to justice, which follows upon it as a metaphysical attempt to ascribe volition and responsibility back onto the ajudicial happening of *genesis/phthora* in the middle-voice. *Dike* names the ordering of coming-to-be as passing-away; it gives voice to the nonhuman apportioning of time that happens in the coming-to-be of passing-away and the passing-away of coming-to-be. The language of metaphysics, rooted in the subject/object bifurcation of doer and deed, follows upon this archaic insight as a way to found a legal order whereby effects can be ascribed to causes and actions to agents. Jean-Pierre Vernant has traced this bifurcation of agent and action as a break with archaic Greece claiming that the very categories of "will" and "decision" find their apotheosis in the Cartesian notion of "the responsible and autonomous subject who manifests himself in and through his actions that are imputable to him."[66] The ancient Greeks had no term for "will," Vernant insists. Instead they understood *dike* in a "border zone where human actions hinge on divine powers and where their true meaning, unsuspected by even those who initiated them and take responsibility for them is only revealed when it becomes part of an order that is beyond man and escapes him."[67] Vernant designates "law," and "will" as ideas that hang upon the notion of "the human subject as agent, the source of actions," a realm of language that follows upon the decline of the archaic Greek order.[68] As the archaic language of middle-voice thinking gives way to the metaphysical language of agency that privileges only active and passive constructions, the *dike* of tragedy succumbs to the justice of law and morality. This overarching narrative about the history of being shapes

Heidegger's reading of the Anaximander fragment against the background of *genesis* and *phthora* that he sees everywhere around him in 1946.

In the midst of Allied commissions and tribunals that everywhere sought to ascribe responsibility to Nazi party officials and private citizens, balancing the scales of justice in considering the guilt of the German *Volk*, Heidegger will turn back to the archaic language of *dike* as a way of preparing a leap (*Sprung*) to the first beginning (*Ursprung, arche*) in the hopes of initiating a turn (*Kehre*) to an "other" beginning.[69] In Anaximander's references to *diken* and *adikias* respectively, Heidegger finds a way of thinking the measure of *physis* in terms of what is measured by being (*seinsmässig*) (EGT, 31/H, 316). *Dike* and *adikia*—traditionally translated into German as *Gerechtigkeit* (justice) and *Ungerechtigkeit* (injustice)—will be thought together by Heidegger as a Heraclitean unity-in-opposition, much like *genesis/phthora*. He will translate *dike* as *Fug* (order) and *adikia* as *Un-Fug* (disorder), attempting to think them in a preconceptual way as the order of being anterior to justice and injustice. On Heidegger's reading, beings come into presence in an order that is simultaneously a disorder. That is, what is present (*das Anwesende*) has its essence (*Wesen*) not in a permanent state of perdurance, but in a transitivity *between* arriving and departing. Beings linger awhile; they experience the transition between a "twofold absence" (namely, their pastness and futurity) that comes to presence in their lingering. Baldly stated, beings "are" in the transitional movement from past to future that is the present. But presence itself is never permanent; it is always already marked by absence: the past has departed, the future has not yet arrived. This "between" of temporal presence and absence, "between coming forth and passing away," between *genesis* and *phthora*, Heidegger names "*der Fug*" (order) (EGT, 41–43/GA 5, 357).

Going back to *Introduction to Metaphysics* where Heidegger first dared to translate *dike* as "Fug," he designated this word as one of his master terms for "being."

> Being, *physis*, is—as sway—originary gatheredness: *logos*.
>
> Being is jointure-giving order [*fügender Fug*]: *dike*. (IM, 171/GA 40, 169)

Furthermore, in his first set of Nietzsche lectures, Heidegger writes that "philosophy is knowledge of *dike*, of the conjoining laws [*Fügungsgesetze*] of the being of beings" (N i, 166/GA 43, 204). In the Anaximander essay Heidegger will explicitly think these "conjoining laws" with reference to the temporally particular "whiling" of beings in their tension between *genesis/*

phthora. Beings linger "between" coming-to-be and passing-away where this "between" functions as a "joining" of each in a jointure (*Fuge*) that sets limits to beings' lingering. *Dike* is the name for this temporal ordering. Beings rebel, however, against this ordering and cling to their own "sheer perdurance" opposing the jointure of being itself. And yet this ontic rebellion against the ontological order of *dike*, one that sets things "out of joint" (*aus den Fugen*) in a way that renders beings *adikias* does not constitute an overturning of *dike*. On the contrary, *Dike* holds sway in and through whatever is *adikias*. That is, being grants a certain temporal fate to beings, marking their coming-to-be with the limit of perishing. This granting of jointure can not be thought of as either a divine or kingly dispensation of anthropomorphic justice, Heidegger claims. It is much more a middle-voiced happening whereby order orders in a way that grants disorder, understanding all the while that disorder belongs to order, is an expression of the originary *polemos* within order itself that comes to presence as disorder. As Heidegger puts it:

> What belongs to that which is present [*Anwesenden*] is the jointure [*Fuge*] of its while [*Weile*], which it articulates [*verfugt*] in its approach and withdrawal. In the jointure whatever lingers awhile keeps to its while. It does not incline toward the disjunction [*Un-Fuge*] of sheer persistence. The jointure belongs to whatever lingers awhile, which in turn belongs to this jointure. The jointure is order [*Die Fuge ist der Fug*].
>
> *Dike*, thought on the basis of being as presencing, is the ordering-enjoining order [*der fugend-fügende Fug*]. *Adikia*, disjunction [*Un-fuge*] is disorder [*Un-Fug*]. (EGT, 43/GA 5, 357)

In the paronomasic language of *Fug*, *Un-Fug*, *fugend*, *fügende*, *verfügend*, *Fügung*, *Gefüge*, *sich fügen*, and other cognate terms, Heidegger tries to bring to language the unity-in-difference of Anaximandran being as *dike*. Rather than seizing upon the standard metaphors of penalty, debt, recompense, or retribution, Heidegger attempts a middle-voiced rendering of justice as an order that appropriates the disorder of temporally particular beings, that grants to them the possibility of letting them be. Being as *dike* lets *adikia* into its order just as, in good middle-voiced reciprocity, *adikia* lets *dike* order it. The polemical play and interplay of *dike* and *adikia*, like that of *genesis* and *phthora*, *presence* and *absence*, order and disorder, lets the jointure of being "get over" (in the sense of *Verwindung*) beings' disorder.[70] Here, Heidegger will venture a rather complex leap into the archaic lexicon of Anaximandran thinking by offering his own rather questionable "translations" of terms such as *to chreon*, *tisis*, and *didonai*.[71] But, at root, what Heidegger seeks in all these daring translations is a language of comportment for a nonmetaphysical *ethos* of dwelling within the polemical order of being, an attunement of letting-be—*Gelassenheit*. This middle-voiced reinterpretion of *ethos* in the late Heidegger thinks *Aufenthalt* not as "ethics," but as a sojourn, dwelling, or abode, that lingers awhile "in" being. The staying power of this *ethos* does not rest on human volition or control. This acquiescing to the order of *dike*, as a "letting-be" is not a mere mood or attitude, but an attuning to being that attunes us in and through our attuning by being. This sense of "being-in" the order of *dike*, of letting ourselves be appropriated by being functions as another of the middle-voiced performances of *Ereignis* that mark Heidegger's thought of the *Kehre*.

In the work after *Beiträge zur Philosophie (vom Ereignis)* (1936–38), Heidegger will attempt a wide-ranging middle-voiced performance of almost all his earlier themes. This will involve a rethinking of active/passive constructions in ways that now focus on pure performativity: on the medial status of language "between" agent and action, subject and object, beings and being. Hence, Heidegger will write in 1945: "*Gelassenheit* [the *ethos* of releasement] lies—if one may speak here of lying—outside the distinction between activity and passivity . . . because it does not belong to the domain of the will" (GA 77, 109). In many of the late Heidegger's various constructions—"*die Sprache spricht*," "*das Wesen der Wahrheit ist die Wahrheit des Wesens*," "*die Haltung des Aufenthalts*," and "*Nähe waltet im Nähern als das Dingen des Dinges*"—we can detect the same attunement to the medial realm "outside" the distinction between activity and passivity (OWL, 124/GA 12, 243; PM, 153/GA 9, 201; GA 55, 206; GA 7, 179). But there are other constructions too that attempt such an attunement, even if they are less obvious. In phrases such as "*es gibt*"—the "there is"/"it gives" of being—"*Geschick*," "*Lichtung*," "*Ereignis*," "*bewahren*," "*wesen*," and others Heidegger offers a new language of appropriation, of that stance "in" being that occurs outside the realm of the active and the passive. In his notebooks of 1938–39, Heidegger explains this in terms of what he calls *Sein-lassen* ("letting-be") and *Inständigkeit* (inabidingness):

> One is of the opinion that letting a being be as how and what it is, is to be simply achieved by being indifferent to beings, by understanding nothing about them and by taking nothing away from them.
>
> But, on the contrary, "letting be" [*Sein-lassen*] presupposes the utmost inabiding [*Inständigkeit*] the truth of the essence of be-ing [*Seyn*].
>
> The more essentially the human being's essence is wrested free of animality and spirituality, the more he is allotted into the

> inabiding, understood as the inner persevering in the grounding of the truth of being.
>
> Letting beings be must be kept at the most distant remove from any intrusion into what is straightforwardly actual as the "effective" and "successful." (M, 86/GA 66, 103; translation altered)

This Heideggerian insistence on our abiding "in" being (in the sense of *Inständigkeit*) as a standing-in and exposing ourselves to the openness of being comprises part of Heidegger's "turn" from the anthropocentric language of *Being and Time* toward the middle-voiced language of *Ereignis* and *Gelassenheit*. In his early Freiburg lectures Heidegger had taken up the notion of "being-in" a situation from the Pauline formulae "I in Christ" and "Christ in me" that pointed to the kairological experience of temporal union with the eternal. In Paul's claim that "it is no longer I who live, but it is Christ who lives in me" (*Galatians* 2:20), Heidegger finds an opening into the phenomenological realm of care (*Sorge*) that would become decisive in his account of "being-in" from *Being and Time* (SZ, 130–80).[72] But this late Heideggerian term, *Inständigkeit*, performs a middle-voiced conversion of the anthropocentric notion of "being-in" as "care" by thinking the belonging-together of be-ing and human being in the appropriative event (*Ereignis*) of being. Hence, Heidegger can write in *Beiträge*:

> The "there" [*Da*] is the open "between" of earth and world that lights up and shelters them. It is the medial point [*Mitte*] of their strife and thus the site of their innermost be-longing and the ground of the "to-oneself," the *self* and selfhood. The *self* is never "I." The *being-with-itself of the self* comes to presence [*west*] as the inabiding in the taking-over of the self in its appropriation [*Er-eignung*]. Selfhood is belongingness to the intimacy of strife as the coming-to-strife of appropriation. . . .
>
> With the grounding of Da-*sein* all relations to beings are transformed and the truth of be-ing [*die Wahrheit des Seyns*] is experienced for the first time. (GA 65, 322)

In this difficult, enigmatic language of *Seyn* and *Ereignis* we can see Heidegger groping for a lexicon to express something of the powerful experience of Pauline-Lutheran faith and National Socialist commitment that shaped his works from 1918–1938. In his fervor to find his way inside the truth of being, to penetrate to its core in a Nietzschean experience of joyful wisdom, Heidegger had understood his own reticence to let go of will, volition, duty, and service (*Dienst*), all of those robust virtues of his Christian, National Socialist, and Nietzschean incarnations. As he rethinks the language of *Inständigkeit*, however, Heidegger begins to find a passage to the world of pre-Socratic experience, of a "standing-in" the openness of being that is marked by an experience of "care" that is non-anthropocentric and that lets the human being be appropriated by the truth of being (PM, 284/GA 9, 374). But this phrase "appropriated by" reflects the passive construction of both a poor translation and the inadequacy of our language (both English and German) to convey the Greek experience of the middle voice. In his attempt to both appropriate and be appropriated by "The Verdict of Anaximander" in its double genitival sense, Heidegger turns to the language of *dike* as *Fug* and its cognates of *Fügung, Verfügung, sich fügen, fügend,* etc. as a way of performing his own middle-voiced turn in the language of metaphysics. Now the human-focused notion of care will be transformed into the pre-Socratic experience of *dike* and *ethos*, of a reciprocal caring and being cared-for, of sheltering and being-sheltered, that comes to presence in the term *Inständigkeit*. In his 1951 essay "Building Dwelling Thinking," Heidegger would bring together this insistent power of dwelling "in" the truth of being with the whole lexical family of words deriving from the master term *Fug*—which attempts to think Anaximander's notion of *dike*. Hence, Heidegger writes:

> The essence of building is letting dwell. The enactment of the essence of building is the setting up [*Errichten*] of locations through the joining [*das Fügen*] of their spaces. *Only if we are capable of dwelling [Wohnen], can we build.* Let us think for a while [*Weile*] of a farmhouse in the Black Forest, which peasant-dwelling built some two hundred years ago. Here the in-abidingness [*Inständigkeit*] of the power to let earth and heaven, divinities and mortals enter in [*einzulassen*] *simple oneness* into things, ordered [*gerichtet*] the house. (PLT, 160/GA 7, 162)[73]

Here, we find a range of terms that attempt a middle-voiced interpretation of "dwelling" akin to the one Heidegger alluded to in "The Letter on Humanism" with his references to *ethos* as the site of dwelling and language as the "house of being" (PM, 253–54/GA 9, 333). For Heidegger, "The way the human being in his proper essence becomes present to being [*anwest*] is ecstatic inherence [*Innestehen*] in the truth of being." Moreover, the site of this in-dwelling in being for the human being is language, which appropriates the human being and, in turn, "is propriated [*ereignet*] by being and enjoined through [*durchfügte*] being" (PM, 254/GA 9, 333). All of these efforts to think through dwelling as an event of appropriation—where being lets human beings enter the openness of a site where they can be appropriated, the fourfold of earth and sky, gods and mortals, the topology of being—attempt to say the words of Anaximander within the nonmetaphysical register of a middle-voiced, poetic saying of *dike*, *ethos*, dwelling, and order. If, in what is proper to us, we let appropriation overtake us by taking up its call, by inabiding in its exposure, we begin to respond to a proper sense of dwelling in the jointure allotted to us. This would be the task of a Heideggerian thinking appropriated by the pre-Socratic experience of order and *dike* that Heraclitus named *harmonia*. In "What is that—Philosophy?" Heidegger tries to show how such an experience is anterior to "philosophy" in its technical sense.

> The Greek word *philosophia* goes back to the word *philosophos*. . . . The word *philosophos* was presumably coined by Heraclitus. This signifies: for Heraclitus there is as yet no *philosophia*. An *aner philosophos* is not a "philosophical" man. The Greek adjective *philosophos* says something completely different from the adjective philosophical. An *aner philosophos* is *hos phile to sophon*, he who loves the *sophon*; *philein*, to love, signifies here, in Heraclitus' sense *homolegein*, to speak [*sprechen*] as the logos speaks, that is, to correspond [*entsprechen*] with the *logos*. This correspondence is in accord with the *sophon*. Accord is *harmonia*. That one being reciprocally joins itself to [*sich fügt*] another, that both are joined to one another in an originary way [*ürsprünglich einander fügen*] because they are ordered and fitted to each other [*zueinander verfügt*]—this *harmonia* is the distinguishing mark of *philein*, of "loving," thought in its Heraclitean sense. (WiP, 14–15/GA 11, 13–14; translation altered)[74]

The thinking that comes both before and after "philosophy," the thinking of the pre-Socratic order of being as *Fug*, *harmonia*, *dikē*, attunes itself to being's withdrawal, to the *lethic* dimension of all that "occurs essentially" (*west*). For such thinking to happen, the human being must let itself be appropriated, must *stand in* (*Inständigkeit*) the truth of being as *aletheia* that opens itself in the reciprocal joining, fitting, and ordering of beings by being—what Anaximander and Heraclitus name *dike* and Heidegger terms *Fug*. If the traditional translations of the Anaximander fragment consider it in a legal and moral sense as an early example of the metaphysics of debt, retribution, and penalty, that is because they fail to think "essentially," Heidegger claims. They merely continue to translate the archaic lexicon of Anaximander with the dictionaries of Aristotelian metaphysics and Christian theology. Hence, they render Anaximander's phrase *didonai diken* as "paying penalty" or "paying retribution" whereas Heidegger will think it as "giving jointure" (*Fuge geben*) where *didonai* says something like "letting belong to" (*Gehörenlassen*) (EGT, 43–44/GA 5, 357). Being—thought of as the "it gives/there is" (*es gibt*)—lets jointure join together what is both in- and out-of-joint. *Dike* functions here as the hinge that holds together all the disjointed beings that have been granted their while upon the earth. Our fate as humans, Heidegger wants to say, is joined by the hinge of *dike* whose articulated movements can unhinge us, given our fragile situation in the while in which we linger. We are not in control of the hinge. We have no *techne* at our disposal (*Verfügung*) that can order the movement of the hinge in accord with a human measure of justice. When we try to fasten the hinge to a temporarily particular while, so as to make it eternal, things come out of joint. We can not simply "overcome" (in the sense of an *Überwindung*) this disjointure (*adikia*) of being by asserting a human order through will and mastery. Rather, the only thing left to us is a "getting over" (*eine Verwindung*) of disjointure.[75]

When beings cling to themselves, Heidegger claims, they "stubbornly follow the inclination to persist in hanging on, and indeed to insist on persisting. [They] aim at everlasting continuance, no longer paying heed to *dike*, the order [*Fug*] of the while [*Weile*]" (EGT, 45/GA 5, 359; translation altered). Only if we let the order of *dike* belong to beings, only if we "let or allow something to be itself"—that is, show it "consideration" (*Rücksicht*) can we "get over" the disjointure of beings. In a complex etymological turn to the Middle High German term *ruoche* which he deems the root term for the word *Ruch* (*reck*), Heidegger finds this sense of letting order belong in the word *care* (*Sorge*) (EGT, 46–47/GA 5, 360–61). But as with all the middle-voiced turnings of the late Heidegger's language, now care, which was the basic mode of "being-in" in *Being and Time*, will be thought in non-anthropocentric terms as being's mode of appropriating beings, as well as beings' way of letting themselves be appropriated. This reciprocal hinge connecting being and beings, Heidegger claims, is thought in Anaximander's word *tisis*—German *Ruch*, English *reck*, which signifies "to have care or concern for," "to take heed of."[76] Beings come to presence (*wesen*) in the hinge of *dike* that lets the enjoining (*Fügung*) between *genesis* and *phthora* belong to the order (*Fug*) that "gives reck" (*Ruch geben*) or care to the whiling of beings. *Ruch* (reck) in this sense is a letting something remain in its essence as what is proper to it—namely, its whiling. Hence, Heidegger claims, "*tisis* as reck corresponds to *dike* as order (*Fug*)" where *dike* names the truth of being itself. All of this happens, Anaximander tells us, "according to necessity" (*kata to chreon*) (EGT, 46/GA 5, 360).

Before Heidegger lays out his own translation of *to chreon*, he simply declares: "*to chreon* is the oldest name in which thinking brings the being of beings to language" (EGT, 49/GA 5, 363). Against the standard translations of *to chreon* as "necessity," "what is compelling," and "that which inescapably must be," Heidegger ventures a radical transfer of its meaning by tracing this term back to *cheir* (hand) and *chrao* ("to place in someone's hands," "to hand over" or "deliver") which he then thinks as "to let something belong to someone" (EGT, 52/GA 5, 366). The operative frame of reference here, Heidegger tells us, is not one of compulsion or constraint, still less of things that "must be." Rather, Heidegger writes, "we will dare a translation that sounds strange and which can easily be misinterpreted: *to chreon*, usage [*der Brauch*]" (EGT, 52/GA 5, 366).

> "Usage" [*Brauch*] as the word that translates *to chreon* should not be understood in these current, derived senses. We should rather keep to the root-meaning: to use is to brook [*brauchen ist bruchen*], in Latin *frui*, in German *fruchten*, *Frucht*. We translate this freely as "to enjoy" which originally means to be pleased with something and so to have it in use. . . . "To use" accordingly suggests: to let something present come to presence as such; *frui*, to brook, to use, usage means: to hand something over to its own essence and to keep it in hand, preserving [*währenden*] it as something present. . . .
>
> As dispenser of portions of the jointure, usage is the destining joining [*das zuschickende Fügen*]: the enjoining of order [*die Verfügung des Fugs*] and thereby of reck. (EGT, 53/GA 5, 367)

This sense of usage as bound up with the order of *dike* opens a pathway into the late Heidegger's understanding of poetic thinking as a way of preparing for a new *ethos* of dwelling. Whereas traditional philosophers think *Brauch* and usage as "custom" (*ethos* in its anthropocentric sense), Heidegger wants to uncover its nonmetaphysical sense as that which lets order presence itself even amidst disorder.[77] Something of this nonmetaphysical understanding of *brauchen* comes to Heidegger through Hölderlin who often uses the verb *brauchen* to signify the belonging together of gods and mortals in their dwelling upon the earth.[78] In *Was heißt Denken?* Heidegger draws upon this Hölderlinian use of *brauchen* from the last stanza of "Der Ister":

> Es brauchet aber Stiche der Fels
> Und die Erd',
> Unwirthbar wär es, ohne Weile;

where Hölderlin thinks of *brauchen* in middle-voiced terms (in John Llewelyn's thoughtful translation):

> It is however meet that the rock be broached
> And the earth furrowed,
> Without welcome would it be else, unabiding;

Again, Heidegger will think here of the primordial connection between *ethos* and *dike* as a nonmoral reciprocity of human beings and being, of the "necessity" of "letting be" as a way of finding the proper measure for dwelling upon the earth. To abide in being between *genesis* and *phthora* means here to find an abode granted by what *physis* allows. This means finding an *ethos*, a proper mode of comportment attuned to the overarching order (*Fug*) of being within which the human being finds it sojourn, stay, or halt (*Aufenthalt*). Heidegger's use of the term *Brauch* points to his larger concern with Anaximander's *dike*—an order of being within which mortals can dwell between *genesis/phthora*, birth/death where the rock and shaft, earth and furrow come together in the poetic rendering of "*es brauchet*" ("it is meet") to form an essential order of belonging within which the human being finds its proper fit. What is "fitting" here is the measured allotment meted out by this order of being. In this "essential belonging" (*Wesenszugehörigkeit*), the dwelling of mortals finds its proper measure (GA 8, 196). In English, the etymological affinity between what is "meet" and the "meting" out of measure finds its resonance in the ancient Greek term *metron* from whence it is formed. As a noun, "meet" signifies a boundary stone that measures what is fitting or proper; as a verb, it designates the process of allotting, distributing, apportioning, and measuring. To express the Hölderlinian relation of essential belonging as what is "meet" means to understand it as a form of poetic dwelling that lets itself belong to what is proper to it. What the Anaximander fragment signifies for Heidegger, then, is a verdict or a "saying the true" (*ver-dictare*) that *lets* the human being *belong* (*Gehörenlassen*) to an order of being that is shaped in the "between" of *genesis* and *phthora*. This order or *Fug* is understood as the jointure (*Fuge*) between approach and withdrawal. *Brauch* in this sense "means: to let something present come to presence as such; *frui*, to brook (*bruchen*), to use (*brauchen*), usage (*Brauch*) means: to hand something over to its essence and as so present, to keep it in hand" (EGT, 53/GA 5, 367). In this "handing something over" we thereby let it properly belong to what is its own. Here, the Hölderlinian echoes of the Böhlendorff letter can be read in Heidegger's interpretation of the Anaximander fragment.

On this reading, originary justice—thought as *Fug/dike*—would constitute the giving/granting of being its due. It would mean that doing justice to beings would be understood as letting them belong to the order of the while—between the absence of the no longer and the absence of the not yet. What letting belong asks of us is to let be, a comportment or *Haltung* of holding oneself up in the "between" of this double absence. The *Haltung* of *Gelassenheit* or "releasement," then, involves us in an original responsibility to other beings to release them from our grasp and to let them belong to an order (*Fug*) that is the order of *dike*. *Dike* here does not constitute a present state of affairs or a standard of justice that can be pointed to as a fixed measure. Rather, *dike* consists in the meting out of balance that is "meet" or that befits us and within which we can abide responsibly as the beings that we are, beings whose stay on earth is measured by the gauge of the between—of heaven and earth, of the no longer and the not yet, of *genesis* and *phthora*. Anaximander's *dike*, like Hölderlin's poetic measure, "measures out the human being's dwelling, its sojourn on the earth beneath the sky" (PLT, 221/GA 7, 199). This "between" is less a permanent state than a relation that is marked by the play of pres-ab-ence and the temporally particular character of our sojourn. *Dike* is formed in this between, in the jointure of how the lingering of the particular is *gefügt* or fitted within the order of being.

The "between" becomes a space for measuring oneself against the godhead, a metric that honors the unknown dimension of the godhead as that which is other and inaccessible. To dwell poetically means here to acknowledge the power of this unknown order that, as *dike*, *fügt* (joins together) and *verfügt* (disposes) an order of responsiveness or responsibility to that which exceeds knowability and control. In the late work, Heidegger attempts to address this issue by calling for an *ethos* of releasement/*Gelassenheit* as a way of fostering an attunement to such a responsibility. In the Anaximander essay Heidegger claims that *adikia*/*Un-fug*/dis-order is the fundamental trait of being. To do justice to this character of being as that which is "out of joint," poetic thinking attunes itself to this lack of order as the unknown and absential dimension of being itself. Here, being gives itself in its granting of the "there is" or "*es gibt*" as that which simultaneously withholds itself. *Brauchen*, then, comes to mean the way being disposes or *verfügt* its order by preserving the play between granting and withholding as a joining together (*fügen*). By translating *to chreon* as *Brauchen*, Heidegger thinks a Hölderlinian order (*Fug*) of justice where "it is meet" that beings come to belong together through a *Haltung* of letting belong, a poetic *ethos* of dwelling that lets order manifest itself in the disorder of temporal whiling.

In *What Calls Forth Thinking?* (WS 1951/52) Heidegger returns to the same problem that he articulated in "The Verdict of Anaximander" by thinking *Brauchen* in terms of releasement. There he writes: "*Brauchen* is: to let something into its essence, is safeguarding it in its essence" (WCT, 187/GA 8, 190). And in these same lectures Heidegger identifies the Hölderlinian poetic phrase "*es brauchet*" ("it is meet") with the "*es gibt*" of the self-giving of being, a middle-voiced event that appropriates the human being into its order, or *Fug*. This whole complex of themes is deeply related to Heidegger's notion of poetic dwelling—understood as the proper way of bringing the human being into this way of being as releasement or as letting *dike* flourish, names that signify the originary event of being. In our belonging to the order of *dike*, being and human being correspond (*entsprechen*) in a way that makes us responsive to the claim that being has upon us. In responding to this claim (*Anspruch*) we become responsible to/for what can never be appropriated, but what remains other, alien, uncanny. In attuning ourselves to this uncanny dimension of being, an attunement that can only happen in and as poetic dwelling, we find ourselves "between" *genesis/phthora* and come to let this uncanny relation belong to us even as we let go of our claims to arrogation and control. In attempting to find this balance of *dike* and a measure for letting this order belong, the human being comes to dwell poetically.

But let us be clear. Heidegger never claims a measure *for* being. On the contrary, he will always emphasize that being is incommensurable with any human measure. Measure happens in that we let ourselves be measured in the "between" of mortals and gods that happens in the event of presencing as *genesis/phthora*. This, Heidegger wants to say, in a language that is barely sayable, is the meaning of *to chreon* as one of the many names for the event of being: presencing (*an-wesen*) as the revealing-concealing play of truth that marks the human being's whiling upon the earth. Hence, Heidegger can write, "Disposing order and reck, usage lets go of each present being into whiling and delivers each to its own whiling" (*Der Brauch läßt, Fug und Ruch verfügend, in die Weile los und überläßt das Anwesende je seiner Weile*) (EGT, 54/GA 5, 368). As he ends his essay on "The Verdict of Anaximander," Heidegger then comes to deliver his own verdict on the state of German guilt and expiation in 1946. Speaking of "rescue" in terms strikingly different from those of his contemporaries, Heidegger writes:

> Is there any rescue? Rescue comes when and only when danger *is*. Danger *is* when being itself reaches its extremity and when the oblivion that issues from being itself, undergoes reversal. But what if being, in its essence, needs to use [*braucht*] the essence of the human being? What if the essence of the human being rests in thinking the truth of being? Then thinking must poetize on the riddle of being. It brings what is to be thought into nearness with the earliest of what has been thought. (EGT, 57–58/GA 5, 373; translation altered)

In the ruins of a Germany devastated by air strikes, Allied occupation, and the trauma of dislocation and defeat, Heidegger offers his own verdict about the truth of German devastation, finding it not merely in homelessness and depredation, but in the essential forgetting of the concealed truth of Anaximander's *Spruch*. Thought essentially, Anaximander's verdict passes a sentence (*Spruch*) on the modern age as one that lacks an eye for originary justice, a justice not of human making, but one that dispenses itself to all beings by handing over what is in each case present into its while (EGT, 55/GA 5, 369). What this verdict signifies remains concealed in the ligatures of Anaximander's language even as it gets further obscured beneath the palimpsest of philological exegesis in the history of metaphysics. Still, Heidegger holds out genuine hope that in the traces or *Spuren* of Anaximander's hidden words, there might be a presentiment of a justice that is not humanly constructed but prevails as the order of a poetic measuring that grants the gift of measure to all that is. To abide in that measure as a way of dwelling upon the earth becomes for Heidegger a way of "saving the earth" as the responsibility of human beings.

HEIDEGGER'S POETIC MEASURE: THE HÖLDERLINIAN *ETHOS* OF DWELLING

Already in the 1930s Heidegger had taken up the thematics of "saving" and "rescue" in his Hölderlin lectures and had intimated that Hölderlin's words might become the language of the future (GA 65, 422). In his 1951 lecture, ". . . Poetically Dwells the Human Being," Heidegger turns to an analysis of Hölderlin's late poem "In lovely blueness" as a way of thinking the thematics of "rescue" as a question about poetic measure and the problem of limits. In a postwar Germany still reeling from the migration, expatriation, and resettlement of diverse ethnic groups within and without the borders of the newly formed German Federal Republic (1949), Heidegger takes up the question of authentic dwelling as a way of addressing the pressing matter of homelessness that shapes the problems of the moment. But, as Heidegger will claim, apart from any issues about the German housing shortage or the rebuilding of devastated cities, the question of dwelling cannot properly be thought of in terms of social or economic dislocation. Rather, the authentic meaning of dwelling has the character of an "event"—in Heidegger's sense of *Ereignis*—an event that measures our present destitution and raises both the question and the possibility of what it means to be human. In "Building Dwelling Thinking" (1951), Heidegger places emphasis on the question of dwelling as a way to come to terms with both the poverty of our historical homelessness and our need to find a home upon the earth. There, he addresses the very question of what dwelling signifies: "To be a human being means: to be on the earth as a mortal. It means: to dwell. . . . Dwelling is . . . the fundamental character of human being. . . . Human being consists in dwelling and, indeed, dwelling in the sense of the sojourn (*Aufenthalt*) of mortals upon the earth." (PLT, 147–49/GA 7, 149–51).

Yet Heidegger is well aware that in the epoch of technological dominion driven by the metaphysics of will and machination, the possibility of genuine dwelling is denied to us. In the face of an age that is marked by frantic production, planning, calculation, and attempts at control and mastery, we experience the uncanny effects of not-being-at-home even in the spheres of experience that are most familiar to us. How are human beings supposed to dwell, then, in a world torn and shattered by the abyssal errancy of world war and national ambition? How are we to find our way through the nihilism that pervades the world's night? What possibilities remain for us in the destitute time of being's withdrawal that has shaped the fates of modern humans? Heidegger attempts to address these questions not by offering timely observations on the plight of modern Germany but, rather, by turning to a meditation on the poetry of Hölderlin, especially his late poem "In lovely blueness," which raises the question about the proper measure for human beings in the age of the gods' withdrawal. For Heidegger, the economic crisis and the housing shortage that besets Germany in 1951 is merely an epiphenomenal manifestation of a long-standing homelessness whose roots go back to the metaphysics of modern technology and its unidimensional grasp of being as "resources" available on constant standing reserve to be calculated, consumed, and stockpiled for instrumental purposes. ". . . Poetically Dwells the Human Being" takes up the challenge of our ontological homelessness while attempting to frame it against the possibility of poetic dwelling, understood as both a sojourn (*Aufenthalt*) and an *ethos*. In his late work, Heidegger variously restates his claim that "[t]hrough their incessant activity, modern technology and the scientific industrialization of the world set about to extinguish every possibility of sojourning (*Aufenthalten*)" (GA 75, 244). Still, in his meditations on Hölderlin's poetry, Heidegger persists in seeking ways to open up new possibilities for dwelling against the devastation and violence wrought by World War II. Only by acknowledging our present destitution and homelessness, Heidegger tells us, can we mortals "bring dwelling to the fullness of its being (*Wesen*)" (PLT, 161/GA 7, 164).

In ". . . Poetically Dwells the Human Being," Heidegger seeks to make us aware of our own situation of homelessness as one caught up in an unpoetic, calculative approach to our existence. Moreover, he claims, "it could be that our unpoetic way of dwelling—its inability to take the measure (*das Maß zu nehmen*)—derives from a curious excess (*Übermaß*) of frantic measuring and calculating" (PLT, 228, 215, 218/GA 7, 207, 195, 196). For Heidegger, authentic dwelling or *Wohnen* is quite unusual (*ungewöhnlich*); it can only come about through what he terms an "other form of building," a building that, as poetizing, genuinely "lets us dwell." Here, Heidegger will think poetizing (*Dichten*) as the authentic form of letting-dwell (*Wohnenlassen*), as that which "first brings the human being onto the earth and to it and in this way brings it into dwelling." Such poetizing is fundamentally nothing other than a measure-taking of the human being's sojourn/*Aufenthalt* upon the earth. Poetry measures the boundaries and limits of what is appropriate for human beings. It shapes the human being's *ethos*, its proper way of dwelling and holding itself within the boundaries of the fourfold. Through poetic measure we discover what fits, what is our due, what is proper. Such measuring lets the human being come into its proper sense of self, its ownness (*Eigenes*): "Only insofar as the human being takes the measure of its dwelling is it able to be commensurate with its essence (*seinem Wesen gemäß zu sein*)" (PLT, 221/GA 7, 199).

In his marginal notations to his own copy of ". . . Poetically Dwells the Human Being," Heidegger writes this addendum to the passage about measure, dwelling, and being commensurate with "i.e., being needed/used and need/use (*d.h, gebraucht und Brauchen*)." But what does Heidegger mean and how can we read dwelling, measure, and *Brauchen* together? There is much that needs to be untangled here. For Heidegger, the human being becomes commensurate with its essence by finding its measure in what is "meet" (*gebraucht*) or what is meted out in the middle-voiced event of commensuration that Heidegger terms "*Brauchen*" ("that which needs/uses"). In *What Calls Forth Thinking?*, written at the same time as ". . . Poetically Dwells the Human Being," Heidegger defines *Brauchen* as "letting into essence and preserving therein" (WCT, 189/GA 8, 192). In this sense, dwelling comes to mean participation in the event of being itself whereby being both needs and uses the human being in a middle-voiced relation that is marked by neither a "subjective" participation nor an "objective" being-used. *Brauchen*, then, marks a certain correspondence (*Ent-sprechen*) between the human being and the event of being in/as a belonging to each other: "In use/need (*Brauchen*), there lies a self-measuring corresponding (*das sich anmessende Entsprechen*)" (WCT, 187/GA 8, 190). This self-measuring undertaken by human beings is marked by profound limitation and finitude, a measuring whereby the human being comes into what is proper to it, what is its own (*das Eigene*). Yet such a measure is not achieved via will or volition; it happens only when we are released over to what Hölderlin calls "the Open" (*das Offene*), that realm where the human being lets the claim (*Anspruch*) of being appropriate it in the middle-voiced event of *Brauchen*. But how is this measuring bound up with dwelling, especially the poetic dwelling alluded to by Hölderlin's "In lovely blueness"?

Heidegger maintains that poetry is, essentially, nothing other than measure-taking, a measure-taking "by which the human being first receives the measure for the breadth of its being" (PLT, 222/GA 7, 200). Poetry measures the limits of what is appropriate for human beings, shaping the contours of our mortal fate. The finitude of this mortality defines our proper sojourn or *Aufenthalt*. Our poetic *ethos* measures our possibilities as beings whose ownmost way of being is a measuring projected upon our death whose inevitability, in turn, shapes our measuring. Much as Hölderlin's poem "In lovely blueness" measures the distance of the sky above the earth through the verticality of the church steeple that both connects and separates gods and mortals, Heidegger measures the unknown godhead against the metaphysical measure of human being. In the play between gods-mortals-earth-sky, Heidegger finds a way of thinking through the proper measure of poetic dwelling.

> What is the measure for human measuring? God? No. The sky? No. The manifestness of the sky? No. The measure consists in the way in which the God who remains unknown, is revealed *as* such by the sky. God's appearance through the sky consists in a disclosing that lets us see what conceals itself, but lets us see it not by seeking to wrest what is concealed out of its concealedness, but only by safeguarding the concealed in its self-concealment. Thus the unknown God appears as the unknown by way of the sky's manifestness. This appearance is the measure against which the human being measures itself. (PLT, 223/GA 7, 201)

As "the inceptual form of building (*das anfängliche Bauen*), poetizing first of all lets the dwelling of human beings into its essence. Poetizing is the originary letting-dwell (*das ursprüngliche Wohnenlassen*)" (PLT, 227/GA 7, 206). But we need to understand Heidegger's sense of "building" in poetic-ontological terms, rather than as the technical activity of masons, bricklayers, engineers, ironworkers, and welders. "The essence of building," Heidegger tells us, "is a letting-dwell" (PLT, 160, 227/GA 7, 162, 193). But such building happens only as a form of poetizing.

> The statement, *the human being dwells in that it builds*, has now been given its proper sense. The human being does not dwell in that it merely establishes its stay (*Aufenthalt*) on the earth, beneath the sky, by raising growing things and simultaneously raising buildings. The human being is capable of such building only if it already builds in the sense of the poetic taking of measure. Authentic building occurs so far as there are poets, such poets as take the measure for the architectonic, the structural enjoining (*Baugefüge*) of dwelling.

Dwelling authentically, Heidegger tells us, happens only when poets take the measure for the structural enjoining of being, for the way human dwelling—as *ethos*—opens a space/clearing for letting the gods appear beneath the sky and upon the earth. That means that only when the human being lets itself be appropriated (*vereignet*) in the event of being (*Ereignis*) can authentic dwelling happen. Such dwelling happens, however, only through poetizing—but not simply "poetry" as a specific literary form. Rather, poetizing here needs to be understood in its originary Greek sense as *poiesis*, a form of being's self-unfolding that lets world come to be. As William McNeill expresses it, "The essence of poetizing can no longer be understood as poetry in the narrow sense of poesy, as the composing of poetic works or poems. In first letting a world appear and come into being, poetizing in its essence originarily configures the dwelling site of human beings, their *ethos*."[79] That is, being manifests itself to us as "the event of an originary *poiesis* of which we are not the origin, yet which, happening in and through us, first enables our dwelling."

When, drawing upon "In lovely blueness," Heidegger writes that human dwelling upon the earth is in its essence "poetic," he means to point to the originary character of being's way of appropriating us to the event of presencing that enables our attunement. This attunement, in turn, is what allows for the possibility of dwelling, of sojourn, of *Aufenthalt*, and of *ethos*. *Physis*, understood as originary *poiesis*, is what Heidegger terms "the architectonic, the structural enjoining (*Baugefüge*) of dwelling" (PLT, 227/GA 7, 206). This structural enjoining does not exist apart from the singularity of being's constant emergence. Rather, it happens as the very event of being that opens up our space of dwelling, an event marked by the temporal particularity (*Jeweiligkeit*) of beings in each particular case. The architectonic of dwelling, then, needs to be understood as the way that each singular event of dwelling fits together for each moment within the Anaximandran play of *genesis/phthora*, birth and decline, a structure that is not fixed and permanent, but that emerges in and through the poetic measure of be-ing. Such a measure emerges in the play of the fourfold between gods and mortals, earth and sky; it can never be reckoned in advance. Hence, it remains incalculable and unknown, eluding the grasp of mortals.

In his short poem "What is God?" Hölderlin poses the enigmatic question of a poetic theophany. God is unknown, the poet tells us, yet despite this concealed dimension, God manifestly reveals his concealedness in a way that remains mysterious and impenetrable. As the poet puts it:

> . . . the more a thing
> is invisible, it yields to what is alien/
> . . . Jemehr ist eins
> Unsichtbar, schicket es sich in Fremdes. (SPF, 270–71)

In ". . . Poetically Dwells the Human Being," Heidegger finds in this alien and unknown dimension of God a hint for understanding the essence of poetic measure. Heidegger tells us that God is not the measure, rather, the measure lies in the unknown dimension of God *as* the unknown manifested by the sky's appearance. In the sky's lovely blueness God's self-concealment appears as that which conceals itself. In this appearance we find traces of a withdrawal and concealment "by which the human being measures itself" (PLT, 223/GA 7, 201).

In poetry we take the measure of this appearance by way of its self-concealment and, in so doing, we let come that which is allotted to us, that which befits the fit of being's structural enjoining. This enjoining lets the justice of being come forth in the proper span of its amplitude.[80] The poetic measure of justice would thus be found not in any human measure, but in the very event of the "*es gibt*" or "*es brauchet*" that happens in the meter of language and the metric of being. Hölderlin's poetry calls us to this poetic form of dwelling: "It waits for mortals to correspond to it. Correspondence leads to the path of a turning that enters into the nearness of the gods who have fled" (GA 4, 195). But this possibility of poetic dwelling, a possibility that defines the essence of human being, can only happen when we let the metric of being unfold as "a letting-come of what has been meted out" (PLT, 224/GA 7, 203). This letting-come as a "releasement" (*Gelassenheit*) toward beings marks our poetic *ethos* as a middle-voiced event that is neither merely passive nor active but a "*Sicheinlassen auf* in the sense of a non-willing engagement that attentively lets beings be themselves."[81] As Heidegger reminds us, "The correspondence to the being of beings always remains our abode (*Aufenthalt*)," our *ethos*, yet often we do not heed this call to respond to such a responsibility (GA 11, 20). On this reading, *ethos* comes to be understood as the correspondence of being and human being and not something that solely applies to, or emerges from, the human sphere. Here, we can speak of the ethicality of ethics as not grounded in subjectivity, but in the relation of the human being to being's withdrawal: the poetics of dwelling in an age where the gods have fled. The poetics of dwelling, then, expresses itself as an *ethos* (*Aufenthalt*) of releasement, a comportment (*Haltung*) of holding-oneself-back (*Ent-halt*) and with-holding (*Vor-enthalt*) marked by reverence, awe, reticence, and sparing. Ethics in its originary form releases us from the subjective "ethics" of rules, directives, and instrumental application and comes to be understood as the safeguarding or preserving of the open site for being's essential occurring (*Wesung*). In this turn from ethics as a habit that we have to an *ethos* or way of *in-habiting* that has us, Heidegger thinks the poetic measure of justice in a way that measures our current metric in terms of the machination of the *Gestell*. But, in the process of deconstructing ethics back to its originary character as the poetic event of being, has Heidegger bypassed the dynamic of justice itself, especially in the way he configures the relation of the poet to the ethics of the Other? This pressing question will emerge for Paul Celan as he tries to read Heidegger's understanding of poetic measure, not from the sheltered precinct of Greco-German affinity, but from the alien sphere of Hebrew ethics marked by profound alterity.

THREE

PAUL CELAN: THE POETICS OF CAESURA

> Justice . . . always has an eschatological dimension.
>
> —Jacques Derrida, *Taste of the Secret*

> Justice won't wait; it is to be done at every instant, to be realized all the time.
>
> —Blanchot, *The Writing of the Disaster*

OF A JUSTICE TO COME: CELAN, DERRIDA, AND THE APORETICS OF JUSTICE

Already at the beginning of philosophy, before Plato conceived the dialogue-form as the most fitting mode of philosophical exchange, the Greeks spoke of *aporia*—of being unable to find one's way out, of being caught in a cul-de-sac without finding the means of egress. To think the *aporia*—or that which is a/porous, without porosity—means to understand the limits of the way or path of thinking itself. But to enter into the *aporia* also means that one confront it not simply *as* a limit or boundary that cuts off the possibility of finding one's way. Rather, it means to dwell at the limit so that limitation itself might be thought of as something productive, as perhaps leading to a way of thinking philosophy as a discourse of the limit that embraces limitation as a positive phenomenology of the threshold and as a way into the horizonality of experience. It is in this sense that Derrida, in his essay "The Force of Law," writes about what he calls "the experience of the aporia":

> As its name indicates, an *experience* is a traversal, something that traverses and travels toward a destination for which it finds passage. The experience finds its way, its passage, it is possible. Yet,

> in this sense there can not be a full experience of aporia, that is, of something that does not allow passage. *Aporia* is a nonpath.[1]

In the *aporia* we confront the impossibility of traversal, of the lack of possibility, of coming up against a roadblock that cuts off the path leading outward. Yet, as Derrida grasps it, this very "experience" of the *aporia*—the *ex* + *peras* as a "venturing outward" (CP, 110–11/GA 65, 159—61)—can also open us up to a tension, paralysis, or blockage that gives birth to the urgent need to act or decide in the very midst of such paralysis. It is as if by acknowledging the impossibility of traversal we come to a decision about what becomes possible, as if the experience of the limit provides the impetus to decide how to negotiate the limit in a new and creative way.[2] In confronting the *aporia* of the non-path, we come to a decision about a possible path for traversing the non-path. It is within this aporetic experience of the impossibility of traversal that the very problem of justice begins.

On Derrida's reading, justice "happens" precisely where it can never happen—in the *present*. For justice always eludes the present. It eludes the axiomatics of calendrical and historical time bursting upon the present as absence itself, as what precipitously demands of us that we decide "now"—but not the now of chronological succession that provides unity and continuity within the historical pageant of calculable time. Rather, the time of justice—if we can venture such a *topos*—is a "now"-time on the order of Walter Benjamin's notion of *Jetztzeit* in his "Theses on the Philosophy of History."[3] For Benjamin, now-time breaks the line of continuity that establishes the order of narrative history; it bursts asunder the rosary-bead sequentiality of the calendar and the clock. With the now-time of Benjamin's philosophy of history we confront the messianic moment of shock that awakens us to the call of what is to come, of a futurity that will never be present but will always be deferred. And yet it is precisely this deferral that elicits the urgent call for a "justice to come." Justice is messianic. It is that which we all await and yet that which never comes. The invocation to justice as a call for what is still to come, what still eludes the all-encompassing grasp of the present, shares with the messianic the character of the *avenir*, of the "to come." In the aporias of the present, where the path to justice is blocked, we confront the impossibility of justice as something incalculable. As Derrida formulates it, justice is inextricably tied to law even as law itself never instantiates justice. The existing order, structure, hierarchy of law inevitably fails to achieve justice; whether in the court room, the hospital, the assembly, the clinic, the barracks, or the prison, law fails to bring about social justice. Indeed, at times such institutions themselves implement or carry out laws to thwart the very possibility of justice (one need only think of *topoi* such as electroshock therapy, lethal injection, apartheid, the labyrinth of institutional health care, U.S. immigration laws and deportation practices). In such cases where "en-forcing" law becomes a matter of co-optation and control, we can perceive all too clearly the astonishing gap that obtains between law and justice.

Yet justice requires law, requires that an attempt be made to performatively enact the judicial injunction to make things right, to find a balance between power and freedom. In this space, gap, or *khora* between justice and law, Derrida finds the opening for a way to deconstruct the law and to hold out the promise of the undeconstructibility of justice: "Justice is not the law. . . . Justice is not reducible to the law, to a given system of legal structures. That means that justice is always unequal to itself. It is non-coincident with itself."[4] In other words, justice is never present to itself in the present but always exceeds presence by demanding that the impoverished state of justice in the present be urgently addressed "now" in terms of the future possibility of justice, of that which is im/possible. Despite the cynical manipulation of the trope of justice in political-juridical-social-economic discourse for immediate gain, Derrida holds out the hope for a "justice to come."

> Justice remains *to come*, it remains *by coming* [*la justice reste à venir*], it *has* to come [*elle a à venir*], it *is* to-come, the to-come [*elle est à-venir*], it deploys the very dimension of events irreducibly to come. It will always have it, this *à-venir* and will always have had it. *Perhaps* this is why justice, insofar as it is not only a juridical or political concept, opens up to the *avenir* the transformation, the recasting or refounding [*la refondation*] of law and politics.
>
> "Perhaps"—one must [*il faut*] always say *perhaps* for justice. There is an *avenir* for justice and there is no justice except to the degree that some event is possible which, as event, exceeds calculation, rules, programs, anticipations and so forth. Justice, as the experience of absolute alterity, is unpresentable, but it is the chance of the event and the condition of history.[5]

What makes justice possible, Derrida wants to say, is its im-possibility, its resistance to the presentist strategies of co-optation that seek to reduce it to a Thucydidean ploy for gaining advantage in the brutal power play of statist politics or civil feud. Justice can not be leveled by mere manipulation, calculation, or the sophistic strategies of either *nomos* or *physis*. Justice exceeds such calculations; its ultimate meaning can be found, Derrida tells us, in the simple definition offered by Levinas in *Totality and Infinity*, where he writes: "The relation with the other [*autrui*]—that is to say, justice."[6] In the otherness of justice, in the alterity of its expectations and retrievals, we find a difference in the very structure of how we experience time. Beyond obligation, beyond debt, beyond repayment or the very structure of exchange, justice "happens"—if it happens at all—as an "event."[7] Within this performative, rather than constative, event-structure, justice comes to us as the infinite possibility of the im-possible. To "perform" justice means to transgress the totalizing metaphysics of the Parmenidean-Hegelian tradition within Western thinking that seeks to gather all things together into a unifying structure. Unlike Hegelian appropriation [*Ereignung*], which always goes back to the subject's self-knowledge and self-identity, Derrida's event (*Ereignis*) of justice opens to the other—the dispossessed, the infirm, the widow, the orphan, the leper, the stranger. Not Hegelian totality, but Eckhartian infinity, marks the Derridean-Levinasian interpretation of justice as that which exceeds all strategies of gathering, *legein*, *Versammlung*. What Derrida seeks to break asunder in his pluralistic deconstruction of justice is the whole Heideggerian impulse to gather everything into a kind of "hyper-unity," as John Caputo puts it.[8] Against this Heideggerian discourse of *Versammlung*, which interprets justice in terms of *Fug*, *fügen*, jointure, junction, and joining, Derrida seeks to show how this very impulse toward "gathering" undermines the possibility of justice since justice never "exists" and always resists being gathered into a stable and sustainable temporal present. Rather than interpret justice in terms of fugal harmony/identity, "of the accord that gathers or collects while harmonizing (*Versammlung*, *Fug*)," Derrida wants to privilege dispersion, dissociation, and disjunction since, on his view, these constitute "the condition for my relation to the other."[9] As he puts it, "Once you grant some privilege to gathering and not to dissociating, then you leave no room for the other, for the radical otherness of the other, for the radical singularity of the other."

In this reading of justice as irrevocably tied to dissociation, plurivocity, dispersion, heterogeneity, and disjuncture, Derrida affirms a justice that can never be found in the present order of things since it is never "there" or "*da*." Derridean justice never collapses into *Dasein*, never "appears" as itself since it can never be gathered together as something present to itself. Hence, because it eludes presence, justice can never come back to itself as "identity," it "can only *come back* or belong to the other."[10] The possibility of justice, Derrida claims, is tied to the radical singularity of the other as "absolute *pre*cedence" or "absolute *pre*viousness," to "what comes before me, before any present, thus, before any past present, but also what, for that very reason, comes from the future or as future: as the very coming of the event."[11] Justice does not exist, cannot exist, since it is not something "present"; it both comes *before* the present and after it. It is "other" than the present, never exhausted "in" the present, absolutely irreducible to the stasis and permanence of presence. Justice disturbs and interrupts the unifying stratagems of the present by constantly pointing back toward the precedence of the past and the coming of the future. But it also disrupts the singularity of "the proper" by opening us up to the other and by transgressing the axiomatics of gathering that are endemic to the Heideggerian reading of *dike* in terms of *legein* and *Versammlung*. By breaking open a crack to the future and to the future's radical alterity, this gesture of disruption gives assent to the messianic hope and possibility of a justice to come. As Derrida puts it:

> As soon as you address the other, as soon as you are open to the future, as soon as you have a temporal experience of waiting for the future, of waiting for someone to come: that is the opening of experience. Someone is to come, is *now* to come. Justice and peace will have to do with this coming of the other, with the promise. . . . This universal structure of the promise, of the expectation for the future, for the coming, and the fact that this expectation of the coming has to do with justice—that is what I call the messianic structure.[12]

What constitutes "the messianic structure" for Derrida is less the traditional religious hope for the coming of a Messiah that characterizes the three "desert" religions of Judaism, Christianity, and Islam. Rather, Derrida wants to dispense with any attempt to determine the Messiah as such—whether in its past form as religious doctrine or in its future form as eschatological revelation. For Derrida the messianic is akin to a Heideggerian "formal indication"—it points toward the phenomenological *structure* of possibilities without filling in such possibilities according to the reigning *Weltanschauungen* of the present. Within this formally indicative structure that Derrida calls a "messianicity without messianism," there is "a call, a promise of an independent future for what is to come, and which comes like every messiah in the shape of peace and justice."[13] This messianic time of the promise, of the possibility of what might come, of what urgently needs to come, opens up the whole structure of time to "the Now" in a way that deconstructs and disrupts both the metaphysics of presence (where Being is always understood as what "is" present) and the metaphysics of gathering and *Versammlung*. As Derrida expresses it, "The Messiah is not some future present," some safe and secure projection of our quotidian order on the grid of the future; rather, the messianic happens "now."[14] But, Derrida insists, "this 'now' is not a present."[15] It is not part of the sequence of historical time, but belongs to an incalculable messianic time. Precisely in this sense the messianic time of justice belongs to "the time of the promise [since] it will always remain, in each of its future times, to come: . . . it never exists, it is never present, it remains the theme of a non-presentable concept."[16] Following Benjamin's discussion of "*Jetztzeit* ('now-time') which is shot through with chips of Messianic time," a messianic "now" where "every second of time was the straight gate through which the Messiah might enter," Derrida holds out the eschatological promise of a justice to come that thinks the future in terms of redeeming the past and all the unjust suffering that haunts the corpses of the absent dead.[17] In this enigmatic understanding of justice that echoes the prophet Amos's call to "let justice flow like a river" (Amos 5:24), to let it break open the present to the "now-time" of both remembrance and expectation, Derrida draws as much on the work of Benjamin as he does on that of the Jewish prophets. In doing so, he attempts to challenge the Platonic metaphysics of substance, essence, and permanence that enshrouds the here-now of temporality within the static metaphysics of permanent presence. Taking up Blanchot's demand that the call of justice be an urgent one, an appeal that always exceeds the reigning measure of the present, Derrida will come to see justice as that which rends historical time, as the very movement of heterothesis and disruption that urgently demands that justice be brought about *now*—even if it can never be made present.[18] For the very possibility of justice, Derrida wants to say, is borne only by the condition of its impossibility. Were the Messiah to come, he would only shut down the hope/promise of his coming. Hence, his coming is always deferred. In this aporetic structure of imminence and deferral, the logic of calculability and reckoning is decisively broken. As what is to-come (*à-venir*), as what is possible, justice eludes the ontological imperative to become present in the stable configuration of temporal presence. As that which can never exist, can never be present, justice remains that which is to come, remains messianic. This is what Derrida tries to get at when he claims that "justice—or justice as it promises to be, beyond what it actually is—always has an eschatological dimension."[19]

In this Derridean reading of justice, a reading that owes much to the whole tradition of Jewish prophecy and messianism, Derrida touches upon a whole series of insights that I hope to show are relevant for pursuing a reading of the poetry of Paul Celan. In one sense this is a problematic reading, for although Derrida has written several essays on Celan's poetry in none of them does he thematize explicitly anything like an interpretation of justice, as he does in his later philosophical work.[20] Moreover, even in Celan's work "justice" does not appear as a major trope or preoccupation in any direct way. Yet I want to show that the whole Derridean problematic of messianic promise, of alterity, of justice as the relation to the other, of *aporia* as well as of mourning and memory will come to play a decisive role in the work of Celan. Like Derrida, Celan draws on the rich prophetic work of the Hebrew tradition, which runs through his poetry like a hidden thread that holds together so much of the dense hermetic language that appears so recalcitrant to the casual reader. For both Derrida and Celan, two exiled Jews whose creative lives were spent in Paris, the question of justice became a way of repositioning their own marginal existence in European society and culture by reframing it in terms of a philosophical dialogue with the fundamental tenets of their Jewish heritage. Such a project involved rethinking "justice" in terms of the onto-theological problematic of the *deus absconditus*, of the post-Hölderlinian god who has fled and abandoned the human being to her singular fate as that being who, as Rilke put it, "is not really at home in the interpreted world."[21] As those who had lost their homeland—El Biar in Algeria and Czernowitz in the Bukovina—Derrida and Celan came to experience in the most concrete ways possible the fate of exiled Jews who had been abandoned to/by the power plays of twentieth-century nationalism, fascism, totalitarianism, and political "justice."[22] Like Levinas, each understands the spiritual history of the West as an irresolvable struggle between the two dominating myths of Athens and Jerusalem—as the tension between the Odyssean myth of return and the Abrahamic myth of exile.[23] If the Odyssean myth can be found in the Parmenidean identity of the self with itself and in the Platonic-Hegelian notion of the spirit's journey as a return to its original home in being, then the Abrahamic myth can be traced in the Kabbalistic notions of exile and "the breaking of the vessels" (*Shevirah ha-kalim*) and in Franz Rosenzweig's *Star of Redemption*, which reveals the infinity of ethical obligation that is always restless and part of the Jewish burden of the nomad, the uprooted, the dispersed.[24] Against the totalizing metaphysics of Graeco-Germanic identity and return, Levinas will emphasize the Hebraic heteronomy of dispersion and infinite obligation, what Derrida will term "dissemination without return."[25]

In this Levinasian ethic of infinite obligation for the radically "other" and for alterity and dispersion rather than identity and totality, Derrida and Celan will come to terms with the concrete historical experience of twentieth-century European Jewry rent apart by the totalitarian-identitarian metaphysics of racial purity and exclusion that, in Levinas's words, "has been struck with a horror of the other that remains other."[26] If this Western metaphysical prejudice in favor of "totality" could allow itself the possibility of a "final solution" to one of its most pressing problems, then perhaps we can understand why Derrida privileges *aporia*—"this impossibility to find one's way"—as "the condition of ethics."[27] Against the universalist vision of a consensus on communitarian ethics, Derrida and Celan will radically underscore the singularity of ethical decision that opens itself in the aporetic realm of crisis, contradiction, and paradox. If law aspires to the universality of the code, the constitution, the contract that applies to everyone, then justice needs to be understood as that which "has to reinvent the law each time" it confronts the singularity of human pain and suffering that is always *his* or *hers* or *mine*.[28] In this Derridean understanding of justice as that which is always irreducibly singular and incalculable, that which always exceeds the present by pointing back to the past and ahead to the future, we can find traces of a singularly Jewish experience of twentieth-century European history, an experience that underlies the poetry of Paul Celan. In the incalculability of Jewish suffering, in the impossibility of its supersession or *Aufhebung*, there Celan comes to grapple with what Giorgio Agamben calls "the aporia of Auschwitz"—namely, the noncoincidence between facts and truth, event and witnessing, where "the impossibility of bearing witness, the 'lacuna' that constitutes human language, collapses, giving way to a different impossibility of bearing witness—that which does not have language."[29] Celan's poetry is undeniably a witnessing—but of what? In what sense can we speak of Celan's poems as "witnesses"? Or is it perhaps more appropriate to speak of his poetry as a Jewish form of Hölderlinian *Andenken* or "remembrance," a vigilant Kaddish for the abandoned Jewish dead in Eastern Europe? How to speak in such a way that in speaking we let the silence of the dead speak through us? This is part of the impossible task of poetic language that Celan confronts in venturing to take up the impossible path of "the aporia of Auschwitz."

In a note from 1966 outlining his plans for a forthcoming volume of poetry, Paul Celan writes: "Titel für den Band 'Übertragungen': FREMDE NÄHE" (Title for the volume 'Translations': STRANGE/FOREIGN NEARNESS).[30] In this oxymoronic phrase Celan hoped to express something of the irreconcilable paradox and contradiction that he believed lay in the work of poetic translation. For in the "carrying over" (*über/tragen*) of meaning from one language to another Celan found a powerful metaphor for the work of the translator. And yet for him the paradox of strange and alien proximity meant something more. As a German-speaking Jew from Romania exiled by the events of World War II from his native Bukovina, Celan knew firsthand what it meant to be a stranger in the homeland. In 1942 his parents died in a German concentration camp in Eastern Europe; during that time he was forced into a series of labor camps and remained there for nineteen months. Exiled from his native city, his family, and his language, Celan came to experience in the deepest way possible the factical meaning of *Fremde Nähe* as the irresolvable aporia of native and foreign that captured the experience of exiled Jews in Eastern and Central Europe during the Nazi and Stalinist purges. In the aporetic tension between identity and difference, native and foreign, proximal strangeness and distant familiarity, Celan came to understand not only his own singular plight, but the fate of Europe itself. As Maurice Blanchot would later put it, beyond its historical meaning as "event," or its aesthetic significance as that which resists the possibility of mimesis or representation, "Celan knew that the Shoah was the revelation of the essence of the West."[31]

To think "after" Auschwitz—following the German sense of "*nach* Auschwitz" in all its doubled and ambiguous forms as "according to," "in conformity with," "in the direction of," "following")—is to confront the unyielding contradictions of Celan's analysis. And yet it is precisely this question of Europe's inability—or unwillingness—to think the Shoah that preoccupied Celan so deeply in his own work, something that we can see in his dealings with the German cultural establishment in the 1950s and '60s, especially his dealings with the German philosopher Martin Heidegger. Celan had a deeply ambivalent relation to Heidegger. He owned more than thirty of Heidegger's works and the notes from his personal library show that he was actively engaged in reading and offering marginal commentary on them.[32] What preoccupied Celan above all was Heidegger's intense focus on the relation between poetry and thinking (*Dichtung und Denken*), a relation that proved so decisive for Celan's own work. Celan learned a great deal from his reading of Heidegger. And yet Celan was deeply troubled by Heidegger's political affiliation with National Socialism and his silence on the question of the Shoah. After finally meeting with Heidegger in 1967 at the philosopher's Black Forest cabin, Celan drafted a letter (that he never sent) calling Heidegger to account for having seriously failed his own project of thinking. Addressing Heidegger directly, Celan charged "that you, through your behavior, decisively undermine the earnest will to responsibility in the realms of the poetic (*Dichterische*) and—if I dare presume to say—the thinkerly (*Denkerische*)" (MSS, 129). For Celan and the generation of Jewish exiles living in Paris in the postwar period, the legacy of Heidegger's work would always be marked by a deep division between its philosophical brilliance and its political barbarity. The history of French philosophy in the years after World War II would be decisively shaped by this division.

How to think "after" the disaster? How to write in such a way that the very act of writing would approach the limit of what could be thought? How to dwell at the threshold of that limit such that dwelling itself would bring the writer/thinker into a strange and uncanny (*unheimlich*) relation to all that is of the homeland and the home (*heimlich*)? These questions of the postwar generation, questions whose shape and form would be bequeathed to them by the writings of Heidegger, would profoundly determine the work of Celan, Derrida, Blanchot, and Emmanuel Levinas. Celan's work in the years after 1945 would be determined by both the shadows of the Shoah and by the writings of Heidegger. In this impossible conjunction between two historical influences whose relation was always defined by a profound and unremitting disjunction, we can trace the history of an author and an epoch.

But there were other disjunctions that Celan would also have to confront as an exiled Jew, a foreigner, an orphan, and a survivor, disjunctions whose own genealogy would be caught up in the very problem of language. As he left his native city of Czernowitz in 1945 to move first to Bucharest, then to Vienna in 1947 and then to Paris in 1949, Celan had decisions to make about the very language in which to express his thoughts. Celan's poetry emerges in the space of that disjunction, keenly aware of the jarring inconsistencies that attend the linguistic problem of lending a name to precisely that which cannot be named. In the teeth of this aporia Celan's work will resist the tradition of identity-metaphysics in Western thinking that finds its expression in the unity of the name, calling into question the process of naming. We find traces of this resistance in his decision to change his own proper name from Antschel to Celan and in his refusal to name the event of his life—and his generation—with the name "Auschwitz" or "Shoah" or "Holocaust" or "Final Solution." Instead, he refers simply to "that which happened" ("*das, was geschah*") and the task it poses to the poet. As he put it in his Bremen speech of 1958:

> There remained in the midst of the losses this one thing: language. It, the language, remained, not lost, yes in spite of everything. But it had to pass through its own answerlessness, pass through frightful muting, pass through the thousand darknesses of deathbringing speech. It passed through and gave back no words for that which happened; yet it passed through this happening. Passed through and could come to light again, 'enriched' [*angereichert*] by all this. (SPP, 395/GW III, 186)

If the name *Auschwitz* could not be named, precisely because in its function as a name it performed the annihilation of the name, then how could a poet attempt to grapple with the enormity of such a void? How to speak about mourning and memory, justice and redemption, when the very *topoi* of ethical reflection had, like the bodies of the Jewish dead, been shattered and disseminated as smoke and ash? How, in the immediate wake of the experience of loss, oblivion, and horror, to give voice to the voiceless without slipping back into the selfsame linguistic and metaphysical structures that had helped prepare the way for the "thousand darknesses of deathbringing speech"? It is within the aporia of such questioning that Celan will take up again the "task of the German poet" to refashion the possibility of speech, but now in a distantiated and deconstructive fashion. In doing so, he will engage the work of Heidegger as a conversation partner who will help him to think through the uncanny relation of language to the *topoi* of terror in ways that both draw upon and strongly undermine Heidegger's own vision of poetic-philosophic dialogue as a way of reconstituting in language the site for the rebuilding of a lost and shattered homeland. In 1946, Heidegger will write three essays that will take up the problem of a postwar European world—"Letter on Humanism," "The Verdict of Anaximander," and "What Are Poets For?" There, he will attempt to grapple with the trope of "darkness"—but now, unlike Celan, not as a way of thinking through the fate of European Jewry. Rather, he will think more broadly of the pervasive nihilism of the postwar world that he thinks in terms of what he calls "the world's night" and the Hölderlinian experience of "the default of God" (*der Fehl Gottes*) (PLT, 91/GA 5, 269). In the profound experience of loss that marked the "event" of World War II, Heidegger detects the traces of a possible way out of the darkness of the world's night. In such an age, Heidegger contends, what is necessary is that there be poets/thinkers who "reach into the abyss," since the turn away from the abyss is possible only if the abyssal as such is first "experienced and endured" (PLT, 92/GA 5, 269). In an epoch where being is thought of as plentitude and presence, Heidegger will think through "the German catastrophe" as an ontological event of Anaximandran *dike*, marked by loss, withdrawal, ruin, absence, and destruction. But he will also think it in terms of the Sophoclean trope of homelessness and the loss of a dwelling place, those uncanny, *unheimlich* dispositions of fate that point to the aporetic disjunctions of the human being upon the earth. On Heidegger's reading, what truly characterizes the darkness of the world's night is our inability to think through these *aporiae* in an originary way. Hence, he turns to the early Greeks and to Hölderlin as sources for the project of "reaching into the abyss." But if Celan could find deep affinities with Heidegger's critique of the metaphysics of presence and with his emphasis on the need for a philosophical-poetic dialogue on the thematics of loss and abyssal absence, then he could not follow the lines of Heidegger's exclusionary Graeco-German axis of affinity or his inability/unwillingness to enter into dialogue about the fate of European Jewry.

Celan learned much from Heidegger, and in what follows I hope to trace the lines of such influence in the writing of several of his most important poems—especially in "Tübingen, Jänner," in "Todtnauberg," and in the "Jerusalem Cycle" of poems from *Zeitgehöft* which will constitute the focus of this chapter. The effect of Heidegger's writing on the work of Celan was deep and profound. Yet at the same time there was a gulf that separated them—the divergent historical fates of an autochthonous Alemannic-Catholic philosopher committed to the ancient Greeks *and* an exiled Bukovinian-Jewish poet who found his spiritual sources in the works of the Hebrew tradition and its later commentators. Like those exiled Parisian Jews, Levinas and Derrida, Celan's relationship to Heidegger would be marked by deep ambivalence, for while Heidegger would become one of the most significant influences on Celan's work, he would also come to embody the selfsame metaphysics of German complicity in "that which happened" that shattered his whole world. In this chapter, I want to look at the work of Celan against the Heideggerian axis of Graeco-German affinity specifically as it relates to two essential themes—firstly, the Heideggerian notion of *ethos*, dwelling, *Aufenthalt* that he finds in Sophocles and Hölderlin read against Celan's retrieval of Hebrew ethics from the Bible, Kabbala, Kafka, Scholem, Buber, and Susman. Secondly, I want to examine the Heideggerian interpretation of *dike* as a nonmoral, nonjuridical concept read against the Celanian commitment to justice that has profound ties to the whole Hebrew tradition of ethics. In this way, I hope to read the Heidegger-Celan conversation as part of a postwar reenactment of Levinas's Odyssean-Abrahamic myths of return and exile that so profoundly characterized the Athens-Jerusalem split in German thought. By reading Celan's poems through and against the Heideggerian-Hölderlinian axis of Graeco-Germanic exceptionalism, I want to show how deeply imbricated they were in the whole Hebraic tradition of justice that runs through the work of Levinas, Derrida, Buber, Rosenzweig, Bloch, Susman, and Scholem. I choose Celan as a crucial source here because it seems to me that his work helps to show both the extraordinary insightfulness of Heidegger's ontological reading of Western history, as well as its deep ethical limitations and dangers. In the marked ambivalence that Celan demonstrated to Heidegger both as person and as thinker, I hope to uncover not only a strained personal relationship, but a way of rethinking the relationship between poetry and philosophy. Celan does this by both drawing upon and challenging the Platonic-Aristotelian legacy of thinking that grasps the human being's relation to the *polis* in *ethical* terms as a fundamental question about justice in the city and justice in the soul. One way to trace the lines of Celan's break with this Graecocentric element in Heidegger's thought is to read it in terms of the Heideggerian notion of *Geworfenheit* as the thrownness of the human being into a singular historical situation that shapes the horizon of *Dasein*'s facticity (SZ, 133). The historical accident of Celan's thrownness, his singular experience as an Ashkenazic Jew born in the epoch between two world wars on the border of a Central Europe in decay, would profoundly shape the poetic-philosophical dialogue that would emerge later.

CELAN'S PNEUMATIC JEWISH IDENTITY

In order to understand the long and complex history of Celan's ambivalent relation to his homeland and to his Jewish heritage, a few basic facts are necessary. Celan was born as Paul Antschel on November 23, 1920, into a middle-class Jewish household in Czernowitz, a city of one hundred thousand residents, half of whom were Jews.[33] Czernowitz was the polyglot capital of the Bukovina, known affectionately to its inhabitants as "Little Vienna." Both his parents grew up near Czernowitz at a time when it constituted the easternmost province of the Austro-Hungarian Hapsburg Empire under Kaiser Franz Josef I. Celan's mother, Fritzi Antschel née Schrager, was raised in Sadagora, which was a center of Hassidic culture, while his father, Leo Antschel, was born in Schipenitz in an orthodox Jewish family with Zionist yearnings. Fritzi, however, insisted on speaking *hochdeutsch* at home and sought a traditional German-Austrian education for her son. She schooled him in the German classics—Schiller, Goethe, Heine, the Brothers Grimm—while Leo insisted that Paul learn Hebrew and prepare himself for his bar mitzvah. In the tension between these competing parental visions, Celan expressed early on the difficulties of bringing together the Jewish-German influence in Central Europe after World War I. The Antschels, like so many middle-class Jewish families in Czernowitz, sought a path of economic-social assimilation into the German cultural establishment of their day. They were not particularly religious; instead, as Celan's biographer Israel Chalfen puts it, their "Judaism served as a moral structure rather than as a religion. Jewish ethics were to shape [Paul's] character and instill the behavior necessary for the social advancement they hoped for him."[34] Still, the family celebrated Sabbaths in both Hebrew and German and the lasting influence of these two competing cultures helped to shape the underlying problematic of his work. Later, as Celan set out on a search for the lost *topos* of his Bukovinian homeland, he would confront the underlying contradictions of a German-Jewish existence in Central Europe in the middle of the last century.

Clearly, Celan had his own personal and familial crises to work through, but the sheer political-historical narrative of Czernowitz was dizzying, shifting from its status as the "Jewish El Dorado" of the Hapsburg Empire to an anti-Semitic Romanian provincial city in the 1920s, then taken over by the Red Army in 1940, and a year later by the SS, which deported fifty thousand Jews to camps in Transnistria, after which it was reconquered by Stalin in 1944 and incorporated into the Ukraine in 1947.[35] Celan would spend the rest of his adult life trying to account for the cultural trauma of his break with "this former province of the Hapsburg monarchy now falling into historylessness" (SPP, 395/GW III, 185). After he left Czernowitz at the end of the war and moved to Bucharest, and then Vienna and finally to Paris, he would find himself in the difficult position of explaining his cultural identity to others. He referred to himself ironically as "a posthumously born Kakanier" orphaned by history and as a "Bohemianized German- and Jewish-Jew from North Bukovina" (MSS, 815, 57). Living as a German-speaking Jew in a nationalist Romania that sought to suppress

German as a language and Jews as a race, Celan developed what he himself described as "strange perspectives":

> What was near lay distant and so one could only then measure the true distance if one stood in the distance oneself. (MSS, 815)

Out of this strange distantiation, Celan came to live in a world of contradiction and paradox—at first breaking with his Jewish heritage when he arrived in Paris in 1948 and later, during the mid-fifties, rediscovering his lost Jewish heritage by turning to Jewish writers such as Gershom Scholem, Martin Buber, Margarete Susman, and others.[36] Initially, Celan attempted to "escape from history" by literally leaving Romania behind and settling in Vienna and Paris and then moving as far away from his middle-class, Eastern European Jewish roots as possible by choosing a French-Catholic wife whose family had deep aristocratic ties. But Celan's attempts at assimilation were undermined both by the cultural milieu in which he lived, as well as by his own deeply ambivalent stance toward his new identity.

As he left Czernowitz behind him with all its memories and scars, Celan was all of twenty-five years old. During his time in Bucharest (1945–47) he wrestled with the changes in his life by trying on different pseudonyms in lieu of his given name of Paul Antschel: "Paul Ancel," "A. Pavel," and then, in an anagram of the Romanian spelling of his name, "Paul Celan."[37] A line from an early poem, "In Praise of Remoteness" (1948), captures something of the labyrinthine contradictions running through Celan's work: "only when faithless am I true" (PCS, 43/GW I, 33).[38]

His decision to leave the Bukovinian world behind him and to establish himself in Paris, the cultural capital of Europe, can be viewed in terms of his yearning to find a place within the prevailing European culture of his day. As he admitted in a radio interview of 1952: "I had always lived on the margin so the center attracted me all the more powerfully" (MSS, 815). Nonetheless, Celan remained ever mindful of his East European Jewish roots. "I am an *Ostjude,*" he told Marie-Luise Kaschnitz.[39] And in a letter to his Jewish relatives in Palestine he tells them, "Perhaps I am one of the last who must live out to the end the destiny of the Jewish spirit in Europe."[40] One of Celan's friends, the philosopher Otto Pöggeler, claims that Celan "did not want to be seen as someone who, though coming from a strange eastern city, had then become emancipated only to take part in the intellectual world of Parisian modernity."[41] On the contrary, Celan's Jewish roots proved ineradicable. In the last year of his life he writes to his by then estranged wife Gisèle: "My Judaism: that which I still (re)cognize in the ruins of my existence" (PC/GL II, 487).

In order to get a better sense of "Celan's difficult and painful relation to his Judaism and to his search for a way of conducting himself as a Jew," I will try to think through not only his Jewish ties or his relation to Israel, but also his complex relation to the German language and to specific German writers and philosophers (Hölderlin/Heidegger) concerning the problem of nearness and distance, one's own and the foreign, *das Eigene* and *das Fremde*.[42] His Jewish lover, Ilana Shmueli, expressed it this way: "I perceived his Judaism as a bitter, enduring struggle with his own Jewish identity: a struggle with himself, a struggle with the world around him. . . . This Judaism had a distinct place in his being, which in his last years constantly throbbed in him and yet given his self-demands it was not always something that he could attain. . . . It was this fact of his *not-being-Jewish-enough* that tore at him and brought conflicts that had something self-destructive about them."[43] But one could also make the case that the same difficulties that he had with his Jewish identity, he also had with his "mother tongue," the German language. As a young kindergartner and elementary school student, Paul spoke German; later, when he was forced to attend a Romanian-speaking grammar school and gymnasium, he was able to participate in a specially expanded German language instruction program for native German speakers (MSS, 819). After he moved to Paris he also had to practice an idiosyncratic form of what he termed "speech hygiene," by which he meant preserving a healthy space for his German language practice amidst a Francophone culture (and household). In a 1954 radio interview with Süddeutschen Rundfunk, he admitted that he "lived in linguistic exile" in France and that what kept his language skills sharp were his activities as a translator (MSS, 189–90). "I translate," Celan claimed, "because it's fun, because it brings me joy, because it makes me more familiar with my own [*eigenen*] language," in contrast to the other foreign languages that he had learned (among which were Romanian, Russian, Hebrew, French, English, Italian, Yiddish). In this linguistic space between one's own and the foreign (the same problematic of *das Eigene* and *das Fremde* as Hölderlin's Böhlendorff Letter), Celan came to think of translation not merely as a way of returning back to oneself by way of the other but, more fundamentally, as a way of searching for that which doesn't exist, an "impossible path" that leads to an encounter (*Begegnung*) with a realm that is "immaterial, yet earthly, terrestrial, something circular, returning upon itself by way of both poles . . . *a meridian*" (SPP, 413/GW III, 202).

Only in the space of his psychological and linguistic exile can we begin to understand Celan's poetry and its inner relation to a tradition of justice that is radically different from, and other than, the tragic-philosophical justice of Hölderlin and Heidegger. Celan experienced in the most concrete way possible the loss of his home—literally, in his parents' deportation to Transnistria and their subsequent deaths, in his compulsory work camp existence in Romania during the war, in his emigration from Czernowitz and difficulties in Bucharest, Vienna, and Paris. These are things that he came to experience as an East European Jew in the time of the dictatorships. But his sense of exile went deeper. "You are at home within your language, your reference points, among the books, the works you love," Celan wrote to the French poet Yves Bonnefoy; "As for me, I am on the outside."[44] This sense of ever being an outsider, a stranger, a foreigner, an exile would leave its imprint upon all of Celan's work, touching on the essential lines of both connection and division that ran through his Büchner Prize speech of 1960, "The Meridian." There he speaks of retracing the lines that lead back to "the place of my own origin" through a poetological form of "*topos* research" that aims at rediscovering his lost homeland—not only in Czernowitz and the Bukovina, but more fundamentally in the German language of his mother's idioms and tales (SPP, 413/GW III, 202). Through the attempted recovery of a lost world that is "immaterial, yet earthly, terrestrial," Celan manages to find a meridian that binds him both to the terrestrial world of his parents' home in Czernowitz and to the spiritual-immaterial realm of the Holocaust dead to which they belong. Yet as part of this *topos* research into his own origins, Celan inevitably confronts the "uncanny strangeness" (*Unheimlichkeit, Fremdheit*) of absence, of the dead victims of the Nazi terror for whom no earthly place or *Ort* marks their passing since their ashes succumb to the scattering forces of the wind (SPP, 411, 406/GW III, 200, 193). No tombstone designates their demise; neither gravesite nor urn preserve their bodies. What once existed, the singular mark of an East European Jewish world, has vanished. Still, Celan writes, there remains "a trace of the ashes" of the lost dead, "*eine Aschenspur*" of their burnt flesh. Amidst these ashes the poet seeks in the shadow of the unspeakable to somehow recover what can never be recovered (MSS, 75). Within this impossible landscape, this "topology of the abyss," as Jean Bollack calls it, Celan dares to suggest that in spite of everything the poem "remains mindful of its dates" (*bleibt seiner Daten eingedenkt*) (SPP, 408/GW III, 196).[45]

Celan's commitment to memory and remembrance needs to be read within the whole congeries of relations that constitute the German-Jewish (non)-conversation around the event(s) of the Shoah. If such a dialogue is possible—and it is precisely its (im)possibility to which Celan's work bears witness—then only as an extension of Gershom Scholem's point that "[n]othing can be more misleading than to apply [the] concept of [a German-Jewish dialogue] to the discussions between Germans and Jews during the last 200 years. This dialogue died at its very start and never took place."[46] Instead, what emerged in Central Europe between the world wars was "the hopelessness of [a] cry into the void" to which no response was forthcoming. It is precisely such hopelessness that will concern us in this chapter as we try to read Celan's poetry in "dialogue" with the thought of Heidegger and (Heidegger's) Hölderlin. For Celan will take up the Heideggerian-Hölderlinian *topos* of remembrance or *Andenken*, but in a radically different and deconstructive sense. Abjuring Heidegger's philhellenic idyll of an Odysseus-like "poetic homecoming" as the "proper" task of the poet, Celan will rather seize on the Levinasian theme of Abrahamic exile as a way to contrast the German-Jewish experience of remembrance (EHP, 123,140/GA 4, 99–100,118). Heidegger will persist in thinking remembrance as an act of "gathering" (*Versammlung*) and preservation, an experience of "the foreign" (*das Fremde*) that "allows what is merely strange in the foreign to be forgotten so that only that foreignness that is to be transformed through what is proper to one is preserved" (EHP, 164/GA 4, 142). Celan will challenge this axiomatics of Heideggerian homecoming, however, by attending to those who remain without a home, those who will never experience the completion of return. As a Jewish poet from the Bukovina, Celan is denied the safe return to that which is "one's own" (*das Eigene*), a return that sustains Heidegger's Hellenic dream of German homecoming. What Celan will remain mindful of is the dates of dissemination, the time of disjunction and annihilation, the dates that he cannot speak of directly, but only by way of his poetics of indirection. He does this so ably in the Büchner Prize speech, "The Meridian." There he will fix upon the poet's task of remembrance in terms of Büchner's novella *Lenz* and come to see Lenz's fate and the fate of German Jewry as bound to the selfsame date—"January 20th."

Through an allusive pirouette of indirection Celan will take the twentieth of January as his nodal point for drawing meridians to the most essential themes in his work. The very first line of Büchner's *Lenz* begins: "On the 20th of January Lenz wandered through the mountains . . . only it sometimes troubled him that he could not walk on his head."[47] Lenz, the historical Lenz, was an eighteenth-century poet who hailed from the Bukovina, but in Büchner's telling he also will be transformed into a symbol of visionary madness. Celan then takes up this trope of poetic madness and links it to his own critique of the madness of German culture in the years of the Shoah. "Whoever walks on his head," he claims, "has heaven as an abyss (*Abgrund*) beneath him" (SPP, 407/GW III, 195). Lenz's journey will end in madness and death and his poetic dream of walking on his head will come to signify for Celan a radical reversal of the ontological grounding that marks Heidegger's *Satz vom Grund* lectures of 1957 (which Celan read closely).[48] If Heidegger will attend to ground (*Grund*), earth (*Boden*), and autochthony (*Bodenständigkeit*) as principles that offer a way of grasping the poetic enterprise, then Celan will take up the Heideggerian notion of the *Abgrund* as a way of thinking both with and against Heidegger. On the one hand, like Heidegger, Celan will identify the Western tradition's preoccupation with ground as part of the onto-theological constitution of both metaphysics and theology. On the other hand, he will think it in terms of the abyssal nihilism of modern existence. As he puts it in the notebooks from his "Meridian" speech, Lenz's abyss—with all its madness and uncertainty—constitutes the uncanny ground of the poem: "In this groundlessness (*Bodenlosigkeit*) lies—archaically enough—the ground (*Grund*) and principle of the poem" (TCA/M, 61).

As this abyssal ground, the poem comes to inscribe not only a sense of void and absence, but also the reversal of the highest values within the tradition. Hence, Celan can write in his notebooks that "if it is true that heaven yearns for the human being, then that can only be something welcome." In other words, if we grant a Nietzschean reversal of the highest values whereby the human being no longer yearns for heavenly escape but heaven itself yearns for the human, then perhaps we might begin to see Lenz's poetic gesture of walking upon his head as a turn toward a time without ground, a time "when you tip over the hour glass" and come to be mindful of "dates and moments that are not to be gleaned from calendars and clocks" (TCA/M, 58). In this time of reversal or *Umkehr*, a time marked by Lenz's gesture of inversion, the poet encounters a circular path of intersecting relations—a meridian (L. *meridies*, "mid-day") that brings the spatial distance of oppositional points into the temporal sameness of a singular date—the twentieth of January (TCA/M, 199).[49] In this impossible encounter between sameness and difference, identity and opposition, Celan will offer a poetic inscription for his own private memories of loss and exile, juxtaposed against the historical dating of German racial exclusion and extermination. This historical encounter will take place at the intersection of yet other encounters: of Celan with the work of Georg Büchner, of Büchner with a mad eighteenth-century Bukovinian poet (Lenz), of Celan with the politically cleansed German literary establishment of 1960 who confer the Büchner Prize on him, of Celan with Adorno's claim that "to write a poem after Auschwitz is barbaric."[50]

In its most basic historical register, the twentieth of January names the date in 1942 of the Wannsee Conference organized by Reinhard Heydrich, head of the Gestapo, and his SS-Obersturmbahnführer, Adolf Eichmann, to find a "Final Solution" to the Jewish problem in Europe. In a palatial villa on the outskirts of Berlin, all of the various branches of the Nazi state bureaucracy and war offices conspired to outline, plan, and execute Hitler's order to eliminate the Jewish presence throughout Europe. Drawing a meridian to his own life, to what he calls "the place of my own origin"—namely, the

Bukovina—Celan juxtaposes the Wannsee Conference's date of planning with the Bukovinian poet Lenz's unplanned walk through the mountains, a walk that ends in madness (SPP, 413). Punning on the grotesque link between *Wann*-see (the place or *Ort* of the Final Solution) and *Wahn* (the German word for "madness" or "delusion") as between the idyllic beauty of the villa and the terror of the camps, Celan is able to circumscribe a meridian linking poetry, madness, and the Holocaust. In doing so, he is able to locate a nodule point to gather and refract all the contending forces in the German-Jewish (non)-dialogue that come to decide his own fate. It is hardly an accident that these issues came to shape his "Meridian" speech so powerfully, precisely in the year 1960. Eight days before the German press announced the winner of the Büchner prize (May 19, 1960), the Israeli secret service captured Adolf Eichmann in Argentina and brought him to Jerusalem to stand trail for crimes against humanity.[51] If Celan doubted whether the Eichmann trial would bring justice for Jewish victims, he did not waver concerning the need to seek justice especially in the teeth of the postwar cover-up by ex-Nazi party members. The whole tenor of his Meridian speech is to situate the Jewish tradition at the margins of his address in an effort to emphasize how marginal it was within the German literary establishment of its time. Hence, he alludes to obscure figures such as the Jewish publisher of Büchner's works—Karl Emil Franzos from the Bukovina—or Moritz Heimann, the little-known Jewish critic, and other, more prominent Jews such as Gustav Landauer, Leo Shestov, Walter Benjamin, and Franz Kafka. But his rhetorical aim is to challenge the comfortable atmosphere of the German literary establishment in Darmstadt that has granted prestige and asylum to many figures whom Celan suspects of having been former supporters of the Reich. In so doing, he will exaggerate a certain form of politeness by repeating the formal address "ladies and gentlemen" often and, at the end, offering a litany of "thank yous" ending with the final sentence: "Ladies and gentlemen, I thank you for your presence (*Anwesenheit*)" (TCA/M, 13). By this subtle and almost imperceptible turn to the cliché of thanks and gratitude, Celan will covertly allude to the reality of Jewish absence (*Abwesenheit*)—not only in the Darmstadt Academy, but within mainstream German history and culture. Juxtaposing presence and absence, *Wannsee* and *Wahn*, Lenz's poetic madness and the madness of the German technocracy of death, Celan will turn the simple observation that "every poem has its '20th of January'" on its head. That is, he will forge a meridianal link between Jewish *Verfolgung* (persecution) and German *Verfolgungswahn* (persecution mania) even as he insists on thinking this link in its unrepeatable singularity, a singularity that can never be leveled by metaphor or archetype. Here the *political* dimension of *Wann/Wahn* will be rethought as an *ethical* question about justice and justice denied. Like Büchner, Celan will think the political *as* ethical as he comes to terms with the madness of German annihilation.

Against the postwar German strategy of cover-up, self-reinvention, and forgetting, Celan will cling to the Jewish theme of remembrance, of a deep-seated duty to the dead—of "remaining mindful of [their] dates" (SPP, 408/GW III, 196). In this sense, the twentieth of January becomes the site of remembrance for those Jewish dead wiped out in the extinction rationally planned at Wannsee. In her insightful book, *Textgräber: Paul Celans geologische Lyrik,* Ute Werner makes a strong case for understanding Celan's poetry as a way of "learning to see (fleetingly) that which has never been seen."[52] On her reading, Celan's poetry offers a *Totengedenken* (a way of "remaining mindful of the dead") that speaks not so much of gas chambers or the sheer brutality of the mounds of corpses, but to the fact of the still unburied status of the millions of murdered Jews who remain without graves.

This fact of the dead corpses' withheld burial leads Celan to focus not merely on the reflective mode of historical recollection for the dead, but on a future responsibility to their burial since in Jewish law an unburied corpse may not enter into the promise of future resurrection.[53] This unsettled and unsettling character of the Auschwitz dead, their never yet having found a resting place, stands as an ethical demand upon us by the other to provide a ground for repose. Hence, for Celan, the memory of Auschwitz presents to us not so much a scar as an "ever open wound" that traumatically calls out to us for healing. In this sense, we can read Celan's poetry as an attempt to create a poetic crypt to receive the scattered ashes of the dead, a gravesite that commemorates and remains mindful of the unburied Holocaust victims who have been wholly (Gk. *holos*) burned (Gk. *kaiein,* to burn, cremate). As Werner tells us, Celan's poems reinscribe a place for the dead, providing "a grave in the text" that becomes a "primary site of/for remembrance/commemoration" bringing the *topoi* of "grave" and "memory" into a profoundly meaningful relationship, one that can be turned back to Greek roots.[54] In ancient Greek, *mnema* ("grave") and *mneme* ("memory") share an etymological connection; in Celan's poetry, a phenomenological one. So much so that Celan literally traces the ashes of the cremated victims geologically back from their chemical particles as the remains of underground water that as calcium carbonate gets crystallized in the caverns and cavities of stone, rock, slate, and granite—hence the profusion of geological imagery in so many of his poems.

Like Sophocles's Antigone, Celan becomes preoccupied with the question of proper burial for the dead, of the ethical responsibility of the survivor who seeks to challenge the political order of the day. Celan strives to unearth a more rooted form of justice, one that does not succumb to the logic of enforced silence, forgetting, or repression in the name of political expediency. In his view, the situation in Germany during the 1950s-1960s was marked by an atmosphere of expedient amnesia, a situation where former Nazi supporters regained their positions of prominence and continued to exert cultural and institutional influence at all levels of German society.[55] In late 1959, in reaction to proceedings in the German Bundestag concerning laws designed to prevent crimes against minority groups, a series of anti-Semitic episodes erupted to challenge the legal rulings. Synagogues were defiled, Jewish cemeteries were desecrated, rocks were thrown through windows, anonymously written pamphlets were distributed attacking Jewish businesses and individuals, including invectives against Celan's publisher, the Fischer Verlag in Frankfurt.[56] Against this background, Claire Goll, the widow of Celan's former patron the poet Yvan Goll, published a letter in January 1960 accusing Celan of plagiarism. She went on to attack him employing a series of stereotypes about the lying, uncreative, and money-grabbing Jew who as the epigone of a worn-out race could only steal ideas from others rather than produce them himself. Moreover, in her letter, Goll alluded to what she termed the "legend" of Celan's murdered parents in the east. Within the anti-Jewish climate of the day, Goll's charges were taken up by a number of German newspapers and journals who attacked Celan. In response, Celan tried to align some prominent German literary figures to publish articles denouncing Goll and defending his good name. As part of this campaign Celan traveled to Tübingen in January 1961 to convince the prominent literary critic Walter Jens to write such a piece. As the first Jew to receive the Büchner Prize, Celan was inordinately sensitive to the manifold meanings behind his selection, worrying that a certain perverse form of anti-Semitism might be attached to the honor.[57] The rise of neo-Nazism in Germany profoundly troubled him, and the Meridian address speaks eloquently to his own ambivalence concerning the status of the (Jewish) poet in contemporary Germany. How to think the relation between poetry and the Holocaust "*nach*" Adorno? How to find a way to mediate our own time with the horror of the past, to find a "middle point" (L. *meri-*) from our "day" (L. *dies*) to a past one, a *meri-dian* to connect German and Jew—even despite the meridian linking the *Wahn* of January 1942 Wannsee with the *Wahn* of neo-Nazi *Wahnverfolgung* in 1961? This is what is at stake in the whole thematics of "January" within Celan's work, the madness of the twentieth of January that links the poet Lenz's walk into the mountains with the *Gestell* of Nazi planning as annihilation. In "Tübingen, Jänner," written in late January 1961 after a brief visit to Jens in Tübingen, the trope of poetic madness (Lenz's-Hölderlin's-Celan's) will be set in tension with the philosophical transmission of poetic prophecy in the form of Heidegger's lectures on Hölderlin. The idyll of a Graeco-Germanic bond between thinking and poetizing (*Denken und Dichten*) will be interrupted and displaced via a turn to Hebraic themes that contrast sharply with the philhellenic axis of German philosophy, theology, and literature. Precisely in this displacement of a place ("Tübingen") that preeminently stands as the classical *topos* of Hellenic-Hesperian affinity, Celan finds a way to respond to the problem of the meridian—of how to memorialize the caesura that splits the idyll of romantic Germany from the neo-Nazi present of persecution.

"TÜBINGEN, JÄNNER"

"Tübingen, Jänner" comes to us as a poem that speaks in fragments about the fragmented discourse of reading and (re-)writing. It shows itself as a multilayered palimpsest written over with inscriptions from an array of languages—not only German, Greek, Latin, and Hebrew, but also the untranslatable, incoherent, and incomprehensible discourse of poetic madness. Celan draws on the well-established position of Tübingen as the site for the flourishing of German Idealism, of the university city where Hegel, Schelling, and Hölderlin all lived together as theology students in the Tübingen Stift, of the bucolic Swabian landscape marked by the gentle flow of the Neckar River. In this sense Tübingen comes to embody a certain exemplary status as a name standing for a theological-philosophical-poetic tradition of Graecophilia that understands German identity as having its roots in its autochthonic bond to ancient Hellas.[58] As part of this tradition it also comes to signify a certain German philosophy of history that draws its eschatological vision of the future from an engaged conversation with the origins and sources of Western thinking in the early Greeks. But Tübingen also signifies something else: the place where the mad Hölderlin lived from 1806–1843 (after a brief stay in the Autenrieth Klinik) in a medieval tower overlooking the Neckar. In this state of benightedness, the mad Hölderlin came to personify a certain romantic vision of the poet as a Cassandra-like prophet whose mantic pronouncements divined a certain tragic order of isolation, withdrawal, and ineffability. Celan's carefully constructed poem brings these oppositional meanings into tension by setting them in a space of contention, a space that, on the one hand, enshrines the memory of Hölderlinian poetics (vv. 4–6) and, on the other, refracts this poetics in a language of blindness (v. 1), drowning (v. 9), stammering (v. 21), and madness (v. 23) that disrupts any consistent attempt at appropriating its meaning. We are left to confront the "riddle" (v. 4) of Celan's relation to Hölderlin as poet and to the "Hölderlin" of the German literary-philosophical tradition. In what follows I would like to offer a reading of "Tübingen, Jänner" as the first in a series of interpretations ("Todtnauberg" and various selections from "The Jerusalem Poems") that will attempt to bring Celan into conversation with

Hölderlin, Heidegger, and the Hebrew tradition. My aim in doing so is to think the problem of memory (*Gedächtnis*) and/as remembrance (*Andenken*) as a way of reflecting on the possibility of a language "of" justice—one that not only speaks "about" justice, as if it were merely a philosophical desideratum, but attempts to enact it in a poetic idiom that measures the Hölderlinian notion of cosmic justice as a form of balance and symmetry (*metron*) that rests on the figure of reversal and inversion. The classical site for such a notion is, of course, Hölderlin's Böhlendorff letter that speaks of the fate of Germany as something that lies in the knowledge of how best to balance the proper relation between what is one's own, native, and national (*das Eigene*) with what is alien, foreign, and other (*das Fremde*).[59] For Celan, we will see, this Hölderlinian discourse about native and foreign, Greek and German, ancient and modern will itself be reversed given his experience as a stateless, exiled foreigner coping with the trauma of the Shoah. What is at stake here, however, is not simply Celan's coming to terms with Germany's inability or unwillingness to acknowledge the other, the alien, the Hebrew. Rather, it involves finding a proper language of remembrance that, out of the wreckage and debris of the Nazi era, might offer an ethics of remembering that does not succumb to the deadening language of the oppressors and their metaphysics of presence, but honors the absence of the other, buried under the rubble of destruction.

"Tübingen, Jänner" is written under the shadow of the twentieth of January, of all its madness and devastation, of all the paradoxes of *Wahn-* and *Wannsee*. In its formal structure it gives voice to a language of disruption, fragmentation, and scission. What it gathers, it disperses; what it recollects is given back as disjuncture. Even in its very title we are provided hints of the doubling and ambiguity that will follow. "Jänner" is an Austrian idiom that indicates "Januar" (January); it is also the same word that Büchner employs in his novella to indicate Lenz's descent into madness on the twentieth of January.[60] But the *Jänner* of the title also alludes to Janus, the Roman god of doors, passageways, gates, and entrances.[61] For Janus the moment of breakthrough and transition is holy. As the god of beginnings and inceptions, Janus was portrayed as a two-headed divinity who looked back to the past and forward to the future. Consequently, as the classical Janus-headed god of mythology, he came to embody the tensions and contradictions that came to presence in phenomena of transition. Perhaps some traces of this discordant opposition can be found in Celan's whole figural use of *Jänner* and *eingejännert* (PPC, 312), which finds him "en-januaried" in the antagonisms of the native and foreign that form the German-Jewish (non-)dialogue. Turned in two directions at once, caught in the cleavages and contradictions of future and past, "Tübingen"—as cultural myth and as historical reality—comes to signify for Celan, like Janus himself, something "doppeldeutig" (literally: "double-meaning" or "ambiguous"/"equivocal"). On the one hand, it becomes the place of German memory ("Erinnerung," v. 6); on the other, precisely owing to—yet in spite of—this memorializing function, Tübingen comes to express the eschatological language of "coming" itself (vv. 12–14), of a "time" (v. 18) given over to the prophetic voice of poets, patriarchs, and philosophers. It will be in terms of this doubling, a doubling that literally enacts a *contra-diction* (L. *contra* "against" + *dictio*, "saying" from *dicere*—v. "to say, pronounce, show"), that Celan lays out the structures of his engagement with Hölderlin and the German literary reception of Hölderlin that finds its culmination in the work of Heidegger.

On this reading, "Tübingen, Jänner" names a place of poetry as a poetry of place bound up in a relation to a specific time. (In the original draft, the title of the poem read "Tübingen, Jänner 1961" [TCA/NR, 36].) If, following Heidegger, Hölderlin's work will conceive poetry in terms of "vocation," of a call to "homecoming, by which the homeland is first prepared as the land of nearness (*Nähe*) to the origin (*Ursprung*)" (EHP, 47/GA 4, 28), then Celan's poem can be thought of as a Janus-like reflection on the *topoi* of homeland, nearness, and origin. For Heidegger, Hölderlin's poetry is less a literary achievement than a philosophical injunction that calls us to genuinely "dwell," where dwelling is understood not as occupying a house but as "the basic character of human existence" (PLT, 215/GA 7, 193). In this sense, poetic vocation, like the homeland itself, is not something already given or achieved; on the contrary, it is "something which is coming" and which can only come via remembrance or *Andenken*. As Heidegger puts it, "If remembrance of what-has-been lets this be in its own essence, and does not disturb it by a hasty misreckoning, trying to bring it into the present, then we experience what-has-been, returning in the *remembrance* as a *re-thinking* (*An-denken*), swinging out beyond our present, and coming to us as something futural" (EHP, 123/GA 4, 100). As those who prepare this futural "advent," the poets foretell "the coming of the holy." We need to understand this poetic vocation in its Greek sense, Heidegger claims, following the etymology of *propheteuein* as *pro* + *phasis* "to speak in advance of," whence we derive the word *prophet*.

The poets are, if they stand in their essence, *prophetic*. They are not, however, "prophets" according to the Judeo-Christian sense of the term. The "prophets" of these religions do not only utter in advance the primordial word of the holy. At the same time they prophesy the God on whom they count for the security of their salvation in eternal bliss (EHP, 136–37/GA 4, 114).

Heidegger would come to think of Hölderlin as the poet who, in foretelling the holy, "opens the time for an appearing of the gods, and points into the location of the dwelling of historical man upon this earth."

In his office as the one who foretells the coming of the gods (*parousia*), the poet stands "*between* gods and mortals" as the "voice of the people (*Volk*)" who receives the holy word and passes it on to the *Volk* (EHP, 63–64/GA 4, 47). Here the poet helps the *Volk* "to remain mindful of (*eingedenk*) its belonging to beings as a whole." Poetry in this sense "belongs to a definite time," Heidegger will claim; yet in mediating between gods and mortals, the poet is able to stand "between the times" as the prophetic voice of the coming of the holy:

> By founding (*stiftet*) anew the essence of poetry, Hölderlin first determines a new time. It is the time of the gods who have fled *and* of the god who is coming. It is the *time of need* (*die dürftige Zeit*) because it stands in a double lack and a double not: in the no-longer of the gods who have fled and the not-yet of the god who is coming. (EHP, 64/GA 4, 47)

Celan was deeply familiar with Heidegger's work on Hölderlin, having read his essay "What Are Poets For?" ("*Wozu Dichter?*"), from *Holzwege*, and his collection *Elucidations of Hölderlin's Poetry*.[62] Moreover, he had read Karl Löwith's book, *Heidegger: Denker in dürftiger Zeit*, even underlining passages that spoke of the "eschatological consciousness" in which "Heidegger thinks toward that which is coming (*ein Kommendes*), toward the awaited *parousia* of being."[63] In this Hölderlinian-Heideggerian *topos* of the thinker-poet in a "time of need," Celan would find a hint for a Janus-like reversal of the eschatological yearning for the *parousia* or the "coming-of-the-Lord." As we saw earlier in our discussion of Derrida and Benjamin, the Hebrew tradition of justice thought of time as messianic, as "the straight gate through which the Messiah might enter."[64] In a certain way Benjamin's rejection of historicist time as something "homogeneous and empty" comported well with Heidegger's own notion of time and historicity. Yet in his "Theses on the Philosophy of History," Benjamin pointed out that "the Jews were prohibited from investigating the future. The Torah and the prayers instruct them in remembrance (*Eingedenken*), however." And it is precisely in terms of remembrance, memory, and "remaining mindful of" that Celan will frame his own relation to Tübingen as the *Denkmal* or "memorial site" to poetic time in its Hölderlinian sense. Like Janus himself, Celan seems to say, memory is schismatic, broken apart by a caesura that splits time itself in half. Within his own life the powerful force of such a caesura would find its expression in the whole enthymeme of "Auschwitz," a word he refrained from using.[65] Writing in the shadow of Adorno's claim about the impossibility of crafting genuine poetry in the wake of Auschwitz, Celan will take up Heidegger's philosophical call for the pressing need of poets in a destitute time, "in the evening of the world's age that has been declining toward its night" (PLT, 91/GA 5, 269). Yet even as he will grant the power of Heidegger's philosophical engagement with poetry and with his critique of language in the epoch of modern technology, Celan will come to see its impoverishment as a way of thinking through the caesura of the twentieth century, the caesura of Auschwitz. Against Heidegger's Hölderlinian idyll about Graeco-German affinity as the site for poetic remembrance, Celan will draw on his traumatic experience as a Jewish survivor to think memory not merely as commemoration, but as annihilation. It is in this sense that, in the shadow of "Tübingen, January 1961" and of other Januarys of madness and genocide, the poem "remains mindful of its dates" (SPP, 408/GW III, 196). No longer can Tübingen stand so innocently as the site of a German-Greek-Christian axis of thinking and poetizing. In the disruptions and scissions of Jewish experience a break appears that Celan will trace on the palimpsest of "Tübingen" in all its cultural-philosophical-poetic meanings.

"ZUR BLINDHEIT ÜBER-REDETE AUGEN"

The poem opens, paradoxically enough, on a note of closure: eyes that normally *see* are "talked-into" closing, persuaded toward "blindness." The German text begins "*Zur Blindheit über-/redete Augen*;" this initial use of the preposition "*zu*" (to, toward)—"eyes talked-toward blindness" literally—can be seen in tension with the very last words of the poem—"*immer-, immer-,/ zuzu*," which Felstiner loosely translates as "ever-ever-/ moremore" (SPP, 158–59). In this latter form, the word "*zu*" functions as an adverb that means "closed" or "shut." In other words, both the first and last words of the poem (apart from the final line that is a citation) turn on the Janus-like image of a door opening/closing. What we find here is a complex language of inversion and involution that remains hypersensitive to the possibilities of opening and closing—of eyes, of memory, of words, and of the eschatological language of a coming time. It is this possibility—and, in Celan's eyes, necessity—of *Umkehr* that will shape the way he reads Hölderlin's words in "Tübingen, Jänner" (TCA/M, 10).

Celan had deep admiration for Hölderlin's poetic craft. He knew his work quite well and owned both the six-volume *Kleine Stuttgarter Ausgabe* edited by Friedrich Beissner and the two-volume *Tempel-Klassiker* edition.[66] Moreover, his own work reveals an ongoing poetic dialogue with Hölderlin—in poems such as "Remembrance," "Tenebrae," "I drink wine," and others. But his affinity to Hölderlin went deeper. Given Hölderlin's personal suffering and his time spent in the Autenrieth clinic, Celan—who had also gone through the gauntlet of various stays in French psychiatric clinics—

strongly identified with Hölderlin's bent toward madness and dissolution. He went so far as to call him his "*Schicksalsbruder*" ("brother in fate").[67] Yet "Tübingen, Jänner" can hardly be read as a poem celebrating Hölderlin or memorializing his time in Tübingen. Playing off the title of Hölderlin's celebrated ode "The Blind Singer," Celan draws on the classical *topos* of poetic blindness/insight that marks the Greek tradition of Homer and Sophocles's Oedipus. But there is more. Celan will set up a self-conscious relation to Hölderlin's "*Der Rhein*" hymn that proclaims:

> The sons of gods, though,
> are the blindest of all. (SPF, 198–99)

On Celan's reading, blindness is intimately caught up with language—the eyes are "talked into" their blindness, a blindness that undermines the purity of poetic insight. The trope of the "pure" will become decisive here. We could even read this relation between eyes and words in the second line as an inversion of Heidegger's notion of "*Ge-rede*" (palaver, idle chatter) where the "*über-redete Augen*" fall victim to the superficial gloss of cover-up that dominated so many areas of postwar German culture.[68] Clearly, we can also detect a biographical reference to the slanderous accusations of Claire Goll, which Celan believed had blinded members of the German literary community to the underlying issues of anti-Semitism. There is no one way of reading the blindness image of the opening verse. So much of the text plays on an intertextual level with references back and forth between Hölderlin and Heidegger and the Greek tradition. In his late poem "In lovely blueness," for example, reflecting on Sophocles's tragic hero, Hölderlin writes that "King Oedipus has perhaps one eye too many"—a line that Celan had underscored in his copy of *Introduction to Metaphysics* where Heidegger calls this a "prophetic word of the seer" (*seherisches Wort*).[69]

However we decide to interpret these opening words about eyes (plural) talked-into blindness—precisely in Tübingen during the month of January—we are left with some troubling allusions. Firstly, we confront the *excess* of speech (*über*-redete or "over-talked") as a failed rhetorical strategy of persuasion. Secondly, we notice an unnerving plurality that will be reinforced in later verses (eye*s*, v. 2, tower*s*, v. 7, visit*s*, joiner*s*, v. 8, word*s*, v. 10, patriarch*s*, v. 16), references that undermine any illusion of unity and cohesion. Everything is doubled, multiple, in excess of measure, symmetry, balance; truth itself and the poetic possibility of truth telling is called into question. Indeed, the very first line "Zur Blindheit *über-*" opens with a tear: an enjambment that breaks the line and rents it from any context of coherence. It is in this poetic fissure, Celan seems to say, that we begin.

There can be no "pure" beginning. And it is in terms of these two figural elements—purity and beginning—that the first stanza unfolds.

> Their—"a
> riddle, what is pure-
> ly arisen"—, their
> memory of
> floating Hölderlintowers gull-
> enswirled. (vv. 3–9)

Here, we are given over to the eyes' twofold possession of Hölderlin: on the one hand, their "memory" of floating Hölderlintowers and, on the other, their possession of a line taken from Hölderlin's ode "Der Rhein." Memory and citation, when thought together with purity and beginning, come to form an intertextual field of encounter for the two poets at the axis of a German history gathered around the madness of the twentieth of January. But what is the function of a citation and how does it figurally play into the possibility of memory? These are questions that Celan addresses here. By citing something from the past one *retrieves* it from its original context and *repeats* it into a new one—such is the double movement of *Wiederholung* (repetition/retrieval) that Celan knew well from his reading of Heidegger's *Being and Time* (BT, 304–306/SZ, 331–33). Citation then, as Anja Lemke reminds us, always signifies "tearing out a verse from its original context, that is transporting/translating (*Übertragung*) what is foreign (*das Fremde*) into what is one's own (*das Eigene*)."[70] But such a transporting of what has been (*das Gewesene*) into the present situation of a new poem never takes place without a breach—hence, Celan's two enjambments in verses 3 and 4, which fracture the very meaning they seem to indicate. Hölderlin's "original" text speaks of "a" riddle; yet Celan's line reads "their—'a / riddle . . .' " ("*Ihre—'ein Rätsel . . .'* ")—in other words, the plural eyes will be juxtaposed against the singular riddle. Moreover, the double hyphens as well as the double quotation marks undermine the illusion of oneness, unity, self-sameness to which the citation appears to speak. That Celan is inverting Hölderlin's original pun about the "pure" (*Rein-*) in a poem entitled "The Rhine" ("*Der Rhein*") can hardly be doubted. What will concern him here, however, is the whole German discourse about purity and the pure as directed toward the twentieth of January. That is, Celan will find in the use of Hölderlin by his later Nazi commentators (such as Kurt Hildebrandt) the ideological impulse to a Juden*rein* (Jew-free) Germany.[71] What remains a riddle or enigma is how the poetic-philosophical yearning for a pure origin will be both transformed and transmogrified into a political desire for a nation that is *Judenrein* and that has gone mad with delusions about *Rassenreinheit* (racial purity). In this way, by *citing* Hölderlin and placing him (or his text) in a new *site* Celan brings to presence the dynamic of the stranger, the foreigner, the Jew in relation to the original text, the native place, the pure.[72]

By rewriting the original text one undermines its originality; citation in this sense becomes recitation. In the act of citing the "purely-arisen," its "source" becomes doubled; the *Ur-sprung* of the citation is negated, "sprung over," as it were, to the new context. We are left with only a replacement of the source, a world where we have only the riddle and enigma of the desire for pure origin. Celan plays with this purity of citation by playing off the homonymic relation between "*rein*" (pure) and "*Rhein*" (Rhine) that Hölderlin originally employed to reinforce the purity of the *arche*. By doubling this as repetition Celan crafts his own practice of citation against the philosophical illusion about the purity and singularity of "an" *arche*. Several poems from *Niemandsrose* (1963) engage this poetic practice of citation. There Celan will "cite" lines from poets as diverse as Dante, Jean Paul, Mandelstam, Villon, Ovid, Büchner, Dickinson, and others.[73] Yet the focus on Hölderlin is striking. In his first draft for the title page of *Niemandsrose* Celan cited another well-known verse from Hölderlin's "Der Rhein"—

> . . . For
> As you began, so you will remain,
> And much as need can effect . . . (TCA/NR, 4; SPF, 198–99)

In Hölderlin's original poem the line from "Der Rhein" that Celan cited in "Tübingen, Jänner"—"what is pure- / ly arisen" (*Rein- / entsprungenes*)—directly precedes this verse and shows Celan's unremitting preoccupation with origin, inception, source, provenance, and what I will call "the discourse of the *arche*." If Heidegger could write nostalgically about Hölderlin's poem "Homecoming" that "the original essence of joy is learning to become at home within a nearness to the origin. . . . The poet comes home by entering into nearness to the origin," then Celan could only remember the breach of any possible homecoming, the impossibility of ever returning home (EHP, 43–44/GA 4, 25). For him, the Graeco-German discourse of the *arche* that found its expression in the autochthonic bond between these two "original" peoples betrayed a brutal impulse to suppress the foreign, the strange, the other. Not consanguineous purity and homogeneity, but racial and linguistic heterogeneity and alterity provided the basis for any kind of poetic translation of difference. Hence, Celan could write in *Atemwende*:

> Yet in you, from
> birth,
> foamed the other spring (*die andre Quelle*). (Joris tr. *Breathturn*, 86–87)

In other words, at the beginning—if one can speak of beginning at all—there reigns otherness, an archeo-heterology of difference. The idyll of the *arche*, sung on the banks of the Neckar by Hölderlin and his later interpreters, rings hollow in the memory of the exiled Jew from Czernowitz. Celan's "Tübingen, Jänner" undermines the myth of the *arche* by constantly inserting hyphens, colons, quotation marks, parentheses, and enjambments. It doubles virtually everything, leaving the dream of Heideggerian *Versammlung* (gathering) and Parmenidean oneness in grave danger. Citation merely reinforces this critique by its very act of repetition/recitation. The myth of origin will be pluralized into multiplicity, undercutting the notion of both purity and presence. Something of this archeo-heterology will be expressed in *Writing the Disaster* where Blanchot remarks: "There is no origin, if origin presupposes an original presence . . . every beginning is a beginning over."[74]

The Janus-like doubling of citation, like the doubling involved in memory and remembrance, works not from an original source that is pure, but from a palimpsest of layered inscriptions tied to various dates of significance. The poetic text of Hölderlin comes to us, then, not as a spotless origin, but as a cicatrix or scar that marks the trauma of a remembered wound. Even memory will be doubled in "Tübingen, Jänner"; in addition to the eyes' "memory of floating Hölderlintowers"—i.e., of their reflection in the pure water of the Neckar—there is Celan's memory of the towers in the water, a mnemological reflection of a reflection as it were. By repeating/retrieving the reflection(s) Celan deconstructs its (their) archaic force.[75] This undermining of a certain German *arche*-metaphysics associated with Tübingen, the Neckar, and the Hölderlin-Rezeption will be reinforced in the water images of stanzas 1 and 2. There, Celan alludes to "swimming" towers, "drowned" joiners, and "plunging" words—all references to the play of surface and depth, of the unstable movement of water that cannot "stand" as a metaphysics of standing presence or ground. Instead, we are immersed in a stream of Heraclitean citation where the "original" words swim in the memory of those who re-cite and re-situate them. The full effect of this immersion is played out in the biographical references to Hölderlin's Tübingen stay:

> Visits of drowned joiners (*Schreiner*) to
> these
> plunging words. (vv. 9–11, SPP, 158–59)

What are we to make of these "visits"—and who are the "drowned joiners"? By now it has been well documented that in the time of his madness Hölderlin lived in a tower on the Neckar taken in by the joiner/carpenter, Ernst F. Zimmer, who looked after him until his death. There is also another biographical reference to the lithographer Johann Georg Schreiner who visited Hölderlin there in 1823 and 1825/26 and drew a portrait of him that Celan later saw.[76] Celan is no doubt alluding to these visits in some inverted way, but why are these two Schreiner "drowned"? And in what sense do they make visits *to* "these / plunging words"? What lies hidden here, below the surface, is an allusion to Heidegger's comment in *Elucidations to Hölderlin's Poetry* that "poems appear like a shrine without a temple" ("*Gedichte erscheinen wie ein tempelloser* Schrein") (EHP, 21, 222/EHD, 7, 194). This onomatic play between *Schrein* (shrine) and *Schreiner* (both as cabinetmaker/joiner and the lithographer who visited the mad poet) will be explicitly addressed in Celan's notebooks where he writes:

> -i- Poems: "temple-less shrine" . . .
> Handwork: hand/reflect on connections
> such as "hand and heart"
> handwork—heartwork
> Beginning: "poetizing as artisanal craft"? The craftsmanship
> involved in poetizing? . . .
> Final Note: Poetry: "a temple-less shrine."
> <Heidegger:Hölderlin> (MSS, 98–99)

Heidegger would make much of the intimate bond he saw between the artisanal handicraft of the carpenter/joiner and the skilled handiwork of the poet. Here, Celan follows this Heideggerian insight but in a direction that decisively undermines Heidegger's dream of the *arche* (WCT, 14–22/GA 8, 17–27).[77] For the German word *Schrein* conveys a range of meanings that betray an underlying connection to the *topoi* of *arche*-metaphysics. Besides its standard renderings as "cabinet," "chest," or "cupboard," it can also be translated as "shrine," "box," or "coffer" for preserving scrolls, reliquaries, and cultic objects going back to its Latin root, *scrinium*.[78] In this sense, it functions as an "archive," "chest," or "ark" (in German: *Arche*) for sheltering the holy *and* also as a "coffin" (*Sarg*) for preserving bodies with ointments or salve (German: *Salbe*), all derived from the Latin *scrinium*. From this diverse field of possible signifiers, Celan sets into motion a poetic tension between the Heideggerian impulse to turn Hölderlin's poetry (and poetry as such, including his own) into a shrine for preserving the *arche*, an archival reliquary that safeguards its sacred meaning *and* the deconstructive force to see such preservation as a kind of entombment, a way of handicrafting a hermeneutic coffin to render the living word dead by turning it into a citation. Within this etymological frame we can now read the line anew: the visits by drowned "Schreiner" can refer to those readers/interpreters who visit the text and drown in the depths of its plunging words. These hermeneutic pilgrimages to the dead Hölderlin's towers and words might also be read as an allusion to those who seek to enshrine the poetic text by turning it into a citation, an archive of/for the *arche*.

The third stanza unfolds as a way for Celan to bring the possibility of such an archive/shrine into tension with the expectation of a prophetic pronouncement from the poet:

> Came, if there
> came a man,
> came a man to the world, today, with
> the patriarchs'
> light-beard: he could,
> if he spoke of this
> time, he
> could
> only babble and babble,
> ever-, ever-
> moremore. (vv. 12–22)

This stanza gives utterance to a conditional hope about the coming of a man who, were he to come, would no longer speak with the prophetic voice of a patriarch, but would only babble and babble. Again, as in the first two stanzas, we are dealing with citation and the way citation can be used to undermine the entombed meaning of a text by those who might wish to preserve it in a reliquary or shrine. The citation here is once more doubled and goes back to Hölderlin and to Heidegger's recollection of Hölderlin's texts for the double German task both of reflecting on the first beginning of Greek metaphysics *and* of preparing the way for an "other" beginning to come.[79] In "Bread and Wine," writing about the time of waiting between the gods who have fled and those who are to come, Hölderlin asks, ". . . and what are poets for in a destitute time?" (". . . *und wozu Dichter in dürftiger Zeit?*") (SPF, 156–57). Taking up this Hölderlinian theme in his essay "What are Poets For?" (1946), Heidegger speaks of the "default of God" ("*der Fehl Gottes*"), or "the god's failure to arrive," as characterizing the epoch of the "world's night," the era of modern nihilism (PLT, 91/GA 5, 269).[80] In his self-conscious use of the German verb *dürfen*—which Felstiner, Hamburger, and Joris all translate as "could"—Celan calls attention to the link between Heidegger's reading of Hölderlin and of Hölderlin's poetological relation to the time of the coming gods. Following Hölderlin, Heidegger understands the poet as a prophet whose vocation consists in "the originary naming of the gods" (EHD, 45/GA 4, 45).[81] "Poetry is a founding: a naming of being. . . . Poetry is the primordial language of a historical *Volk*" (EHP,

60/GA 4, 43). Given Celan's historical experience, we can understand his skepticism concerning the poetic language of both primordiality and the *Volk*. The language of the third stanza is decidedly nihilistic in that it raises the Hölderlin question—"What are poets for in a destitute (*dürftige*) time?"—but it offers a far less ennobling answer. Even if we were to want to retrieve Hölderlin's poetological mandate of announcing the *parousia* or Second Coming in Heidegger's name, then the language of such a hope could only take the form of babbling or glossalalia (Greek: *glossa* "tongue" + *lalein* "to prattle").[82] "*Nach* Auschwitz" (in all its senses as "after," "following," "in accordance with," "subsequent to"), any form of poetic mimesis would be absurdly impossible—not only because the very language of the "*Volk*" and of "primordiality" would be so befouled by its misuses and perversions as to be impossible. But it would also be owing to the fact that the very message of Christian eschatological salvation would be so poorly attuned to the tragic dimension of Jewish messianism. Hölderlin reinforces this naming function of the poet in "At the Source of the Danube" where he speaks of naming as something "compelled by the holy" (SPF, 180–81; EHP, 216/GA 4, 188). But Celan will, of course, refrain from naming a prophet or patri-*arch*, leaving him nameless, referring to him twice merely as "*ein* Mensch" (my italics), "*a* man".

The very temporality of the messianic call "come, come" shows itself as fragmented, broken, and inchoate—hence the language of the third stanza with its difficult line-breaks and enjambments. The poet can no longer speak with the voice of the prophet and call for the return of the gods to come. In the post-Nietzschean, post-Auschwitz era of the "world's night," the eschatological idiom of a coming salvation reveals itself only in/as a repetitive, doubling, and ambiguous language of stammering, stuttering, babbling. The sacral word of the poet-prophet-patriarch, these figures who seek to recover the ruling power of the origin as *arche*, will take the form of an incoherent citation, quoted secondhand by one of the hermeneutic pilgrims ("Pallaksch. Pallaksch"). Again, as has been well documented, Celan knew the account in Christoph Theodor Schwab's biography (reported by Wilhelm Michel in *Das Leben Hölderlins* and underlined by Celan in his copy) about the later years of the mad Hölderlin who, when addressed by visitors, would respond in a private language of incoherent stammering.[83] Schwab reported that "one of his favorite expressions was the word 'Pallaksch.'" As Celan would later observe in a letter to Ilana Shmueli, "A word of Hölderlin already appeared once in a poem of mine, 'Tübingen, Jänner.' There at the end it reads 'Pallaksch' by which Hölderlin, in the time of his madness, meant Yes and No at the same time."[84] As a code word for a certain kind of poetic undecidability and as a testament to the madness of the poetic vocation, the final verse of "Tübingen, Jänner" comes to stand for a world of binary opposition without the possibility of Hegelian *Aufhebung* or unity. That is, it places two opposite meanings against one another without the hope of dialectical reconciliation/overcoming into a higher third term. The purity of the *arche* and the native stands opposite the impurity of the foreigner, the madman, the babbler. There can be no clear separation between these realms; they simply imply and call for one another.

This unremitting image of doubling repetition without the hope of unity is reinforced in a number of ways in the last four lines of the poem. The doubling incoherence of *lallen* (babble), followed by the truly incoherent utterances of a coming patriarch—"immer-, immer- / zuzu"—gives voice to the mad speech of a failed prophet who is in a binary relationship with a mentally deranged murderer. These two lines refer back to an indirect citation from Büchner's *Woyzeck* where Marie (Woyzeck's beloved) calls out, "Immer, zu, immer zu" as she, in the arms of another, dances past Woyzeck—words that Woyzeck then later repeats when, in his madness, he murders her.[85] By bringing madness and murder together in yet another citation, Celan weaves back to the double theme of Lenz's madness (*Wahnsinn*) and the murderous planning of the Wannsee Conference of January 20 alluded to in the title "Tübingen, Jänner." Following this Büchner citation is yet another Hölderlin citation in the last line—("Pallaksch. Pallaksch")—that stands in an intimate relation with the first citation (vv. 3–5) from "Der Rhein"—"ein/Rätsel ist Rein-/entsprungenes." Both citations play with the theme of doubling—the pun on "*Rhein/rein*," the repetition of "Pallaksch," the repetitive act of citation itself, the fact that there are two citations from Hölderlin in the poem. At the same time, this poetic doubling occurs precisely as a way of undercutting the illusion of purity, *arche*, order, and meaning. For each time the citation is doubled it serves as a disruption, fragmentation, and tearing asunder of the quote from its "original" context, even as it calls into question the strange/foreign sense of its "new" context. Such a repetitive form of interruption gives voice to a repeated trauma. Moreover, Celan sets the two citations into an unmistakable binary relation: the riddle of the purely arisen (*arche*-metaphysics, *Judenrein* politics, the language of the sacral, and their enigmatic relation) *and* the incoherent utterance of a mad poet whose voice is less that of a prophet than of a stammering babbler. Placed within parentheses, interiorized in the space of madness, the words function literally as an *Er-innerung* (both as memory of, and an interiorizing of, madness, murder, genocide, and the breakdown of language that both leads into and follows from them).

"Tübingen, Jänner," then, appears as a poem that remains mindful of memory, recollection, and memorializing the fate of the Jewish people. It also stands as the holy site of German poetry and philosophy symbolized topographically by "Tübingen" and thought within the temporal frame of a "January"—"today" (v. 14) as a recollection about a different January (January 1942) in anticipation of yet more eschatological Januarys to come, "of this time" (vv. 17–18).[86] Against this background, "Tübingen, Jänner" comes to us as a poem about memory that gives voice to the fragmentation, incompletion, and brokenness in the line of history without seeking to reestablish a lost unity from the past (historical recollection) or prophetically project a coming unity in the future (eschatological hope). In the teeth of historical catastrophe, Celan calls for and calls forth a salvific power within memory/recollection that re-members the suffering of the dead and the injustice done to them. In this sense, "Tübingen, Jänner" seeks to enact justice as an ethical duty to remember the scattered corpses of the unburied dead in spite of the caesura of Januarys past. Against the Heideggerian impulse toward "gathering" or *Versammlung* as a way of finding a path back to the *arche*, *Heimat*, and homeland, Celan underscores dispersion, fragmentation, and his own irrevocable exile from a Czernowitz homeland.[87] In the years following "Tübingen, Jänner," Celan will reframe these questions about loss, mourning, and caesura in terms of both a renewed conversation/*Auseinander-setzung* with Heidegger and/as an impossible dialogue with the Auschwitz dead. His 1967 poem "Todtnauberg," written right after his visit to Heidegger's famous "*Hütte*" in the Black Forest, gives testimony to just such an impossible conversation.

"TODTNAUBERG": THE CONDITIONS OF THE (IM)POSSIBILITY OF DIALOGUE

The years between the writing of "Tübingen, Jänner" (1961) and "Todtnauberg" (1967) were difficult ones for Celan. He suffered a number of psychological breakdowns and was subjected to stays in psychiatric clinics where he underwent a battery of different drug therapies as well as electroshock treatment for his depression. In January 1967 (precisely in that month that proved so difficult for him) he had a chance encounter with Claire Goll at the Paris Goethe Institute and five days later attempted to kill himself by thrusting a knife into his heart.[88] Some six months later he came to Freiburg at the behest of Professor Gerhart Baumann to give a reading of his poetry and while there was invited by Heidegger to come to his Black Forest cabin for a visit. Yet from February 13, 1967, until the time of his visit to Freiburg on July 24 Celan was confined to the Sainte-Anne psychiatric clinic in Paris.[89] Everything that followed—the meeting in Freiburg after the reading, the car ride to Todtnauberg the next morning, the interrupted walk on the moor, the visit in the cabin, the exchange of letters afterward—needs to be put into this context of severe psychological crisis and instability. Celan was a difficult person whose traumatic experience from the war years was always with him, making it ever more difficult to come to closure about the past. His well-documented ambivalence about meeting Heidegger—his misgivings before, during, and after, as well as his obvious interest in conversing with a world-renowned philosopher who admired his work and shared his passion for the thoughtful dialogue between philosophy and poetry—was hardly a unique episode. As we will see later in our discussion of Celan's visit to Jerusalem in 1969, ambivalence marked much of his personal experience. And yet this ambivalence needs to be understood in its larger context, for what characterizes the text of "Todtnauberg" is not merely an individual's ambivalence regarding a personal meeting, but a linguistic-historical-cultural-phenomenological ambivalence about the (im) possibility of a German-Jewish dialogue in the wake of the Shoah. The language of "Todtnauberg" is notoriously difficult, marked everywhere by ambiguity and undecidability, of a poetic idiom that can be read both as a tribute to Heidegger's thinking—and as a serious *Auseinandersetzung* or "critical engagement" with it.

That Celan had some positive feeling about their historic encounter can be seen partly in his letters and the fact that he had a special bibliophilic printing of "Todtnauberg" made of fifty copies, the first of which he sent to Heidegger in January 1968 with a personal dedication. He also had written to his wife a few days after the meeting telling her that he and Heidegger had "a serious conversation with clear words on my part" (PC/GL I, 479). He added: "I hope that Heidegger takes up his pen and will write a few pages that relate to our conversation that will serve as a warning against the Nazism that is once again thriving." Several days later, Celan also wrote to his friend Franz Wurm reporting that "everything went well in Germany, including the meeting with Heidegger with whom I had a long and very forthright conversation" (PC/FW, 87–88).[90] Yet there are also documents that attest to the difficulties Celan was having with Heidegger: a conversation with his host Gerhart Baumann on the eve of his meeting that he was having doubts about visiting Heidegger in Todtnauberg; his expressed wish that he not be photographed with Heidegger (which he later withdrew); his notebook entries critical of Heidegger, and his drafts of the poem.[91] Nor were these ambivalent reactions hard to understand. Celan knew of Heidegger's political support of National Socialism from his readings of Löwith and the collection of political speeches, *Nachlese zu Heidegger*, edited by Guido Schneeberger.[92] But he also sensed that the poetic sensitivity of Heidegger was something rare and philosophically worth engaging. He had long wanted to visit Heidegger, and his notebooks and correspondence from the 1950s and early '60s give evidence of a long-term engagement with Heidegger's work as well as an earnest desire to carry out a dialogue with him about poetry's place in the epoch of technological nihilism. Celan shared many of Heidegger's views on the transmogrification of language in an age of cybernetic reckoning marked by the loss of a connection to place, landscape, earth, and homeland. But he was also deeply troubled by Heidegger's commitment to a philosophy of rootedness and autochthony that privileged the "purity" of the *arche* and its political idyll of a *Volk* with its primordial connection to the language of *Heimat* and soil.[93] Celan's friend Jean Bollack, in his essay "Vor dem Gericht der Toten" ("Before the Court of the Dead"), reports how much Celan suffered under the veil of silence that Heidegger had employed to deflect questions concerning his entanglement in National Socialism. Moreover, Bollack relates how much Celan hoped for a word from Heidegger (both private and public) that would break this silence.[94] The text of the poem he wrote reflects just such an attitude.

"Todtnauberg" is a poem about a place, a specific *Ort*, "site," or *topos* whose landscape comes to express the underlying contradictions of a German-Jewish dialogue about homeland and homelessness. Both Celan and Heidegger had reflected long and carefully about the notion of place. In his work of the postwar years Heidegger writes about the "topology of being," by which he means a fourfold relation of earth, sky, mortals, and gods gathered in a place or *topos*.[95] In his "Meridian" speech, which draws heavily on this Heideggerian language of topology, Celan will explicitly speak of poetry as a kind of "*Topos* research" that is intimately bound up with the specificity of place (SPP, 411–13/GW III, 199–202). He will go so far as to state that his particular form of *topos* research is a "seeking . . . the place (*Ort*) of my own origin." This kind of searching, he concedes, is nothing other than an "impossible path, [a] path of the impossible" since "none of these places is to be found, they do not exist." The landscape of his Czernowitz home, now "fallen into historylessness" (an*heim*gefallenen), the one obliterated by the ravages of war and the calculus of genocide, can never be recovered. The poet who has been violently expelled from his homeland, "driven from [his] world" (*weltvertrieben*), remains ever the stranger, the exile, the Jew (GW III, 185; PC/FW, 143).[96] This inextinguishable identity as the homeless wanderer is one Celan would never put behind him. If Heidegger could write in reverent terms about the poet as "the one who has been cast out" (*der Hinausgeworfener*) so that he might consecrate the poetic word of his *Volk* in a time of need, for Celan the implications would be read quite differently (EHP, 64/GA 4, 47). As he well knew, being cast out of his land meant "an obliteration of a sense of place" that would always bring to memory the loss (and impossible recovery) of his Czernowitz home and landscape.[97] Just so, "Todtnauberg" can be read as a kind of *Widerruf* (revocation/disavowal) of the whole idyll about landscape, language, and *Volk* that underlies Heidegger's well-known essay of 1933, "Creative Landscape: Why I Remain in the Provinces."[98]

But it also offers a poetic critique of the late Heidegger's discourse about homelessness, dwelling, rootedness, and *ethos*.

In his late essays Heidegger speaks of dwelling as "the fundamental character of human existence" (PLT, 215/GA 7, 193). Written in the time of the post–World War II housing shortage in Germany where millions were resettled from urban areas destroyed by Allied bombing, Heidegger undertakes a critique of the merely sociological, demographic, and political-economic responses to this problem. For him, the genuine problem of dwelling needs to be thought in terms of the possibility of poetizing since "poetizing is what truly *lets* us dwell (*Wohnenlassen*)." As he puts it in his essay of 1951 "Building Dwelling Thinking":

> However hard and bitter, however hampering and threatening the lack of houses remains, the *real plight of dwelling* does not lie merely in a lack of houses. The real plight of dwelling is indeed older than the world wars with their destruction. . . . The real plight of dwelling lies in this, that mortals ever search anew for the nature of dwelling, that they *must ever learn to dwell.* What if humanity's homelessness consisted in this, that humanity still does not even think of the *real* plight of dwelling as *the* plight? Yet as soon as humanity *gives thought* to its homelessness it is a misery no longer. Rightly considered and kept well in mind, it is the singular summons that calls mortals into their dwelling. (PLT, 161/GA 7, 163–64)

For the late Heidegger "dwelling" could be understood in terms of what he calls our "stay" upon the earth, our *Aufenthalt,* which in turn can be read as being bound up with our capacity to poetize, since "poetry and dwelling belong together" (PLT, 227/GA 7, 206). In the "Letter on Humanism," he thinks *Aufenthalt* in conversation with the texts of Sophocles and Heraclitus as "ethos" or "originary ethics"—not ethics in its calculative sense as a system of rules or directives, but the site of "dwelling" where one abides in the "abode" of being as a "sojourn" between birth and death, natality and mortality (PM, 269–71/WM, 184–88). Going back to his early Freiburg lectures on Aristotle, Heidegger thought of *ethos* not merely as a "habit" that might be gained via knowledge (*episteme*), skill (*techne*), or virtue (*arete*); rather, he thought it as the habitat that forms our way of "having" such that our "be-having" is less the accomplishment of subjective initiative than the attuning to the site from which we dwell.[99] Habits that have us, such as language, form the habitat in which we find ourselves, what Heidegger in *Being and Time* termed *Befindlichkeit* ("attunement") (BT, 126–34/SZ, 134–42). *Ethos* in this sense constitutes nothing theoretical, fixed, or permanent; it involves, rather, a constant reinterrogation of the site in which we are situated, the dwelling in which we come to find ourselves through the recursive praxis of being found. For the later Heidegger what attunes us to such being-found is poetry. Hence, in a primordial sense, poetry offers a way of interrogating the condition of our homelessness, of attuning us ever more powerfully to the fact that we are *not* at home, but are "*un-heimlich*," uncanny, un-settled, thrust from the settlements of habit and habitat.

Celan had learned much from Heidegger about the attunement of *ethos* and its relation to poetic craft. From his readings of the late essays and *Introduction to Metaphysics*, he knew of the unsettling plights of Oedipus and Antigone who had been thrust out of their homeland by questions of birth and politics, themes that he undoubtedly read differently than Heidegger. Yet it is precisely these questions that Heidegger either would not or could not address that form (both literally and figuratively) the landscape of "Todtnauberg." As a native Jew thrust from his homeland in the Bukovina, Celan would suffer the fate of ontological homelessness in Heidegger's sense, but always in terms of its specific historical, political, and linguistic *topoi*. The language of "Todtnauberg" will take up these *topoi* and read them in and against the *topos* of the Black Forest cabin on the high moorland with woodland turf. What comes to language in the poem is a discourse about what did not come to language in the meeting between the poet and the philosopher, but which lies buried beneath the topography of the damp earth that covers over the secrets that lie underground. Celan was preoccupied by the Heideggerian question of *ethos* and even understood it in terms of the philosopher's own idiosyncratic idiom. In a letter to Werner Weber he writes: "Language, above all in the poem, is *ethos*—*ethos* as a fateful projection of truth" (*schicksalhafter Wahrheitsentwurf*).[100] As Celan thinks it, poetry and translation need to be understood less as the subjectivist experience of an egological reader/writer, than as exercises in "waiting for the address of language (*ein Warten auf den Zuspruch der Sprache*), if I can let the words of Martin Heidegger speak here." Yet, like Heidegger, Celan understood that the occlusions of modern technology undermined the proper attunement of poetic listening:

> We already have a cybernetic form of lyric poetry—we will also probably soon have (long live logical consistency!)—a lyrical cybernetics. . . .
>
> No more language, no more conversation—no, only Information, word systems with exact specifications of the wave-lengths necessary for "reception," a sterile "formal designing" [in original] for an adjustable "eye-complex."[101]

If *ethos* in this sense designates an uncanny relation to language whose uncanniness or *Unheimlichkeit* rests precisely in our inability to find our proper site of dwelling upon the earth, then Celan's poetry can be understood as a Heideggerian address (*Zuspruch*) to the claim (*Anspruch*) that language makes upon us. It is not we who have language, Heidegger famously tells us in "Building Dwelling Thinking"; rather, it is language that has us (PLT, 146/GA 7, 148). If we think of language as a human achievement, as the self-subsistent activity of a speaking subject, then we miss the ontological play of appropriation (*Ereignis*) and engagement that happens in the very possibility of speaking, listening, writing, reading, and remaining silent. For Heidegger, language happens as a claim upon us where "thinking lets itself be claimed by being (*vom Sein in den Anspruch nehmen*) so that it can say the truth of being" (PM, 239/GA 9, 313). In this sense, "language is the highest event (*Ereignis*) of human existence" (EHP, 58/GA 4, 40). But wherein does this "event" of language occur? Heidegger claims that it happens in the play of dif-ference between speech and stillness, between the self-subsistent speaking of mortals and the letting be still of language itself.

> At the proper time it becomes unavoidable to think of how mortal speech and its utterance take place in the speaking of language as the peal of the stillness of the dif-ference. . . . The structure of human speech can only be the manner (*melos*) in which the speaking of language, the peal of the stillness of the dif-ference, appropriates mortals by the command of the dif-ference. (PLT, 208–209/GA 12, 28–29)

In "Todtnauberg" Celan would take up this question of language as the play of dif-ference between speech and stillness, conversation and silence—now understood not only ontologically but through landscape, topography, botany, and geology. In the cleft of difference as the play between an *ethos* of poetic dwelling *and* an ethics of poetic exile, Celan hews away at the woodpaths that shelter Heidegger's provincial Black Forest retreat.

"TODTNAUBERG": A READING

At its most basic level, "Todtnauberg" can be read as a set of "lyrical stenographic notes" describing the excursion to Heidegger's cabin in the Black Forest on the day after Celan's triumphant reading before an audience of 1,200 listeners at the University of Freiburg on July 24, 1967.[102] The entire poem of twenty-six verses consists of only one sentence; most of the verses contain three words or less. In an admirably economic fashion that mimics a stenographer's outline, Celan describes the visit in a fragmented, clipped language that is short on adjectives and sparse in its diction. He soberly recounts the physical setting of Heidegger's hut: the flowers and landscape that surround it; the fountain that stands behind it; the star-die that sits beside it; the guestbook that lies within it. In the last four stanzas of the poem he tells of the chauffeured car ride that he and Heidegger shared to the Horbacher moor near Todtnauberg that was then interrupted by bad weather. Nothing of seeming consequence "happens" in the poem. There are no direct charges laid at Heidegger's feet for his Nazi past, no poetological declarations about the need for an *Auseinandersetzung* between poetry and philosophy as a way of coming to terms with the fate of Germany and the German language post-Auschwitz. But who would expect such directness from Celan? Anyone who is conversant with his late verse post-*Breathturn* knows how parsimonious and austere his language can sometimes be. And yet "Todtnauberg" is one of the longest poems in the collection *Lichtzwang* or "Light-Compulsion." What are we to make of this language? And how can we read its diction in ways that do justice to both the directness and indirectness of its verses?

The poem can be read on any number of levels: as a celebration of a historic meeting between Germany's leading poet and philosopher; as a call for future conversation and understanding; as a bitter account of a failed (and impossible) conversation—not only between Heidegger and Celan, but between Germans and Jews post-Auschwitz; as a document of ambivalence and ambiguity that moves between hope and despair, celebration and condemnation; as a poem about the possibility of memory and remembrance thought through the topography of landscape as a way of coming to terms with an ethics of remembering the dead.[103] I want to look at the *ambivalence* in this text as a way of thinking the aporia that constitutes what Derrida calls "the experience of the impossible" and which he thinks serves as nothing less than "the condition of ethics."[104] In this "experience of aporia"—what Celan in "The Meridian" termed "the path of the impossible" that "leads to encounter" (*Begegnung*)—we might even find hints of the (im)possibility of justice, since in Derrida's sense "aporetic experiences are the experiences, as improbable as they are necessary, of justice" (SPP, 413/GW III, 202).[105] Concealed in the halting, fragmented language of "Todtnauberg"—a *Berg* (mountain) of *Tod* (death)—is a poem that calls for the impossible: of the re-burial of those thrown into mass graves, of the re-collection of the ashes of the cremated corpses, of the re-membrance for both Jew and German of their loss, and of the re-cognition of German complicity in authorizing the annihilation of Jewish life in Europe. Yet despite these fragile hopes, we are left to consider whether in his reading of Heidegger's postwar work Celan comes to recognize the impossibility of his "hope, today / for a thinker's / (un- / delayed coming) / word / in the heart" (vv. 12–16).

The poem begins cryptically enough by naming two flowers in succession—"arnica" and "eyebright"—without any context and without any relation to a subject. Each of these are strategically placed at the beginning because they serve as the portal or threshold from which to read the entire poem. "Arnica" is the Latin name for a healing herb that serves as a salve and tincture for the treatment of wounds and bruises. Its German name "*Wohlverleih*" means "conferring or granting prosperity and well-being." "Eyebright" is likewise a healing plant that is used against eye ailments for those who have been wounded, afflicted with dim vision, or blinded. The German word *Augentrost* literally translates as "eye-consolation;" the Greek name for eyebright, *euphrasia* meaning "cheerfulness" or "serenity," goes back to the Greek root *phrazein* "to speak," "thoughtfully reflect" and *eu* "well, good."[106] Given all these various shadings and intonations, how are we to read this? Is Celan hoping for a healing encounter with Heidegger that will bring a salve to his psychic wounds and relief to eyes stung with tears spent mourning his parents' death? Or should we read these opening words as an indictment of Heidegger's blindness and as an indication of the need for healing because of the wounds already afflicted? There is, of course, biographical evidence in support of both readings. In a letter to his wife from 1962 Celan writes of having taken a walk in the mountains and having come across "*Augentrost-euphrasia*," which reminded him of his work-camp experience during the war in Moldavia. In 1942 he had written a poem, "Herbst," about his trauma at that time that refers to "*Augentrost*," and clearly the sight of this flower conjures memories of atrocities from the past (PC/GL I, 126; DG, 397). Moreover, there are other allusions that reinforce this connection between work/death camps, memory, and flora. Arnica is a star-shaped yellow flower that reminds him of the yellow star that Jews were forced to wear in the Nazi years, imagery that gets played out in verse 3 with the allusion to the "star-die" on Heidegger's fountain. Moreover, eyebright is a flower that is "half parasitic" holding echoes of both the NS-discourse of parasitic Jews as well as a geological reference to organisms that live from the dead.[107] Out of the chthonic depths of the Todtnauberg soil these botanical secrets hold the key to the reading that follows.[108] Celan stands ambivalently between hoping for consolation from his host and being held hostage by the traumas of the past.

> . . . the
> drink [*Trunk*] from the fountain with the
> star-die on top. (SPP, 315)

We could read the language of verses one and two of *Augentrost* and *Trunk* in "Todtnauberg" as allusions to eyes and drowned (*ertrunkener*) joiners in "Tübingen, Jänner" with all its references to Hölderlin and the failure of a Heideggerian poetics of prophetic vocation—and, I think, there is a good case to be made for this. Hölderlin was decidedly on Celan's mind as he was composing this poem. In an early draft that he did not include in the bibliophilic edition he sent to Heidegger, Celan cites the famous line from "Friedensfeier" that Heidegger had quoted in his essay "Hölderlin and the Essence of Poetry":

> Since we have been a conversation and have heard from one another. (SPF, 214–15)

For Heidegger this line came to be read as an insight that "the being of the human being is grounded in language; but this actually occurs only in *conversation* . . . language is essential only as conversation" (EHP, 56–57/GA 4, 38–39). In this way, "speaking, then, mediates our coming to one another. . . . We are a conversation, that always also signifies that we are *one* conversation. The unity of a conversation consists in the fact that in the essential word there is always manifest that one and the same on which we agree, on the basis of which we are united and so are authentically ourselves." But it is precisely on this point of unity that Celan can not give assent. In his draft he writes:

> Since we have been a conversation
> on which
> we choke
> on which I choke
> that
> drives me out of myself, three times, four times. (TCA/LZ, 49)

In this double citation from Hölderlin, through Heidegger, the very *topos* of dialogue and conversation is inverted such that what might have been an occasion of open exchange with real risk for both parties is now viewed as a moment of near-suffocation. Drawing on imagery from Nietzsche's *Thus Spoke Zarathustra* where in "Of the Vision and the Riddle" the young shepherd chokes on the thought of eternal return, Celan here recounts his choking on both Heidegger's *Gerede* and his silence.[109] Even in the seemingly bland and descriptive lines

> in the
> hut, (vv. 4–5) (SPP, 314–15)

we can find traces of this choking. In the word *Hütte*, the German noun for hut, we can find an echo from the German verb *hüten*—to "watch," "protect," "to be on one's guard," but also "to keep a secret"—so that when

Celan enters the sanctuary of Heideggerian *Heimat*-philosophy he finds a thinker who both shelters his past and stands guard over its long-withheld secrets. Against this background we can now reread the first verse as alluding to the need for healing in multiple senses. The two plants are named in succession—"Arnica, Eyebright"—standing next to one another in close proximity yet separated by a punctuation mark, much as the poet and philosopher are brought together only to remain apart. This sense of two flora being joined in their disjunction appears again in verse 18—"Orchis and Orchis, singly"—where Celan reinforces this perception of two individuals ("singly") who are next to one another (sharing much in common) yet impossibly separate and apart. The Orchis mentioned here is a flower with crimson red blossoms whose roots are bulb-shaped, formed like testicles or scrotal sacks. In "Radix, Matrix" Celan had already made a connection between testis and Jewish roots destroyed in the Shoah. Here again he comes back to the bond between testicle and bulb as a way of juxtaposing German rootedness against Jewish roots cut off at their source even as he alludes to blood lost (SPP, 166–67). Could there also be a subtle hint here of other oppositions—of Christian versus Jew, of Greek versus Hebrew, Alpha and Omega versus Aleph and Tav? Might we read the two pairs of plants whose German names begin with "A" and the two flowers whose names begin with "O" as a subtle allusion to a Christian eschatology of Alpha and Omega that had such profoundly threatening implications for German Jews?

The next verse speaks of taking a drink at a "*Brunnen*" (fountain, well, spring) outside Heidegger's cabin, the one with a star-die on top. The language here, so plain and descriptive on the surface, harbors a number of difficult and obscure connections. The fountain functions as a source or spring, but also stands for the *arche*-metaphysics that shapes Heidegger's vision of the German homeland as rooted in the autochthony of both language and soil. But "*Brunnen*" also alludes to Celan's own homeland of birth, the Bukovina, which in German translates as "Brunnenland," the land of springs, fountains (DG, 46). If Heidegger is a philosopher with strong connections to place, region, and dialect, then Celan can be read as the poet of no-place, of exile, and of a language cut off from its living source or spring. In just this way the mere mention of the bare *facta* of Heidegger's life-world in Todtnauberg—the hut, the fountain, the flora, the star-die, and the woodland turf—provides a way of thinking through, and placing into relation, two fundamentally different ways of experiencing the world that hang upon nothing more profound than arbitrary chance or accident. This factically random plight that shapes our world at birth—that we are "thrown" into a world of factical existence, a language, a culture, a historical epoch that is not of our own making—what Heidegger in *Being and Time* will term "thrownness" or *Geworfenheit*, will get played out in the allusion to the *Sternwürfel* (which needs to be read through both Mallarme's *Un Coup des Des* and the star-imagery of Heidegger's late work).[110] The fate of the Celan-Heidegger meeting was already fated in the way the die fell in 1889 in Messkirch and in 1920 in Czernowitz. In juxtaposing two different interpretations of the star we find two opposing visions of Christian-Hebraic eschatology: Heidegger's motto "to head for a star—only this" with its Christian imagery of light and salvation *and* Celan's Jewish Star of David with its kabbalistic symbolism of "illuminating the path of life and reconstruction" after a "path of humiliation and horror" (PLT, 4/GA 13, 76).[111] But the star might also be an allusion to a passage from *The Gay Science* where Nietzsche writes that in the wake of the death of God the deed of his murder is so far that it is "still farther than the farthest stars," since "the light of the stars requires time."[112] What Celan cannot have known, could not have surmised from the image of the star-die atop the fountain, was the trace of something absent there, the carved swastika in the wooden block that had formerly adorned Heidegger's fountain during the NS years, as Rainer Marten has reported.[113] This archaic symbol of the fourfold, of the turning cycle of all life that had spelled death for those born under the Star of David, remained covered over and concealed in the shelter of the *Hütte*, one of the uncanny, *unheimlich* aspects of the facticity that kept the thinker and the poet from ever truly encountering the other.

The next stanza once again takes up the same sober, descriptive style that characterized the opening lines. There, Celan recounts in simple language something that appears almost incidental: a description of his written entry in Heidegger's guestbook, which sits on a table in the cabin. On July 25, 1967, during his visit to Heidegger's cabin Celan wrote:

> In the cabin-book, with the view of the fountain-star,
> with a hope for a coming word in the heart
> 25th of July, 1967
> Paul Celan.[114]

In a later revision of this entry in his poem Celan changes this to read:

> into the book
> —whose name did it take in
> before mine?—
> the line written into
> this book about
> a hope, today,

for a thinker's
(un-
delayed coming)
word
in the heart, (SPP, 314–15)[115]

Here again, as in "Tübingen, Jänner" we are dealing with the poetics of citation, but now Celan cites himself through temporal distance and in doing so underscores the urgency of "today." If in the earlier poem Celan alluded to both Hölderlin's and Heidegger's eschatological hopes of a "Second Coming" of the gods who had fled, here he situates this hope in the temporal now of the present—"today"—which he then interrupts by placing in brackets his hope for an "(un- / delayed coming)." The enjambment here is telling; it is as if Celan already knows that this hope will not proceed immediately in seamless fashion but will suffer delay in coming, if at all. Here again we find the irremediable ambivalence. On the one hand, there are positive allusions to Heideggerian language: the paratactic Heideggerian style; the homophony of verse 7—"*wessen Nahmen nahms auf*"—that is endemic to the late Heidegger; the question mark at the end of verse 8 that alludes to Heidegger's well-known privileging of questions; the emphasis placed on "word" by having it constitute a single line (verse 15)—with allusions to Heidegger's own underscoring of Heraclitean *logos*; and the culmination of the entire stanza leading to the word "heart" (with Heideggerian allusions to Augustine's "restless heart" and to "the thinking heart" in the work of Meister Eckhart and Pascal).[116] But there are other, more troubling allusions buried under the surface here as well.

For Celan, the heart is an organ of memory.[117] What the poet cannot forget as he writes his name in a book that assuredly contains names of former Nazi sympathizers is the bond between "name" and "book"—that finds its culmination in the Nazi registries of Jewish names collected in a book before their deportation. Or perhaps we can also read this as a matter of variance between guest and host where the host can gather names in a book that offers continuity and preservation, whereas the guest experiences only the caesura of a nameless aggregate of bodies without identity and a sense of place? In his later work Derrida writes of the guest-host relationship as one that involves a singular ambivalence: the host (*hospes*) opens his house to the stranger or foreigner (*hostis*) in a gesture of hospitality that remains ever in tension with a certain kind of hostility.[118] For Derrida, genuine hospitality emerges at the threshold of hostility in an aporia that forces us to confront the possibility that the guest will never leave, but will become a parasite to the host, a condition that Derrida playfully terms "hostipitality."[119] In this hidden contradiction between guest and host, where hospitality functions "like a promise as much as like a threat," who is held hostage? Is it Celan who then becomes part of Heidegger's attempt to expunge all traces of his National Socialist affiliations? Or is it an allusion to those held hostage by the past, by an inability or unwillingness to grant a place of rest for those who no longer live, a "hospitality as mourning," as Derrida calls it?

Heidegger never genuinely accepts the risk of real hospitality with Celan—that is, opening oneself or one's home to the other, the stranger, the foreign at the threshold of alterity. He never was able to break his studied silence on the topics so dear to Celan's heart. Instead, he retreated back into the conventions of hospitality that posed little risk at all. If there is ambivalence to be read at the margins of "Todtnauberg," then perhaps that is because Celan never was able to *enter* into its *topos*, despite his allusions to being "*in* the hut," writing "*in* the book," and awaiting a word "*in* the heart." The interiority of Heidegger's world would not admit entry by a foreign stranger. Here perhaps is where the reading of "Todtnauberg" put forward by Hans-Georg Gadamer appears most problematic. Gadamer will envision Celan as one of "the many pilgrims who went up to Todtnauberg," a guest come to take in the "consolation of the eyes" and a refreshing drink from the fountain.[120] But it would be too simple to consider Celan a pilgrim—a wanderer perhaps, a foreigner, or even an uprooted exile, but not a pilgrim. In the second half of the poem this underlying ambivalence attending Celan's visit will be reinforced.

> Woodland turf (*Waldwasen*), unleveled,
> Orchis and Orchis, singly
>
> crudeness, later, while driving,
> clearly,
>
> the one driving us, the man
> who hears it too, (SPP, 314–15)

Again, here we find the stenographer's notes transformed into a cryptic commentary on the topography of ambivalence—notes on the landscape, the interrupted walk on the moor, the crudeness of speech and of rustic provinciality. In a poetic idiom of serrated verse Celan provides a shorthand for his deep ambivalence during his visit to Heidegger's hut. In Celan's use of the rare German term *Waldwasen*—"woodland turf"—we find traces of two dominant Heideggerian motifs: the Schwarz-*wald* or "Black Forest" and the philosophical discourse on *Wesen*—"essence"—so prominent in Heidegger's work. Here, we might understand this as a discourse on the essence of the Black Forest that lies hidden in the landscape. The word *wasen* is a term that in Northern German dialect means "damp or moist turf" or "the moist earth." In the *Grimms' Dictionary*, *wase* is a term from forestry that has etymological ties with the Latin word *fascis* (German: *Faschine*)—a "bundle of wooden sticks"—from which the word *fascism* derives.[121] But *Grimms'* also notes that *wasen* is "the parcel of land where the knacker or flayer disembowels the livestock and hurriedly buries its carcass just below the surface of the earth, also known in Southern Germany and on the Rhine as the 'knacker's [or butcher's] yard.'" Moreover, it is "under the *wasen* (sod, turf) that the human being finds its last place of rest"; in this sense, *wasen* alludes to "those dead corpses one secretly carries to the garden and later buries under the *wasen*." Tracing this whole lexicon of turf, sod, and knackery through its many allusions to the Southern German landscape and its underground secret burial rites, we can see how for Celan such a landscape would bring back memories of other concealed slaughter inflicted on the Jewish dead by their German knackers. Hence, we can now read the innocent term "unleveled" in another sense—as a reference to the mass of corpses hastily buried in unleveled graves by German soldiers in World War II.

Against this background Celan's friend Jean Bollack reads his trip to Todtnauberg as "a journey to the land of the dead," a Hebrew reenactment of a Greek *nekyia* modeled on the journey to the underworld undertaken by Odysseus in the *Odyssey* and Socrates in the *Republic*.[122] Bollack interprets the unleveled woodland turf not merely as a damp meadow but as a cemetery with countless unleveled hills. On his reading, the two men make a journey to Hades and come before the tribunal of the dead, accompanied by a third figure—a "driver" (*Fahrer*), "the one driving us"—whose significance becomes plain when we view it in terms of the word-complex for "*führen*": *Der Führer*, Ein-*führung* (in *die Metaphysik*). Within this context the driver (Gerhard Baumann's graduate assistant, Gerhard Neumann) becomes a "witness" to the (non-)conversation between poet and philosopher while chauffeuring them to their interrupted visit to the Horbacher moor. The double reference to driving and to the one who (co-)hears underscores the significance of witnessing, of simply being present for the testimony of one who is there. What remains unspoken here between the two men, of course, is precisely this notion of witnessing as a philosophically meaningful process. For Heidegger, the significance of witnessing was made clear in his essay "Hölderlin and the Essence of Poetry" where he writes:

> Who is the human being? He is the one who must bear witness [*zeugen*] to what he is. To bear witness can signify to testify [*Bekunden*], but it also means to be answerable for what one has testified in one's testimony. . . . But what should one testify to? To his belonging to the earth. (EHP, 54/GA 4, 36)

Going back to his early Aristotle lectures, Heidegger had identified "witnessing" with the topic of *ethos* whereby he understood *ethos* as the bearing, comportment, or attitude that allows one to become a witness (GA 18, 165). But it is Heidegger's inability to truly become "answerable for" his own past—in its German sense of *Verantwortung* or "taking responsibility"—that animates Celan's reference to the driver as witness in verses 21–22. Instead of resolutely responding to the call of conscience, which in *Being and Time* he identifies as a mark of authentic existence, Heidegger will only provide the unrefined, "crude" (v. 19), and "rough-hewn" discourse that one might associate with the rustic landscape of Todtnauberg. Instead of witnessing, there will only be a continuation of the covering over and concealment that constitutes the late Heidegger's carefully orchestrated defense of his own silence. It is this crudeness that becomes "clear" to Celan "later, while driving" (vv. 19–20).

But there is another dimension to the "covering over" of the past that lies hidden in the topographic details of the poem that Heidegger undoubtedly missed when he received it as a gift. This concerns the whole discourse of "the high moorland" with its "dampness" that relates back to the first line of the poem and its botanical references to arnica and eyebright, as well as to the first line of the second half of the poem (v. 17) with its reference to "woodland turf." Moorland and the whole thematic complex of moors—"quaking bogs," "peat," "turf," "moorpool," "peatorgan," "raised bog," "moorbody," and others—give voice to how prominent this theme becomes within Celan's corpus.[123] The highmoors surrounding Todtnauberg and Horbach bring to Celan's mind a memory of his own youth in Czernowitz which had similar moorlands. Moreover, the very *topos* of a moorland carries with it the traces of the Jewish dead whose names echo at the margins of these moors.[124] These moorlands are formed geologically when dammed-up water under airtight pressure from the soil helps in the partial decomposition of vegetation, turning it into turf or peatbog. This dark brown substance made from rotting plants is then used as fertilizer or fuel.[125] In a poem written about a year before his visit to Todtnauberg, Celan alluded to the "moor soldiers of Masada" by which he sought to bring together a whole range of associations from the prisoners of the Papenburg-Börgermoor concentration camp to Jewish freedom fighters versus ancient Rome, to a Jewish song of freedom cited in a book by Eugen Kogon on *Der SS-Staat*, as well as an acknowledgment of the Israeli troops' victory in the Six Day War of 1967.[126] That these starkly Jewish themes concerning moorlands as a site of Jewish suffering and death appear juxtaposed against the crude, rustic landscape of Heidegger's Black Forest cabin can here be read "clearly" (v. 20). The paths of genuine encounter were only "half-trodden"; neither poet nor philosopher could break through the silence of the dead whose traces lay buried beneath the peatbog of the moorland turf. In this sense, both Celan and Heidegger came to fulfill Gershom Scholem's prophecy about the impossibility of any genuine German-Jewish dialogue.[127] In the space between "hope and grief" that Scholem identified, the fact remained that no dialogue ever occurred, and was never likely to occur, given the brutal conditions under which it was attempted. Heidegger's hospitality as hostility was played out on a landscape whose contours betrayed an unleveled field on which its "log-paths" (*Knuppel- / pfade*) permitted no passage.[128] (*Knüppel* or "cudgels" can also be used to strike the persecuted. Felstiner notes that "translating *Night and Fog* [Celan] had used that word for death camp prisoners 'bludgeoned awake' at 5 AM.") Against this background we can better understand an early draft of "Todtnauberg" that Celan did not include in the final version:

Temple-ashes	*Im Ohr Wirbelnde*
Swirling in the ear	*Schläfenasche, die eine, letzte*
patiently suffer the last	*Gedankenfrist duldend.*
deadline for thinking. (TCA/LZ, 49)	

The ashes from the temples/skulls of the dead Jews continue to swirl in Celan's ear as he patiently awaits the deadline for a "thinker's / (un- / delayed coming) / word / in the heart."

In the terse language of the last two verses

dampness
much. (SPP, 314–15)

we are brought back to the opening lines of the poem. The hoped-for eye-consolation at the outset ends in much dampness. Under the entry for *feucht* (damp, wet, moist) in the *Grimms' Dictionary* we find two telling references:

> "wet eyes . . . their eyes became wet, are wet from tears . . ."
> "a wet death, to find a wet grave, to perish in water."[129]

Celan can not forget the many tears he has shed for his parents' death and the loss of millions of other lives who found a wet grave buried under the moors of concentration camp peat-bog. In earlier poems he had likewise associated the word *feucht* with "eyes," "ashes," and even the "drink/draught" (*Trunk*) from the fountain, all themes that would get played out again in "Todtnauberg" (SPP, 82–83; 122–23). But in the *Grimms' Dictionary* there is a third reference that will get played out in much more detail in the later Jerusalem poems—a reference to the *Book of Job* (8:6–11):

> If thou wert pure and upright surely now God would awake for you and once again set your dwelling place aright for justice's sake (um deiner *Gerechtigkeit* willen). . . . Can the rush grow up where there is no *dampness*? Can the reed-grass grow where there is no water? They that hate thee shall come to shame and the hut (*Hütte*) of the godless shall come to naught. (8:22)

Could the allusion to "dampness / much" from *The Book of Job* be read in terms of the justice that Celan so yearned for? "Much could / Be said about this," as Hölderlin so cryptically put it in "The Ister" (SPF, 256–57). Read against the German text we can think *viel* here as another indication of the *Viel-deutigkeit* or "ambiguity" of Celan's position. The many tears for the many corpses brings to language the plurality that reigns through the poem—the plurality of flora on the moor (v. 1), names entered in the book (v. 7), lines written of hope (v. 10), log-paths interrupted (v. 24), as well as the doubling of herbs (v. 1) and orchis (v. 18) and the repetition of the words *Buch* (vv. 6 and 9) and *Fahren/fährt* (vv. 19 and 21). The singular vision of German inclusivity that excluded Jews will be deconstructed through the plurality of *facta* from Heidegger's lifeworld. The log-paths that did not bear Jewish footprints, the ones that led to much dampness, appear here, like Heidegger's *Holzwege* or "woodpaths," as merely half-trodden (like the half-lives of those who were unable to share Celan's ambivalent hope for a coming word). But there is not simply doubling here but, rather, ambiguity. The poet comes to the thinker for a heartfelt word, but he cannot forget that this conversation is half-trodden, blocked, by the juxtaposition that obtains between them: in nearness and distance, through German rootedness and Jewish exile, as perpetrator and victim.

As near as they are in their need for thinking through a poetic relation to the catastrophe of modern European nihilism, these two remain as "Orchis and Orchis, singly." Unable to find common ground in thinking *the* caesura of modern Western culture that happened on the moorlands of Eastern Europe, they stand apart from one another as native dweller in the homeland and foreign wanderer in exile. For Heidegger, poetry provides a measure for human dwelling, a way of attuning ourselves to our appropriate place within the fourfold of being's unfolding. For Celan, poetry provides a way to measure the measureless suffering of those who have perished, a way to find a resting place to commemorate the scattered ashes of the dead whose exilic traces can be found in the "temple-ashes" of memory (TCA/LZ, 49). In this sense "the poem counts as that which remains mindful of the dead" (*des Todes eingedenk bleibende*) (MSS, 151). In this abyssal cleft between Hölderlinian and Hebraic "Andenken" the hoped-for conversation *as* reconciliation perished. What separated Heidegger and Celan was the caesura of Auschwitz—of the one who remained silent and of the one who endured the silence of commemoration. The echoes of the dead clamoring for justice would not find resonance on the high moorland of Todtnauberg. And if we can start to make sense of this immense chasm separating the two men then perhaps it is against this question of justice. In *Writing the Disaster,* Blanchot reflects on the troubling relation between homogeneity and heterogeneity as the opening of a possibility that enables the disaster. Reflecting on "the holocaust, the *absolute* event of history," Blanchot asks: "How can it be preserved, even by thought? How can thought be made the keeper of the holocaust where all was lost, including guardian thought?"[130] For him, the question remains—"Can one maintain any distance at all when Auschwitz happens? How is it possible to say: Auschwitz has happened?" In the face of such an interrogation Blanchot explores the messianic injunction that "justice won't wait; it is to be done at every instant, to be realized all the time. . . ."

In the wake of Auschwitz, Celan was overwhelmed by the pressing need to render justice to the dead, to provide a resting place for their remains and to gather the remnants of their ashes in the gravesite provided by the poem. For him this was a matter of ethical responsibility. In "remaining mindful of the condition of being-other, being-different, being-severed," he found a way of thinking through the paradoxical, contradictory relation of "strange nearness" (*Fremde Nähe*), a contradiction that remains decisive in his Todtnauberg encounter with Heidegger.[131] In the poems that he composed after his trip to Jerusalem in the fall of 1969 we can find the traces of a more developed response to Heidegger, particularly as it relates to the question of justice. In working through his own relation to his Jewish roots, especially against the unspoken Athens/Jerusalem themes that split the ground between philosopher and poet, Celan comes to speak in a different way about the themes that lay submerged under the Todtnauberg peat-bog.

THE JERUSALEM POEMS: *EROS* AS ESCHATOLOGY

When Celan left Paris in late September 1969 for Israel he was at a crossroads in his life. His marriage to Gisèle was in ruins; he was forced to move out and live alone in a studio apartment in the Latin Quarter of Paris. Writing in really low spirits to Franz Wurm he confessed that "Paris is a burden to me—which, I know, I can not shake off" (PC/FW, 124). "I am very much alone," he tells his childhood friend from Czernowitz, Petre Solomon.[132] His psychological troubles continue to haunt him and he worries about his growing isolation and sense of homelessness and exile. Yet, as ever with Celan, the fears of loss and displacement were met with strands of hope and possibility. In the summer of 1969 he had received an invitation from the Hebrew Writers Association in Tel Aviv to give a reading of his poetry and he accepted. In his speech to this group he struck a simple yet profound note: "I have come to you in Israel because I needed to" (SPP, 414/GW III, 203).

Given the disappointments of 1968—the failures of the student movements in Paris and Berlin in May and the Soviet suppression of Czech freedom in the Prague Spring uprising—Celan turned his hopes to Israel as a way of identifying with the possibility of a *Heimkehr,* a return home to the lost community of his youth.[133] He writes to a friend: "I need Jerusalem, as I needed it before I found it." While there Celan met an old friend from Czernowitz with whom he had been in contact the year before in Paris. Ilana Shmueli became his lover and through her he was able to express his deep-rooted metaphysical yearning for a home. The poems he sent her—the so-called Jerusalem Poems—bring to expression the yearning for love and home that runs throughout his work. Through her Celan finds a way to articulate the inchoate hopes from a past that remain fragile, though inextinguishable. These hopes take the form of what, in his letters to Ilana, he calls "Jerusalem"—both a place and a name for an unnameable hope without place. Shortly after his return to Paris, he writes to her "that Jerusalem would be a turning, a caesura in my life—*that* I knew. What I didn't know is that there I would be gifted with you" (PC/IS, 14). A few days later he adds this codicil:

> I wanted to add something to a longer letter to warn you about me and about us—but then came your face as I saw it in Jerusalem and in N'we Awiwim and I knew: what brought us together is something primary, something above everything else—.
>
> Your face, Ilana. Your Jewish face. Your face.
>
> Jerusalem raised me up and strengthened me. Paris oppresses me and wears away at me. Paris, through whose streets and houses I've had to drag the burden of so much madness, so much reality, all these years. (PC/IS, 16)

We can read the Jerusalem poems as documents of an erotic yearning for completion—not only for sexual union with a lover who represents the possibility of a return home to the shelter of a lost Czernowitz, but also for an eschatological union with Jerusalem itself as the Bride of Solomon, the Shekinah spoken of in Jewish mysticism, "the city of the Lord, the Zion of the Holy One of Israel" prophesied by Isaiah (Isa. 60:14). This overlapping of the erotic and eschatological—or perhaps of the eschatological as erotic—can also be read in the utopian hopes that Celan brought to his Jerusalem cycle. These were hopes not only for reconstituting the lost community of Czernowitz (he met several old friends and relatives from his youth there) or for constituting a new community of Jewish survivors of the Shoah who, like him, had lost those dearest to them. It was also a way of healing the wounds from a lifetime of separation and exile, a way of easing the "burden of so much madness, so much reality." "Jerusalem," in this utopian sense, enabled him to give a name to his hope for a way of memorializing the lost dead of the Shoah, a way to give poetic voice to the yearning for redemption from the past and for justice for the dead. In this way the poetic trope of "the lovers" comes to stand for the possibility of an encounter that anticipates the utopian vision of a future society without violence, domination, and racial hatred, a vision whose lineaments we can detect in Celan's many references to political oppression in his work: the Spanish Civil War (SPP, 74, 188), Viennese Social Democracy (SPP, 74), Rudi Dutschke and the Student Revolt of 1968 (DG, 326–29), the Vietnam War (LD, 70), Karl Liebknecht, Rosa Luxemburg, and the Spartacist Revolt of 1919 (SPP, 328), the cold war and the threat of the Atomic Bomb (SPP, 122), and the Six Day War in Israel (SPP, 316). In all its symbolic power, Jerusalem came to function as the lost mother, the bride awaiting the bridegroom, the hoped-for community of the living and the dead, a political vision of peace, the possibility of messianic redemption. All of these various dimensions of hope and expectation came to play their role in the crafting of the Jerusalem poems. Celan came to Israel burdened with questions about his Jewish identity, questions that were framed in the contradictory language of poetic ambivalence. For years he had been reading the works of Gershom Scholem on the Kabbalah, of Buber on the Hassidic piety of Eastern European Jewry, of Margarete Susman on the fate of the Jewish people post-Auschwitz, of Franz Rosenzweig on the relation between *pneuma, ruach,* and "breath" (*Atem*), of Hugo Berman and the Bar Kochba Circle in Prague on the significance of holy names, of Osip Mandelstam on the persecution of European Jewry, of Franz Kafka on the contradictions of Jewish existence, and of a diverse range of sacred texts from the Psalms, the Song of Songs, Job, Isaiah, apocalyptic theology, and the mystics.[134] All of these texts had a profound influence on the way Celan would configure the question of Jewish identity in the wake of the Shoah as well as on the poetic-philosophical question about language, topology, and dwelling that he had appropriated from Heidegger and Hölderlin.

As a Jew from Eastern Europe whose own existence had been grievously altered by the historical realities of martial conquest, forced labor, the loss of one's homeland and institutional identity, as well as the murder of one's own family members, Celan well knew the Pindaric-Hölderlinian problem of native and foreign, familiar and strange, *oikos* and *allotrios* that we have been exploring in the last three chapters. The traces of this Hölderlinian yearning for home, *Heimat*, *Volk*, and nation can be found on virtually every page of his corpus. Yet this hope for belonging to a community with which he could identify was powerfully undermined by the facts of twentieth-century European politics—of Wilson's Fourteen Points that reshaped the Bukovina as "Romania" in the name of "national self-determination;" of the ensuing racial politics of Romanian nationals who sought to oppress the native Jewish population of Czernowitz; of the marauding German and Russian armies whose designs for resettlement and racial purification led to so many deaths; of the postwar imposition of a Soviet-controlled Ukraine that appended Czernowitz to its cold war vision of East Bloc solidarity. As a result of these historical tribulations, Czernowitz existed for Celan only as a lost site on a child's map, a place no longer to be found except through the drawing of a meridian to an "immaterial" other (SPP, 413/GA III, 202). How to connect the boulevards of Paris to his lost home in the Bukovina? How to find a way of drawing a meridian to connect his present site of loneliness and exile to his lost home, lost language, lost family, lost community, and lost self? Jerusalem came to offer a name for such hopes, a name for reconnecting to a lost world and place. Despite all the positive associations with "Jerusalem" as the "name for this metaphysical homeland," however, there remained deep contradictions within Celan's work about the possibility of just such a hope.[135]

Three days before he was scheduled to leave Israel, he decided to break off his stay and return to Paris immediately. Soon after his return, the familiar themes of ambivalence emerge in both his personal correspondence and in his poetry. He worried about the frayed relations with his old friends and relatives after so many years of separation, about the reality of leaving Europe for a new life in Israel. He even toyed with the idea of living on a kibbutz, of starting a new life with Ilana, of living among other Jews and speaking mainly Hebrew. But the old fears and ambivalence would not let him loose from their grip. After his great hopes were dashed and the future receded from view, he realized that the one possibility he allowed himself—the hope of a redemptive "homecoming" to Jerusalem—was shattered. Within a few months he committed suicide. The Jerusalem poems stand in the shadow of these contradictions and ambivalence, offering a vision of what Celan would term his "pneumatic Judaism," a singularly personal engagement with his family traditions and, beyond them, with the intellectual-spiritual sources of twentieth-century Judaism. In a letter to Gershom Schocken, son of the great Jewish publisher Salman Schocken, Celan tried to dispel the rumor that he had ever tried to hide his Jewish identity—either in Paris or Germany—by posing as a "crypto-Jew." "My poems imply my Judaism," Celan claimed; "for me, especially in a poem, Jewishness is sometimes not so much a *thematic* as a *pneumatic* concern"

(MSS, 945).[136] In a letter to Ilana he insists that "of course, in the midst of everything, my Judaism is self-evident;" and in a note from his journal he writes—"my Judaism: that which I still (re)cognize in the wreckage of my existence" (MSS, 126).

This distinction between a "thematic" and a "pneumatic" Judaism will be crucial for understanding Celan's work. By "pneumatic" Celan means the immediate connection of *pneuma-spiritus-Atem*-breath uniting "Geist" or "spirit" to the physical breath of life that animates the human body. Celan came to prize the essentially Jewish dimension of this spiritual-physical relationship in the writings of Franz Rosenzweig who saw in it a relation that "stretches beyond the spiritual (*seelisch*)-physical life of individual human beings and even beyond their lifetime and that connects individuals to a spiritual (*geistigen*) community."[137] In his poem "Benedicta," Celan writes:

> Hast—
> thou hast drunken
> what came to me from our fathers
> and from beyond our fathers:
> —Pneuma. (SPP, 174–75)

In earlier drafts of this poem Celan had written—"Pneuma—: / Sperma." alluding to a citation from the Jewish philosopher Philo about the *logos spermatikos* that he had discovered while reading Ernst Bloch's *The Principle of Hope* (DG, 692; TCA/NR, 74–75): "[O]nly the pure one, transformed through its own reversal, possesses the power to wake the dead . . . to renew and to awaken. Through the sacred water, the *logos spermatikos*, he gives it back to *Dasein* and leads it upward, purified, until everything below is transformed into something elevated" (TCA/NR, 74–75; DG, 692).[138] In this profound bond to the community of the dead, which could only be awakened through the living word that came through the fathers and beyond them, Celan forged his own pneumatic version of Judaism. A pneumatic Judaism implied not only a "breath turn" toward a new possibility of communication and encounter; it also functioned as a turn to the community of "breath" as *ruach*—the breath of communion that linked Jewish survivors to those lost in the flames of the Holocaust. Against this understanding we can read Celan's discourse on "the breathturn" through its Jewish sources. In his notes to the Meridian Speech he writes: "[T]o judify" (*verjuden*) means "to-recognize-oneself-in-the-other; it is a holding communion with others as a holding communion with oneself. It is a reversal (*Umkehr*)" (TCA/M, 199). In this notion of "Judification," which Celan claims is "to be recommended for an understanding of the poetic," we can find traces of Levinas's ethical imperative toward the other. We can also hear echoes of this Jewish ethical understanding in Celan's well-known citation from the Russian poet Marina Tsvetayeva—"All poets are Jews" (PCS, 93/DG, 164).

Celan's pneumatic Judaism existed in a profound tension with the sources of his own tradition—a tension between the hope for messianic redemption in a time of exile *and* the Kafkaesque fear that the absurdity of modern existence leaves no place for such hope. Jewish alienation, pain, and exile will be juxtaposed here with the hope for a reconstituted community of Jewish victims. We can recognize the deep conflicts and contradictions of Celan's pneumatic Judaism in the description set out by his lover Ilana Shmueli:

> I perceived his Judaism as an ongoing, bitter struggle about his Jewish identity, a struggle with himself, a struggle with his environment. There were so many worlds that made a claim upon him and his pressing demand for the absolute brought him time and again to discord. This Judaism had a distinct place in his being which, in his last years, constantly throbbed in him—and yet it was not always attainable for him, not in the way that he demanded of himself.
>
> He lacked authenticity. He characterized himself as "a goy Yid" (*gojischer Jid*) with a self-derision that was, with Celan, often pushed to the extreme. He was ashamed of the faults and weaknesses of the Jewish community, faults that he too bore as being his own. But every criticism about Jews coming from the outside he interpreted as anti-Semitic and condemned them—oftentimes rightly, but also oftentimes wrongly. He lacked the evidence that he needed. It was his "Not-being-Jewish-enough" that tore him apart and brought conflicts that had something self-destructive about them.[139]

In *Jenseits von Schuld und Sühne*, Jean Amery writes of "the necessity and impossibility of being a Jew" in the postwar epoch as he attempts to negotiate the paradoxes of a nonreligious Jew who comes to an understanding of Jewishness in recognizing that "as a Non-non-Jew, I am a Jew."[140] Amery puts forward his own singularly elusive definition of Judaic identity for the generation of Jews who experienced the horrors of the death camps. "For me," he writes, "being a Jew means to feel the tragedy of yesterday as a heavy burden upon oneself." In one of his notebooks from the time he was reading Amery, Celan jots down this note:

> Amery
> The Auschwitz number and the Old Testament. (MSS, 121)

This entry corresponds to a passage from *Jenseits von Schuld und Sühne* where Amery confesses: "I bear on my left forearm the Auschwitz number; it can be read in less time than either the Pentateuch or the Talmud and yet it contains more fundamental information. It is also more binding as the fundamental formula of Jewish existence." In his personal copy of Amery's book Celan noted this passage and another one, which he not only underlined but marked five times—

> It is not "being" that oppresses me or "the nothing" or "God" or the absence of God—only society: for society and only society brought about the disruption of my existential balance. . . . Society and only society took from me my trust in the world.[141]

As with Amery, Celan's Judaism was profoundly influenced by the historical and societal forces that compelled him to recognize his own Jewishness. In the bond of solidarity with those who were persecuted through the violence of words/deeds because of their Jewishness, Celan came to form his own pneumatic community. These pneumatic ties to Judaism constituted for Celan a "community of those who have no community."[142] In all these ways "Jerusalem" comes to signify for Celan the place for those who have been denied a place, a site of memory and hope where mourning and redemption meet in the intersection of the earthly and heavenly city bequeathed by the fathers.

> The place where they lay, it has
> a name—it has
> none. (SPP, 120–21)

If the terrain of Jewish suffering in Eastern Europe has a name (Auschwitz), yet has none (it is merely "grass written asunder" [SPP, 118–19]), then Jewish identity will be formed in the shadow of this paradox. Celan traces this shadow in the topographic details of these poems, finding the lineaments of Jewish history and prophecy in the plazas, walls, gates, doors, monuments, and landscapes of the city. Through his description of the quotidian sights of this Jewish metropolis Celan limns a portrait of the historical grief and messianic urgency that shapes his understanding of Jerusalem as the "city of justice" (Isa. I:26).[143]

"ZEITGEHÖFT": HOMESTEAD OF TIME

Celan died before the Jerusalem poems could be published and he never came to a final decision about titles, arrangements, ordering, and sequence. Nonetheless, he did choose a title for the collection—"*Zeitgehöft*," a difficult compound noun that has been variously translated as "homestead of time," (SPP, 345) "Timehalo" (DCS, 136), "Farmstead of Time" (LP, 155), and "time-court" (PPC, 323)—yet which means more literally "homesteaded by time." Beginning with poems from *Light Duress* (LD, 138) and *Snow Part* (SP, 60), Celan began employing the word *Zeithof*—"court of time"—as a term that sought to understand poems as sites, places, *Orte*, *Höfe*, where time finds its homestead, where it shows itself as a "court" or "farmstead" for placing memory and hope, mourning and expectation. In his lectures on the *Phenomenology of Internal Time Consciousness*, Husserl termed this phenomenological relation to past and future "retention" and "protention."[144] Celan had read Husserl's book with its phenomenological insights into "the present: [as] something which, in the future, will have been," something that alters the contours of the moment as it undergoes the diachronic process of recollection and/as projection. There, Celan underlined the word *Zeithof* in a passage about expectation/protention: "The now-point again provides consciousness with a *time-court* (*Zeithof*) that comes to pass in the continuity of apprehended memories." In this image of a time-court of memories that brings together the abstraction of "time" with the concretion of a homestead, Celan brings together spatial-temporal themes that proliferate in the Jerusalem poems. Yet the image of a time-court can also be read as a vision of time that finds no place, that remains without place or site, perhaps even the non-place of utopia. In this eschatological vision of time as memory and as end-time, Celan gives voice to his hopes for finding a bond with a Jewish community and to his fears about remaining trapped in the shell of "Jewish loneliness" (SPP, 414/GW III, 202).

"There Stood"

The first poem of the so-called Jerusalem Cycle, "Almonding One," is an erotic text sent to Ilana just after Celan returned to Paris. It speaks to the newfound sexual union between the two against the backdrop of Jerusalem and ends with a Hebrew word: *Hachnissini* (SPP, 352) which means "take me into you." The word can be traced to a melancholy song beloved by East European Jews from the poet Chaim Bialik that speaks of shattered dreams, lost love, and the hope for refuge in a resettled Jerusalem. The first verse of the Bialik poem alludes to themes that will be played out over the range of Celan's Jerusalem cycle:

> Take me in under your wing,
> Be mother and sister to me,
> Let your womb be a refuge for my head,
> A nest for my disdained prayers. (PC/IS, 171)

In the second poem of the cycle, "There Stood," Celan will draw on this erotic image of the lover as both mother and sister—"my sister, my love"—from "The Song of Songs" (5:2) as a way of giving voice to both his love for Ilana and his vision of a redeemed Jerusalem of the soul:

> There stood
> a splinter of fig on your lip,
>
> there stood
> Jerusalem around us,
>
> there stood
> the bright pine scent
> above the Danish skiff we thanked,
>
> I stood
> in you. (SPP, 354–55)

Beyond all the erotic images of longing—the erect male phallus standing in the female lip (*imago vulvae*) with the fructuous possibilities of union—we can find a range of allusions to the eschatological hope for another kind of union: with the dead mother and father and the lost Hebrew tribes condemned to perish. The fig here can stand archetypally for the feminine sex but, as Jean Bollack notes, beyond its significance as a symbol for erotic ecstasy, it can also be read in terms of the remembrance of the dead.[145] For Celan, the fig conjures memories of Hölderlin's poems "Remembrance" and "Mnemosyne," which speak of the "fig tree" and of his own poem "Remembrance" (1954) that draws a connection between figs, standing, and memory (SPF, 250, 260). But if Hölderlin's fig tree evokes memories of Achilles's death and of the fertile Greek landscape, Celan's figs summon images of Jerusalem and of his own father's death in a frozen Transnistrian winter, since Leo Antschel had always embraced Zionist dreams of resettling in Jerusalem where fig trees flourish. But there are other images here that also evoke the remembrance of the dead. "The Danish skiff" (v. 7) refers to the *kikar Dania* ("Danish Square") in Jerusalem where there stands a memorial of a boat to commemorate the Danish resistance movement's rescue from Nazi occupation of more than seven thousand Jews who were shuttled to safety in Sweden by fishermen in October 1943. A plaque in the square reads:

> Danish courage and Swedish generosity gave indelible proof of human values in times of Barbarism. Israel and Jews everywhere will never forget.[146]

In some sense, Celan crosses the political and the erotic here by comparing the Danes' role in rescuing Jews with Ilana's role in saving him. The reference to "the bright pine scent" reinforces this image of remembrance in that it refers to the smell of pine trees that line the hill where the Jewish Holocaust Memorial Museum, Yad Vashem, is located. Celan visited Yad Vashem—which means "hand/memorial" and "name"—with its reference to Isaiah's eschatological vision of granting "a place and a name" to those who yearn for a home: "for my salvation is near to come, and my justice is to be revealed" (Isa. 56:1–5). Celan's political call for justice, like his erotic call for loving union with the sister/bride, can be read as an expression of hope for union with a "Thou"—with Ilana, with his dead mother and father, with the Jewish community who have perished, with the earthly and heavenly "Jerusalem around us" (v. 4). Pöggeler also notes a connection between the "bright" (*hell*) pine scent and the Jewish notion of a "*Hall*-jahr"—the messianic-utopian year of fulfillment, "the jubilee year" which "proclaims liberty throughout all the land unto all the inhabitants thereof" (Lev. 25:10). These apocalyptic tones will also echo in another erotic love poem that Celan sent to Ilana, "The Heat."

"The Heat"

Much like "There Stood," this poem narrates in polysemic fashion the details of a walk by Celan and Ilana through the Old City and then in the Kidron Valley under the East Wall in Jerusalem on a blazing hot day in October. "The Heat" ("*Die Glut*") invokes meteorological images of the famed Arabian Hamsin, the seasonal hot wind that blows and carries with it the passion of lovers in heat. Again, Celan turns a reference to a sacred text, "The Song of Songs," into a poetic vision of eros and thanatos:

> Set me as a seal upon thine heart as a seal upon thine arm: for love is strong as death; passion as incapable of being overcome as the realm of the dead. Its heat ("*Ihre Glut*") is fiery and a flame of the Lord. ("The Song of Songs" 8:6; my translation from the Luther Bible)

This heat carries with it a number of contrasting and contradictory associations: Hölderlin's oriental "fire from heaven" (BL, 165/SA VI, 427); the heat of love and passion; the Shoah's burning ovens; the Atomic heat of Hiroshima and cold war missile politics.[147] The first stanza brings out all these contrasts. Employing the communal pronoun, Celan writes:

> The Heat
> counts us together

in the shriek of an ass at
Absalom's Tomb, here as well. (SPP, 356–57)

Ilana writes that on their walk past Absalom's Tomb in the midday heat they heard no sound—except "the shriek of an ass."[148] This image of the ass—Absalom was killed while riding an ass; Jesus enters Jerusalem on an ass—also alludes to a long-held negative symbol of the Jew as "ass" or beast of burden. His shriek can thus be heard as a protest against being made to bear a terrible weight, the fate of Jewry. The tomb was built by Absalom himself, who rebelled against his father King David and was murdered and buried as a criminal (anticipating the fate of so many later Jews). The tomb was built, Absalom claimed, "to keep my name in remembrance" (II Samuel 18:18). In Celan's language the heat "counts us together"—a reference to an earlier poem "Count Up the Almonds" where the poet, in attempting the impossible task of enumerating the innumerable Jewish dead in the concentration camps, adds: "count me in too" (SPP, 48–49). Like Absalom's Tomb, Celan's poem stands as a monument to the murdered victims, even as it expresses his own sense of inconsolable suffering with the community of the dead.

The next verse continues the references to suffering in the allusion to Gethsemane:

Gethsemane, yonder,
circled around, who
does it overwhelm? (SPP, 356–57)

On their walk Celan and Ilana decided not to visit Gethsemane, the garden where Jesus prepared himself for the agony of his crucifixion, but "circled around" it. The poet asks, however, "whom does it overwhelm?" How are we to understand this question? That there are messianic implications here for understanding the relation between Christ as savior and the Christian rejection of the Jews because of their alleged "murder" of Jesus, is clear. Celan, like so many Jews, is overwhelmed by the centuries-long myth of Jewish complicity in the death of Jesus propagated in the Fourth Gospel (Jn 19:6–21). For him, the messianic energies of Christian apocalypse are complicit in the persecution of Jews from the Middle Ages through Luther and the nineteenth century leading up to the German Final Solution. Choosing to visit the Jewish site of Absalom's Tomb "here" (v. 4) rather than the Christian memorial of Gethsemane "yonder" (v. 5), Celan still does not forget the historical implications of the two-thousand-year narrative of Jewish persecution that overwhelms both him and Ilana.

The next stanza, though only a single line, brings the whole poem into focus:

At the nearest gate nothing opens up. (SPP, 356–57)

As they continue their walk outside the walls of Jerusalem near the foot of the Mount of Olives, Celan and Ilana pass the Eastern Gate—called by Jews "the Gate of Mercy" and by Christians "The Golden Gate." Within this spiritual-pneumatic topography Celan offers an archeology of Jewish messianism. For Jews, this is the gate—very near the site of the original Temple—through which the messiah will enter when he comes (Ezekiel 44:1–3). For centuries pious Jews from all the world have let themselves be buried here beneath the slopes of the Kidron Valley so that they might be nearer to the Messiah to ask for mercy at the end of time.[149] Christians, on the other hand, believe that Jesus, the Messiah, has already come and thus they designate it "the Golden Gate." But Celan's allusion also needs to be understood against the Moslem tradition as well, since in 1541 the Ottoman Sultan Suleiman I walled off the Eastern Gate to the city, thus choking off all Jewish hopes for a Messianic liberation of Jerusalem. It is in terms of this twofold legacy of the gate's redemptive opening and apocalyptic closure that Celan can write:

through you, Open one, I bear you to me. (SPP, 356–57)

Celan had written to Ilana in late October 1969 an erotic line about "being entwined in you at the gates of all fertility, in spite of this" (PC/IS, 15), hinting at how their love might enable him to pass through the blocked-off gate of salvation. As the sister/bride, the "you" here comes to symbolize the Shekinah, the mystical kabbalist doctrine of the feminine element within God, the "in-dwelling of God in the world," specifically in Jerusalem.[150] The Shekinah is often associated with the "great fire" ("the Heat" of v. 1) from which the human soul emerges. In Kabbalist myth the Shekinah takes the form of an active potency that animates everything: "[I]t is the spark that dwells in everything, or is trapped or captive in everything—but the Shekinah is in exile there."[151] It is this notion of exile that appears in early Jewish texts where the Shekinah becomes so closely associated with Israel that "wherever Israel was exiled, it is as if the Shekinah were exiled with them." In erotic terms the union between the Shekinah and the Godhead, the Shekinah and Israel, the Shekinah and the trapped energy of thingly existence, bears the mark of immanence and transcendence, the earthly Jerusalem and the heavenly one. Celan will draw heavily on this tradition in the Jerusalem poems. After reading Scholem's *On the Mystical Shape of the Godhead* in 1967–68, Celan will turn to the cryptic world of Kabbalistic imagery to express his own sense of exile and abandonment in a world cut off from the sparks of the Shekinah. Passing through the gates of Jerusalem, finding entry into both the city and his beloved, Celan finds "the Open one," the portal that will allow him to cross over the threshold separating the living and the dead.

For Celan, the Shekinah assumes the Gestalt of the in-dwelling of the divine in the world, the heavenly Jerusalem that is cut off from its source and forced to live in exile in the earthly Jerusalem. Only through a loving union of souls in the "Open"-ness of an encounter (v. 9), a union where the self is brought to itself through the other, in bearing the other to the self, can the hidden potencies of the divine bring about the possibility of justice. From Scholem, Celan drew on the erotic language of the Jewish mystics who understood this possibility as one where

> the good oil flowing from the "white head" . . . mingle therein and the deeds of the just are emanated from there, and the seeds of peace are sown there. For the seed is drawn from the brain and reaches the tip of the phallus, and is emptied into its mate; and this is the secret of its bearing fruits, by way of the mystery of true union and unification. And the cause of all this lies in the deeds of the just, who ascend upwards with the perfection of their mediation. . . .[152]

In this sexual symbolism of procreative energy Celan uncovers a way of commemorating the Jewish dead. In the union between the Just One (*Tsaddik*—the seventh *Sefira* of the ten potencies/logoi of God) and the Shekinah (the tenth *Sefira*, the feminine manifestation of the heavenly Jerusalem and, paradoxically, its Exilic Other), the scattered sparks of divine energy that lie trapped and inert in the tangible form of things are repaired in a sacred act of redemptive restoration, the *tikkun* of Jewish mysticism. In another version of the myth, after the destruction of the Temple in Jerusalem, the Shekinah was sent into exile with Israel and will be reunited with the *Tsaddik* only at the time of redemption. Drawing on this elaborate mystical symbolism Celan interprets erotic union as a promise of a justice to come, a justice which repairs the rivenness of a world out of joint and holds out the possibility of spiritual redemption. The Shekinah, in this sense, comes to stand for "the secret of the possible," the Open possibility of a gate that allows entry.[153] Celan had written of just such a possibility in a poem from *Threadsuns*, "Out of Angel-Matter":

> Out of Angel-Matter, on the day
> of ensouling, phallically
> united in the One
> —He, the Enlivening-Just One, slept you towards me,
> sister—upwards
> streaming through the channels, up

into the rootcrown:
parted,
she hoists us up, co-equal . . .
strewn from the East, to be harvested in the West,
  co-equal . . . (TS, 198–99)

Here we see not only the spiritual-pneumatic force of the world coupling with its material other in a phallic union, but we are also given a vision of a scattered Judaism from the East (Jerusalem/Bukovina) being harvested in the West (Paris) animated and enlivened through the active potency of a messianic justice that yields the hope of a co-equal, equiprimordial relation to being. A fuller reading of this poem would also explore Celan's ambivalence about such hoped-for justice and connect it to his deteriorating psychological health with allusions to the electroshock treatments he was receiving for his depression—"a bolt of lightning sews our skulls aright" (vv. 10–11). Nonetheless, what emerges out of "The Heat" is a vision of messianic justice that is inextricably bound up with Celan's erotic union with Ilana, a vision that has its sources in the mystical texts of the Kabbalah that Celan was working through in his Scholem readings. Celan's erotic images in "Out of Angel-Matter" bring together the impulses of Jewish mysticism and the fate of Eastern Jewry in the Holocaust, a hoped-for restitution of justice for the dead. In Jewish mysticism, if there is a God, then he must be just; as Otto Pöggeler puts it:

> He must reverse the judgment concerning the murdered victims, that their lives were worth nothing, and mete out justice to the dead. In the Tree of Life from Jewish mysticism it is this Sefira, the Enlivening-Just One who is united with the Shekinah, the exiled and regal one who, in her love and succor, can only be made present from out of justice.[154]

Celan's poems stand in an intimate relation to the union of the Just One and the Shekinah, expressing in their vital, erotic energy a way into and through the closed-off/walled-up Gate of Mercy that blocks the messiah's promised return. As prayers of hope for the possibility of reunion, they function as part of the "mending of the world" so essential to the task of mystical *tikkun* and so much a part of the erotic union between the Tsaddik and the Shekinah. Bearing his lover to him (v. 9) becomes a way of bearing the corpses of the murdered dead across the threshold of the Gate of Mercy to their proper burial place in a "reunited" Jerusalem, one that as "the Open one" promises a "*Heimkehr*" or return homeward for all the victims of Nazi persecution, including his father, his mother, and himself. In this sense, the poem itself enters into the promise of reparation as it seeks the possibility of an eschatological promise of justice for those who have been violated beyond any measure imaginable. Celan's "Jerusalem" thus emerges from the messianic promise of what is to come, built upon the memory of suffering and exile that the Jewish people have been compelled to endure. In this struggle to think Jerusalem in the tension between what is to come and what has been, Celan echoes Derrida who asks—"Am I in Jerusalem? This is a question to which one will never respond in the present tense, only in the future or in the past anterior."[155]

"That Shining"

Before turning to a reading of the two most powerful poems of the Jerusalem Cycle—"The Shofar Place" and "The Poles"—I should like to offer some thoughts on a short poem written by Celan on November 7, 1969. Like the other poems in this cycle, "That Shining" presents a narrative account of a tourist's visit to the Holy City, in this case an excursion to Abu Tor, "a Jewish quarter situated on the top of the mount overlooking the Old City and its environs. The Arabic name Abu Tor means 'Father of the Ox.' "[156] But the view of the Old City afforded by the distant perch of Abu Tor reveals to Celan more than the tourist's breathtaking view of the Golden Dome or "Mosque of Omar." From his poetic vantage the cupola of the dome rises up like a golden buoy from out of the "Temple depths" (v. 7) in such a way that for him it "measured the danger that fell / still beneath us" (vv. 8–9). Against this promontory he could measure the weight of Jerusalem's past against the hopes for its future, knowing full well that the dangers surrounding Jerusalem in the wake of the Six Day War were only those on the surface. The genuine dangers were buried deep beneath in the palimpsestic layering of Jerusalem's history, since the Golden Dome was built upon the same rock where the Temple of Solomon once stood and where Jews believe Abraham had tried to sacrifice Isaac and where Jacob saw the ladder to heaven. The endless lamentations of the Jewish people about the destruction of the Temple and their ensuing exile and Diaspora confront here their messianic hopes about a rebuilt temple in a Jerusalem of peace. Within Judaism itself there is a rich tradition of light metaphors that offer the promise of redemption—the eternal light in tabernacles and synagogues; the Menorah lamp; the light aura of Jerusalem; Isaiah's call: "Arise, shine, for Thy Light is come" (Isa. 60:1); the Kabbalistic *Ziv* that yields the "primordial light" from which the Shekinah is emanated; "the good light stored away for the righteous," among many other examples.[157] But there is also a tradition steeped in affliction and mourning, one that follows from the enslavement in Egypt through the Babylonian Captivity and the destruction of the Temple by Nebuchadnezzar (586 BCE) and the Romans (70CE) to the pogroms and persecution of Jews from the Middle Ages through the Holocaust. In this tension *between* the eschatological promise of a light that will bring "that shining" (v. 1), the *Ziv, and* the nihilistic dread of a light that will come with the nuclear conflagration of another Arab-Israeli war, Celan finds solace in the "hand roots" of his and Ilana's tradition. Cut off from his roots as the Westernized exile from Paris whose commitment to writing in German prevents him from moving to Israel, the orphan of history finds a trace of light in the shared hopes of another orphan, even as he recognizes "the danger . . . beneath us" (vv. 8–9). Here, he is "in search of light as much as in search of you," as he wrote to Ilana (PC/IS, 44). Standing watch over Jerusalem at the line of demarcation between east and west, antiquity and modernity, city of peace and city of apocalypse, Celan looks below at the abyss of danger that threatens to capsize the golden buoy that is *his* Jerusalem.

"The Shofar Place"

The Shofar Place	*Die Posaunenstelle*
deep in the glowing	*tief im glühenden*
text-void,	*Leertext,*
at torch height,	*in Fackelhöhe*
in the timehole:	*im Zeitloch:*
hear deep in	*hör dich ein*
with your mouth.	*Mit dem Mund.* (SPP, 360–61)

"The Shofar Place" takes up this threat of apocalypse and hears in it the trumpet blast of the Hebrew ram's horn, the Shofar, that sounds the call for a new beginning. Traditionally, the Shofar announces the beginning of the liturgy for Jews as well as the New Year festival, Rosh Hashanah; but it also announces the Hebrew *Jubeljahr* or "Jubilee Year" which is understood as the onset of a messianic era. Here, the Shofar signals a turn in time itself, a shift from the secular time of historical chronology to the messianic time of redemption, Benjamin's "*Jetztzeit*" or "time of the now."[158] In this sense, the trumpet sounds the call of hope—but it can also be heard as a warning signal for danger from an approaching enemy. When the Israeli army overtook the Western Wall during the Six Day War, General Shlomo Goren sounded the Shofar to celebrate the return to Israel of the sacred remains of the temple.[159] Celan will hear in this sounding of the trumpet a call for taking up the revolutionary possibility of transformation, of attending to the ram's horn as a relic from the ancient past buried deep in the "timehole" (v. 5) of Jerusalem's history that lay beneath the temple walls.

"The Shofar Place" is a poem constructed in seven lines, a structure that borrows from the apocalyptic book of Joshua, which speaks of seven priests blowing seven rams' horns for seven days, at which time the Jewish people circled the city of Jericho seven times shouting until the walls of Jericho fell down and the people took the city (Joshua 6:4–20). Yet there is another Biblical reference here that helps to place Celan's poem into the context of his poetic apocalypse of Jerusalem. This concerns the text from Exodus where, at the sound of the ram's horn, Moses hears the voice of Jahweh speaking to him delivering the Ten Commandments (Ex. 19:16–20). In this theophany that exceeded the limits of human speech, Celan finds a way of expressing the limits of poetic expression and of human longing. One of the sources for his taking up the theme of the Shofar was Margarete Susman, whose book *Deutung Biblischer Gestalten* Celan had read intensively. For Susman the revelation on Mt. Sinai was less in the spirit of a legalistic-authoritarian command than a reciprocal expression of love, especially the love for the homeless, for strangers, and for the dispossessed. Citing the text of Leviticus 19:34

> But the stranger that dwelleth with you shall be unto you as one who is born among you, and thou shalt love him as thyself,

Susman interprets the trumpet blast of the Shofar as a sign of "healing, reconciliation, redemption" where everyone who is homeless will once again find a home.[160] Celan would hear in this reading a way of coming home to his lost mother, birthplace, and Jewish identity through his love of another exiled Jew from Czernowitz, the "*Du*" of nuptial merger at whose "wedding" feast the festive torch of union would be lit.[161] And, like the other poems in the Jerusalem Cycle, this one can be read as a love poem with erotic references to "depth"-"void"-"hole"-"mouth." But it can also be read as an expression of an apocalyptic nihilism that hears in the trumpeting of the ram's horn the signs of a hollow tradition that has been emptied of meaning, the abyssal time of a coming conflagration. The tensions in Celan's Jerusalem poems run deep. On this reading, we can think of the "empty text" (*Leertext*, v. 3) as the Hebrew Book whose meaning has been voided in the "timehole" that signals the caesura of historical time brought on by the "glowing" (v. 2) fires of the Shoah. How to begin to ask the question of historical meaning after Auschwitz? With what language or tongue could we hope to address the irretrievable loss of hope and possibility?

Celan struggles with these questions in as compressed a poetic idiom as possible. To move from the unspeakable atrocities of the Holocaust to the messianic promise of fulfillment requires, above all, a "breath turn" (*Atemwende*), a poetic in- and ex-halation that "remains mindful" of what has transpired even as it initiates a turning to an Other that sets the estranged I free (SPP, 407–408/GW III, 195–96). The breath required for the trumpeting of the Shofar holds forth such a possibility for Celan in that its horn announces a "turning" of/in time, a time of eschatological redemption—a "timehole" of messianic peace. In *Deutung Biblischer Gestalten* Susman writes of these "messianic tidings" that announce the inception of a new era of justice, one that is singular in its Hebraic form. In the Greek form of justice, she claims, "the cosmic as well as the tragic has a *visual* form; it is a justice that one beholds." Hebrew justice, on the other hand, the justice of the prophets, is one that does not yet exist but must be realized through the ethical actions of individual human beings.[162] Juxtaposing Anaximander and Heraclitus with Isaiah and Daniel, Susman argues that whereas Greek justice employs metaphors of paying penalty and repentance, of war as the father of all things, Hebrew justice calls for the attainment of peace and of an ethical commitment to the other as a bond for such a possibility. Celan's "breath turn" draws on this Hebrew tradition of justice with its call for an ethical community of peace as a way of initiating a turn within time from history to eschatology. Here, we can understand the time of the Shofar blast as one that announces the end of racial genocide and atomic warfare. Within this messianic temporality the possibilities of a future are gathered in a "homestead of time" that offers the hope of a homecoming. Such a breath turn requires more than merely hearing the trumpet's blast; it demands a new way of speaking/writing where the "*Du*" is called to a transformative kind of synesthesia: "hear deep in / with your mouth" (vv. 6–7) (Deut. 6:1–7). Ilana hears this as a "command for absolute attentiveness to the text, the 'empty-text' which bears within itself the glowing enigma."[163]

"The Poles"

The Poles
are within us,
insurmountable
while we're awake,
we sleep across up to the Gate
of Mercy
I lose you to you, that
is my snow-comfort,
say, that Jerusalem *is*,
say it, as if I were this
your whiteness,
as if you were
mine,

as if without us we could be we,
I leaf you open, forever,
you pray, you lay
us free. (SPP, 362–63)

"The Poles" is perhaps the most enigmatic of all the poems from the Jerusalem Cycle and takes up the theme of attentiveness in an erotic way even as it renders it in terms of the selfsame topology of gates and passageways that we have seen in other poems from the collection. On November 19, 1969, Celan back in Paris receives a letter from Ilana in Jerusalem that speaks candidly about the difficulties of a long-distance relationship. She acknowledges that his Jerusalem trip was a "gift" and "much more" but she writes: "I want to go farther, beyond Jerusalem. I believe I can do it, we could do it, we could once again get beyond the poles and go back there" (PC/IS, 43). Taking up this image, Celan writes his poem two days later about the poles separating him and Ilana and transforms it into a cipher about the polarities within Jerusalem and within his own experience of it as the historical city of strife/conflict *and* the messianic city of eternal peace. What is Jerusalem? or rather: What is "Jerusalem"? A city of suffering and destruction? A site of shelter, refuge, and community? Is it the earthly city mourned by the Psalmist who weeps at its memory while in captivity, singing: "If I do not remember thee, let my tongue cleave to the roof of my mouth; if I prefer not Jerusalem to my chief joy" (Ps. 137:6)? Is it the heavenly city of peace (Ps. 122:6–8)? As we have seen with so many of Celan's poems, instead of definitive answers we find only the tensions and fissures that must first be worked out in relation to so many conflicting memories, fears, and hopes. In this sense we can see how the trip to Jerusalem serves as a form of *Trauerarbeit* for Celan—a way of enacting the "work of mourning" for what can no longer be and for those murdered victims who will have to wait until the messianic redemption at the end of time. Within this context the Jerusalem poems serve as both a coming home and a leave taking, texts that await their gathering in the "homestead of time."

In Ilana's image of the poles Celan finds a way of thinking through the Hölderlinian oppositions of "one's own" and "the foreign" that marked "Tübingen, Jänner" and "Todtnauberg." From the optic of Jerusalem he now sees these in a polar relation that both separates and unites east and west, Czernowitz and Paris, "*Ich und Du*," individuality and community, the memory of the past and the hope for the future. But he also constructs these polarities in such a way that they are not to be understood simply as that which lies outside himself or his union with Ilana. Rather, "the poles / are *within* us," he tells her. The tension between nearness/distance, heaven/earth, speech/silence, life/death can not be sublated through a "supersession." As

Celan seems to hint, only in tension/opposition itself can we hope to keep each element alive. It can never be simply a matter of thinking *either* the Jerusalem we experience *or* the Jerusalem we hope for. Both are necessary; both exist only in tension with the other. Drawing on an image from Franz Rosenzweig's *Zweistromland*, Celan understands Israel as the "Land of Two Rivers," the land of two poles.[164] While "we" are awake, he tells Ilana—that is, while we remain tethered to the factical world of consciousness, the earthly Jerusalem of history—we cannot surmount the opposition of the poles. Only through the erotic-mystical promise of sleep can the antipodes be brought together. In the "Enlivening-Just One's" sleep "towards" his sister/bride, the Shekinah, Celan finds the possibility of erotic union and a way of finding justice for the dead, a way of enabling the living to commune with the dead across the passageway of time (TS, 198–99). At this threshold of encounter that Celan names "the Gate /of Mercy," there is itself a split, as the enjambment between verses 5 and 6 suggests. But the image is yet more complicated. Not only does the Gate of Mercy have a double arched doorway, but it is only one of two doorways that make up the ancient gate. This is the same gate that Celan had alluded to in "The Heat," the one that had been closed off by the Muslim Sultan Suleiman to prevent the messiah from entering the city and bringing hope to Jews.[165] Here again, Celan will bring into play both the hope of messianic redemption and its denial. His language is precise: "we sleep across, *up to* (*vors*) the Gate / of Mercy." *Vors* here can be read as "on the verge of," "at," "in front of," "before,"—but *not* across. Sleeping across up to the Gate brings the poet and his beloved to a threshold or portal that serves as a site of intersection between the living and the dead, between those who are awake and those who sleep. Because for the wakeful the gate is permanently walled up and blockaded, it is only in sleep that they can find a path of ingress. But what is blocked is not only the realm of the living from the realm of the dead. So too is time. In this sense, just as the wall cuts off the living from the dead so too does it separate the past and the future, making any contact between them impossible. This leaves the poet in an abyss of the present where memory is cut off from hope and the recollection of the dead's suffering remains insurmountable, a burden that can never be redeemed. We hear traces of this burden in the poet's reference to his "snow-comfort" (v. 8). It is here that the intersubjective temporality of *Ich und Du* intersects with the larger communal temporality that is named in the gates of Jerusalem.

In a poem written in 1943 entitled "Black Flakes," Celan writes about the death of his mother in a Transnistrian work camp during a bitter Ukrainian winter. For him, the black snow flakes bring with them a "snowdrift" that, he writes, "sifts your father's / bones, hooves crushing / the Song of Cedar" (SPP, 14–15). Celan's father was likewise murdered in winter and the

Song of Cedar refers to a popular Zionist song that alludes to Palestine as "my dear homeland," "there where the ashes of my father rest" (DG, 589). As a young man Celan had rebelled against his father's orthodoxy and his visions of a Zionist homecoming and yet in the Jerusalem poems we can find numerous allusions to his own sense of *Heimkehr* in Jerusalem, a *Heimkehr* to and through his parents. In "The Poles" this *Heimkehr* will be expressed as a union with his *Du,* Ilana, the Shekinah of his sleep-dreams who offers her own kind of mercy in the wake of his parents' deaths. "I lose you to you" he writes; "that / is my snow-comfort" (vv. 7–8). But what is this loss? And how can it be rendered in the idiom of a gate? The Gate of Mercy as the entryway of erotic union and of commemorating the dead who lie buried outside its portal, comes to function here as a contested site of juncture. For if, on the one hand, it serves as the place in whose vicinity pious Jews are buried to await the messiah's coming, on the other, it also serves as a Muslim place of burial to block the coming Jewish messiah. Such are the paradoxes and contradictions that are embodied in this oldest of Jerusalem's gates. Outside the gate there reigns the historical time of conquest and contention. Inside the gate there holds sway the messianic time of peace, mercy, and redemption. Yet the poet and his Shekinah lie together *at* the gate, on the threshold of this possibility, as if they have not yet earned the right of entry, as if there were still some impediment to their own union and, through them, to a union with the remembered dead. The conditions for the possibility of passing through this impediment lie in the paradoxical language of "loss" rather than in one of "gain." In losing Ilana to herself, Celan finds a path of possibility for establishing a bond to an other, a bond that he hopes will serve as a way (back) into the Jewish identity/community he has lost, amidst the wreckage of so many other losses.

In a letter to Ilana that he wrote the day after he composed "The Poles," Celan noted: "Yes, that is my—passionate—wish: that you bring forth what lies within you; that you make of yourself what you are" (PC/IS, 44). In this Pindaric-Nietzschean injunction to "Become who you are!" Celan finds a source of comfort or, as he calls it, "snow-comfort"—the consolation of another Jewish survivor from Czernowitz being able to embrace a future of possibilities, a future denied to Leo and Fritzi Antschel. Desert heat, winter snow, the bifurcation of *Ich und Du*—these are only two of the numberless poles that stand in tension here. As elsewhere, Celan writes in a way that grants the Other its own singularity which, from his perspective, means its own alterity; rather than appropriate his lover to him and his own ipseity, Celan lets go of any strategies of conquest, entering into an ethical bond with Ilana that grants to her what is her own. Drawing on the prophetic language of Isaiah—"As one whom his mother comforteth, so I will comfort you; and ye shall be comforted in Jerusalem" (Isa. 66:13)—Celan finds in

Ilana's own egological self-determination a source for an intersubjective community of love and filial union, the sister/bride of the "Song of Songs." Celan will express something of this paradoxical understanding of community as an ethical bond without bondage, of an I:Thou relation at the threshold of union, but still marked by distance, in one of his letters to Ilana:

> There is so much distance between us that we will never again lose ourselves—so near are we to each other.[166]

At the very edge of his own self, at the boundary-line of a gate that is both open and closed, Celan utters an impossible command that is, at the same time, a hope for a way through the portal:

> say, that Jerusalem *is*. (SPP, 362–63)

Relayed in the imperative form, this utterance is, however, less a command of duty than an injunction of hope. If "Jerusalem" is to be, if the hoped-for messianic possibility of peace and justice is to reign upon the earth, then Ilana (we) must be able to *say* that it *is*. This hope must be given a place and this place of hope must be given a name. Because the earthly Jerusalem is a place of war and violence it cannot serve this function. Only in the affirmation of the heavenly Jerusalem, of Jerusalem as it *should* be, not as it *is*, can the possibility of such a Jerusalem ever come to be. This messianic vision of Jerusalem demands that we think the impossible—but not in such a way that we thereby render it possible. On the contrary, it is precisely the impossibility of the heavenly Jerusalem, the Jerusalem of justice, that enables us to move past the merely factical situation of injustice that prevails in our historical situation. Only as something that cannot be calculated, cannot be projected onto the screen of the future as an attainable blueprint for planning and execution, can we say that the justice of Jerusalem *is*.

Calling into question the whole edifice of the Western metaphysics of presence that privileges the stable configurations of identity and noncontradiction, Celan speaks to the absence of justice as a condition of calling for its (impossible) fulfillment. "Jerusalem" *is* not, hence it *must* be. Say it! Say it as if the very act of imagining its possibility were enough to open up this possibility itself. This, it could be argued, is what animates Celan's poetic call to the Other as much as anything. Celan's Jerusalem, like Derrida's justice, eludes closure and finality; it is that which must be pronounced even in the face of the impossibility of its pronouncement. Much as justice exceeds the possibility of its being instantiated in law, Jerusalem exceeds the possibility of its being instantiated in language. Nonetheless, it must be said, much as the law must attempt to render justice even when it recognizes that it must inevitably fail to do so. We are left with a contradiction—something that *speaks* (*dictare*) *against* or *contra* its own possibility. To borrow Derrida's terms, Celan's "Jerusalem" present us with an aporia—that which "we shall not be able to pass."[167] The "Gate of Mercy" blocked by the Muslim Suleiman can not be traversed; it is a *non*path. Yet precisely at this gate, at the threshold of promise that speaks of the Jewish messianic hope of justice for the dead, Celan calls for the formation of a community of mercy that will grant them justice. This expression of an ethics of remembrance, of an ethics of a Jerusalemic "we" that promises comfort and consolation, comes to the poet as a way of redeeming the promise of his dead parents and his lost homeland. But again, this utopian hope for justice at the opening of the Gate of Mercy also needs to be read against the blockage of such hope, a blockage that Celan knew from the story of the gatekeeper in Kafka's "Before the Law," (a text that Celan had translated into Romanian).[168] The impossible call for justice here meets the impossible entry into "the gateway of the Law." Naming Jerusalem, saying that it *is*—or rather, *can be*—functions as what Derrida will call "an experience of the impossible."[169] This experience, the one he shares with Ilana of the impossible conjunction between two lives near and far, lies at the heart of "The Poles" and of the Jerusalem Cycle as a whole—literally, since the call to "say, that Jerusalem *is*" lies precisely in the middle of the poem (verse 9 of 17) and the poem lies in the middle of the cycle (poem 11 of 20). As the poetic-eschatological center of Celan's hope, the very saying of Jerusalem's name centers "The Poles."

Within the modality of "say"-ing Jerusalem, the dead will pass through the gates, the lovers will find each other, the poet will come home, there will be a community within which the *Ich und Du* will embrace and be embraced. "Say it," he bids Ilana, say it "as if I were this / your whiteness, / as if you were / mine" (vv. 10–13). Here again we find the split between an "I" and a "you"—although the language bespeaks a hope of whiteness. Within the Jewish tradition the color white stands as a symbol of creation and redemption. Gershom Scholem writes of the "white robes of the just and pious in the resurrection" and of the kabbalist interpretation of white as a sign of the highest of the ten Sefiroth and of "the absolute mercy of the Godhead."[170] But the white alluded to here also serves as an index of the poet's own writerly encounter with the absolute otherness of the blank page, the abyss of the nothing from which the poet climbs every day, as he once wrote to Franz Wurm (PC/FW, 231). Hence, he can tell Ilana:

> I leaf you open, for ever, (v. 15)

as if Ilana were the book from which Celan could read his Jewish identity. The poles that lay within each of the lovers, the insurmountable ones, are crossed in the sleep of a promise that redeems each of them. The last stanza gives voice to this hope:

> you pray, you lay
> us free.

The English translation by John Felstiner nobly attempts to capture something of the resonance and interplay of the two German verbs *beten* and *betten*: "to pray" and "to bed" (as in to sleep with someone, erotically). It is as if Celan were saying that in the erotic solace that he finds in Ilana's bed the very promise of Jerusalem opens to him and enables the I to join in community with the Thou. This is a dream that emerges out of Celan's earlier "Meridian" Speech with its allusions to the utopian hopes of Gustav Landauer and Peter Kropotkin, as well as to the philosophical messianism of Walter Benjamin. There, Celan claims that the poem, like a meridian, "wants to reach an Other, it needs this Other, it needs an Over-against" (SPP, 409–10/GW III, 198). But to reach the Other the poem requires a special kind of "attentiveness" (*Aufmerksamkeit*) which it "dedicates to all its encounters"; such an attentiveness, he writes, "is a concentration that stays mindful of all our dates." With clear allusions to the brutality of the concentration camps (KZ) as well as to the twentieth of January, Celan here conceives of the poem as a site to both contest the violence of the KZ and to commemorate the suffering of the dead. He then cites (and re-situates) a line from Benjamin's essay on Franz Kafka. "Attentiveness," he repeats, "Attentiveness is the natural prayer of the soul (*Gebet der Seele*)." In "The Poles," the prayer spoken in Ilana's bed brings together the attentiveness of a concentration on encounter and remembrance with the attention to an eschatological liberation of the souls of the dead now rendered free through the prayer of Celan's poem. Here, the leaves of a book, the whiteness of a page that allows entry through poetic attention, offer a site of burial for the dead and a portal of entry for the erotic energy of the living.

But the affirmation of ecstatic union is only one half of Celan's polar disposition, as we have seen all too often in our reading of his work. "I Drink Wine," one of the last poems of the Jerusalem Cycle, offers a different view of messianic justice, one rendered by a "lottery drum."

"I Drink Wine"

> I drink wine from two glasses
> and plow away at
> the king's caesura
> like that one

at Pindar,
God turns in his tuning fork
as one among the least
of the Just,
the lottery drum spills
our two bits. (SPP, 366–67)

"I Drink Wine" opens with an image from the Seder feast of the Jewish tradition that takes place at Passover. According to Hebrew custom, the Paschal table is laden with a variety of foods that symbolize the passage from slavery (bitter herbs) to freedom (wine). Typically, the father sits at the head of the table to recite the *Haggadah* or "telling" of the story of the Jewish people's exile in Egypt, their wandering in the desert, and their salvation in Israel. At the father's table place there stand two glasses of wine—one to be drunk in celebration of freedom from exile and one to be left unconsumed for the prophet Elijah who, according to biblical promise, will be sent as a messenger to announce the coming of the Messiah:

> For behold the day cometh that shall burn as an oven. . . . But unto you that fear my name shall the Sun of Justice arise with healing in its wings.
>
> Behold I will send you Elijah the prophet before the coming of the great and dreadful day of the Lord. . . . (Malachi 4:1–5)

As Leo Trepp puts it in his book *Das Judentum*: "This goblet is called 'the cup of Elijah.' We do not drink from it, rather we take it merely as a sign through which we are admonished 'to remain mindful of the Torah, of the laws of Moses' in order thereby to hasten the coming of the breakthrough of peace for humankind. The past here reaches across the future."[171] As part of their ceremonial festivities those at the Seder table recall the sufferings of their forebears, chanting, "This year here, next year in Jerusalem. This year slaves, next year free." Against this rich background of Hebrew tradition the poem begins. Celan's own exile from his homeland, his remembrance of the dead, his hope for redemption and for the possibility of finding a way across "the poles" of his bifurcated identity as German and Jew will all find voice here. Moreover, following the word of Malachi, he too will seek healing from the Sun of Justice for the sufferings inflicted on him and his brethren.

The first stanza opens with this image from the Hebrew world of the Seder festival but then moves to the Graeco-German world of Pindar and Hölderlin, the archetypal poets of the festival. Celan writes that he continues to "plow away at / the king's caesura" and he compares this plowing away to "that other one's" own plowing away at Pindar. The reference here is clear. While reading Wilhelm Michel's *Das Leben Friedrich Hölderlins*, Celan marked a passage that cited a letter written in 1805 by the Hamburg privy councilor Johann Gerning describing the translations Hölderlin was engaged in: "Hölderlin, who is always half-crazy, also plows away (*zackert*) at Pindar."[172] In a letter to Ilana he explains: " 'That one': what is meant there is Hölderlin about whom an ill-minded person once wrote: he 'plows away' [*zackere*] (probably: dabbles, bungles [*pfusche*]) at Pindar" (PC/IS, 58). The first stanza points to two activities of the poetic "I": drinking and plowing away. Each of these activities is separated by a break, the dividing conjunction "and," which also brings them into relation. The dizzying number of binaries in this one short stanza include the two glasses of wine, the drinking/plowing away, this one (Celan) and that one (Hölderlin), Hölderlin:Pindar, all of which get thematized in the "king's caesura." As in "The Poles," Celan points toward the break, split, or schism that he experiences as his bifurcated identity: the exiled East European Jew living in the West, married to a Catholic with whom he speaks French, cut off from his language, his homeland, his family (the caesura of his break with Gisèle), caught in the caesura between German being-at-home and Jewish wandering. But there is a deeper caesura here, a "king's" caesura. At the same time that he must drink wine from two glasses, he must also confront a caesura that runs more deeply than the world of his poetic "I"; this is, as Lacoue-Labarthe puts it, "the caesura of our times": Auschwitz.[173] The German compound noun for king's caesura, *Königszäsur,* bears within it the encoding "KZ"—which stands for *Konzentrationslager* ("concentration camp"). Celan confesses to Ilana that: "In the king's caesura, there we lie, that's where we stand now, you and I" (PC/IS, 58). What separates him from Hölderlin, precisely as regards the notion of the caesura, is the question of the "king"—the Christian savior as king, the king of the Jews, the one in whose name the persecution of Jews as the murderers of Jesus, is carried out. This king's caesura, by which is meant "the cut" or "wound" that the Christian tradition has, in the name of its King, inflicted upon the Jews, splits the tradition in half, into two poles, or glasses as it were: the Hebrew and the Greek. If Hölderlin will interpret the caesura as one rooted in Greek tragedy and Pindar, Celan will plow away at a different caesura—the one known to him through Jewish mysticism and Scholem's writings.

For Hölderlin, the "caesura"—by which he means a "counter-rhythmic interruption" in both poetic meter and in tragic action—serves as a way of designating a break between two realms. In Sophoclean tragedy Hölderlin understands this as the moment when Teirisias interrupts Creon during the action in *Antigone* and shifts the center. In so doing, he "tragically removes man from his orbit of life, the very mid-point of his inner life, to another world, and tears him off into the eccentric orbit of the dead"

(E&L, 318/SA V, 196). In *Oedipus*, as well, it is Teirisias's interruption of the proceedings that shifts the rhythm of the play. There, Teirisias, who in Hölderlin's translation of the play is called "König" (king), challenges Oedipus who, as Hölderlin puts it, "is tempted to *nefas*" having "interpreted the oracle too infinitely (*zu unendlich deutet*)." It is precisely on this issue of the king's caesura (KZ) and of *deut*-en that Celan will focus his energy. As part of his work on caesura, Hölderlin had translated a fragment from Pindar that he entitled "The Highest":

> The law
> King of all, mortals and
> Immortals; it indeed drives
> Powerfully, for that reason,
> Justice most just with the highest hand. (SA V, 285)[174]

If, for Pindar, the Law is "the king of all," the force that drives the highest form of justice, then, for Hölderlin, this law needs to be understood in terms of "strict mediation" (*strenge Mittelbarkeit*), of a break between mortals and justice as between immortals and justice. An im/mediate relation to the highest justice is impossible; Oedipus's attempt to interpret justice as if he were already one with it shows this all too clearly. There is a caesura between the highest and the realm of mortals, as between the realm of the immortals and mortals. Hence, unlike Pindar's original text which placed the terms "mortals" and "immortals" on the same line, Hölderlin's translation separates them into a caesura: "mortals and / immortals . . ." (vv. 2–3).[175] Hölderlin's translation, then, not only recognizes this caesura, but precisely in a bold attempt at trans-lation/*Über-setzung* it enacts the caesura. Celan will attempt his own poetic form of translation here as he plows away at the king's caesura that separates his own notion of Hebraic justice from the Graeco-German version of *dike* and *Gerechtigkeit* put forward by Pindar and Hölderlin. For Hölderlin, justice will be understood in poetological-tragic terms as that which provides a proper measure—in the sense of both tragic excess (Oedipus's overinterpretation of the oracle) and balanced poetic meter. What the caesura brings to light is the very need for a break in a text or plot/narrative so that one does not fall victim to the Oedipal illusion of immediacy with the divine. Justice is always what is impossible to achieve, what eludes immediacy. Even the gods are not the masters of justice, which is the highest of all. But where Hölderlin and Celan find common ground is in the understanding of caesura as what the Swabian poet calls "the pure word" (*das reine Wort*) (E&L, 318/SA V, 196). For both of them poetry serves as this "pure word," the word that breaks open the normal rhythms of life and provides a counter-rhythmic gesture of dissent, what Celan in his "Meridian" speech terms a "counter-word" (*Gegenwort*). For Celan such a counter-word can be found in Büchner's play *Danton's Death* when the character Lucile, in protest against the Jacobins' condemnation of her beloved Camille at the guillotine, shouts out suddenly: "Long live the King!" (SPP, 402–403/GW III, 189–90). In this one gesture, a gesture that is literally art-less (since Lucile, as Celan acknowledges, "is blind to art"), Celan perceives an "act of freedom." Here, in a poetic caesura that announces itself suddenly and without art or artifice as "the pure word," Celan finds an expression for his "breath turn," the *Atemwende* that initiates a shift in human perception, an *ethical* act that affirms "the Majesty of the Absurd," as it succeeds in "testifying/witnessing to human presence." In all its senses as an ethical act of witnessing, as a counter-rhythmic protest against the totalitarian domination of the human spirit, Celan's pure poetic word sees itself as a kind of "king's caesura," a way of articulating Lucile's kingly counter-word to the forces that threaten life itself. As he drinks his poetic wine from the two glasses of German-Jewish tradition, Celan plows away at the king's caesura, hoping to find the proper poetic language of witnessing that will help to initiate a breath-turn of freedom, a way of remembering the dead that will provide a measure of justice. But as always with Celan, the caesura of freedom will carry with it the scar of its "wound." The polar tensions between hope and despair remain, manifesting themselves in a deep ambivalence about the possibility of genuine freedom in the shadow of the Shoah. These tensions emerge with real force in the second stanza of the poem in such a way that we might even speak of a caesura between the two stanzas.

If the opening stanza lays focus on an egological "I" who drinks and plows away at a king's caesura that eludes its grasp, the second stanza will shift terrain. Now the I has disappeared and in its place we are left with a "God" whose kingly identity has been undermined, to say the least. In a post-Nietzschean world where the *deus absconditus* leaves little trace of his departure save the empty churches that echo his *requiem aeternam deo*, God has turned in his "tuning fork." In this stanza we encounter the sources of Celan's Jewish identity, the texts that he reads against the Graeco-German notion of the king, especially the writings of Gershom Scholem and Margarete Susman. From Scholem he takes up a Kabbalist understanding of a God who retreats from the workings of history in a primordial act of "self-contraction" known as *tsimtsum*. The consequences of this Kabbalist understanding of divine withdrawal for Celan's experience of exile and for his understanding of the king's caesura are profound. On Scholem's telling, Kabbalist myth—especially in the work of Isaac Luria—constitutes a response to the Jewish experience of exile and to the "expulsion of the Jews from Spain, an event which, more than any other in Jewish history down to the catastrophe of our time, gave urgency to the question: why the exile of Jews and what is their vocation in the world?"[176] In Lurianic Kabbala, however, exile is not merely a historical experience of the Jewish people; rather, "exile [is] an element in God Himself." For Luria, God's first act is neither creation nor emanation, but rather withdrawal. The *Ein Sof* or "Infinite One" withdrew its presence, thereby creating a vacuum that functioned, paradoxically, as a site for creation. Into this vacuum the *Ein Sof* emanated a ray of light that generated the primordial Adam from whose cranial orifices there emerged the ten Sefiroth, including the Shekinah. This bond between the Sefiroth is broken, however, when the lower ones, which are referred to as "vessels," are unable to contain the power of this divine light and shatter in a primordial event known as "the breaking of the vessels" (the *shevirah*). As Scholem describes it, "This is the decisive crisis of all divine and created being, the 'breaking of the vessels,' which Luria identifies with the Zoharic image of the 'dying of the primordial kings.'"[177] But how are Jews to respond to this primordial kingly caesura? For Luria, this task consists in the "mending" or "repair" of the breaking of these original vessels known as *tikkun*. The doctrine of the *tikkun* stresses that human beings must act to repair the damage done to the divine realm of the ten Sefirot, a realm that lies everywhere in shards and fragments, exiled from its primordial essence. This cannot be done by God alone. Hence, the responsibility to act ethically falls to the human realm to heal the caesura within being itself through acts of justice and mercy. As Scholem explains it:

> Everything that humanity does influences this very complicated process of *tikkun* at any given point . . . which is why Luria declares that worlds in all their externals are dependent on religious deeds and on the enactment of the commandments in the Torah. . . . And so in a certain sense we are not only masters of our own destiny and fundamentally responsible for the continuation of the exile (*Galut*) ourselves, but we also fulfill a mission which reaches far beyond that. (translation altered)[178]
>
> *Tikkun* [is] the restoration or reintegration of all things to their original condition, as intended in the divine plan of Creation; a plan that was never realized, because it was hindered by the Breaking of the Vessels, on an ontological level and by Adam's fall on a human plane. The completion of the process of *tikkun* is redemption; any act of *tikkun* is thus an act toward salvation.[179]

Within this Lurianic understanding of the *tikkun*,

> everything that happens, happens according to the secret law of the *tikkun*, depending upon whether it is enacted or not. At every

> stage Biblical history offers an opportunity for redemption, but at the decisive point humanity always fails to take advantage of it. . . . But the essential function of the Law . . . is to serve as an instrument of the *tikkun*. Every human being who acts in accordance with this Law brings home the fallen sparks of the Shekinah and of his own soul as well. . . . Thus fundamentally every human being and especially every Jew participates in the process of the *tikkun*. This enables us to understand why in Kabbalistic myth the Messiah becomes a mere symbol, a pledge of the Messianic redemption of all things from their exile. For it is not the act of the Messiah as executor of the *tikkun*, as a person entrusted with the specific function of redemption, that brings Redemption, but my action and yours. . . . For Luria the coming of the Messiah means nothing other than co-signing a document that we ourselves write. (translation altered)[180]

Against this background of the Lurianic Kabbalah we can read Celan's "I Drink Wine" as an ambivalent response to the injustice that he sees everywhere around him. Confronted by a receding divinity who has absconded and left the world in disrepair, turned in his "tuning fork," Celan acknowledges the human responsibility for the caesura of the Shoah as well as the need for its ontological repair. In the act of writing poetry, in the co-signing of a document written as a call for messianic redemption and for a homecoming out of exile, Celan embraces the ethical responsibility of the human subject in a world where God has receded. To "say, that Jerusalem *is* . . . ," to write as if the very act of writing were a way of enacting the redemption of the *tikkun*, that is Celan's poetic affirmation of a hope that is besieged on all sides by the irredeemable memories of loss and despair. Celan's poetic "I" is, in this sense, not a heroic subject who overcomes all odds to assert its own mastery over the world around it but, rather, an embattled soul whose own ambivalence remains caught in the poles of a contradiction. Living in a world marked by the breaking of the vessels, caught between the historical exile of the Jewish people and the mystical exile of the Shekinah, the poet undertakes the ethical repair of the world through an act of remembrance. In this turn to the Other, to the lost dead whose scattered remains call out for burial and wholeness, Celan seeks a breath-turn. Even here the Kabbalist language of *tsimtsum* helps to express something of the paradoxical phenomenon of the *Atemwende* that Celan affirms as an "act of freedom" (SPP, 403/GW III, 189). For, in his withdrawal from the world, God "contracted the essence of [His] presence into a handbreath"; "this act of withdrawal or inhalation," which the Kabbalists take as the primordial withdrawal of the Shekinah in her exile from God, will function for Celan as a fertile myth for understanding the "absential" as a defining characteristic of Jewish experience.[181] As Celan reads it, such a turn will constitute nothing less than a refiguration of Western culture through the Hebrew tradition of ethics and justice rather than through the Graeco-German measure of *dike* and *Gerechtigkeit*. We can see traces of these concerns in "I Drink Wine" that reflect the whole question of theodicy in the Jewish interpretation of the Holocaust, especially Margarete Susman's work, *Das Buch Hiob und das Schicksal des jüdischen Volkes*.

Celan read this work carefully, became friends with Susman and entered into a correspondence with her.[182] Her work on Spinoza from 1913, "Spinoza und das jüdische Weltgefühl," presented him with a thoughtful account of Jewish identity for a generation of post-assimilationist Jews. In this essay Susman had written: "The sentiment for an earthly home is not as profound as that for a metaphysical one. . . . The Jews are uprooted from their earthly home, yet it is not this one, but the metaphysical one about which they have to decide concerning their ability to endure life and be able to justify it."[183] More than thirty years later Susman will take up this question of justification and theodicy in her book on Job that deals with the question of the Holocaust. For her the question is: How, if at all, is it possible to justify the unthinkable suffering of the Shoah? How are we to make sense of this, to find a language that would not always already betray the traces of its own inadequacy? How, "in this moment of world-catastrophe that has led humanity in both its life and its knowledge to the edge of suicide," can we begin to frame again the question of "justice"?[184] Of God's justice in the eyes of humanity? Of human justice in the eyes of God? In a world where "for the Jewish people, as for Job, divine and human justice have been broken asunder," and where "every Jew is stigmatized by the reality of rejection," the question remains—why? "As no other people on earth the Jewish people thus exist purely in a question; they exist, like Job, in the unanswerable question about the form of existence imposed upon them." If Job can attest that "the arrows of the Almighty are with me" (Job 6:4), then the Jewish people can claim an affinity with this "same grim entanglement." In the shadow of Job's legacy, Susman writes, "there are no great accomplishments of Judaism in exile right through the late writings of Kafka . . . that are not in essence a theodicy, an attempt at a justification of God before his people or a justification of the people before God."[185] Against this impossible question, the very act of writing and speaking itself becomes ever more questionable. Susman attempts to revive Job's question (and with it the questionability of such a question) as a way of thinking through the unspeakable question of the Shoah: "In the face of this event every word is no doubt a word too-little and a word too-much." Between these two poles Susman attempts to find the proper measure for the word, understanding all the while that throughout their history the Jewish people "have affirmed excess (*Übermaß*) as their measure (*Maß*)."

Celan took up this question of the Shoah as a question concerning language and its proper measure in one of his most famous poems, "Zürich, Zum Störchen." Playing off Susman's own formulation from the opening paragraph of her Job book, Celan describes a conversation he had about the question of justice and the Shoah with the Jewish poet Nelly Sachs:

> Of too-much was our talk, of
> Too-little. (SPP, 140–41)

In Celan's poem Susman's words are reversed; if she begins her book with an emphasis on the "too-little," Celan seeks to underscore the point that any attempt to put the question of the Shoah into language is a question of "too-much." And yet despite his differences with both Susman and Sachs, and his rejection of what he terms "your God," Celan still valued their willingness to engage him in conversation and to continue to use the terms of Job's "cavilling word" (*haderndes Wort*) (v. 18) as the basis for a way of working through the question of the Shoah. Celan was deeply skeptical about the attempt. He remained wary about the value and possibility of giving expression to the impossible constellation of despair that remained clustered around the synecdoche "Auschwitz." And yet, as Ilana Shmueli tells us, "For Celan the Shoah never ceased."[186] The pressing question of justice needed to be reformulated in terms of Nietzsche's proclamation of a final accounting of the *deus absconditus*. If both Susman and Sachs retained their belief in the God of the Old Testament and his justice, Celan remained ever skeptical. As he put it in the last stanza of "Zürich, zum Störchen":

> We
> really don't know, you know
> we
> really don't know
> what
> holds true. (SPP, 140–41)

In one of the last poems from *Lightduress*, "Treckshutenzeit" ("Trek-scow-time"), Celan takes up again the question of the *deus absconditus*, "the dis-elevated one," the one "cast from the throne," the same question that will be addressed in "I Drink Wine" with its focus on the "God [who] turns in his tuning fork" (v. 6).[187]

As he plows away at the king's caesura, the crack in time and history marked by the abyssal difference between human and divine justice, Celan takes up the question of the tuning fork. Tuning forks measure proper pitch on a musical scale and attempt to find this measure in a balance of notes, sounds, expressions that resonate between two prongs or tines. By indicating that God has turned in his tuning fork, Celan points to God's renouncing of his ability to measure the proper tone between the insurmountable poles that separate human and divine, Hebrew and German, "the Highest" (*Höchste*) of Hölderlin and Pindar from the one taken down from the heights of the Highest (*enthöht*) by the "world-catastrophe" of Auschwitz. Precisely because this once elevated being can no longer provide a way of balancing the extremes on a world scale, we are unable to find a measure between the too-little and the too-much. Having turned in his tuning fork, God now stands "as one among the least of the Just" (vv. 7–8). This cryptic reference from the legends of East European Hassidism can be taken in two ways. On the one hand, this can mean that God has lost his status as the kingly arbiter of justice and has retreated into hiding as merely one other figure among the least of the just. On the other hand, it could also signify a way of taking away ethical responsibility for injustice from God and placing it firmly back in the realm of ordinary human beings and their life-praxis. As he comes to consider the relationship between human beings and God on the issue of justice, Celan draws on an old Hebrew legend that he knew, taken up by Gershom Scholem in his essay, "The Tradition of the Thirty-Six Hidden Just Men." As Scholem relates "this legend, widespread in Jewish folklore, speaks of thirty-six *Zaddikim,* or just men, on whom—though they are unknown or hidden—rests the fate of the world."[188] "According to several of these legends, one of the thirty-six hidden men is the Messiah. If the age were worthy of it, he would reveal himself as such." What this tradition of Ashkenazic wisdom stresses is precisely the unknown nature of the workings of justice, that it is not manifest in the great events of history but rests in the hands of "your neighbor and mine whose true nature we can never fathom." This "anarchic morality," as Scholem terms it, puts the responsibility for justice and ethical action in the hands of ordinary human beings who may not be aware that they are part of the group of thirty-six *Zaddikim,* so hidden is this secret. By stressing that God is "one among the least / of the Just," Celan both undermines the metaphysical foundation of a *deus absconditus* as well as stressing the need for human participation in the decisions about justice. Scholem's essay reaffirms this view that, as the passage from Proverbs puts it, "The Just man is the everlasting foundation of the world" (Prov. 10:25). But Celan will express it ambivalently in "I Drink Wine," underscoring the necessity of human justice as what the tradition demands of us, even as he questions whether there ever can be anything like a "foundation" upon which any truth can stand. In the last stanza of the poem this radical skepticism will be reflected in the anarchic venture of a game of chance where

> the lottery drum spills
> our two bits [*unser Deut*]. (SPP, 366–67)

That the fate of the European Jews would be a matter of luck, that is something Celan knew all too well.[189] But there are other dimensions to this image of the *Deut*—which could signify an allusion to *Deutsch* (German), *Deutung* (interpretation), or Deuteronomy. In colloquial German, the phrase—"*keinen Deut wert*"—means "not worth a farthing" since "*Deut*" is a Dutch coin with little value.[190] As a reference to *Be-deutung* (meaning, significance), we could read this verse to mean that instead of providing meaning, the whole discourse of the first two stanzas—the polar tension between the "I" who forms the subject of the first *and* "God" who stands as the subject of the second—has little worth, since God has absconded and left us to suffer in silence. In a world bereft of meaning and measure, where the fate of justice falls to us rather than to an elevated deity, it is simply not enough to let the lottery chips fall where they may. Or, as Celan put it in one of his notebooks, it is not enough to accede to a world where one can say "he did his duty, but *not even one farthing (Deut) more*" (DG, 876). To stand in the king's caesura, to dwell in the cleft brought on by the KZ, signifies nothing less than to take upon oneself the ethical responsibility to be one of "the least of the Just." Caught between hope and despair, between what Susman terms "the time wholly abandoned by God" and the time of "messianic hope," Celan ambivalently plows away at the Hölderlinian caesura as a way of expressing his impossibly contradictory position between Hebrew ethics and German philosophy.[191] Hölderlin well understood that "this is the time of kings no longer" (SA IV, 62), that the age of the French Revolution would bring with it a revolution in poetic practice, one in which the responsibility would fall to the poet in a time where,

> . . . the solid letter
> Be given scrupulous care, and the existing
> Be well interpreted (*gedeutet*). (SPF, 242–43)

If Hölderlin understood by this that poetic measure would serve as a way of building a revolutionary order of balance and harmonic tension, then Celan would interpret this differently. For him, the task of the poet involved writing in a language that would affirm justice yet in such a way as not to make it "present," but to honor its absential power, the power of the hidden

Shekinah. Poems for him served as instantiations of the *tikkun*, of the hidden repair of the world that would help to welcome the Shekinah back from the exile into which she had fallen. Forced to live in the bifurcated world of polar oppositions between German and Jew, heretic and mystic, earthly and heavenly Jerusalem, Celan focuses on the apophatic language of withdrawal to express his hopeless relation to a future cut off from its past. Something of this tradition will be reflected in Scholem, who draws on the Kabbalist interpretation of the Just One for a way of grasping the contradictions within the Hebrew tradition.

> The *Zaddik* (Just One) stands in the realm of nothingness; this paradoxical statement . . . combines a purely mystical element with a moral one, fluctuating in emphasis toward one side or another. This nothingness is the divine nothing (*Ayin*): it is that sphere within the Godhead from which all true creation springs. It is also the end of the road that the Kabbalist traverses during his absorption in the *Sefiroth*. On his road toward the divine nothing, he must cast off all individual qualities and distinctiveness, making himself infinitesimally small, indeed, nothing, in order to pass through the "Gateway of Nothingness."[192]

As "one among the least of the Just," the *Zaddik* confronts the injustice and senselessness of the world in a hidden, enshrouded way, not drawing attention to his deeds but plowing away in silent obscurity. At the very threshold of time itself, caught between the memory of the dead and the messianic hope for homecoming, Celan finds in the *topos* of "Jerusalem" a way to attend to the "solid letter" of Hölderlin's "Patmos" hymn. In the caesura between the departed king and the apocalypse to come, Celan poetizes justice in a hidden language of gates, doorways, thresholds, poles, caesuras, shofars, and wine glasses. Against the attempt of Susman "to unify Jewish and Christian metaphysics" in an ethic of reconciliation and forgiveness, Celan confronts "the glowing text-void" that is the nihilism of post-Shoah flames (SPP, 360–61).[193]

What the Jerusalem Poems open to us is a way of confronting the impossible caesura that measures the distance between these traditions and helps us to begin to raise again the ethical question of how to endure the abyssal world of Judaic despair, the one in which, Kafka writes, "there is no room for justice."[194] But in this void, this glowing text-void, the one where absence reigns and where the sureties of faith are never made present, Celan scribbles his poetic "letter in a bottle" and sends it out to sea (SPP, 396). By attending scrupulously to his poetic craft, by adhering to the Hölderlinian cultivation of the solid letter and by painstakingly interpreting (*gedeutet*) "the existing" (*bestehendes*), Celan turns poetry into an ethical act. Though he can never be sure of where his *Flaschenpost* may land, Celan sends it seaward in an act of faith that is not free of despair. The Jerusalem poems come to language in that same space, a space of hope that is walled in by despair. Celan needed the meridianal lines of connection to Jerusalem from his Paris co-ordinates in order to find a way of linking his past and his future. But the weight of that past would prove to be too great a burden. Six months after he returned from Jerusalem, Celan chose his own death on April 19, 1970, the night of the Passover Seder feast that he would never celebrate. In this place Celan found himself so cut off from his Czernowitz family Seder that he could no longer find a way back, nor attempt a way forward.[195] In the margins of the Jerusalem Poems we can read the apocalyptic cries for release and redemption, entreaties that are calls for "a justice to come" for himself and for the lost dead whose own cries resound in the poems. Celan attempts the impossible. He attempts to bear witness to that which, as Giorgio Agamben claims, "it is not possible to bear witness": Auschwitz.[196] And he does so in a language that withdraws into the king's caesura of witnessing (in both its genitival senses). Not Athens, but Jerusalem becomes the site for this witnessing of the absential—an impossible contradiction of hope and despair that gets expressed in the love poems for Ilana and the justice poems for the absent dead. "Testimony," Derrida insists, "implies faith or promise"; it is an affirmation of the hope for something to come.[197] Like a messianic promise whose arrival never comes—since to instantiate hope means to imprison it within the metaphysics of presence—Celan's poems call for a justice that is impossible to realize, a justice that urgently calls "come, come" even as it always recedes into a future that never arrives. To learn to wait for this absential justice to come, even now, in a present that never arrives—that is the impossible aporia of Celanian justice that echoes in the entreaty, "say, that Jerusalem *is*."

POSTSCRIPT

A *posteriori*—that's how everything begins.

—Georg Büchner, *Leonce and Lena*

Isn't there justice?

—Emmanuel Levinas, *Nine Talmudic Readings*

Justice recedes from being grasped. As what eludes the reach of the human, it fails to appear as something that could be subsumed under the category of presence. Justice happens, if it happens at all, in the shadow of absence, in a time other than the present—as mourning and memory, as expectation and as promise. Celan well understood the temporality of justice as belonging to what Derrida calls "the time of the promise [since] it will always remain, in each of its future times, to come: . . . it never exists, it is never present, it remains the theme of a non-presentable concept."[1] In both expectation and memory we find hope and mourning, traces of the absential in what is no longer and in what is yet to come. Where traditional ontology thinks of being as self-identical presence, Derrida thinks of it as a spectral ghost that haunts the temporalities of the future and the past that are not "mine," but the temporal specters of the other. In Celan's poems we have traced the outlines of these specters, *revenants* of the dead, those phantoms whose spectral forms haunt us with their unspeakable suffering. In the absential spaces between the lines of his verse we find the (absent) markings of the ghosts who return again to claim both our memory and our mourning. In this mourning we leave behind the lost possibilities of the past even as we claim the traces of the ghosts who live on in us. For both Derrida and Celan the force of such mourning is aporetic. On the one hand, it leaves behind what cannot be retrieved in the present or in the future; on the other, such mourning carries out the work of just such a retrieval by making us responsible to the dead in a way that exceeds the present or any future that could be made present. It is this sense of responsibility that is *before* us and *beyond* us that characterizes the work of mourning, opening us both to those who are no longer and to those who are not yet.

Mourning needs to be understood here as both a lament for the justice denied to the victims of the past *and* as a call for a justice to come, a messianic justice "beyond all living present, within that which disjoins the living present, before the ghosts of those who are not yet born or already dead."[2] As Derrida defines it, this form of justice, a justice that does not let itself be deconstructed back into the propositions of metaphysics or the calculations of legal redress, "is always unequal to itself. It is non-coincident with itself."[3] Justice in this sense is always absential, always non-coincident with the present or with any semblance of presence, never exhausted in self-identity, but ever open to the other in a time that is other, to perhaps "the time of the other." Derridean justice is marked by the power of absence that takes the form of "the messianic: the coming of the other, the absolute and unpredictable singularity of the *arrivant* [the one still to come] *as justice*."[4] This "absolute dissymmetry" of justice—its refusal to fall into the structure of calculation, economy, exchange, equivalence, assimilation—renders it disproportionate and incalculable. Justice exceeds "values, norms, prescriptions" in its infinite demand that there be justice *now*, without delay or interruption. And yet, at the same time, "justice remains *to come*, it remains *by coming*, it *has* to come, it is to-come, the to-come [*à-venir*]. . . . It will always have it, this *à-venir*, and always will have had it." Justice, then, comes to us in the form of an aporia as "an experience of the impossible," an experience haunted by a messianic promise and an urgency that "does not wait. It is that which must not wait."

In this experience of the aporias of justice we are ever and again brought back to the irremediable mourning of those whose names have been expunged from history, those whose ghosts continue to haunt us beyond the calculation of numbers and names.[5] Mourning too belongs to justice in that its aporias follow the same structure as those of justice. That is, genuine mourning needs to work through the appeals of ipseity and presence, focusing not on *my* memory in the present moment, but on the alterity of the other who is no longer present. Mourning thus is neither an act of introjection nor one of incorporating the mourned within me but, rather, a rupture, break, or scission that rends the other from me in a way that "over-takes" me as "sur-prise." Mourning, like justice, is due the other in ways that I cannot predict or foresee. In the trauma or wound that the departure of the mourned brings with her, in her singular withdrawal, I am claimed by a responsibility that is incommensurate with traditional norms, ethics, and justice. Hence, it is not *my* experience of loss that is at stake in mourning, but the responsibility to the other whose absence confronts me as a futural call and promise for a fragile justice to come. In responding to that call, in confronting the ghosts of the dead who refuse to remain interred in the crypts that confine them to a final resting place, these specters return to haunt us in the name of a justice denied, a justice whose very name serves as a shibboleth for a messianic promise to come.

Celan's poetry shares with Derrida this thought of the spectrality of justice, of a justice that is both infinite and impossible to circumscribe within the boundaries of the present moment. For Celan, justice eludes the present as it recedes from being instantiated in any equivalent gesture or act. Like mourning, justice is impossible and marked by aporia, paradox, enigma, and disruption. The traces of Celanian justice, if we could even speak of such a thing, take the form of geological deposits whose sediment has been dislodged from the fissures within rock and stone only to be carried away from their native environs, in flight, and displaced by forces that extend far beyond them. Here, monoliths fracture into microliths.[6] Within this geological process stones erode and break down into particles that get transported by currents and then deposited as sediment within a new geological configuration in a cycle of departure without return. In this way the stones function as host sites for other organisms to form there, sites of "hospitality" that offer Celan a powerful poetic metaphor for the understanding of an originary geopoetics of disintegration, loss, and destruction—even as they point to a distant, precarious hope for a future that restores balance and offers the possibility of renewal.[7] In this aporia between loss and hope, possibility and impossibility, Celan sends forth his poems as missives that take the form of "primeval messages in a bottle" (*urweltliche Flaschenpost*), geological alluvia that carry tectonic traces of a world that has disappeared and fallen into oblivion. From the "wound of the earth" (*Wunde der Erde*), Celan draws a meridian, searching for his lost place of origin, a place that no longer exists, that he hopes will lead to an "encounter," somewhere "north of the future" (SPP, 226–27; 413/GW III, 202).[8]

Against the settledness or *Seßhaftigkeit* of Heideggerian dwelling, Celan's geopoetical *Flaschenpost* bears witness to the loss of the home and the unsettled status of the unburied dead whose microlithic remains demand burial—if not in the ground, then in the crypt offered by the poem. The poem functions as a textual gravesite, a place of mourning for the lost dead whose suffering can never be properly set aright, despite the need to do just that. Celan's poems call out for a justice to come, a justice that exceeds law, presence, instantiation, and totality. Like Derrida, he will think justice as absential, as incalculable, illimitable, and infinite—a justice riven by aporia, since its very possibility demands that it be made present. And yet, as infinite, it always remains as what is to come. Celan was preoccupied with the absolute, unrepeatable singularity of factical life in all its forms. His poetry offers countless examples of the way language refuses to find a covering law for the unburied dead, but instead encodes that suffering in an idiom suffused with rupture, disjunction, and caesura. At the heart of his experience of justice is aporia: the impossibility of finding a path through the contradictions of the moment.

Only there, where the way is blocked, in a moment that calls out for decision and action, can we genuinely confront the abyssal depths of justice's infinite demands upon us. It is this aporetic moment that Celan points to in his two poems on a shared theme, "Shibboleth" and "In One," where he thinks the impossibility of passage, "*No pasarán*," in terms of a shibboleth that, when spoken, cuts into "*die Fremde der Heimat*" (the strangeness/foreign land of the homeland) (SPP, 74–75). As Derrida reminds us, Celan's "Shibboleth" performs the aporia of estrangement, "strangeness, estrangement in one's own home, not being at home, being called away from one's homeland or away from home in one's homeland, this not passage (*ce pas du 'ne pas'*), which secures and threatens every border passing in and out of oneself."[9] As the word that cuts one off from the homeland, the shibboleth both gathers and disperses; it comes to mark the date of what is irreplaceably singular even as it repeats the date as an act of commemoration and return. Celan's shibboleth thus offers the aporia of singularity and repetition, of what can only come once and of what returns. In this sense, Celan's poem "Shibboleth" becomes itself a shibboleth that marks the date of specific, singular events—in February 1934 when Viennese workers rebelled against the Austro-fascist regime of Dollfuß and the events of February 1936 and 1939 when Spain's Popular Front challenged Franco—*and* calls out for a futural hope to come against all future fascisms of the spirit.[10] In the aporia between the time of commemoration and the time to come—what Celan in "And with the Book from Tarussa" terms "*die Stundenzäsur*" (the caesura of the hours)—we find a poetry measured and weighed upon "the language-scale, the word-scale, the homeland-/scale of exile" (PCS, 95/DG, 165). This "*double edge* of a shibboleth" renders the caesura "of belonging and of exclusion" that tears at the heart of Celan's poetic mourning.[11] "Like unburied words" for the unburied dead whose mourning will never cease, Celan's poems call out for a "decision of justice" whose coming may never come (DG, 164). Celan's call for justice can, however, hardly be understood as utopian. In an aphorism from his collection *Gegenlicht* that shows traces of Kafkaesque absurdity, Celan writes: "Our talk of justice is empty until the largest battleship has foundered on the forehead of a drowned man" (CP, 11/GW III, 163). And yet Celan was always mindful of the need to think hope and despair as belonging together in the same aporetic configuration:

> Speak—
> But do not sever No from Yes
> Give your verdict (*Spruch*) this meaning as well:
> Give it the shadow. (SPP, 76–77)

Against the specter of those unburied shades who haunt us through their return, Celan holds forth the fragile promise of a justice to come, a justice out of accord with our own time, a justice for a time that is itself out of joint. This spectral justice of/for ghosts counters the No with a Yes and in holding out this promise provides an opening to the future.

Celan's work would be difficult to understand apart from his readings of both Hölderlin and Heidegger. As I have tried to show, so much of his writing (including "The Meridian" speech) shows traces of Heideggerian and Hölderlinian influence. And yet the irreparable caesura that separates Celan from each concerns this promise for a spectral justice to come, a justice marked by scission and circumcision, the mark of a shibboleth separating one tribe from another. In Celan's offer of a promise we find deep traces of a Heideggerian commitment to "what is coming" (*das Kommende*), to "advent" (*Ankunft*), and to "the coming of the holy" (*das Kommen des Heiligen*) (EHP, 136/GA 4, 113–14). Understood from its etymological roots in Latin, *promise* (*pro* + *mittere*) signifies a "sending forth," a "releasing," a "letting go" of something: a word, a thought, a hope. In this sense, Heidegger's understanding of the future takes the form of a promise that poets will send forth the word that "opens the time-space for an appearing of the gods and points towards historical humanity's dwelling place upon this earth" (EHP, 137/GA 4, 114). And while Celan shares Heidegger's hope for an opening to the future, and a promise for a historical dwelling place, his poems hold out the memory of exile, banishment, and deportation. Still, in a letter to his wife that speaks of his visit to Heidegger's hut at Todtnauberg, he references the topic of hope for a future commitment from Heidegger on questions about Germany's past, writing: "I hope that Heidegger will take up the pen and write some pages that relate to our conversation and in view of the re-emerging Nazism will also be a warning" (PC/GL I, 479).

Such hopes would never come to fruition. And yet, Heidegger and Celan shared a deep hope for an "other" beginning—even if they each framed this hope differently. Each of them wrote of this hope in the face of a world shaped by loss, abandonment, and destitution, a world bequeathed them by Hölderlin in his laments about the departed gods and the loss of the homeland. What solidified their bond was this shared sense about the role that technology played in the instrumental triumph of language as one of the most powerful forces in destroying the homeland. But it is precisely this question of technology and its dangers in the face of an "other" beginning that profoundly separate Heidegger and Celan as they come to confront the specter of the loss of the homeland. Heidegger's habitual attempts to think *ethos* as an originary kind of dwelling confront Celan's poetics of exile at the meridian of a strange and distant nearness, the "Fremde Nähe" of an impossible dialogue, a "despairing conversation" made ever more despairing by Heidegger's entrenched silence (SPP, 410/GW III, 198). But what of their respective ways of approaching the question of justice? How are we to think the poetic measure of this difference that marks their respective paths of questioning?

Clearly, the meridian of silence that separates Heideggerian homecoming from Celan's exile renders a caesura that threatens the very possibility of promise, hope, and renewal. Yet despite this caesura we can also find traces of affinity between the Jew from the Bukovina and the *Landsmann* from the Black Forest. Heidegger's thinking can be read as a way of finding our just place within the configurations of being, configurations to which we must adjust if we are to find our proper home. Heidegger's repeated discussions about *ethos*, sojourn, and *Aufenthalt* would all be offered in the spirit of taking up questions of "ethics" and "justice" in a nonmetaphysical register that would address the very issue of an originary form of human dwelling upon the earth. In a profound sense, Heidegger's notion of *ethos* as dwelling signifies an openness to the strange, the unfamiliar, the foreign, and the other. In the *Letter on Humanism*, Heidegger translates Heraclitus's fragment *ethos anthropoi daimon* as: "The (familiar) abode for humans is the open region for the presencing of god (the un-familiar one)" (*Der [geheure] Aufenthalt ist dem Menschen das Offene fur die Anweisung des Gottes [des Un-geheuren]*) (PM, 271/GA 9, 356). *Ethos* here signifies a kind of dwelling in and with the proper, the ownmost, *das Eigene* that opens up to the improper, the foreign, *das Fremde*. Such an *ethos* allows the other as other to come to presence; it lets otherness be. From *Being and Time* through the later writings on *Gelassenheit*, Heidegger's thinking opens to the otherness of being as a letting be and as a sense of responsibility to the event (*Ereignis*) of being that lets *Dasein* be appropriated (*ereignet*).

In a profound sense, Heidegger understands responsibility as the very ethicality of being that emerges in and from the open region where the human being dwells, a region open to the otherness of the other. In belonging to being, in letting the event of being appropriate me as *Ereignis*, I am responsible for preserving (*bewahren*) this openness—which is nothing other than the "truth" (*Wahrheit*) of being. As Heidegger puts it in "Building Dwelling Thinking": "Mortals dwell insofar as they save the earth . . . saving properly means: to release something (*freilassen*) into its proper essence" (PLT, 150/GA 7,152). Responsibility to the other means *freilassen*, releasing the other to its own proper *Wesen* or way of essentially prevailing. Responsibility, then, does not originate with the egoicity of the Cartesian subject as an enclosure out of which I come; rather, I am called to take over being's singular way of self-showing, and be responsible for it. "Ethics," in this sense, does not reside with the subject, but belongs to being—phrased differently, being has its own ethicality that has nothing to do with the "ethics" of an autonomous subject. Hölderlin's poetry points to this ethicality in ways that depart from the metaphysics of subjective ethics and toward the openness of being (*das Offene*) as what calls the poet to the task of measuring. Poetic measure for Hölderlin measures this infinite, incalculable openness as it engages the singularity of human dwelling. This Hölderlinian poetic measure does not provide a normative measure valid "once and for all," but attunes itself, rather, to the immeasurability of being's withdrawal. In the figure of "the trace of the gods who have fled," Hölderlin points to the unknowable measure of/for poetic attunement (SPF, 158–59). Paradoxically, Hölderlin finds in the gods' withdrawal a measure for their self-manifestation; in the lovely blueness of the sky he sees traces of a measure beyond the reach of the poet. In some lines from his late hymn "The Only One" (First Version), he indicates something of this inability of the Cartesian subject to appropriate any proper measure:

> Much though I wish to, never
> I strike the right measure. But
> A god knows when it comes, what I wish for. . . . (SPF, 222–23)

To dwell poetically for the human being means accepting "the limits/Which god at birth assigned/To him for his term and site (*Aufenthalt*)" (SPF, 202–203). The human sojourn upon the earth is shaped by these limits which provide a measure for how to dwell in the absence of any fixed or immutable measure. Like Pindar, who grasps the human being as "creature of a day" (*Tagwesen*), that being who is but a "shadow of a dream," Hölderlin finds his poetic measure in accepting the "term and site" for human dwelling, the lot or portion (*moira*) that we have received (DKV II, 750). And in his translation of Pindar's Second Olympian Ode he renders the Greek term *moira* as *Fügung*—"enjoining," the way things fit together, the just fit (DKV II, 697).[12] As Hölderlin understands it, poetic measure helps us to learn how to dwell within the just fit allotted to us in our *Aufenthalt* or sojourn upon the earth. Heidegger interprets this to mean that through poetizing, "the human being first receives the measure for the breadth of its being" (PLT, 222/GA 7, 200). At the heart of such receptivity Heidegger identifies a "letting-come of what has been meted out" (*Kommen-lassen des Zu-Gemessenen*) (PLT, 224/GA 7, 203). Much as Hölderlin, who follows Pindar in interpreting "measure" in poetic-ethical terms, Heidegger thinks it as a form of dwelling filled with a measured relation to the appropriate fit of the human being within the structural enjoining of being as *dike* or *Fug* (order) (P, 92–93/GA 54, 137; N i, 166/N I, 194). Yet neither Heidegger nor Hölderlin simply takes over the Greek idea of *dike* as the just measure that sets limits; rather, each situates it within the singular site of the human sojourn upon the earth. Here, "justice" is less a set structure of reigning principles than a jointure (*Fuge*) open to the play of the event (*Ereignis*) that comes to be each time in a singular way. Poetizing happens as a way of keeping open the Open (GA 4, 103). And yet for Heidegger the very discourse of "ethics," "justice," "rights," "values," and "virtue," cuts off the possibility of abiding in this openness by attempting to calculate, outline, posit, and confirm the basic principles of a prescriptive ethics of quotas and utility.

Heidegger's attempt to rethink justice as poetic justice, or the poetic measure of justice, seeks to challenge these metaphysical gestures by attuning us to poetry's way of opening us to *Ereignis*, the middle-voiced appropriating event of granting/withholding that prepares a site for human dwelling. In this way, poetry—as poetizing—opens to the poetic measure of being that grants an opening within which human beings can dwell beneath the sky and above the earth. Poetizing, in this sense, is not something that humans accomplish, but a gift granted to us that lets us dwell poetically.[13] As Hölderlin puts it:

> Filled with what is our due, yet poetically
> The human being dwells upon the earth
> [*Voll Verdienst, doch dichterisch wohnet*
> *Der Mensch auf dieser Erde*]. (PF, 788–89)

By attending to what is our due, poetizing measures the fit of human beings within the whiling of being, the way we fit into what is fitting. In "The Verdict of Anaximander," Heidegger calls this fit "*dike*, the order of the while" (*den Fug der Weile*) (EGT, 45/GA 5, 359). There, Heidegger writes of *dike* as being bound up with reck (*Ruch*) or care for other beings, a comportment that "lets reck in each singular case belong to the other, lets reck belong in its relation to each other" (EGT, 47/GA 5, 360). What pervades this whole discourse of reck and care is a form of poetic dwelling that takes responsibility for the other, for the *Ereignis* of the other that is always coming again in its singularity.

Here we are both near to and distant from the poetics of Paul Celan who understands poetry as a gift to the stranger, an act of hospitality that reaches out to the other. For Celan, poetry is like a handshake, a gesture of welcome that opens the word, opens the heart, to the other in the hope of something coming (GW III, 177). I have chosen, like Derrida, to read this welcoming gesture about what is coming as Celan's fervent hope for a "justice to come." This gesture of welcome offered by the poem opens the future in a way that cannot be anticipated, in a way that breaks open the present, and disjoins presence from the gathering gesture of totality. Celan's poetry thus offers a justice not only for those who are yet to come; it also opens such justice to the ghosts of the dead, those spectral shades who haunt the present and who lay claim to a justice denied them. In this way, Celan's poetry opens a dwelling place, an *Aufenthalt* for those denied an *Aufenthalt* in the political designs of the autochthonous *Volk*. Celan writes from this position of exile, suspended "between homeland and abyss" (*zwischen Heimat und Abgrund*), a place suffused with mourning where the poet can barely think the possibility of hope (SPP, 152–53).[14] Like Hölderlin, who knew intimately the burden of despair, Celan thinks hope against despair as a way of preparing the poetic gesture of mourning.

In one of his lectures on Hölderlin, Heidegger writes that the fundamental mood of poetry is "sacred mourning," a mourning that, in the wake of the departed gods, binds us to the homeland (GA 39, 87–88). This homeland, he stresses, is not to be understood as "simply a birthplace, also not merely as a familiar landscape, but rather *as the power of the earth*, upon which the human being—each according to its particular historical *Dasein*—'dwells poetically.'" This sacred mourning is open to that which holds sway over the human being, that which runs through us and encompasses us as an "indwelling." It is in "such a homeland that the human being first experiences itself as belonging to the earth." At the heart of this understanding of mourning we can find perhaps the most profound points of both conjunction and disjunction that bind and divide Heidegger the thinker to/from Celan the poet. On one side we can find traces of an ecological sense of justice, of an openness to the powers of a *physis* that does not follow the rules or principles of human justice, a justice open to the unanticipated arrival of the other, that lets the other be in its otherness. And yet, as we have seen, Heidegger's privileging of the homeland will be interpreted by Celan as a gesture that reinforces his own irremediable sense of exile and exclusion. Celan's banishment from the "homeland," from the "birthplace," and from the "familiar landscape," attunes him to a justice not of the present order, a justice that never accepts the status quo of the present as a possible site for its coming to be. Rather, Celan's call for justice emerges from the depths of an exile so abyssal that it conceives of the very hope for justice as im/possible. Precisely as impossible, this call for justice becomes ever more necessary. As Walter Benjamin so poignantly put it, "It is only for those without hope that hope is given."[15]

In the teeth of such hopelessness, Celan acknowledges that "the poem . . . can be a message in a bottle, sent out to sea in the—not always greatly hopeful—belief that somewhere and sometime it could wash up on land, on heartland perhaps. Poems in this sense too are underway (*unterwegs*): they are headed toward (*sie halten auf etwas zu*)" possibilities (SPP, 396/GW III, 186). Even here in a gesture toward what is coming that abandons the soil of the homeland for the infinite and unforeseeable possibilities of the sea, we find Celan drawing on the language of Heidegger in his allusions to being underway (*unterwegs*) on a sojourn (*Aufenthalt*). And perhaps here we can find some space of encounter between Celan and Heidegger, one that shares an understanding of their present age as a time of destitution, an impoverished epoch ruled over by the metaphysics of a modern technology that threatens the very possibility of poetic utterance. Within such an age we find ourselves unequal to the task of uttering the promise of justice, the hospitable gesture welcoming the arrival of the unexpected, the incalculable, and the unprethinkable.

In the shadow of Anaximander's verdict on the fit and jointure of being, both Heidegger and Celan, like Hölderlin before them, encounter a world with little understanding about the poetic measure of justice. Each abandons the metaphysical measure of permanent presence for a measure attuned to the letting-come of what has been meted out in the play of singularity and difference. Here, poetic measure lets the creative play of *physis* emerge in the event or *Ereignis* of justice that happens as what Nietzsche, following Heraclitus, called a *Weltspiel*: the play of the world as what renders justice each time again, infinitely. Perhaps no modern philosopher has expressed this poetic measure of justice as incisively as Jean-Luc Nancy. In his essay "Cosmos Basileus" (The Sovereignty of the World), Nancy maintains that there is no justice external to the world as its measure. As he puts it, "Justice is the return to each existent its due according to its unique creation, singular in its coexistence with all other creations. . . . Justice must therefore be rendered both to the singular absoluteness of the proper and the absolute impropriety of the community of existents. It must be rendered the same to each: such is the play (or the sense) of the world."[16] Here, justice is rendered as the sharing of the gift that is being, the gift of the "*es gibt*"—an infinitely giving gift that is exposed in its singularity to coexistence, "to alterity and to alteration."[17] This exposure to the event of creation—what Anaximander terms *genesis*—happens once even as it happens forever, again and again, singularly. This gift of singularity is what is proper to each existent. From within this Anaximandran world, justice gives the measure of jointure to each proper existent in its *genesis* as part of the cosmic play that lets beings come to presence. But Anaximandran justice also thinks beings in terms of *phthora*, perishing, absence, and withdrawal. To think this absence through the improper, the strange, the exiled, the abandoned, and the suffering—this is to hear the call of a justice to come. In the exhortations of the Old Testament prophet Amos, this means "to let justice flow like an inexhaustible stream" (Amos 5:24).

If we were to heed such a call in all its due measure, it would mean that we would need to abandon the name *justice* as a master name even as we would incessantly pursue "a just measure of the incommensurable."[18] Such a justice would always need to be written with ellipses that would trail off into an openness incommensurable with its inscription. This justice of the ellipsis that never coincides with anything present, that solicits us to follow an "impossible path, the path of the impossible," attends not only to the openness of the future, however (SPP, 413/GW III, 202). It also traces the mark of absence, of that which is elided, left out, omitted, or eradicated. Celan employs these ellipses in his "Meridian" speech again and again to testify to the absence and effacement of the Jew from German life. But the ellipsis also marks the trope of an Abrahamic exile without the hope of an Odyssean return, the impossibility of Celan's return home to the Bukovina. It is in this sense perhaps that we can read Celan's relation to Heidegger as one marked by ellipses—especially Heidegger's inability to think the ellipsis of the Jew in his Graeco-Germanic history of being. We could perhaps, borrowing the phrase from the last line of "Engführung," read this ellipsis of exile as the mark of rupture where presence and absence, German and Jew, Heidegger and Celan, are "written asunder" (*auseinandergeschreiben*), never to find jointure (SPP, 130–31).

And yet, as he comes to closure in his Büchner prize speech, Celan once again employs the ellipsis as a way to point toward a hope that will not be extinguished, a hope that he does not cease from pursuing to "find . . . a meridian" (SPP, 413/GW III, 202). Such a meridian traverses the path of an impossible hope, one echoed in "Todtnauberg" where Celan writes of:

> a hope, today.
> for a thinker's.
> (un-
> delayed coming)
> word
> in the heart. (SPP, 314–15)

Heidegger too will employ the ellipsis as a way of pointing toward the Hölderlinian readiness for "that which is to come" (*das Kommende*) (GA 4, 47). In "*Aus der Erfahrung des Denkens*," pointing the way as it were, Heidegger compresses his hope for what is coming in lapidary form: "To head for a star . . . ," he writes (GA 13, 76), a hope that echoes Hölderlin's own poetic invocation for "the coming God," the god whose coming is *to* come, can only *be* as this coming (SPF, 152–53). If, with Derrida, I have chosen to read justice in this way as "a justice to come," it is not with an ambition to erase the ruptures between Heidegger and Celan or to gather their differences together in order to reconcile them through a reading of Hölderlin. Acknowledging the aporias, at times pointing toward them, at other times insisting upon them, I have tried to think these aporias in all their difficulties, finding in the singularity of each poem or essay a way of rethinking the enigmas of justice that persist as enigmas. If the work of justice, like the work of mourning, will never have ceased from needing to be done, then with Celan we will need to take up this task ever again with an urgency that does not admit of delay. With Derrida and Celan we could then say: there is an infinite need for justice, an infinite need for justice's infinity. To write in the name of this justice would mean to ceaselessly measure the incommensurability of a justice written with ellipses, a justice beyond our ken, a justice that would abandon the very name of justice to take on a measure of hope—perhaps even a poetic measure. It would be the call of this justice that we would then hear in the call of the poet, who once called—"we will never be done with hope."[19]

NOTES

INTRODUCTION

1. F. W. J. Schelling, *Die Weltalter: Fragmente*, ed. Manfred Schröter (Munich: Beck, 1979), 211. Heidegger treats this in CPC, 95, 150/GA 77, 146, 231.

2. In his Nietzsche lectures Heidegger writes: "Experienced in a Greek way, the man of the basic relationship with beings is *metron*, 'measure,' and he lets his confinement to the restricted radius (restricted for each respective self) of the unconcealed become the basic trait of his essence" (N iv 94/ N II, 138–39).

3. Heidegger variously calls Hölderlin simply "the" poet, as well as "the poet of the poets," "the poet of the essence of poetry," and "the poet of the other beginning" (GA 70, 159–60, 166).

4. "Martin Heidegger-Takehiko Kojima: Ein Briefwechsel," in *Japan und Heidegger*, ed. Hartmut Büchner (Sigmaringen: Thorbecke, 1989), 225; cf. also GA 11, 160.

5. In Hölderlin's translation of Sophocles's *Antigone* he renders Ismene's description of Antigone as *kyndyneuma* with the German term *vermessen* SA V, 206. In his English translation of *Hölderlin's Sophocles* (Northumberland: Bloodaxe Books, 2001), 72, David Constantine translates this as "you reckon recklessly."

6. In his *Introduction to Metaphysics*, Heidegger writes, "We understand fittingness first in the sense of joint (*Fuge*) and structure (*Gefüge*); then as arrangement (*Fügung*), as the direction *that* the overwhelming gives to its sway; finally, as the enjoining structure (*fügende Gefüge*) which compels fitting-in (*Einfügung*) and compliance (*Sichfügen*)" (IM, 171/EM, 123).

7. On this problem of thinking the untranslated possibility of justice and ethics, see the work of Dennis Schmidt, *On Germans and Other Greeks* (Bloomington: Indiana University Press, 2001); *Lyrical and Ethical Subjects* (Albany: State University of New York Press, 2005); "What We Didn't See," in *The Pre-Socratics After Heidegger*, ed. David Jacobs (Albany: State University of New York Press, 1999), 153–70.

8. Jean-Luc Nancy, *A Finite Thinking* (Stanford: Stanford University Press, 2003), 173.

9. François Raffoul, *The Origins of Responsibility* (Bloomington: Indiana University Press, 2010), 223.

10. In GA 55, 326, Heidegger writes: "Being is the sole measure of beings." In *Was ist das-die Philosophie?* Heidegger will also claim: "The correspondence to the being of beings does, to be sure, continually remain our abode *(Aufenthalt)*." (Pfullingen: Neske, 1956), 35.

11. Raffoul, *The Origins of Responsibility*, 248.

12. Jacques Derrida, *The Gift of Death*, 2nd ed. (Chicago: University of Chicago Press 2008), 95.

13. Jean-Luc Nancy, *A Finite Thinking,* 136. In French *hanter*—"to frequent"; in German one sees this connection in the words *Heim* (home) and *heimsuchen* (to haunt—as of ghosts). Cf. *Dudens Etymologie* (Mannheim: Duden, 1963), 257. For an excellent discussion of the sources of *ethos,* cf. Charles Scott, *The Question of Ethics* (Bloomington: Indiana University Press, 1990), 142–47.

14. For an insightful critique of this technological application of ethics, cf. the work of William McNeill, esp: *The Time of Life: Heidegger and Ethos* (Albany: State University of New York Press, 2006) and "A Scarcely Pondered Word," in *Philosophy and Tragedy,* ed. Miguel de Beistegui and Simon Sparks (London: Routledge, 2003), 165–92.

15. In "The Way to Language," Heidegger cites Novalis: "Precisely what properly characterizes language . . . no one knows" (BW, 397/GA 12, 229).

16. Hans-Georg Gadamer puts it best: "What one recovers from (*verwindet*) does not simply lie behind one as something overcome (*überwindet*) or surmounted (*aufgehoben*), but keeps determining one henceforth" *Gesammelte Werke,* IV (Tübingen: Mohr-Siebeck, 1987), 483.

17. H. W. Petzet, ed., *Martin Heidegger/Erhart Kästner Briefwechsel, 1953–1974* (Frankfurt: Insel, 1986), 59–60.

18. On the topic of volition in Heidegger cf. Bret Davis, *Heidegger and the Will* (Evanston: Northwestern University Press, 2006).

19. In the "Letter on Humanism," Heidegger writes: "Thinking is related to being as what arrives (*l'avenant*)" (PM, 275/GA 9, 363).

20. Raffoul, *The Origins of Responsibility,* 276–81.

21. Jean-Luc Nancy, "Cosmos Basileus," in *The Creation of the World* or *Globalization* (Albany: State University of New York Press, 2007), 110–11, 55. Compare the earlier translation in *Being Singular Plural* (Stanford: Stanford University Press, 2000), 186–87.

22. Charles Kahn, *The Art and Thought of Heraclitus* (Cambridge: Cambridge University Press, 1979), 62–63, cf. also fragment B51, 64–65.

23. *Pres-ab-sence* is a term coined by Thomas Sheehan to designate the fateful play between presence and absence within the selfsame happening, cf. "Martin Heidegger" in *A Companion to the Philosophers,* ed. Robert Arrington (Oxford: Blackwell, 1999), 288–97 and "Heidegger's Topic: Excess-Recess-Access," *Tijdschrift voor Filosofie* 41, no. 4 (1979): 615–35.

24. Liddell-Scott, *Greek-English Lexicon* (Oxford: Oxford University Press, n.d.), 1841; Alois Vanicek, *Griechisch-Lateinisches Etymologisches Wörterbuch* ((Leipzig: Teubner, 1877), 91; Christoph Horn, ed., *Wörterbuch der antiken Philosophie* (Munich: Beck, 2002) 201–202.

25. Charles Kahn, *The Art and Thought of Heraclitus,* 44–45.

26. Dennis Schmidt, "The Ordeal of the Foreign and the Enigma of One's Own," *Philosophy Today* 40, no. 1 (1996): 189.

27. Emmanuel Levinas, "The Trace of the Other," in *Deconstruction in Context,* ed. Mark C. Taylor (Chicago: University of Chicago Press, 1986), 345–59, here 345, below 348.

28. Emmanuel Levinas, *Proper Names* (Stanford: Stanford University Press, 1996), 44.

29. Jean-François Lyotard, *Heidegger and "the Jews"* (Minneapolis: University of Minnesota Press, 1990), 93.

30. Theodor Adorno, *Gesammelte Schriften*, IV (Frankfurt: Suhrkamp, 1980), 42.

31. Paul Celan, *Microlithen sinds, Steinchen* (Frankfurt: Suhrkamp, 2005), 129 (hereafter: MSS).

32. Reiner Schürmann, *Broken Hegemonies* (Bloomington: Indiana University Press, 2003), 351–63.

33. Paul Celan, MSS, 126.

34. Paul Celan, SPP, 408–409/GW III, 196–98.

35. In chapter 3 I will focus on the background to "Todtnauberg" in greater detail.

36. Hadrien France-Lanord, *Paul Celan und Martin Heidegger: Vom Sinn eines Gesprächs* (Freiburg: Rombach, 2007) and James Lyon, *Paul Celan and Martin Heidegger: An Unresolved Conversation, 1951–1970* (Baltimore: Johns Hopkins University Press, 2006), as well as Anja Lemke, *Konstellation ohne Sterne: Zur poetischen und geschichtlichen Zäsur bei Paul Celan und Martin Heidegger* (Munich: Fink, 2002).

37. Paul Celan's letter to Werner Weber, March 26, 1960, in *Fremde Nähe: Celan als Übersetzer*, ed. Axel Gellhaus (Marbach: Deutsche Schillergesellschaft, 1997), 397–99.

38. For Heidegger's essays on Hebel cf. GA 16, 491–548 and Charles Bambach, "Heidegger, Technology, and the Homeland," *Germanic Review* 78, no. 4 (Fall 2003): 267–82.

39. Axel Gellhaus, ed., *Fremde Nähe: Celan als Übersetzer*, 398.

40. *Paul Celan/Gisèle Celan-Lestrange Briefwechsel* I, ed. Bertrand Badiou (Frankfurt: Suhrkamp, 2001), 479.

41. Paul Celan, *Lichtzwang: Historisch-kritische Ausgabe* IX, ed., Rolf Bücher (Frankfurt: Suhrkamp, 1997), 107.

42. For some of Heidegger's references to the Böhlendorff Brief, cf. GA 4, 87–88, 157–58; GA 39, 136, 290–94; GA 43, 122; GA 52, 135; GA 53, 154–55, and Peter Trawny, *Heidegger und Hölderlin oder der Europäische Morgen* (Würzburg: Königshausen und Neumann, 2003), 85–169.

43. Theodor Adorno, *Negative Dialectic* (New York: Continuum, 1973), 191/*Negative Dialektik* (Frankfurt: Suhrkamp, 1973), 192.

44. Cf. Heidegger's comment on the "enemy" in the context of his discussion on Heraclitus GA 36/37, 90 which echoes comments from Carl Schmitt.

45. Emmanuel Levinas, *Totality and Infinity*, 50–51.

46. Franz Rosenzweig, *Star of Redemption*, trans. Barbara Galli (Madison: University of Wisconsin Press, 2005), 20–21; 54–58; *Stern der Erlösung* (Frankfurt: Suhrkamp, 1999), 14–15; 50–54.

CHAPTER ONE. THE HÖLDERLINIAN MEASURE OF POETIC JUSTICE

1. Charles S. Halsey, *An Etymology of Latin and Greek* (New York: Caratazas, 1983), 126; J. B. Hofmann, *Etymologisches Wörterbuch des Griechischen* (Munich: Oldenbourg, 1950), 389.

2. Gisela Wagner, *Hölderlin und die Vorsokratiker* (Würzburg: Triltsch, 1937), 68–90; and Dieter Bremer, " 'Versöhnung ist mitten im Streit': Hölderlins Entdeckung Heraklits," *Hölderlin Jahrbuch* 30 (1996/97): 173–99.

3. Ulrich Gaier, *Hölderlin: Eine Einführung* (Tübingen: Francke, 1993), 97–101; Jürgen Link, "Asymmetrie und Ekzentrizität bei Hölderlin," *Kulturrevolution: Zeitschrift für angewandte Diskurstheorie* 6 (1984): 56–58; Lawrence Ryan, *Hölderlins Hyperion: Ekzentrische Bahn und Dichterberuf* (Stuttgart: Metzler, 1965), 11–15.

4. Immanuel Kant, *Schriften zur Anthropologie* (Darmstadt: Wissenschaftliche Buchgesellschaft, 1968), 34.

5. The poet does not stop in the "center" (i.e., Cyprus) but diverges from it "off-course" toward Patmos "ek-centrically."

6. "There is a time for love . . . as there is a time to live in the happy cradle. But life itself drives us forth" (H, 117/SA III, 87).

7. *Der Kleine Pauly* (Munich: Deutscher Taschenbuch Verlag, 1979), IV, 550.

8. Alois Vanicek, *Griechisch-Lateinisches Etymologisches Wörterbuch* (Leipzig: Teubner, 1877), 379; Menge-Güthling, *Enzyklopedisches Wörterbuch der griechischen und deutschen Sprache* (Berlin: Langenscheidts, 1957), 316.

9. On *deus absconditus* cf. Wolfgang Janke, *Archaischer Gesang: Pindar, Hölderlin, Rilke* (Würzburg: Königshausen und Neumann, 2005), 161–70; On *Trauer* cf. Anselm Haverkamp, *Leaves of Mourning* (Albany: State University of New York Press, 1996).

10. Jean-Luc Marion, *The Idol and the Distance* (New York: Fordham University Press, 2001), 102–103.

11. Johann Bengel, *Gnomon: Auslegung des Neuen Testamentes in fortlaufenden Anmerkungen* (Berlin: Evangelische Verlagsanstalt, 1959).

12. Howard Gaskill, "Meaning in History: Chiliasm in Hölderlin's 'Patmos,' " *Colloquia Germanica* 11 (1978): 19–52. Gerhard Schäfer, "Der speculative Württembergische Pietismus" in *Hölderlin und Nürtingen*, ed. Peter Härtling and Gerhard Kurz (Stuttgart: Metzler, 1994), 48–78.

13. Kerstin Keller-Loibl, ". . . gib ein Bleiben im Leben, ein Herz uns wieder": *Der Frieden in Hölderlin's Werk* (Tübingen: Francke, 1995).

14. Halsey, *An Etymology of Latin and Greek*, 68.

15. Vanicek, *Griechisch-Lateinisches Etymologisches Wörterbuch*, 197; Franz Passow, *Handwörterbuch der griechischen Sprache* (Leipzig: Vogel, 1841), 363; Indra McEwan, *Socrates' Ancestor* (Cambridge: MIT Press, 1997).

16. W. K. Guthrie, *History of Greek Philosophy*, I (Cambridge: Cambridge University Press, 1967), 33; McEwan, *Socrates' Ancestor*, 35; Diels-Kranz, *Fragmente der Vorsokratiker* I, (Berlin: Weidmann, 1903), 15.

17. Diogenes Laertius, *Lives of Eminent Philosophers*, I (Cambridge: Harvard University Press, 1970), 131.

18. Johann Bengel, *New Testament Word Studies*, I (Grand Rapids: Kriegel, 1971), xiv.

19. G. W. F. Hegel, *Lectures on the Philosophy of World History*, trans. H. B. Nisbet (Cambridge: Cambridge University Press, 1975), 197; *Vorlesungen über die Philosophie der Weltgeschichte*, I (Hamburg: Meiner, 1955), 242–43.

20. T. G. Tucker, *Etymological Dictionary of Latin* (Chicago: Ares, 1985), 172.

21. On "Hesperia" cf. Hermann Timm, "Weisheit aus dem Abendland: Hölderlins evangelische Dichtertheologie," *Zeitwende* 63, no. 3 (1992): 162–72; C.

Schrevelii, *Lexicon Manuale: Graeco-Latinum et Latino-Graecum* (New York: Collins and Hannay, 1825), 218.

22. Menge-Güthling, *Enzyklopedisches Wörterbuch der griechischen und deutschen Sprache*, 28; *Benselers Griechisch-Deutsches Schulwörterbuch* (Leipzig: Teubner, 1904), 908.

23. René Descartes, *Discourse on Method* (Indianapolis: Hackett, 1993), 35.

24. On this notion of "the holy" as a poetic-philosophical theme see: Michel Haar, *Song of the Earth* (Bloomington: Indiana University Press, 1993); and Vincent Vycinas, *Earth and Gods: An Introduction to the Philosophy of Martin Heidegger* (The Hague: Martinus Nijhoff, 1961).

25. For the inordinate influence of Herder's philosophy of history on Hölderlin see Peter Nickel, *Die Bedeutung von Herders Verjüngungsgedanken und Geschichtsphilosophie für die Werke Hölderlins*, dissertation Universität Kiel 1963; and Ulrich Gaier, *Hölderlin: Eine Einführung*, 350–56 and 417–19.

26. Although the PF and the SA versions have only fourteen stanzas, the newer text of DKV: 227–29 and 644–47 has fifteen. On the relationship between Hölderlin and Pindar see Maurice Benn, *Hölderlin and Pindar* (The Hague: Mouton, 1962); and Albrecht Seifert, *Untersuchungen zu Hölderlins Pindar-Rezeption*_(Munich: Fink, 1982); as well as Dieter Bremer, "Hölderlin als Pindar-Übersetzer," in *Hölderlin: Philosophie und Dichtung* (Tübingen: Hölderlin Gesellschaft, 2001), 157–73.

27. Charles Kahn, *The Art and Thought of Heraclitus* (Cambridge: Cambridge University Press, 1981), 66–67; and Diels-Kranz, *Die Fragmente der Vorsokratiker*, 162.

28. *Poems of Hesiod*, trans. R. M. Fraser (Norman: University of Oklahoma Press, 1988), 94; Hesiod, *Theogony, Works and Days*, ed. Glenn Most (Cambridge: Harvard University Press, 2006), 86–89; Hesiod, *Sämtliche Gedichte* (Zürich: Artemis, 1970), 307. On the topic of *eris* in Hesiod compare Nietzsche's essay "Homer on Competition," in *On the Genealogy of Morality* (Cambridge: Cambridge University Press, 1994), 187–94/ KSA 1, 783–92.

29. Another possible source for this myth in Hölderlin is Plato's *Timaeus* 22a ff. or the compilation of Benjamin Hederich, *Gründliches mythologisches Lexikon* (Darmstadt: Wissenschaftliche Buchgesellschaft, 1996), 898–903, originally published in Leipzig in 1770.

30. For an analysis of the influence of Rousseau on Hölderlin, cf. Jürgen Link, *Hölderlin-Rousseau: Inventive Rückkehr* (Opladen: Westdeutscher Verlag, 1999).

31. Cf. Johann Gottfried Herder, *God: Some Conversations* (Indianapolis: Bobbs-Merrill, 1940), 177–79; *Schriften zu Philosophie, Literatur, Kunst, und Altertum* (Frankfurt: Deutscher Klassiker Verlag, 1994), 779–80; cf. also Elena Polledri, ". . . *immer bestehet ein Maas": Der Begriff des Masses in Hölderlins Werk* (Würzburg: Königshausen und Neumann, 2002), 73–75.

32. In referring to the fragments of Heraclitus, I will use the numbers standardized in Diels-Kranz, *Fragmente der Vorsokratiker*, even though I will often use the translations of Charles Kahn, *The Art and Thought of Heraclitus*.

33. Benjamin Hederich, *Gründliches mythologisches Lexikon*, 1701–07.

34. Pindar, *Nemean Odes, Isthmian Odes*, ed. William Race (Cambridge: Harvard University Press, 1997), 176–79.

35. In *Hyperion*, 165–66/SA III, 155, Hölderlin describes Germans as "impious."

36. In chapter 2 I will pursue a more extensive reading of Heidegger's notion of *Fug/Fügung* in his reading of "The Anaximander Fragment."

37. Charles Kahn, *The Art and Thought of Heraclitus*, 48–49.

38. Pindar, *Olympian Odes, Pythian Odes*, ed. William Race (Cambridge: Harvard University Press, 1997), 234–35 (translation altered); Hesiod, *Works and Days*, v. 200; cf. also SA V, 71.

39. Albrecht Seifert, *Untersuchungen zu Hölderlins Pindar-Rezeption*, 516–18.

40. For a penetrating analysis of this Cartesian stance cf. Reiner Schürmann, *Broken Hegemonies* (Bloomington: Indiana University Press, 2003).

41. It is hardly a coincidence that both Hölderlin and Celan write poems about "Kolomb" (Columbus) as anticipating the mode of a "Cartesian" explorer.

42. Dennis Schmidt, *On Germans and Other Greeks: Tragedy and Ethical Life* (Bloomington: Indiana University Press, 2001), 276.

43. Werner Peters, "Mitte und Mass," in *Die Mitte: Vermessungen in Politik und Kultur*, ed. B. Guggenberger and K. Hansen (Opladen: Westdeutscher Verlag, 1992), 31–37.

44. Sophocles, *Oedipus the King*, trans. David Grene (Chicago: University of Chicago Press, 1991), 45.

45. Werner Peters, "Mitte und Mass," 34.

46. Sophocles, *Oedipus the King*, trans. David Grene, 24.

47. F. E. Valpy, *Etymological Dictionary of the Latin Language* (London: 1928), 231; and T. G. Tucker, *Etymological Dictionary of Latin*, 141; as well as Vanicek, *Griechisch-Lateinisches Etymologisches Wörterbuch*, 826; and Alois Walde, *Lateinisches Etymologisches Wörterbuch* (Heidelberg: Winter, 1910), 431.

48. On the very same day Hölderlin writes to his brother Karl: "[N]ever in my life was I so attached to my Fatherland . . . but I feel it is better for me to be abroad" (SA VI, 424).

49. F. E. Valpy, *Etymological Dictionary of the Latin Language*, 373; and Karl Ernst George, *Kleines Deutsch-Lateinisches Handwörterbuch* (Hannover: Hahn, 1911), 1758.

50. Johann Winckelmann, "Thoughts on the Imitation of the Painting and Sculpture of the Greeks," in *German Aesthetic and Literary Criticism*, ed. H. B. Nisbet (Cambridge: Cambridge University Press, 1985), 33.

51. Ibid.

52. Dennis Schmidt, *On Germans and Other Greeks: Tragedy and Ethical Life*, 139; and Marc Froment-Meurice, *That Is to Say: Heidegger's Poetics* (Stanford: Stanford University Press, 1998), 135.

53. Cf. Ernst Mögel, *Natur als Revolution: Hölderlins Empedokles Tragödie* (Stuttgart: Metzler, 1994), 200–203.

54. Hermann Timm, "Weisheit aus dem Abendland: Hölderlins evangelische Dichtertheologie," 162–72.

55. *Pindar's Victory Songs*, trans. Frank Nisetich (Baltimore: Johns Hopkins University Press, 1980), 165; and Pindar, *Siegeslieder*, trans. Dieter Bremer (Munich: Artemis und Winkler, 1992), 124–25; as well as Pindar, *Siegesgesänge und Fragmente*, trans. Oskar Werner (Munich: Ernst Heimeran, 1967), 124–25.

56. For an etymology of the Greek term *moira* cf. Hjalmar Frisk, *Griechisches Etymologisches Wörterbuch* (Heidelberg: Winter, 1973), 196–97, 249.

57. Ibid., 355–56.

58. Johann Joachim Winckelmann, *Geschichte der Kunst des Altertums* (Vienna: Phaidon, 1936), 321.

59. Peter Szondi., "Hölderlin's Overcoming of Classicism," *Comparative Literature* 5 (1983): 262.

60. Hölderlin's Böhlendorff Brief (SA VI, 425–26), trans. Dennis Schmidt, in *On Germans and Other Greeks: Tragedy and Ethical Life*, 165–66.

61. On Heracles's journey cf. Alexander Honold, *Nach Olympia: Hölderlin und die Erfindung der Antike* (Berlin: Verlag Vorwerk 8, 2002), 192–204.

62. Charles Halsey, *An Etymological Dictionary of Latin and Greek*, 149; and T. G. Tucker, *Etymological Dictionary of Latin*, 175.

63. Alexander Honold, *Nach Olympia: Hölderlin und die Erfindung der Antike*, 181 and "'Der scheinet aber fast/ Rükwärts zu gehen': Zur kulturgeographischen Bedeutung der 'Ister'-Hymne," *Hölderlin Jahrbuch* 32 (2000/2001): 175–93. Cf. also Eva Koczisky, *Hölderlin's Orient* (Würzburg: Königshausen und Neumann, 2009), 107–23.

64. Charles Kahn, *The Art and Thought of Heraclitus*, 74–75.

65. Anke Bennholdt-Thomsen, "Antike und Moderne in der Landschaft des Spätwerks," *Hölderlin Jahrbuch* 33 (2004): 145–52.

66. Johann Gottfried Herder, *Sämmtliche Werke*, ed. Bernhard Suphan (Berlin: Weidmann, 1877–1913), vol. XIII, 406; and Peter Nickel, *Die Bedeutung von Herders Verjüngungsgedanken und Geschichtsphilosophie für die Werke Hölderlins*, 188–200; cf. also Hölderlin's remark: "so the word came down to us from the East" (SPF, 178–79).

67. Johann Gottfried Herder, *Another Philosophy of History* (Indianapolis: Hackett, 2004), 31; *Schriften zu Philosophie, Literatur, Kunst, und Altertum*, 40–41; on stream and source, August Langen, *Der Wortschatz des deutschen Pietismus* (Tübingen: Niemeyer, 1954), 153–55; F. Mauer and F. Stroh, *Deutsche Wortgeschichte* II (Berlin: de Gruyter 1959), 120; and Hesiod *Theogony*, vv. 335–40 alludes to the Ister.

68. Jean-Pierre Vernant and Pierre Vidal-Naquet, *Myth and Tragedy in Ancient Greece* (New York: Zone Books, 1988), 27.

69. Charles S. Halsey, *An Etymology of Latin and Greek*, 148–49.

70. Friedrich Beissner, *Hölderlin: Reden und Aufsätze* (Weimar: Böhlau, 1961); and Wilhelm Michel, *Das Leben Friedrich Hölderlins* (Darmstadt: Wissenschaftliche Buchgesellschaft, 1963).

71. Jean-Pierre Vernant, *Myth and Society in Ancient Greece* (New York: Zone Books, 1990), 260.

72. I would argue that Hölderlin's endorsement of a "mythology of reason" shows itself as a poetic myth of reversal/inversion without *Aufhebung*, synthesis or ultimate "reconciliation."

73. T. G. Tucker, *Etymological Dictionary of Latin*, 205; and Charles S. Halsey, *An Etymology of Latin and Greek*, 156.

74. Hjalmar Frisk, *Griechisches Etymologisches Wörterbuch*, 570–72.

75. Cf. W. F. Otto, *Theophania: Der Geist der altgriechischen Religion* (Hamburg: Rowohlt, 1956), 7–27.

76. Maurice Blanchot, *The Work of Fire* (Stanford: Stanford University Press, 1995), 121, 118–19.

77. Charles S. Halsey, *An Etymology of Latin and Greek*, 49–50.

78. Diels-Kranz, *Fragmente der Vorsokratiker* I, (5th ed.), 419. See also Robert Otten, *Metron, Mesos, and Kairos: A Semasiological Study*, dissertation, University of Michigan, 1956, 37–38, 114; and Kathleen Freeman *Ancilla to the Pre-Socratic Philosophers* (Oxford: Blackwell, 1952), 121.

79. Thomas Hubbard, *The Pindaric Mind: A Study of Logical Structure in Early Greek Poetry* (Leiden: Brill, 1985), 22 and chapter 1, "Relations of Measure," 11–70; Michael Theunissen, *Pindar: Menschenlos und Wende der Zeit* (Munich: Beck, 2000), 808–11.

80. Robert Otten, *Metron, Mesos, and Kairos: A Semasiological Study*, 60; and Michael Theunissen, *Pindar: Menschenlos und Wende der Zeit*, 803–11.

81. Wolfgang Janke, *Archaischer Gesang*, 177–83.

82. For references to Hölderlin's use of the term *Prüfung* cf. SA VI, 401, 406, 430–31 and SA II, 600 (line 30); as well as Alexander Honold, "'Der scheinet aber fast/ Rükwärts zu gehen': zur kulturgeographischen Bedeutung der 'Ister'-Hymne," 137.

83. Johann Gottfried Herder, *Sämmtliche Werke*, ed. Bernhard Suphan, XIII, 37.

84. Wolfgang Binder, "Hölderlin's Namenssymbolik," in *Hölderlin Aufsätze* (Frankfurt: Insel, 1970), 134–260.

85. Cf. for example the film by the Australian filmmakers Daniel Barison and Daniel Ross, *The Ister*, which offers both a geographical and philosophical account of the Ister's course.

86. Heidegger, HHI, 137–47/GA 53, 171–84; and Charles Bambach, *Heidegger's Roots: Nietzsche, National Socialism, and the Greeks* (Ithaca: Cornell University Press, 2003), 232–40.

87. Charles Segal, *Tragedy and Civilization: An Interpretation of Sophocles* (Cambridge: Harvard University Press, 1981), which analyzes the puns and ironies involved in Oedipus's name.

88. Rainer Nägele, *Hölderlins Kritik der poetischen Vernunft* (Basel: Engler, 2005), 82.

89. See the translation in David Constantine, *Hölderlin's Sophocles* (Northumberland: Bloodaxe Books, 2001), 117, 114.

90. For a helpful discussion of *oikos/allotrios* cf. Thomas Hubbard, *The Pindaric Mind*, 33–60.

91. Ilya Pfeijffer, *Three Aeginetan Odes* (Leiden: Brill, 1996), 311–12.

92. Thomas Hubbard, *The Pindaric Mind*, 33.

93. Emile Benveniste, *Indo-European Language and Society* (London: Faber and Faber, 1973), 57.

94. One of the sources of Hölderlin's knowledge concerning Zeus *xenios* was Benjamin Hederich, *Gründliches mythologisches Lexikon*, 2494; cf. also Michael Theunissen, *Pindar: Menschenlos und Wende der Zeit*, 954–55.

95. Martin Heidegger, "Why Do I Stay in the Provinces?" in *Heidegger: The Man and the Thinker*, ed. Thomas Sheehan (Chicago: Precedent, 1981), 27–30/GA 13, 9–13.

96. Both poems employ the same language of "invitation"; cf. "Der Ister," v. 28 and "Die Wanderung," v. 98.

97. *Popularität* is not, as ELT, 152 has it "popularity," but "the capacity for openness and communicability towards others." Cf. DKV III, 921–22 for Jochen Schmidt's commentary.

98. This can also be translated as "Become who you are." Cf. Friedrich Nietzsche, *Ecce Homo: Wie man wird, was man ist*, KSA 6, 155.

99. Emmanuel Levinas, *Totality and Infinity* (Pittsburgh: Duquesne University Press, 1969), 50, 77, 86.

100. Charles Kahn, *The Art and Thought of Heraclitus*, 62–63; cf. also 84–85 Diels, Fragment 10, which explores the *sym/dia-pheromenon* issue.

101. Pindar, *Olympian Odes, Pythian Odes*, ed. William Race, 337 (translation altered); and *The Odes of Pindar*, ed. G. S. Conway (London: Dent, 1972), 144; and Michael Theunissen, *Pindar: Menschenlos und Wende der Zeit*, 45–81.

102. Johann A. Bengel, *New Testament Word Studies*, I (Grand Rapids: Kriegel, 1978), xiv.

103. *The Poems of Hesiod*, trans. R. M. Fraser, 134; Hesiod, *Sämtliche Gedichte*, 339; Hesiod, *Theogony, Works and Days*, ed. Glenn Most, 142–43.

104. Miguel de Beistegui, *Truth and Genesis* (Bloomington: Indiana University Press, 2004), 179.

105. Pindar, *The Odes*, trans. C. M. Bowra (Harmondsworth: Penguin, 1982), 78; and Pindar, *Olympian Odes, Pythian Odes*, ed. William Race, 84–85.

106. Maurice Blanchot, *The Infinite Conversation* (Minneapolis: University of Minnesota Press, 1992), 94.

107. Albrecht Seifert, *Hölderlin und Pindar* (Eggingen: Isele, 1998), 133.

108. Peter Szondi, *Poetik und Geschichtsphilosophie* (Frankfurt: Suhrkamp, 1974), 266.

109. Albrecht Seifert, *Hölderlin und Pindar*, 131.

110. Charlie Louth, *Hölderlin and the Dynamics of Translation* (Oxford: David Brown Books, 1998); Dieter Bremer and Chrsitiane Lehle, "Zu Hölderlins Pindar-Übersetzung," in *Neue Wege zu Hölderlin*, ed. Uwe Beyer (Würzburg: Königshausen und Neumann, 1994), 71–112; Maurice Benn, *Hölderlin and Pindar*; and William Fitzgerald, *Agonistic Poetry: The Pindaric Mode in Pindar, Horace, Hölderlin, and the English Ode* (Berkeley: University of California Press, 1987).

111. Charlie Louth, *Hölderlin and the Dynamics of Translation*, 145.

112. *Pindar's Victory Songs*, trans. Frank Nisetich, 256. Cf. also M. Theunissen, *Pindar: Menschenlos und Wende der Zeit*, 225–36.

113. Pindar, *Nemean Odes, Isthmian Odes*, ed. William Race, 128–29.

114. In the following I will divide the poem "In lovely blueness" into sections I-II-III with line numbers. Here, section III, line 19.

115. Cf. Gerhard Kurz, ed., *Hölderlin: Die Gedichte* (Stuttgart: Reclam, 2000), 602, n. 2.

116. For references to Platonic *katabasis* cf. *Republic* 327a and 614b-e.

117. "Absonderung" and "Abgeschiedenheit" were part of the vocabulary of Swabian Pietism; cf. August Langen, *Der Wortschatz des deutschen Pietismus*, 140–41, 402, 408; Meister Eckhart, *Werke*, II (Frankfurt: Deutscher Klassiker Verlag, 2008), 435–59; see also Mark Roche, *Dynamic Stillness: Philosophical Conceptions of* Ruhe *in Schiller, Hölderlin, Büchner, and Heine* (Tübingen: Niemeyer, 1987).

118. Jean-Luc Marion, *The Idol and Distance*, 80.

119. Pindar, *The Olympian and Pythian Odes*, ed. Basil Gildersleeve (New York: American Book Company, 1885), xxv–lxxvi; and Fitzgerald, *Agonistic Poetry*, 11–13.

120. On this relation between *Verdienst* and the Stoics cf. Christoph Horn and Christof Rapp, eds., *Wörterbuch der antiken Philosophie* (Munich: Beck, 2002), 110.

121. Wolfgang Pfeiffer, *Etymologisches Wörterbuch des Deutschen* (Berlin: Academie, 1989), 282–83, pursues the linkage between *dienen, Verdienst,* as what one appropriates through work ("durch Arbeit erwerben"). We can find traces of such

a connection in Hölderlin's early essay "Parallele zwischen Salomons Sprichwörten und Hesiods *Werken und Tagen*" (SA IV, 185–86). The English word *merit* here has links to the Greek word *meros* (Eng., "part") and *moira* (Eng., "lot" or "fate").

122. On the linguistic punning in Sophocles's *Oedipus* cf. Simon Goldhill, *Reading Greek Tragedy* (Cambridge: Cambridge University Press, 1986), 215–20; and Charles Segal, *Oedipus Tyrannus: Tragic Heroism and the Limits of Knowledge* (New York: Twayne, 1993), 50–56.

123. Sophocles, *Oedipus the King-Antigone*, trans. David Grene, 174–75; and Sophocles, *Antigone*, ed. Hugh Lloyd-Jones (Cambridge: Harvard University Press, 1994), 34–35; and Hölderlin SA V, 219, vv. 349–50, as well as FHA XVI, 298–99.

124. For background on this Greek citation from the *Suidas* cf. Hölderlin, DKV, II, 1390–91.

125. For references to the Greek word *kelis* ("stain," "Fleck") cf. *Oedipus Tyrannus*, vv. 883, 1384; and *Oedipus at Colonus*, v. 1134; for references to *miasma* cf. Sophocles, *Oedipus Tyrannus*, ed. Hugh Lloyd-Jones (Cambridge: Harvard University Press, 1994), 334, 346, 354, 428 (vv. 97, 241, 313, 1012).

126. Jean-Pierre Vernant and Pierre Vidal-Naquet, *Myth and Tragedy in Ancient Greece*, 37–38.

127. Hesiod, *Theogony, Works and Days*, ed. Glenn Most, 112–13; Hesiod, *Sämtliche Gedichte*, 320; Hesiod, *Works and Days*, ed. T. A. Sinclair (Hildesheim: Georg Olms, 1966), 34.

128. Hesiod, *Theogony, Works and Days*, ed. Glenn Most, 142–43; Hesiod, *Sämtliche Gedichte*, 338–39; Hesiod, *Works and Days*, ed. T. A. Sinclair, 71.

CHAPTER TWO. HEIDEGGERIAN "JUSTICE" AS DIKE

1. Jacques Derrida, *Specters of Marx* (New York: Routledge, 1994), 21.

2. Maurice Blanchot, *Friendship* (Stanford: Stanford University Press, 1997), 185.

3. For Heidegger's reading of the history of being cf. EP, 1–74/N II, 399–479; CP, 83–84, 120–34, 161–62/GA 65, 119–20, 171–91, 227–28. See also Dieter Thomä, ed., *Heidegger Handbuch* (Stuttgart: Metzler, 2003), 274–78.

4. Martin Heidegger, "Das Wesen der Wahrheit: Zu 'Beiträge zur Philosophie,'" *Heidegger Studies* 18 (2002): 16 and 18.

5. *Lichtung* can be understood as "the clearing that lights up/manifests beings" in such a way that human beings are appropriated in the very process of such self-manifestation. For a helpful account of *Lichtung* cf. Dieter Thomä, ed., *Heidegger Handbuch*, 164–67.

6. Heraclitus, Fragment 53, Hermann Diels, ed., *Fragmente der Vorsokratiker* (Berlin: Weidmann, 1903), 74. For Heidegger's various translations of this fragment, GA 40, 68; GA 7, 284; GA 39, 125, and Kenneth Maly and John Sallis, eds., *Heidegger on Heraclitus: A New Reading* (Lewiston: Edwin Mellen, 1986). On this topic cf. also Gregory Fried, *Heidegger's* Polemos*: From Being to Politics* (New Haven: Yale University Press, 2000), 21–42.

7. Karl Jaspers's letter of December 22, 1945, cited in Hugo Ott, *Martin Heidegger: Unterwegs zu seiner Biographie* (Frankfurt: Campus, 1988), 316.

8. Cf. the insightful essay by Robert Bernasconi, "Justice and the Twilight Zone of Morality," in *Heidegger in Question: The Art of Existing* (Atlantic Highlands, NJ: Humanities, 1993), 40–55.

9. For some helpful background on the essay "Letter on Humanism" cf. Anson Rabinbach, "Heidegger's *Letter on Humanism* as Text and Event," *New German Critique* 62 (1994): 3–38; and Tom Rockmore, *Heidegger and French Philosophy* (London: Routledge, 1995), 81–103.

10. Ethan Kleinberg, *Generation Existential: Heidegger's Philosophy in France, 1927–1961* (Ithaca: Cornell University Press, 2005).

11. For Heidegger's lectures on Sophocles cf. GA 40, on Aristotle GA 18-GA 19; on Hölderlin GA 39-GA 52-GA 53; and on Heraclitus GA 55.

12. Norbert Ehrenfreund, *The Nürnberg Legacy: How the Nazi War Crimes Trials Changed the Course of History* (New York: Macmillan, 2007), 17.

13. On this whole topic cf. two books by W. G. Sebald, *On the Natural History of Destruction* (New York: Random House, 2003) and *Campo Santo* (New York: Modern Library, 2005), 65–96.

14. Wolf Lepenies, *The Seduction of Culture in German History* (Princeton: Princeton University Press, 2006), 128–53.

15. Friedrich Meinecke, *The German Catastrophe* (Boston: Beacon Press, 1963).

16. Theodor Adorno, *Jargon of Authenticity* (Evanston: Northwestern University Press, 1973); and Hermann Mörchen, *Adorno und Heidegger* (Stuttgart: Klett, 1981), 176–86.

17. Cf. Aristotle, *Politics* 1253A where the human being is defined as *zoon logon echon*—that being alone among beings who has speech/reason—*ratio/oratio*.

18. For an excellent discussion of human beings versus animals and Heidegger cf. William McNeill, *The Time of Life: Heidegger and Ethos* (Albany: State University of New York Press, 2006), 1–52 (esp. 46–48).

19. Wolfgang Pfeiffer, *Etymologisches Wörterbuch des Deutschen* (Berlin: Academie, 1989), 94, 672.

20. Pindar, 8th Pythian Ode, v. 85; and C. S. Halsey, *Etymology of Latin and Greek* (New Rochelle: Caratzas, 1983), 95.

21. C. T. Onions, *Oxford Dictionary of English Etymology* (Oxford: Oxford University Press, 1966), 93.

22. Sophokles, *Dramen: Griechisch und Deutsch*, ed. Wilhelm Willige (Munich: Artemis, 1985), 214–15, where the German translation renders *deinos* as *ungeheuer*. Hölderlin too will translate *deinos* as *ungeheuer* in SA V, 219.

23. On the relation of Heidegger and Hölderlin cf. the insightful study by Stuart Elden, *Speaking Against Number: Heidegger, Language, and the Politics of Calculation* (Edinburgh: Edinburgh University Press, 2006); and William McNeill, *The Time of Life*, as well as Dennis Schmidt, *Of Germans and Other Greeks*.

24. Theodore Kisiel, *The Genesis of Heidegger's "Being and Time"* (Berkeley: University of California Press, 1993), 283. Cf. also T. Kisiel and Thomas Sheehan, eds., *Becoming Heidegger* (Evanston: Northwestern University Press, 2007), 219–20. Helpful articles on the relationship between Heidegger and Aristotle on the question of rhetoric include: P. Christopher Smith, "The Uses and Abuses of Aristotle's Rhetoric in Heidegger's Fundamental Ontology: The Lecture Course, Summer, 1924," in *From Phenomenology to Thought, Errancy, and Desire*, ed. Babette Babich

(Dordrecht: Kluwer, 1995), 315–33; P. Christopher Smith, "*Phronesis*, the Individual, and the Community: Divergent Appropriations of Aristotle's Ethical Discernment in Heidegger's and Gadamer's Hermeneutics," in *Gadamer Verstehen/Understanding Gadamer*, ed. Mirko Wischke and Michael Hofer (Darmstadt: Wissenschaftliche Buchgesellschaft, 2003), 169–85; and Theodore Kisiel, "Heidegger's Einsetzung der rhetorischen Politik in seine 'urpraktische' Ontologie," in *Metaphysik der praktischen Welt: Perspektiven im Anschluss an Hegel und Heidegger*, ed. Andreas Grossmann and Christoph Jamme (Amsterdam: Rodopi, 2000), 165–75; "Rhetoric, Politics, Romance: Arendt and Heidegger, 1924–1926," in *Extreme Beauty: Aesthetics, Politics, Death*, ed. James Swearingen and Joanne Cutting-Gray (New York: Continuum, 2002), 95–109; "Rhetorical Proto-Politics in Heidegger and Arendt," in *Heidegger and Rhetoric*, ed. Daniel Gross and Ansgar Kemmann (Albany: State Univeristy of New York Press, 2005), 131–60.

25. Theodore Kisiel, *The Genesis of Heidegger's "Being and Time,"* 293, 492.

26. Theodore Kisiel, "Rhetorical Proto-Politics in Heidegger and Arendt," 140.

27. Theodore Kisiel, "Rhetoric, Politics, Romance: Arendt and Heidegger, 1924–1926," 108.

28. Heidegger, GA 19, 21–64; cf. Otfried Höffe, *Aristoteles Lexikon* (Stuttgart: Kröner, 2005) and *Aristoteles* (Munich: Beck, 2006); Theodore Kisiel, *The Genesis of Heidegger's "Being and Time,"* 265–308.

29. Aristotle, *On Rhetoric*, trans. George Kennedy (New York: Oxford University Press, 1991), 37–39.

30. Heidegger draws out this formally indicative power of speech in relation to Aristotle in a lecture entitled "Wahrsein und Dasein (Aristoteles *Ethica Nicomachea* Z)," which is scheduled to be published in GA 80. For an English translation cf. "Being-There and Being-True According to Aristotle," in *Becoming Heidegger: On the Trail of His Early Occasional Writings, 1910–1927*, ed. Theodore Kisiel and Thomas Sheehan (Evanston: Northwestern University Press, 2007), 214–37. See also the discussion in John van Buren, *The Young Heidegger* (Bloomington: Indiana University Press, 1994), 227.

31. Cf. Charles Bambach, *Heidegger's Roots: Nietzsche, National Socialism, and the Greeks* (Ithaca: Cornell University Press, 2003), 57–63, 292–93, 310–13.

32. William McNeill, *The Time of Life*, 2.

33. Theodore Kisiel, "Rhetoric, Politics, Romance: Arendt and Heidegger, 1924–1926," 108.

34. Charles Kahn, *The Art and Thought of Heraclitus* (Cambridge: Cambridge University Press, 1981), 94. I would add the emendation that although Heidegger concurs with Heraclitus that the structure of the world is "eternal," he understands it as ever attuned to the temporally particular and singular event character of beings.

35. Kant's Third Critique would have profound significance for ethics in the continental tradition, as Dennis Schmidt argues in "Can Law Survive?," *Toledo Law Review* 26, no. 1 (Fall 1994): 147–58. Cf. also Francois Raffoul, *The Origins of Responsibility*, 58–79.

36. Immanuel Kant, *Groundwork of the Metaphysics of Morals*, 1; Martin Heidegger, GA 55, 235.

37. Hermann Diels, "Anaximanders Kosmos," *Archiv für Geschichte der Philosophie* 10 (1897): 228–37; and Karl Joel, *Geschichte der antiken Philosophie* (Tübingen: Mohr, 1921), 257.

38. Werner Jaeger, *Paideia*, I (Berlin: Walter de Gruyter, 1936), 220.

39. Hermann Fränkel, *Dichtung und Philosophie des frühen Griechentums* (New York: American Philological Association, 1954), 347.

40. Walther Kranz, *Geschichte der griechischen Literatur* (Leipzig: Dietrich, 1939), 92.

41. For an account of Theophrastus's influence on Simplicius cf. Charles Kahn, *Anaximander and the Origins of Greek Cosmology* (Indianapolis: Hackett, 1994), 4–7; see also Robert Bernasconi, *Heidegger in Question*, 42–44.

42. Here, Nietzsche follows the translation of *dike* as *Gerechtigkeit* given in the highly influential study by Ferdinand Lassalle, *Die Philosophie Herakleitos des Dunklen von Ephesus* (Berlin: Duncker, 1858), I, 549–83.

43. Heidegger makes a similar claim about *dokeonta* in N iii, 28–29/N I, 05.

44. Heidegger repeats this view of justice in QCT, 92; GA 5, 246–47; N iii: 141/N I, 636.

45. For Nietzsche's own views on *dike* and Heraclitus cf. PPP: 63–64/ KGW II, 4: 271–72.

46. Cf. Gianni Vattimo, *The End of Modernity* (Baltimore: Johns Hopkins University Press, 1988), 172–275 for a discussion of *Verwindung* in Heidegger.

47. Compare the translations of this same fragment in Charles Kahn, *The Art and Thought of Heraclitus* (Cambridge: Cambridge University Press, 1979), 61; and Wilhelm Kapelle, *Die Vorsokratiker* (Stuttgart: Kröner, 1968), 140.

48. For etymological sources here cf. Charles Halsey, *An Etymology of Latin and Greek* (New Rochelle: Caratzas, 1983), 72; T. G. Tucker *Etymological Dictionary of Latin* (Chicago: Ares, 1985), 205; Alois Vanicek, *Griechisch-Lateinisches Etymologisches Wörterbuch* (Leipzig:Teubner,1877), 778; and F. E. Valpy, *An Etymological Dictionary of the Latin Language* (London: Longman, 1828), 397–400.

49. Heidegger will make similar claims in EP, 97/GA 7, 83–84 and P, 58/ GA 54, 85 where he asserts, "In Hegel's metaphysics and in Nietzsche's, i.e., in the nineteenth century, the transformation of *veritas* into *certitudo* is completed. This completion of the Roman essence of truth is the proper and hidden meaning of the nineteenth century."

50. Heidegger will translate this Diels Fragment 80 in both EM, 127 and GA 39: 126. For an English version consult Kenneth Maly and Parvis Emad, eds., *Heidegger on Heraclitus: A New Reading*, 52. Cf. also the book by Günter Wohlfart, *Also Sprach Herakleitos: Herakleitos Fragment B 52 und Nietzsches Heraklit-Rezeption* (Freiburg: Alber, 1991), which deals with Nietzsche's interpretation of *Spiel* and *Weltspiel*.

51. Nietzsche will discuss the notion of *Horizont* in PTAG, 72/ KGW III, 2, 332; and UTM, 60–67/KSA 1, 248–57.

52. For Heidegger's translation of Diels's Fragment 51 cf. GA 39, 123 and GA 55, 147; for an English translation cf. Maly and Emad, eds. *Heidegger on Heraclitus*, 39.

53. Compare GA 55, 147.

54. On the "es gibt" in Heidegger, cf. Jacques Derrida, *Given Time* (Chicago: University of Chicago Press, 1992), 20–24; John Caputo, *The Prayers and Tears of Jacques Derrida* (Bloomington: Indiana University Press, 1997), 160–211; Sascha Bischof, *Gerechtigkeit-Verantwortung-Gastfreundschaft: Ethik-Ansätze nach Jacques Derrida* (Fribourg: Academic Press Fribourg, 2004); Matthias Flatscher, "Derridas '*coup de don*' und Heideggers '*Es gibt*,'" in *Kreuzungen Derridas: Geistergespräche zwischen Philosophie und Theologie*, ed. Peter Zeillinger and Matthias Flatscher (Vienna: Turia and Kant, 2004), 35–53.

55. For an account of Heidegger's personal travails during the period of French occupation in Freiburg after the war, cf. Hugo Ott, *Martin Heidegger: Unterwegs zu seiner Biographie* (Frankfurt: Campus, 1988), 291–327.

56. Martin Heidegger, "The End of Philosophy and the Task of Thinking," in *Basic Writings*, ed. David Krell (San Francisco: HarperCollins, 1994)/GA 14, 67–90.

57. In EGT, 21–22/GA 5, 331–32, Heidegger rejects the "philosophy of nature" interpretation.

58. My whole point here is to argue that Heidegger's "Anaximander Fragment"—much as his "Letter on Humanism"—needs to be situated historically within the context of the Nürnberg Trials of 1946 and the discussion of Allied "justice."

59. Writing on May 8, 1945 (the day World War II ended in Europe), Heidegger noted: "The War at an end, nothing changed, nothing new, on the contrary. What has long subsisted must now noticeably come out"; "The War decides nothing" (CPC, 157, 160/GA 77, 241, 244).

60. Cf. Heidegger's discussion of *Geschichte/Historie* from "Wilhelm Dilthey's Research and the Struggle for a Historical Worldview," in *Supplements*, ed. John van Buren (Albany: State University of New York Press, 2002), 147–76.

61. See especially Heidegger's comment from "The Turning" where he claims, "All mere organizing of the world conceived and represented historiographically in terms of universality remains truthless and without foundation[*bodenlos*]" (QCT, 48/GA 79, 76).

62. Wolfgang Pfeiffer, *Etymologisches Wörterbuch des Deutschen*, 387.

63. Heidegger used the German text of John Burnet, *Die Anfänge der griechischen Philosophie* (zweite Ausgabe) (Leipzig: Teubner, 1913), from the English original, *Early Greek Philosophy* (London: Black, 1892).

64. Tucker, *Etymological Dictionary of Latin*, 235; Walde, *Lateinisches Etymologisches Wörterbuch*, 755; Charles Krauth, *A Vocabulary of the Philosophical Sciences* (New York: Sheldon, 1881), 168–70 and 654–55; Wulff Rehfus, ed., *Handwörterbuch der Philosophie* (Göttingen: Vandenhoeck und Ruprecht, 2003), 339–41.

65. Charles Scott, *On the Advantages and Disadvantages of Ethics and Politics* (Bloomington: Indiana University Press, 1996), 49.

66. Jean-Pierre Vernant, *Myth and Tragedy in Ancient Greece*, 50. Cf. also the excellent study by Bret Davis on volition in Heidegger and its relation to *Gelassenheit*: *Heidegger and the Will* (Evanston: Northwestern University Press, 2006).

67. Ibid., 27.

68. Richard Macksey, ed., *The Structuralist Controversy* (Baltimore: Johns Hopkins University Press, 1972), 151–52; John Peradotto, *Man In the Middle Voice* (Princeton: Princeton University Press, 1990), 133–34.

69. For some references to Heidegger's "first" and "other" beginning cf. BQP, 108–30/GA 45, 124–50; GA 65, 175–98; and Gregory Fried, *Heidegger's Polemos*, 117–35.

70. For another interpretation of *Verwindung* in the 1946 essay cf., W. J. Korab-Karpowicz, "Heidegger's Anaximander: *to chreon* and the History of Being," *Existentia* XII (2002): 377–405.

71. For standard German translations of the Anaximander fragment: Wilhelm Capelle, *Die Vorsokratiker* (Stuttgart: Kröner, 1968), 82; Jaap Mansfield, *Die Vorsokratiker* (Stuttgart: Reclam, 1987), 73; Michael Grünwald, *Die Anfänge der abendländischen Philosophie: Fragmente der Vorsokratiker* (Munich: Deutscher Taschenbuch Verlag, 1991), 52; M. Laura Gemelli Marciano, *Die Vorsokratiker* I (Düsseldorf: Artemis und Winkler, 2007), 37.

72. Adolph Deissmann, *Die neutestamentliche Formel "in Christo Jesu"* (Marburg: Elwert, 1892), which Heidegger read in 1918; and Charles Bambach, "The Hermeneutics of Origin," *Philosophy Today* 41 (Summer 1997): 313–24, esp. 319, where the Christian formula "love *of* Christ" will be read as a genitive of fellowship in much the same way that the later essay "Der Spruch *des* Anaximander" will be read in terms of a middle-voice of belonging.

73. Heidegger here is playing with the German phrase *"mit Fug und Recht"* which means something like "justifiably so" or "with justice" to have a right to do something.

74. Compare also Jean Wilde and William Kluback's translation of Martin Heidegger, *What Is Philosophy?* (New Haven: College and University Press, 1956).

75. *Verwindung* is a term in the late Heidegger's lexicon to suggest that metaphysics is not something that can be "overcome" since any attempt at "overcoming" (*Überwindung*) is always already caught within the question-frame it seeks to surmount.

76. *Webster's New World Dictionary of the American Language* (New York: World Publishing, 1970), 1186; Wolfgang Pfeiffer, *Etymologisches Wörterbuch des Deutschen*, II, 1446.

77. John Llewelyn, *The Middle Voice of Ecological Conscience* (New York: St. Martin's Press, 1991), 125–27.

78. For Hölderlin's use of *brauchen* cf. SA II, 47, 92, 145, 191–92, 219.

79. William McNeill, *The Time of Life*, 143, xvii and GA 5, 62 for Heidegger's discussion of poesy and *Dichten* in regard to originary *poiesis*.

80. For some thoughtful reflections on this interplay between justice and measure cf. Krystof Ziarek, "Poietic Justice," in *Law and Art: Justice, Ethics, and Aesthetics*, ed. Oren Ben-Dor (London: Routledge, 2011), 33–44.

81. Bret Davis, "Will and *Gelassenheit*," in *Key Concepts: Heidegger*, ed. Bret Davis (Durham: Acumen, 2010), 199.

CHAPTER THREE. PAUL CELAN

1. Jacques Derrida, *Acts of Religion* (New York: Routledge, 2002), 244.

2. John Felstiner, *Paul Celan: Poet, Survivor, Jew* (New Haven: Yale University Press, 1995), 282, which cites the title of Samuel Beckett's work "I can't go on, I'll go on."

3. Walter Benjamin, "On the Concept of History," in *Selected Writings* IV (Cambridge: Harvard University Press, 2003), 397/*Gesammelte Schriften* I (Frankfurt: Suhrkamp, 2001), 704; and John Caputo, ed., *Deconstruction in a Nutshell: A Conversation with Jacques Derrida* (New York: Fordham University Press, 1997), 157–59, 179.

4. John Caputo, ed., *Deconstruction in a Nutshell*, 16–17.

5. Jacques Derrida, "Force of Law," in *Acts of Religion*, 256–57.

6. Ibid.; Emmanuel Levinas, *Totality and Infinity* (Pittsburgh: Duquesne University Press, 1969), 89/ *Totalité et Infini* (The Hague: Martinus Nijhoff, 1974), 62.

7. Jacques Derrida and Maurizio Ferraris, *A Taste for the Secret* (Cambridge: Polity, 2001), 4.

8. John Caputo, ed., *Deconstruction in a Nutshell*, 151–55.

9. Jacques Derrida, *Specters of Marx* (New York: Routledge, 1994), 27; John Caputo, ed., *Deconstruction in a Nutshell*, 14.

10. Jacques Derrida, *Specters of Marx*, 27.

11. Ibid., 28.

12. John Caputo, ed., *Deconstruction in a Nutshell*, 22–23.

13. "For a Justice to Come" (Interview with Jacques Derrida), April 5, 2004: The Brussels Tribunal http://hydra.humanities.uci.edu/derrida/brussels.html.

14. John Caputo, ed., *Deconstruction in a Nutshell*, 22–23.

15. Jacques Derrida and Maurizio Ferraris, *A Taste for the Secret*, 21.

16. Jacques Derrida, *The Politics of Friendship* (London: Verso, 1997), 306; and Nicholas Royle, *Jacques Derrida* (London: Taylor and Francis, 2007), 117.

17. Walter Benjamin, "On the Concept of History," in *Selected Writings* IV, 397/*Gesammelte Schriften* I, 704.

18. Jacques Derrida, *Specters of Marx*, 33; John Caputo, ed., *Deconstruction in a Nutshell*, 24.

19. Jacques Derrida and Maurizio Ferraris, *A Taste for the Secret*, 20.

20. For example, Jacques Derrida, *Sovereignties in Question: The Poetics of Paul Celan* (New York: Fordham University Press, 2005).

21. Rainer Maria Rilke, *Duino Elegies* I, v. 12–13; on the problematic of the *deus absconditus* cf. Hans-Georg Gadamer, *Gadamer on Celan: "Who Am I and Who Are You?"* (Albany: State University of New York Press, 1997), 80–82/*Gesammelte Werke* 9 (Tübingen: Mohr, 1993), 393–95; John Caputo, *The Prayers and Tears of Jacques Derrida* (Bloomington: Indiana University Press, 1997), 9, 289, 320.

22. We can read this exile politically against the ideology of Wilson's "Fourteen Points," which redrew the map of Europe after World War I, the new world order set up after 1945 by the United Nations charter, as well as French aggression in Algeria in the postwar period.

23. Emmanuel Levinas, "The Trace of the Other," in *Deconstruction in Context*, ed. Mark Taylor (Chicago: University of Chicago Press, 1986), 348.

24. Franz Rosenzweig, *The Star of Redemption* (Madison: University of Wisconsin Press, 2005); and Gershom Scholem, "Wider den Mythos vom deutsch-jüdischen Gespräch," *Judaica* 2 (Frankfurt: Suhrkamp, 1970), 7–11.

25. Jacques Derrida, *Given Time* (Chicago: University of Chicago Press, 1991), 100.

26. Emmanuel Levinas, "The Trace of the Other," 346.

27. Jacques Derrida, "Hospitality, Justice, and Responsibility," in *Questioning Ethics*, ed. Richard Kearney (London: Routledge, 1998), 73.

28. Jacques Derrida, "Villanova Roundtable," in *Deconstruction in a Nutshell*, ed. John Caputo, 17.

29. Giorgio Agamben, *Remnants of Auschwitz* (New York: Zone Books, 2002), 12, 39.

30. Axel Gellhaus, ed., *Fremde Nähe: Celan als Übersetzer* (Marbach: Deutsche Schillergesellschaft, 1997), 389.

31. Maurice Blanchot, "Penser l'Apocalypse," *Le nouvel Observateur*, 22–28 January 1988, 79, cited in Ethan Kleinberg, *Generation Existential: Heidegger's Philosophy in France, 1927–1961* (Ithaca: Cornell University Press, 2005), 242.

32. Paul Celan, *La Bibliothéque philosophique/Die Philosophische Bibliothek* (Paris: Éditions Rue d'Ulm, 2004), 338–418.

33. For biographical information on Celan I have drawn on John Felstiner, *Paul Celan: Poet, Survivor, Jew*; Israel Chalfen, *Paul Celan: A Biography of His Youth* (New York: Pesea Books, 1991); and Ilana Shmueli, *Sag, dass Jerusalem ist: Über Paul Celan* (Eggingen: Edition Isele, 2000); as well as Markus May, Peter Gossens, Jürgen Lehmann, eds., *Celan Handbuch: Leben-Werk-Wirkung* (Stuttgart: Metzler, 2008), 8–10.

34. Israel Chalfen, *Paul Celan*, 37.

35. For two excellent accounts of Paul Celan's Jewish tradition cf. Lydia Koelle, *Paul Celans pneumatisches Judentum: Gott-Rede und menschliche Existenz nach der Shoah* (Mainz: Matthias Grünewald Verlag, 1997); and Elke Günzel, *Das wandernde Zitat: Paul Celan im jüdischen Kontext* (Würzburg: Königshausen und Neumann, 1995); as well as *Celan Handbuch*, 16–17, 227–49.

36. Christine Ivanovic, *Das Gedicht im Geheimnis der Begegnung: Dichtung und Poetik Celans im Kontext seiner russischen Lektüren* (Tübingen: Niemeyer, 1996), 60–61.

37. *Celan Handbuch*, 10.

38. Lydia Koelle, *Paul Celans pneumatisches Judentum*, 17–19.

39. Ibid.

40. John Felstiner, *Paul Celan*, 57.

41. Otto Pöggeler, *Spur des Wortes: Zur Lyrik Paul Celans* (Freiburg: Alber, 1986), 351.

42. Ilana Shmueli, "Paul Celans Judentum und Israel," in *Unverloren. Trotz Allem: Paul Celan-Symposion Wien 2000*, ed. Hubert Gaisbauer et al. (Vienna: Mandelbaum, 2000), 288.

43. Ilana Shmueli, *Sag, dass Jerusalem ist*, 78–79.

44. John Felstiner, *Paul Celan*, 94.

45. Jean Bollack, *Poetik der Fremdheit* (Vienna: Zsolnay, 2000) 73.

46. Gershom Scholem, "Against the Myth of the German-Jewish Dialogue," in *On Jews and Judaism in Crisis* (New York: Schocken, 1976), 62/*Judaica*, 2, 8.

47. Georg Büchner, *Lenz* (Stuttgart: Reclam, 1950), 3.

48. James Lyon, *Paul Celan and Martin Heidegger: An Unresolved Conversation, 1951–1970* (Baltimore: Johns Hopkins University Press, 2006) 67–80.

49. Alois Walde, *Lateinisches Etymologisches Wörterbuch* (Heidelberg: Carl Winter, 1910), 480.

50. Theodor Adorno, *Prismen*, in *Gesammelte Schriften* 10.1 (Frankfurt: Suhrkamp, 1997), 30.

51. *Celan Handbuch*, 288–89.

52. Uta Werner, *Textgräber: Paul Celans geologische Lyrik* (Munich: Wilhelm Fink, 1998), 8.

53. On Jewish burial customs cf. Arthur Cohen and Paul Mendes-Flohr, eds., *20th Century Jewish Religious Thought* (Philadelphia: Jewish Publication Society, 2009), 131–36.

54. Uta Werner, *Textgräber*, 9.

55. For the background to this political situation cf. Barbara Wiedemann, *Paul Celan: Die Goll Affäre* (Frankfurt: Suhrkamp, 2000).

56. Ibid., 830–31. The irony here is that Claire Goll was a Jew who tried to hide her own Jewish origins and pass herself off as a non-Jew, cf., *Celan Handbuch*, 20–23.

57. Perhaps Celan imagined it this way: as if by granting a Jew such a prize erstwhile German National Socialists could point to how Germany had progressed so much from the Hitler era, and in this way forestall any genuine changes. Again and again, Celan feared that neo-Nazism was growing in Deutschland.

58. Charles Bambach, *Heidegger's Roots: Nietzsche, National Socialism, and the Greeks* (Ithaca: Cornell University Press, 2003); Suzanne Marchand, *Down from Olympus: Archaeology and Philhellenism in Germany, 1750–1970* (Princeton: Princeton University Press, 2003); Walter Jens, *Eine deutsche Universität: 500 Jahre Tübinger Gelehrtenrepublik* (Munich: Kindler, 1977).

59. See my discussion in chapter 1, section 3 on Hölderlin's Böhlendorff letter.

60. Georg Büchner, *Lenz*, 3.

61. Arno Barnert, *Mit dem fremden Wort: Poetisches Zitieren bei Paul Celan* (Frankfurt: Stroemfeld, 2007), 226–27; *Der Neue Pauly* V (1998): 858–61; and Alois Walde, *Lateinisches Etymologisches Wörterbuch*, 394.

62. Joachim Seng, "Celans Heidegger Rezeption Zwischen 1953–1960," in *Auf den Kreis-Wegen der Dichtung* (Heidelberg: Carl Winter, 1998), 158–60.

63. Paul Celan, *La Bibliothéque philosophique/Die Philosophische Bibliothek*, 498–99; Karl Löwith, *Heidegger:Denker in dürftiger Zeit* (Göttingen: Vandenhoeckh und Ruprecht, 1960), 45.

64. Walter Benjamin, "On the Concept of History," in *Selected Writings* IV, 397/*Gesammelte Schriften* I, 704.

65. Philippe Lacoue-Labarthe, *Heidegger, Art, and Politics: The Fiction of the Political* (Oxford: Blackwell, 1990), 46.

66. *Celan Handbuch*, 293; and Sieghild Bogumil, "Celans Hölderlinlektüre im Gegenlicht des schlichten Wortes," *Celan Jahrbuch* I (1987): 81–110.

67. Elke Günzel, "Die versäumte Begegnung im Engadin: Paul Celan's Auseinandersetzung mit Friedrich Nietzsche," in *Nietzscheforschung* III (Berlin: Akademie, 1997), 175–92, here 183. Günzel notes that the poet Nelly Sachs called Celan "the Hölderlin of our time."

68. Martin Heidegger, *Sein und Zeit* (Tübingen: Niemeyer, 1949) 167–70.

69. Paul Celan, *La Bibliothéque philosophique/Die Philosophische Bibliothek*, 343, where Paul Celan underlined this in his copy of Heidegger's *Einführung in die Metaphysik*.

70. Anja Lemke, *Konstellation ohne Sterne: Zur poetischen und geschichtlichen Zäsur bei Paul Celan und Martin Heidegger* (Munich: Fink, 2002), 323.

71. Kurt Hildebrandt, *Hölderlin: Philosophie und Dichtung* (Stuttgart: Kohlhammer, 1939); and Claudia Albert, *Deutsche Klassiker im Nationalsozialismus: Schiller, Kleist, Hölderlin* (Stuttgart: Metzler, 1994). For other examples of NS-era readings of Hölderlin's work, cf. also Werner Bartscher, *Hölderlin und die deutsche Nation: Versuch einer Wirkungsgeschichte Hölderlins* (Berlin: Junker und Dünnhaupt, 1942); and Walther Allgöwer, *Gemeinschaft, Vaterland und Staat im Werk Hölderlins* (Frauenfeld: Huber, 1939).

72. For the Latin etymology of cite as *citare* "to arouse, summon" and *ciere* "to put into motion, rouse" and site as *situs*, cf. Alois Walde, *Lateinisches Etymologisches Wörterbuch*, 159–60, 164, 718–19.

73. Cf. the extensive commentary in Barbara Wiedemann, ed., *Die Gedichte: kommentierte Gesamtausgabe in einem Band* (Frankfurt: Suhrkamp, 2003), 671–718.

74. Maurice Blanchot, *Writing the Disaster* (Lincoln: University of Nebraska Press, 1995), 117.

75. Paul Celan will do this using the old Heideggerian strategy of *Destruction/Abbau* and *Wiederholung* from *Sein und Zeit*, secs. 6 and 66.

76. Arno Barnert, *Mit dem fremden Wort: Poetisches Zitieren bei Paul Celan*, 255.

77. Celan notes in a letter to Hans Bender that "craft (*Handwerk*) . . . is the condition of all poetry" (GW III, 177).

78. Anja Lemke, *Konstellation ohne Sterne*, 325; Alois Walde, *Lateinisches Etymologisches Wörterbuch*, 690; and Alois Vanicek, *Griechisch-Lateinisches Etymologisches Wörterbuch* (Leipzig: Teubner, 1877), 1079; T. G. Tucker, *Etymological Dictionary of Latin* (Chicago: Ares, 1985), 217.

79. For some references to Heidegger's "first" and "other" beginning cf. BQP, 108–30/GA 45, 124–50 and GA 65, 175–98; and Bret Davis, ed., *Martin Heidegger: Key Concepts* (London: Acumen, 2009).

80. Hölderlin writes of "the deficiency of holy names" ("es fehlen heilige Namen") in "Heimkunft," SPP, 164–65.

81. The English translation leaves out this key sentence; it should have appeared on page 63 of EHP.

82. Alois Vanicek, *Griechisch-Lateinisches Etymologisches Wörterbuch*, 133, 771–72.

83. *Hölderlin Sämtliche Werke*, ed. Norbert Hellingrath, Ludwig von Pigenot, and Friedrich Seebass (Berlin: Propyläen, 1923), VI, 444; Wilhelm Michel, *Das Leben Hölderlin* (Frankfurt: Insel, 1967), 436–37.

84. Ilana Shmueli and Thomas Sparr, eds., *Paul Celan/Ilana Shmueli Briefwechsel* (Frankfurt: Suhrkamp, 2004) 58.

85. Georg Büchner, *Dantons Tod und Woyzeck*, ed. Margaret Jacobs (Manchester: Manchester University Press, 1988), 91–93.

86. Alois Walde, *Lateinisches Etymologisches Wörterbuch*, 475, 479; Alois Vanicek, *Griechisch-Lateinisches Etymologisches Wörterbuch*, 1204–05; T. G. Tucker, *Etymological Dictionary of Latin*, 154.

87. For a critique of Heideggerian *Versammlung* cf., Jacques Derrida, *Specters of Marx*, 27–28.

88. Pierre Joris, "Introduction," in Paul Celan, *Lightduress* (Los Angeles: Green Integer, 2005), 13; and *Celan Handbuch*, 15.

89. For details on this and other aspects of the Heidegger-Celan meeting cf. James Lyon, *Paul Celan and Martin Heidegger: An Unresolved Conversation, 1951–1970*, 159–91.

90. Otto Pöggeler, *Spur des Wortes: Zur Lyrik Paul Celans*, 151: "Celan took up Heidegger's work not only in a polemical, but also in a positive sense." Barbara Wiedemann, ed., *Paul Celan/Franz Wurm Briefwechsel* (Frankfurt: Suhrkamp, 1995), 87–88.

91. Gerhart Baumann, *Erinnerungen an Paul Celan* (Frankfurt: Suhrkamp, 1992), 58–75, esp., the report of Marie-Luise Kaschnitz, 72; James Lyon, *Paul Celan and Martin Heidegger: An Unresolved Conversation, 1951–1970*, 155–72; MSS, 129, 633–34; and Hadrien France-Lanord, *Paul Celan und Martin Heidegger: Vom Sinn eines Gesprächs* (Freiburg: Rombach, 2007), 139–48.

92. Karl Löwith, *Heidegger—Denker in dürftiger Zeit* (*Sämtliche Schriften*, 8) (Stuttgart: Metzler, 1984), 124–234; Guido Schneeberger, *Nachlese zu Heidegger: Dokumente zu seinem Leben und Denken* (Bern: self-published, 1962).

93. Cf., EM, 131, "Die Sprache ist die Urdichtung, in der ein Volk das Sein dichtet." See also Heidegger's writings on Hebel in GA 16, 491–548; and the "Postscript" to Charles Bambach, *Heidegger's Roots*.

94. Jean Bollack, "Vor dem Gericht des Toten," *Neue Rundschau* 109 (1982): 127–56; *Celan Handbuch*, 257.

95. Otto Pöggeler, "Metaphysics and Topology of Being in Heidegger," *Man and World* 8 (1975): 3–27; and Jeff Malpas, *Heidegger's Topology: Being, Place, World* (Cambridge: MIT Press, 2008).

96. On the topic of landscape and terrain in Paul Celan's "Todtnauberg" see the insightful reading of Ulrich Baer, *Remnants of Song: Trauma and the Experience of Modernity in Charles Baudelaire and Paul Celan* (Stanford: Stanford University Press, 2000), 211–56.

97. Ulrich Baer, *Remnants of Song*, 227.

98. Charles Bambach, *Heidegger's Roots*, 1–5, and GA 13, 9–13.

99. On this whole topic see Theodore Kisiel, "Rhetoric, Politics, Romance: Arendt and Heidegger, 1924–1926," in *Extreme Beauty: Aesthetics, Politics, Death*, ed. James Swearingen and Joanne Cutting-Gray (New York: Continuum, 2002), 95–109.

100. Axel Gellhaus, ed., *Fremde Nähe: Celan als Übersetzer*, 398.

101. Ibid., 399.

102. For more on this theme cf. Wolfgang Emmerich, *Paul Celan* (Hamburg: Rowohlt, 1999), 142; and James Lyon, *Paul Celan and Martin Heidegger*, 175.

103. A representative sample of differing interpretations includes: Otto Pöggeler, *Der Stein hinterm Aug: Studien zu Celans Gedichten* (Munich: Fink, 2000), 159–88; Axel Gellhaus, "Seit ein Gespräch wir sind: Interpretation des Gedichtes 'Todtnauberg,'" in *Interpretationen: Gedichten von Paul Celan* (Stuttgart: Reclam, 2002), 161–74; Anja Lemke, *Konstellation ohne Sterne*, 317–38; Robert Andre, *Gespräche von Text zu Text* (Hamburg: Meiner, 2001), 216–22; Jean Bollack, "Vor dem Gericht des Toten," 127–57; as well as the two book-length studies by James Lyon, *Paul Celan and Martin Heidegger*, and Hadrien France-Lanord, *Paul Celan und Martin Heidegger*.

104. Jacques Derrida, "Hospitality, Justice, and Responsibility," in Kearney, ed., *Questioning Ethics*, 73.

105. Jacques Derrida, "Force of Law," in *Acts of Religion*, 244.

106. Alois Vanicek, *Griechisch-Lateinisches Etymologisches Wörterbuch*, 553; J. B. Hofmann, *Etymologisches Wörterbuch des Griechischen* (Munich: Oldenbourg, 1950), 403; and K. Jacobitz and E. Seiler, *Griechisch-deutsches Wörterbuch* (Leipzig: Melzer, 1862), 1767.

107. Wilhelm Schacht, *Blumen Europas* (Hamburg: Parey, 1976), 180.

108. Jean Bollack, "Vor dem Gericht des Toten," 129–34.

109. Friedrich Nietzsche, KSA 11, 201.

110. We can trace the thematics of star imagery from Heidegger's famous utterance, "Auf einen Stern zugehen, nur dieses," from *Aus der Erfahrung des Denkens* (GA 13, 76) to the image of the star on Heidegger's grave in the Messkirch cemetery, H. W. Petzet, *Auf einen Stern zugehen: Begegnungen und Gespräche mit Heidegger 1929 bis 1976* (Frankfurt: Societäts Verlag, 1983), 183.

111. Gershom Scholem, "The Star of David: History of a Symbol," in *The Messianic Idea in Judaism* (New York: Schocken, 1971), 257–81, here 281.

112. Friedrich Nietzsche, KSA 3, 481–82.

113. Rainer Marten, "Heideggers Geist," in Jürg Altwegg, *Die Heidegger Kontroverse* (Frankfurt: Atheneum, 1988), 225.

114. Cited in Otto Pöggeler, *Spur des Wortes*, 259.

115. This version, printed in Felstiner, is the one Celan sent to Heidegger in the bibliophile edition, but it is not the one that appeared in the published version of *Lichtzwang*. Cf. DG, 282, which left out the line ("un-/gesäumt kommendes"/ "un-delayed coming"); and Heino Shmull, ed., *Lichtzwang: Vorstufe-Textgenese-Endfassung* (Frankfurt: Suhrkamp, 2001), 48–51.

116. For a connexus between heart and Heidegger cf. Byun-Chul Han, *Heideggers Herz* (Munich: Fink, 1999); and Otto Pöggeler, *Spur des Wortes*, 264–65.

117. Jean Bollack, *Dichtung wider Dichtung: Paul Celan und die Literatur* (Göttingen: Wallstein, 2002), 384; and K. Nielsen and H. Pors, *Index zur Lyrik Paul Celans* (Munich: Fink, 1981), 106–107.

118. Jacques Derrida, *Of Hospitality* (Stanford: Stanford University Press, 2000), 45; as well as Emile Benveniste, *Indo-European Language and Society* (London: Faber and Faber, 1973), 71–83.

119. Jacques Derrida, "Hostipitality," in *Acts of Religion*, 358–59.

120. Hans-Georg Gadamer, "Im Schatten des Nihilismus" (1990), in *Gesammelte Werke* 9, 375–78; and Philippe Lacoue-Labarthe, *Poetry As Experience* (Stanford: Stanford University Press, 1999), 92–94.

121. Jacob and Wilhelm Grimm, *Grimms Wörterbuch*, 27 (Leipzig: Hirzel, 1854–1960), 2275–86; and Pierre Joris, "Translation at the Mountain of Death," http://wings.buffalo.edu/epc/authors/joris/todtnauberg.html. The reference to *Wasen* that the Grimms cite is a book entitled *Von Hüttenwerken* by Schlüter, which of course continues the referential chain back to *Hütte*.

122. Jean Bollack, "Todtnauberg: Vor dem Gericht des Toten," *Dichtung Wider Dichtung*, 378–79.

123. For a full list of moor and turf words in Paul Celan cf. K. Nielsen and H. Pors, *Index zur Lyrik Paul Celans*, 157 and 236; as well as SP, 69, 105, 107; LD, 160; and *Threadsuns*: 185, 258.

124. Gerhart Baumann, *Erinnerungen an Paul Celan*, 72, remarks on the astonishing similarity between the unforgettable landscape of Celan's youth in the Bukovina and Heidegger's mountain hut at Todtnauberg.

125. *Brockhaus Taschenbuch der Geologie* (Leipzig: Brockhaus, 1959), 563; and DG, 852.

126. Pöggeler, *Spur des Wortes*, 386; DG, 790; and Eugen Kogon, *Der SS-Staat: Das System der deutschen Konzentrationlager* (Munich: Alber, 1946), 52.

127. Gershom Scholem, *Judaica*, 2: 11.

128. That this image also plays on Heidegger can be seen in the first draft of the poem where Paul Celan writes of *Knüppelwege* and *Holzwege*; log-paths use transversely crossed logs to enable one to walk upon wet ground without sinking into the bog; cf. Otto Pöggeler, *Spur des Wortes*, 267; and John Felstiner, *Paul Celan*, 247.

129. Jacob and Wilhelm Grimm, *Grimms Wörterbuch*, 3, 1577–87.

130. Maurice Blanchot, *Writing the Disaster*, 47, 143.

131. Axel Gellhaus, ed., *Fremde Nähe*, 397, 389.

132. John Felstiner, *Paul Celan*, 263.

133. Wolfgang Emmerich, *Paul Celan*, 147–58, also Felstiner, *Celan*, 268.

134. For an account of Paul Celan's ties to Judaic culture, religion, and history besides the works of Lydia Koelle, *Paul Celans pneumatisches Judentum*, and Elke Günzel, *Das wandernde Zitat:Paul Celan im jüdischen Kontext*, see: Joachim Schulze, *Celan und die Mystiker* (Bonn: Bouvier, 1976); *Celan Handbuch*, 235–48; Beth Hawkins, *Reluctant Theologians: Franz Kafka, Paul Celan, Edmond Jabès* (New York: Fordham University Press, 2002); and Jean Bollack, *Paul Celan unter judaisierten Deutschen* (Munich: Siemens Stiftung, 2005).

135. Lydia Koelle, *Paul Celans pneumatisches Judentum*, 333.

136. Felstiner, *Paul Celan*, 280–81; Ilana Shmueli, *Sag, dass Jerusalem ist*, 77–78; and MSS, 593 where, in a letter to Hanne Lenz, Celan writes: "Ich bin Jude."

137. Franz Rosenzweig, *Zweistromland: Kleinere Schriften zu Glauben und Denken* (Dordrecht: Nijhoff, 1984), 12; and Lydia Koelle, *Paul Celans pneumatisches Judentum*, 69–71.

138. Paul Celan, *La Bibliothéque philosophique/Die Philosophische Bibliothek*, 321; and Ernst Bloch, *Das Prinzip Hoffnung* I, (Frankfurt: Suhrkamp, 1973), 752 and DG, 692.

139. Ilana Shmueli, *Sag, dass Jerusalem ist*, 78–79.

140. Jean Amery, *Jenseits von Schuld und Sühne* (Munich: Szczesny, 1966), 148–49.

141. Paul Celan, *La Bibliothéque philosophique/Die Philosophische Bibliothek*, 459; Jean Amery, *Jenseits von Schuld und Sühne*, 158; and Lydia Koelle, *Paul Celans pneumatisches Judentum*, 349.

142. Georges Bataille, *Oeuvres complètes*, V (Paris: Gallimard, 1970–1988), 483.

143. In the Luther Bible this is translated as "eine Stadt der Gerechtigkeit," in *Die Bible: Nach der Übersetzung Martin Luthers* (Stuttgart: Deutsche Bibelgesellschaft, 1984), 670.

144. Edmund Husserl, *Phenomenologie des inneren Zeitbewusstseins* (Halle: Niemeyer, 1928), 25, 30; Paul Celan, *La Bibliothéque philosophique/Die Philosophische Bibliothek*, 421–22.

145. Jean Bollack, *Herzstein* (Munich: Hanser, 1993), 52; cf. also Otto Pöggeler, *Der Stein hinterm Aug*, 68–69; Robert Andre, *Gespräche von Text zu Text*, 156–57. On the etymological link between *Stunde* and *stehen* (past tense: *stunden*) cf. *Kluge Etymologisches Wörterbuch der deutschen Sprache* (Berlin: Walter de Gruyter, 1995), 805; and *Der Grosse Duden* VII: *Etymologie* (Mannheim: Bibliographisches Institut, 1961), 691–92.

146. Lydia Koelle, *Paul Celans pneumatisches Judentum*, 280.

147. Otto Pöggeler, *Die Frage nach der Kunst* (Freiburg: Alber, 1984), 364.

148. Ilana Shmueli, *Sag, dass Jerusalem ist*, 34.

149. Otto Pöggeler, *Spur des Wortes*, 392–94.

150. Gershom Scholem, *On the Kabbalah and Its Symbolism* (New York: Schocken, 1996), 105; *Zur Kabbala und ihre Symbolik* (Darmstadt: Wissenschaftliche Buchgesellschaft, 1960), 140; and *Major Trends in Jewish Mysticism* (New York: Schocken, 1993), 113; *Die jüdische Mystik in ihren Hauptströmungen* (Zürich: Rhein, 1957), 59.

151. Gershom Scholem, *On the Mystical Shape of the Godhead* (New York: Schocken, 1991), 195, 148; *Von der mystischen Gestalt der Gottheit* (Frankfurt: Suhrkamp, 1973), 190, 144.

152. Gershom Scholem, *On the Mystical Shape of the Godhead*, 113/ dt., 108.

153. Daniel C. Matt, *Essential Kabbalah* (San Francisco: HarperCollins, 1995), 9.

154. Otto Pöggeler, *Der Stein hinterm Aug*, 68.

155. Jacques Derrida, *Psyche: Inventions of the Other*, II (Stanford: Stanford University Press, 2008), 152.

156. Zev Vilnay, *The Guide to Israel* (Jerusalem: Da'at Press, 1969), 100. This is from a standard tourist guide issued in the very year of Celan's journey.

157. Gershom Scholem, *On the Mystical Shape of the Godhead*, 147, 167/*Von der mystischen Gestalt*, 143, 162.

158. Walter Benjamin, "On the Concept of History," *Selected Writings* IV, 397/ *Gesammelte Schriften* I, 704.

159. Otto Pöggeler, "Mystical Elements in Heidegger's Thought and Celan's Poetry," in *Word Traces: Readings of Paul Celan* (Baltimore: Johns Hopkins University Press, 1994) 92; John Felstiner, *Paul Celan*, 272 for an archaeology of the Jerusalem wall.

160. Margarete Susman, *Deutung Biblischer Gestalten* (Stuttgart: Diana, 1964), 46–47; Axel Gellhaus, "Marginalien: Paul Celan als Leser," in *Der glühende Leertext*, ed. Christoph Jamme and Otto Pöggeler (Munich: Fink, 1993), 54–55.

161. Paul and Ilana were never married. Among several complicated psychological reasons was the simple one that Celan never obtained a legal divorce.

162. Margarete Susman, *Deutung Biblischer Gestalten*, 155–56, 150.

163. Ilana Shmueli, *Sag, dass Jerusalem ist*, 42.

164. Franz Rosenzweig, *Zweistromland: Kleinere Schriften zu Glauben und Denken.*

165. Otto Pöggeler, *Spur des Wortes*, 392–94.

166. Ilana Shmueli, *Sag, dass Jerusalem ist*, 34.

167. Jacques Derrida, *Acts of Religion*, 244.

168. Franz Kafka, *Erzählungen* (New York: Schocken, 1946), 158–62; *Celan Handbuch*, 304.

169. Jacques Derrida, *Acts of Religion*, 144.

170. Gershom Scholem, *Judaica* III (Frankfurt: Suhrkamp, 1973), 113, 143; and Lydia Koelle, *Paul Celans pneumatisches Judentum*, 310.

171. Leo Trepp, *Das Judentum* (Hamburg: Rowohlt, 1982), 215.

172. Wilhelm Michel, *Das Leben Friedrich Hölderlins*, 435. Paul Celan marked this passage three times in his private copy, cf. DG, 875.

173. Philippe Lacoue-Labarthe, *Heidegger, Art, and Politics*, 46.

174. English translation by A. Tarnowski in Philippe Lacoue-Labarthe, *Poetry As Experience*, 112.

175. Aris Fioretos, ed., *The Solid Letter: Readings of Friedrich Hölderlin* (Stanford: Stanford University Press, 1999), 19.

176. Gershom Scholem, *On the Kabbalah and Its Symbolism*, 110, 113; *Zur Kabbala und ihre Symbolik*, 148, 151.

177. Gershom Scholem, *On the Kabbalah and Its Symbolism*, 112; *Zur Kabbala und ihre Symbolik*, 150.

178. Gershom Scholem, *Major Trends in Jewish Mysticism*, 274/ *Die jüdische Mystik in ihren Hauptströmungen*, 301.

179. Gershom Scholem, *On the Mystical Shape of the Godhead*, 242; *Von der mystischen Gestalt der Gottheit*, 227.

180. Gershom Scholem, *On the Kabbalah and Its Symbolism*, 115–17; *Zur Kabbala und ihre Symbolik*, 155–57.

181. This passage on *tsimtsum*, the divine withdrawal, is from the thirteenth-century Kabbalist Moses Nahmonides, *Commentary on Sefer Yetsirah*, in *Qirat Sefer* 6, ed. Gershom Scholem (1925): 402–403. Cf. also Daniel Matt, *The Essential Kabbalah* (San Francisco: Harper Collins, 1993), 93, 194.

182. For an account of the relationship between Paul Celan and Margarete Susman cf. Lydia Koelle, "Hoffnungsfunken erjagen: Paul Celan begegnet Margarete Susman," in *Unverloren. Trotz Allem*, ed. Hubert Gaisbauer et al., 85–145.

183. Margarete Susman, "Spinoza und das jüdische Weltgefühl," in *Vom Judentum*, ed. Verein jüdischer Hochschulen Bar Kochba in Prag (Leipzig: Kurt Wolff, 1913), 51–70, 52.

184. Margarete Susman, *Das Buch Hiob und das Schicksal des jüdischen Volkes* (Freiburg: Herder, 1968), 31, 72–74.

185. Ibid., 78–79, 31.

186. Ilana Shmueli, "Paul Celans Judentum und Israel," in *Unverloren. Trotz Allem*, ed. Hubert Gaisbauer et al., 299.

187. Pierre Joris, LD, 194–95; Katherine Washburn and Margaret Guillemin, trans., *Paul Celan: Last Poems* (Berkeley: North Point Press, 1986), 100–101.

188. Gershom Scholem, *The Messianic Idea in Judaism*, 251, 255–56.

189. For the story of Celan's survival and of his parents deaths cf. Israel Chalfan, *Paul Celan*, 146–60.

190. *Kluge Etymologisches Wörterbuch der deutschen Sprache*, 105; and *Der Grosse Duden* VII: *Etymologie*, 174.

191. Margarete Susman, *Das Buch Hiob und das Schicksal des jüdischen Volkes*, 215–16.

192. Gershom Scholem, *On the Mystical Shape of the Godhead*, 133–34; *Von der mystischen Gestalt der Gottheit*, 128–29.

193. Cf. the letter of Gershom Scholem to Margarete Sussman where he writes, "You will never succeed in unifying Jewish and Christian metaphysics," cited in Elke Günzel, *Das wandernde Zitat:Paul Celan im jüdischen Kontext*, 7.

194. Franz Kafka, *Hochzeitsvorbereitungen auf dem Lande* (New York: Schocken, 1953), 117.

195. Elke Günzel, *Das wandernde Zitat: Paul Celan im jüdischen Kontext*, 325.

196. Giorgio Agamben, *Remnants of Auschwitz*, 13, 34–39.

197. Jacques Derrida, "Hospitality, Justice, and Responsibility," in *Questioning Ethics*, ed. Richard Kearney, 82.

POSTSCRIPT

1. Jacques Derrida, *The Politics of Friendship* (London, Verso, 1997), 306.

2. Jacques Derrida, *Specters of Marx: The State of the Debt, the Work of Mourning, and the New International* (New York: Routledge, 1994), xix.

3. Jacques Derrida, "The Villanova Roundtable: A Conversation with Jacques Derrida," in *Deconstruction in a Nutshell*, ed. John Caputo (New York: Fordham University Press, 1997), 17.

4. Jacques Derrida, *Specters of Marx*, 78; "The Force of Law," in *Acts of Religion* (New York: Routledge, 2002), 250, 247, 256, 244, 255.

5. Yet we also see the way that mourning can be undone through the mechanical repetition of numbers—"6 million"—and names such as "9/11," which become forms of metonymy that unthinkingly pass for a commemoration. Jean-Luc Nancy, *Being Singular Plural* (Stanford: Stanford University Press, 2000), 178; and Jacques Derrida, "Autoimmunity: Real and Symbolic Suicides—a Dialogue with Jacques Derrida," in *Philosophy in a Time of Terror*, ed. Giovanna Borradori, ed., (Chicago: University of Chicago Press, 2003), 85–88.

6. One of Paul Celan's prose collections, *Mikrolithen sinds, Steinchen: Die Prosa aus dem Nachlass* (Frankfurt: Suhrkamp, 2005), draws on his preoccupation with geological metaphors.

7. In one of the geological texts that Celan read, Franz Lotze's *Geologie* (Berlin: de Gruyter, 1955), 162, we find this claim: "The Earth is restless and vital and still in the process of developing further, striving for new formations in the future." Cf. also Erika Schellenberger-Diederich, *Geopoetik* (Bielefeld: Aisthesis, 2006); and Uta Werner, "Das Grab im Text: Paul Celans Lyrik im Imaginationsraum der Geologie," in *Shoah*, ed. N. Berg (Munich: Fink, 1996), 160; on Paul Celan's reference to "message in a bottle," SPP, 396/GW III, 186.

8. In an interview from 1993, "The Deconstruction of Actuality," Jacques Derrida writes that "the question of the ghost is also the question of the future as a question of justice," in *Negotiations: Interventions and Interviews, 1971–2001* (Stanford: Stanford University Press, 2002), 107.

9. Jacques Derrida, "Shibboleth for Paul Celan," in *Sovereignties in Question: The Poetics of Paul Celan* (New York: Fordham University Press, 2005), 31.

10. Here, "shibboleth" functions as the codeword for life/death, since the mispronunciation of the syllable "sh" will result in execution. The story is told in Judges 12:4ff.

11. Jacques Derrida, "Shibboleth for Paul Celan," 63, 60–61.

12. Compare Heidegger's own translation of Pindar's Eighth Pythian Ode, vv. 92–97 in: *Der Spruch des Anaximander*, GA 78, 326–27.

13. On this issue of poetic dwelling cf., William McNeill, *The Time of Life: Heidegger and* Ethos (Albany: State University of New York Press, 2006), 143–52; and John Llewelyn, *The Middle Voice of Ecological Conscience* (New York: St. Martin's Press, 1991), 113–28; cf. also Heidegger, EGT, 43/GA 5, 357.

14. In his draft of the late hymn "Vom Abgrund nämlich," Hölderlin too writes of his poetic exile between the abyss and the homeland, an exile that echoes in Celan's poem "Radix, Matrix," vv. 3–4, SPP, 166–67.

15. Walter Benjamin, *Selected Works*, I (Cambridge: Harvard University Press, 2003), 356; *Goethes Wahlverwandtschaften* (Frankfurt: Fischer, 1964), 106.

16. Nancy does not cite Anaximander here or Heidegger's essay on "The Verdict of Anaximander," but these texts are constantly in play within his work.

17. Jean-Luc Nancy, *The Creation of the World*, 110.

18. Jean-Luc Nancy, *The Experience of Freedom* (Stanford: Stanford University Press, 1993), 75.

19. Edmond Jabès, "Enlarging the Horizon of the Word," in *The Sin of the Book: Edmond Jabès*, ed. Eric Gould (Lincoln: University of Nebraska Press, 1985), 37.

INDEX